ADVENTURES

IN

PHILOSOPHY

AT

NOTRE DAME

ADVENTURES

in

PHILOSOPHY

at

NOTRE DAME

KENNETH M. SAYRE

University of Notre Dame Press

Notre Dame, Indiana

Library of Congress Cataloging-in-Publication Data

Sayre, Kenneth M., 1928–
Adventures in philosophy at Notre Dame / Kenneth M. Sayre.
pages   cm
Includes bibliographical references and index.
ISBN-13: 978-0-268-01784-2 (pbk. : alk. paper)
ISBN-10: 0-268-01784-0 (pbk. : alk. paper)
1. University of Notre Dame. Department of Philosophy—History.
2. Philosophy—Study and teaching (Higher)—Indiana—Notre Dame—
History. 3. Philosophy teachers—Indiana—Notre Dame—History.
4. College teachers—Indiana—Notre Dame—History.   I. Title.
B52.65.N68S29   2014
107.1'177289—dc23
2013044544

To Ernan, Ralph,

and other companions

on the journey.

CONTENTS

This is a story about the University of Notre Dame's Department of Philosophy. It covers a period extending roughly from the mid-1930s through the first decade of the new millennium. I have been a member of this department since 1958.

The story is based on my own memories, on the memories of other early department members, on documents in Philosophy Department files and in the University of Notre Dame Archives, on books and other published accounts dealing with academic matters during this period, and on material currently available on the Internet. Whenever possible, these sources are documented in endnotes.

I am pleased to thank the following colleagues for prearranged interviews: Scott Appleby, Ani Aprahamian, Brian Daly, Bernard Doering, Thomas Flint, Philip Gleason, Theodore Hesburgh, John Jenkins, Edward Malloy, Marvin O'Connell, Alvin Plantinga, John Robinson, Kristin Shrader-Frechette, and Catherine Schlegel.

I am especially grateful to the following both for prearranged interviews and for several unscheduled conversations related to the book: David Burrell, Cornelius Delaney, Michael Loux, Vaughn McKim, Timothy O'Meara, David Solomon, and Paul Weithman. Special thanks are due Delaney, Loux, and McKim for reading large portions of the manuscript in draft form.

Other colleagues who have been helpful on occasion include Patricia Blanchette, Sheilah Brennan, Alfred Freddoso, Patrick Gaffney,

Gary Gutting, Donald Howard, Lynn Joy, John O'Callaghan, David O'Connor, Alice Osberger, Phillip Sloan, and Leopold Stubenberg.

Former colleagues and students who contributed by email, by telephone, or in direct conversation include Richard Conklin, Andrew Chronister, James Doig, Milton Fisk, Richard Foley, Stanley Hauerwas, Guido Küng, Anita Pampusch, and Charles Quinn.

Others from outside the university whose input has been especially valuable include Julia Annas, Marcia LeMay, Kevin McDonough, and Anthony Simon.

Seemingly endless support in gathering data has been provided by Montey Holloway, LinDa Grams, and the staff of the University of Notre Dame Archives.

I am especially indebted to Ernan McMullin, whose contributions to the book proved indispensable. During the last year of his life, Ernan spent many hours with me in a series of prearranged interviews. He also sent me several recorded tapes and emails sharing his memories of the early department. Particularly helpful was his reading of several chapters in draft form for accuracy.

Above all, I am grateful to my wife, Patricia Ann White Sayre, for her untiring help in the composition of this book. A consummate philosophy teacher and keen literary critic, Patti has been personally involved in affairs of the Philosophy Department since 1980. She read each chapter critically through several stages of composition, and made many insightful suggestions about the emerging narrative shape of the story overall. Countless hours spent discussing the project with her as it developed contributed importantly to its accomplishment.

The image of Fr. Joseph M. Bochenski, OP, is reproduced with permission of the copyright holder, Fribourg State University Library (Switzerland). I am grateful for that privilege. I thank the University of Notre Dame Archives for permission to copy the seven other photographs reproduced in the text.

It should be noted finally that the views expressed in this book are my own and are not necessarily shared by the University of Notre Dame, by all members of its Philosophy Department, or by the University of Notre Dame Press.

Prologue

Time present and time past
Are both perhaps present in time future
And time future contained in time past.
—T. S. Eliot, *Burnt Norton*

Time passes at Notre Dame like everywhere else, despite the aura of eternal presence projected by the Golden Dome. Constructed of iron and steel with a thin overlay of almost pure gold, the Dome is probably the best-known campus landmark in the world. It is held in awe by generations of loyal ND fans, a good number of whom have been my students.

I confess I had not heard of the Golden Dome before arriving at ND to begin teaching in the fall of 1958. And once on campus, a week or so must have passed before I even noticed it. I had come from a Protestant background and received degrees from distinctly non-Catholic institutions (Grinnell College, BA; Harvard University, MA, PhD). What is more, these institutions had failed to endow me with the slightest interest in college football. So when I arrived at ND to begin my new job, I had no prior association with its culture for the Golden Dome to symbolize.

The reader might well ask how such an unlikely prospect found his way to the home of the Fighting Irish in the first place. This is a question I used to ask myself. The answer begins with Fr. Henri Dulac, a diocesan priest who taught philosophy at the University of St. Thomas in Minnesota. Fr. Dulac had arranged a leave of absence that enabled him to teach a year at ND and then to spend a year at Harvard (1956–57) as a visiting scholar. We often spent time together discussing philosophy. One day he surprised me by asking whether I might consider teaching at ND after completing my PhD. It seemed that ND was looking for a few people to teach contemporary philosophy, and Fr. Dulac thought I was a plausible candidate.

Surprised though I was, the prospect of spending a year or so at ND was intriguing, and I decided to pursue the matter further. The next step came when Fr. Herman Reith, then chair of ND's Philosophy Department, found room in a busy New England tour to interview me in a quiet corner of Harvard's graduate student lounge. This conversation went well enough for Fr. Reith to arrange a subsequent interview with Fr. Ernan McMullin, another ND philosopher then spending a brief time at nearby Weston Seminary. Although only four years older than I, Fr. McMullin struck me as being very self-assured and worldly-wise. This conversation also went reasonably well. Having been vetted by three priests, I eventually received an offer to begin teaching at ND the following fall. I decided to accept, and within a year became the first non-Catholic member of ND's welcoming and congenial Philosophy Department.

I hope the reader does not conclude from these remarks that I lack the proper background to write the account that follows. On the contrary, my initial remove from the ND mystique may well have imparted a kind of neutrality that will make the story I have to tell more compelling. The reader should realize from the outset, at any rate, that what follows is not an "official" account commissioned by the Philosophy Department or some other branch of the university. The account was written entirely on my own initiative, and I alone am responsible for the views its expresses.

What follows, at least by intent, is a narrative history of ND's Philosophy Department as it developed from humble beginnings over seventy years ago into one of the most prominent departments in the country today. The development of any given academic department, of course, depends substantially on the development of the university including it. Accordingly, the account that follows has things to say also about the growth of ND University itself.

During the years covered by the story, the university changed dramatically. When I first came, it was a relatively small operation run by a few dedicated and generally quite competent individuals. Administrators usually were drawn from the faculty or the CSC (Congregation of Holy Cross) order, to which they returned when their appointed times were over. Academic focus was on undergraduate teaching, and teachers could still count class preparation as a form of research in their annual reports. There was an actual community meriting the designation "ND family" in which everyone associated with the university had a recognized place.

All this changed in later decades of my stay. Student body and academic faculty have doubled in size, while the physical plant has expanded roughly twice that again. Administrative staff has grown even more extensively, in the areas of fund-raising, public relations (PR), and information technology especially. ND today is a vast bureaucracy, staffed in key places by "specialists" with backgrounds in business. Published research overshadows undergraduate teaching, and faculty are allotted compensation with an eye toward increasing the university's national standing. "ND family" still plays a part in PR rhetoric, but the organization overall functions more like a corporate business.

I hasten to add that similar changes have taken place in other large American universities as well, usually with effects more detrimental than those at ND. It should also be added, rhetoric aside, that ND retains more of the old familial spirit than any other research university I know in the country today. All in all, my time at ND has been both pleasant and productive. Yet the ND of the 1960s and 1970s was a better fit for my own scholarly temperament than the ND of more recent decades.

There will also be occasion in the account that follows to say something about pervasive changes in American higher education generally. Just as development of an academic department depends on that of the university including it, so the development of a university depends on that of the academic culture in which it participates. Readers from other colleges and universities may thus expect to encounter trends and influences already familiar within their own institutions. This is the case with readers from other philosophy departments in particular. For the forces that shaped ND's department in the 1970s and 1980s were active throughout the field of professional philosophy at large.

Despite occasional excursions into broader contexts, however, the following account is concerned primarily with ND's Department of Philosophy and with the people who taught in it during roughly the last seventy years. Indeed, it may be more a story about the people than about the department itself. An academic department as such is a lifeless abstraction. If this account were nothing more than the history of such an entity, it would be preoccupied mostly with facts and figures. It would record the arrival and departure of faculty members, the conduct of faculty meetings, faculty publications and grants, undergraduate and graduate enrollments, and other matters of merely factual character. Such an account might be informative, but it would be largely devoid of human interest.

Instead of this facts-and-figures approach, I have chosen to depict the high points and shortcomings of the department in the form of a nonfiction story. The account is nonfictional in being confined to events that actually happened. The events it recounts are things I have read about, things told me by other people, and things recalled from my own store of memories. While none of these sources is infallible, to be sure, the story that follows is based exclusively on events I have good reason to think actually took place.

The account takes the form of a story, on the other hand, insofar as the events it narrates converge nicely into an ongoing plotline. Things occurring in the 1990s and the decade following show themselves as culminations of things that happened decades earlier, and things that happened earlier are seen to have consequences unforeseeable at time of occurrence. The account is story-like, furthermore, in focusing on what people in the department were like, on how they got along with each other, and on how their personal predilections and ambitions affected the affairs of the department overall. In effect, the following account is a story about a group of intriguing people who figured in the life of this often fascinating department.

In keeping with a narrative structure based on personalities, the following account of ND's Philosophy Department is organized around some of its most prominent members. Each of the eight chapters highlights one key personality. Chapter 1, summarizing the decades prior to 1950, features poet and renegade Thomist Fr. Leo R. Ward, who ushered the department into the twentieth century. Chapter 2 deals with the 1950s, featuring the earth-shaking Dominican priest Fr. I. M. Bochenski, who set the department on its present course during his one-year visit from Fribourg University in Switzerland.

Chapter 3 deals with the 1960s, and features fiction writer and arch-Thomist Ralph M. McInerny. Ralph's uncompromising opposition to any form of modernity remained a force in the department until the year of his death (2010). Chapter 4, which deals with the 1970s, features charismatic Irish priest Ernan McMullin, who continued the course that Fr. Bochenski had initiated. Fr. McMullin was a mover and shaker who made other people actually enjoy following his lead. Chapter 5, dealing with the 1980s, features mountain climber and Reformed polemicist Alvin Plantinga, who turned ND's Center for Philosophy of Religion into the world's foremost center of Christian Reformed thought.

The 1980s provide the topic of chapter 6 as well. It features soft-spoken liberal activist Philip Quinn. More than any other single person, Quinn was responsible for bringing the ND department into line with the dictates of the American Philosophical Association (APA). Chapter 7, in turn, deals with the 1990s and features reclusive celebrity Alasdair MacIntyre. The interrupted presence of MacIntyre in the department late in this decade had a direct impact on its rankings in the *Philosophical Gourmet Report*. Dealing with the final decade, chapter 8 features evenhanded and unflappable Fr. John Jenkins, ND's current philosopher-president. Other philosophers have been heads of universities, but few as intrepid as Fr. Jenkins.

Of these eight key individuals, two continued to play major roles in department affairs well after the respective decades they serve to personify. As these roles played out, they came more and more into conflict with each other. Ernan McMullin's continuing contribution was to keep nudging the department in the direction of the robust pluralism initiated during his chairmanship in the 1960s and 1970s. In response to the increasingly progressive turn of the official department under McMullin's influence, on the other hand, Ralph McInerny intensified his efforts to impose a conservative counterbalance. Within months of being appointed director of ND's Jacques Maritain Center in 1979, Ralph began putting together an "unofficial department" that soon rivaled the regular department in overall impact. Viewed synoptically, the story of philosophy at ND during the last three decades has been largely the story of the conflicting interests of these two charismatic Irishmen.

McInerny and McMullin were both devoted to causes that dominated their professional lives. As with many other crusaders for a cause, however, their efforts led to consequences they may later have considered unfortunate. Ralph spent the last months of his life bitterly denouncing his previously cherished university for honoring President Barack Obama in its 2009 commencement. Fr. Ernan likewise spent his final years estranged from the institution that had granted him an honorary degree only a few years earlier. In my estimation, however, both had been rescued from these disaffections by the time their respective parts in the story were over.

As author of the story, I too experienced some sort of redemption in seeing past events take a shape I had not recognized previously. Whereas previously I had viewed my long experience here as a litany of frustrations, by the time the narration was complete I had reached a state of genuine gratitude for my part in the story of this remarkable department. Among colleagues from early years, I hope some may feel the same after attending to the story.

Redemption takes place in time, being a restoration of what time has let stray in passing. Disaffections of time past are set right in time future, with time present hovering uncertainly in between. As T. S.

Eliot cautioned, "If all time is eternally present / All time is unredeemable."

The only candidate for eternal presence at ND, however, is the Golden Dome, and its aura of eternality is only illusory. So the very fact that time passes at ND leaves room for redemption in this story about ND philosophy. I hope the reader enjoys hearing the story as much as I have enjoyed telling it.

PART I

From Thomism to Pluralism

CHAPTER 1

A Bastion of Thomism

JOE BOBIK AND THE POPE

Joe Bobik was the first new colleague to greet me when I arrived at ND in the fall of 1958. Joe had joined the department two years earlier, having previously taught at Marquette University in Milwaukee. Within the next few months we became close friends. We played piano duets together (he was much better than I), went to restaurants together with our wives, and began making plans for a joint research project. Our coauthored "Pattern Recognition Mechanisms and St. Thomas' Theory of Abstraction" came out in 1963. Although we saw each other less frequently as our careers diverged, Joe and I remained good friends until his death some fifty years later.

Encouraged by our mutual goodwill, I once asked Joe how he happened to become a Thomist. My conception of Thomism at the time was rudimentary, but I knew it had something to do with relying on the works of St. Thomas as the best guide to philosophic truth. I had left Harvard with a deep suspicion of philosophic "isms" (idealism, pragmatism, logical empiricism), which struck me as ready-made answers to artificial problems, prepackaged for consumption by trendy philosophers. Why, I wanted to know, had Joe bought into the package called "Thomism"?

Joe's answer was immediate and unabashed. He thought Thomism had the right answers to most philosophic questions; and the reason he thought this, Joe said, was that "the Pope said so." This response was surprising, to put it mildly. I had never heard of people adopting wholesale philosophic positions simply because they were instructed to do so. Although our conversation soon turned to other things, I was left pondering questions like why a pope would instruct people to embrace a particular philosophy, and why an intelligent person like Joe would cheerfully comply.

The pope in question was Leo XIII, author of the encyclical *Aeterni Patris* (1879). This document responded to a growing malaise in Catholic intellectual circles at that time over the spreading influence of the Enlightenment. Particularly troublesome to Catholics was the Enlightenment's unqualified confidence in the power of reason, its hostile attitude toward things supernatural, and its emphasis on freedom from the sort of authority popularly associated with the Catholic Church. A major theme of *Aeterni Patris,* by way of rejoinder, is that reason is limited to the realm of natural truth, whereas supernatural truths can be grasped only by faith through revelation. In the view of Leo XIII, spiritual well-being requires a proper balance between faith and reason which the teachings of Saint Thomas are uniquely able to provide.

For reasons such as these, Pope Leo ordained that Thomistic philosophy should be adopted as the foundation for training priests in Catholic seminaries and for educating lay students in Catholic colleges and universities. In the words of *Aeterni Patris,*[1] we are told that "the Church herself not only urges, but even commands, Christian teachers to seek help" from Thomistic philosophy. Thus supported by the teaching of the "Angelic Doctor" (Thomas Aquinas), the pope announced, Catholic scholars will be better prepared to interpret Scripture, to understand the church fathers, and to combat heresies and errors spawned by less adequate philosophies.

Joe Bobik had various reasons for taking Pope Leo at his word. For one, he had spent several years in a seminary before marrying and coming to ND as a graduate student in 1948. Like all Catholic seminarians in North America during this era, he had been taught to view Thomism as the bedrock of Catholic theology. Another reason was that ND's Philosophy Department was almost entirely Thomist when Joe arrived, which must have reinforced his conviction that Thomism was the best bet for a budding Catholic philosopher. A further consideration was that Joe was Catholic through and through. He had been in the church all his life and seldom questioned its teachings. Since Pope Leo had said explicitly that Catholic philosophers should rely on the teachings of Saint Thomas, "because the Pope said so" was exactly the answer I should have expected when asking Joe how he happened to become a Thomist.

Having decided earlier not to enter the priesthood, Joe viewed the presentation of Saint Thomas in the classroom as his own sacred calling. He regularly taught courses for both graduate students and undergraduate majors. The courses for which he came to be known best, however, were specially tailored to football players and other student-athletes. Often weary from practice the night before, these students required extraordinary means to keep them awake in class the next morning.

One eye-opening tactic Joe employed was to open each lecture with a joke. This practice apparently got him interested in jokes as a research topic. A theory of jokes resulting from this research was published posthumously under the title *Jokes, Life after Death, and God.*[2] A sample joke from that volume is: "This guy comes into a bar with a frog on his head. The bartender asks, Where did you get that? And the frog answers, It started out as just a little lump on my butt." Another is: "This skeleton walks into a bar and says, 'Give me a beer—and a mop.'"

One might guess that jokes by themselves were not enough to keep student-athletes happy in Joe's classes on Saint Thomas's metaphysics. Another expedient he employed toward that end was to assure his students that taking a course in metaphysics would not lower their grade-point average. Whereas some teachers with axes to grind give out only A's, and others refuse to assign grades at all, Joe gained the reputation of being good for a solid B+. Thus it came about that hallmark ND sobriquets like "Faircatch Corby" and "Touchdown Jesus" were joined by a reassuring "B+ Bobik."

Joe and his wife, Theresa, raised five children, and had to augment Joe's salary to provide for their upkeep. Sometime in the early 1970s they bought a small farm where they grew enough produce to last the family through most of the year. They later acquired a Baskin-Robbins ice cream outlet, staffed by Theresa and the older children. Joe's most intriguing contribution to a balanced budget, in turn, was an annual trip to Las Vegas. He had worked out a system, so he said, that enabled him always to return with more money than he had taken with him. As the years went by, the gaming establishment caught on and would no longer allow him to play. By the time this happened, however, he had been promoted to professor and enjoyed a salary adequate to meet his family's needs.

Joe had to cope with fragile health most of his life. During his early days at ND he developed chronic hyperventilation syndrome, which made him infirm ahead of his time. I remember once appearing unexpectedly at his office door to find him with a paper bag over his head. As the years went on, his frame became more skeletal and his skin more translucent. Because of his unfailing smile, these changes produced a visage that was increasingly beatific. This made his passage from life to death almost seamless when it occurred on March 17, 2009. There was no visitation before his funeral in Sacred Heart Parish Crypt.

PHILOSOPHY AND FOOTBALL

When Joe arrived in 1956, as noted previously, the department was staffed almost exclusively by Thomist philosophers. A notable exception was A. Robert Caponigri, who had joined the department in 1946. Caponigri's philosophic guide was Giambattista Vico instead of Thomas Aquinas.[3] But Caponigri was only one of more than two dozen full-time department members during that time. So it remains accurate to describe the department at the beginning of the 1950s as a bastion of Thomist philosophy.

What accounts for this remarkable homogeneity? A partial explanation, of course, is that many of his colleagues were Thomists for the same reason as Joe himself—"because the Pope said so." But there was more to it than this. The exhortations of *Aeterni Patris,* after all, had not made a Thomist of Caponigri, nor of many other Catholic philosophers in other countries.

Strange as it may appear initially, another reason for the monolithic character of ND's Philosophy Department had to do with the success of its football program in the first half of the century. The era of ND football in question, of course, is that dominated by teams under Knute Rockne and Frank Leahy. During his tenure as football coach from 1918 to 1930, Rockne chalked up five unbeaten and untied seasons, produced twenty first-string All-Americans, and achieved an overall winning percentage of 88 percent, the highest ever for either college or professional coaches. When Frank Leahy took over in 1941, he resumed the pattern with six undefeated seasons, four national titles, and four Heisman Trophy winners. His overall winning percentage was 81 percent.

As ND gained national prominence as a football power, it came to serve as a cultural icon for recent immigrants with Catholic backgrounds. Along with the fact that most of these newcomers were poor, their religion set them apart from established mainline society. In many communities (particularly along the east coast), they lived in "shanty towns," had low-paying jobs, and were generally looked down upon by their Protestant neighbors. Given such circumstances, a well-publicized victory by the "Fighting Irish" would count as a blow in defense of these underprivileged Catholics.

Although ND played this surrogate role for Catholic immigrants generally, it was held in especially high esteem by the struggling Irish. This is because the university had by then assumed the identity of a distinctively Irish institution. Founded in 1842 under the leadership of Fr. Edward Sorin of the Congregation de Sacre Coeur (the CSCs), a French missionary order, the university was led next by Fr. Patrick Dillon (1865–66), and then Fr. William Corby (1866–72; Fr. Corby was president from 1877 to 1881 as well). And beginning with Fr. Patrick Colovin (the fifth president) in 1872, there was an unbroken succession of eleven presidents with Irish names, ending only in 1952 with the appointment of Fr. Theodore Hesburgh.[4] As might be expected, the ethnicity of ND's leadership was mirrored in its faculty and student body. The nickname "Fighting Irish" dates from the pre-Rockne era, reflecting the usual preponderance of Irish players on its football teams.

ND served the Irish immigrant community in other respects as well. For families that could find means to send their sons to college, ND was a place to study without risking one's faith. And when its graduate program began to take shape in the 1940s, it became a natural place for priests and nuns from other religious communities to continue their higher education. What Harvard was to Puritans in the seventeenth century, ND was to Catholics in the early 1900s.

One more factor must be brought to bear in explaining the monolithic character of the Philosophy Department when Joe Bobik joined it. In *Aeterni Patris,* Leo XIII explicitly speaks of philosophy as "a handmaid and attendant to faith" (sec. 8). Whatever else this amounts to, it means that philosophy plays a key role in developing one's religious faith and in protecting it from error. In listing philosophers who have defended the faith most notably, Pope Leo gives special notice to Saint Augustine, who "combated most vigorously all the errors of his age" (sec. 13), and to the "angelic St. Thomas" who (now quoting Pope Sixtus V) "by unwearied diligence" strengthened the safeguards of the church with "scholastic theology" (sec. 14).

Other sections of *Aeterni Patris* were even more graphic in describing the role of Catholic philosophy in defending the faith. Noting in section 7 that the enemies of Catholicism borrow their weapons from the arguments of "sophistic philosophers," Pope Leo anticipates the triumph of Christian philosophy "in using human reason to repel powerfully and speedily the attacks of its adversaries." In section 15 he observes that, given the prevalence of present-day "blasphemers" and "seducers," there is a "very great need of confirming the dogmas of Catholic faith and confuting heresy." And in section 27, he expresses his resolve that Catholic philosophers "become habituated to advance the cause of religion with force and judgment."

Faithful Catholics as they were, ND's Irish were accustomed to fighting the good fight in the classroom as well as on the gridiron. Given ND's mission of guarding the Catholic faith in a still largely Protestant society, and given the role of Thomistic philosophy in sup-

porting that mission, there seemed to be little room in the ND department for philosophers uncommitted to the cause of a militant church.[5]

THE CAGE

Beyond assigning it the role of supporting theology as "handmaid,"
Aeterni Patris made philosophy responsible for "defending the truths
divinely revealed" against enemies who draw "their weapons from the
arguments of philosophers" (sec. 7). The complicit philosophers in
question, presumably, were those of the Enlightenment, and in particular those behind the French Revolution, with its dire consequences
for the established church. Leo XIII's encyclical called on Catholic philosophers to protect the faithful against attack by their wayward secular
counterparts. Another expedient employed by the church to safeguard
its faithful was the *Index Librorum Prohibitorum,* or *Index of Prohibited
Books*—the *Index* for short. Although lists of condemned writings had
been promulgated by the church as early as the Council of Nicea
(AD 325), the first edition of the *Index* emanating from Rome appeared in 1559, following the Council of Trent. Updated at roughly
one-hundred-year intervals thereafter, the *Index* was issued in a revised
version by Leo XIII in 1900 (thirty years after the first Vatican Council). Another edition came out in 1948 under Pope Pius XII.

Most books on the *Index* were works of theology and literature,
but numerous philosophic writings were included as well. Some were
listed individually, such as Kant's *Critique of Pure Reason,* Locke's *An
Essay concerning Human Understanding,* and Bergson's *Two Sources of
Morality and Religion.* In other cases, an author's entire corpus would
be prohibited. Examples are the works of Descartes, Hobbes, Hume,
and Sartre. Other well-known philosophers affected include Francis
Bacon, Blaise Pascal, and George Berkeley, along with such renowned
scientists as Copernicus and Galileo.

Until the mid-nineteenth century, prohibitions of the *Index* were
generally enforced by the Congregation of the Holy Office of the In-
quisition,[6] which was responsible for the infamous trial of Galileo in
1633. By the twentieth century, however, enforcement was generally

left to local authorities. At ND in the 1950s, the most evident means of enforcement was the cage (also called "the grill") on the bottom floor of the library overlooking St. Mary's Lake.

The cage was just what its name implies—an area surrounded by iron bars and secured by a gate. On the outside were ordinary books on open shelves, ready to be handled by any interested passerby. But on the inside, displayed forlornly, were all books in the library's possession that happened to be entered on the prohibited list. These were accessible only with a key that unlocked the gate. On the occasion of my first visit to the cage, I recall being let in by a stern-faced librarian. Once I became known as a responsible member of the faculty, however, I could obtain the key at the librarian's desk and browse the forbidden titles without being monitored. The experience was similar to one I had savored, as a college chemistry student, of being allowed free access to a storeroom of toxic chemicals.

My reasons for visiting the cage were entirely straightforward. I had been asked to teach an epistemology course to an uncommonly bright group of mathematics students. Being fresh out of graduate school, I had not taught a course like this before and had yet to acquire personal copies of all the texts I wanted to consider as possible readings. Thus I had to rely on library holdings to pick out texts for classroom use. Texts from ancient and medieval periods posed no particular problem, since everything I wanted to look at from those periods was shelved in open stacks. But when it came to philosophers of the modern period and the early twentieth century, the only convenient way I had of examining their offerings required opening the cage. In the reading list that resulted, as might be expected, works from the cage were well represented.

When the image of a militant church was introduced previously, it may have seemed natural to picture Thomism as an intellectual force protecting the ramparts against an invading army. Taking the cage in the library as our guiding metaphor, on the other hand, we might think of Thomism as a jailer watching over an imprisoned enemy. Regardless of prevailing image, however, removing the barriers relieves Thomism of its defensive duties. And as Catholicism moves into the 1960s, barriers of this sort are about to come down.

Regarding ND's Philosophy Department in particular, it may be described as in the grips of a "cage mentality" as long as it continued to view Thomism as the appointed defender of Catholic orthodoxy. The department maintained this mentality through the 1930s and 1940s, when being a Thomist was a matter of "them or us." By the end of the 1950s, however, university leadership had begun to realize that Catholic intellectual life could benefit from other approaches to philosophy as well. We return to this topic in subsequent chapters.

Having assembled the reading list for my epistemology course, at any rate, I had no further occasion to visit the cage. So I have no first-hand information about its subsequent dismantling. What I do know is that, having received the reading list, my students were able to buy books in ND's bookstore by both Berkeley and Kant. The only permission required was a blanket statement from the dean saying that students could read any books assigned in their courses. Moreover, when the new university library opened in 1963, it contained no cage.

These largely unheralded events at ND were followed in 1966 by Pope Paul VI's proclamation abolishing the *Index*. Good Catholics were still advised to bear in mind that certain books could be dangerous to read, advice non-Catholics might want to heed as well. But there was no further enforcement of reading restrictions by either church or university authorities.

THE EARLY CURRICULUM

According to *University Bulletin* announcements of the late 1930s, the handmaid Philosophy was kept quite busy. To graduate with a BA degree, all Arts and Letters (A&L) students were required to earn eighteen credit hours in the Philosophy Department. Comparing this load with requirements for a minor in philosophy seventy years later, we can say without exaggeration that during this earlier period all A&L students were required to minor in philosophy.

Moreover, Business College candidates were required to take exactly the same philosophy courses in exactly the same sequence. First in order was a three-hour course in Aristotelian logic, which is to say the logic of syllogisms. Next came a course in something called "general psychology." Unlike anything taught in psychology departments today, this course would provide a classification of mental faculties (sensation, imagination, memory, judgment, etc.) and then move on to topics such as mind and body, free will, and immortality. Both of these courses were offered during the sophomore year. It was not until the 1940s that students were expected to take logic during their first year in college.

Having learned how to think logically as sophomores, students would move on to metaphysics and cosmology during their junior year. Metaphysics most likely would begin with topics from Aristotle (act and potency, being and essence, form and matter, etc.), move through early scholastics such as Anselm and Abelard, and climax with Saint Thomas's five proofs of the existence of God. Cosmology, in turn, would deal with the physical world, covering matters to which the previous course relates as "meta." Moving on to the 1940s, cosmology morphed into natural theology, and then into philosophy of nature in the 1950s. By the 1960s it had been succeeded by philosophy of science.

The final two courses were philosophy of mind and ethics, taken during the senior year. Philosophy of mind might be described as an advanced version of general psychology, dealing with the role of intellect or mind in both the natural and the spiritual order. Topics dealing with the natural order might include the so-called "common sense" by which ideas originating in the several physical senses (vision, touch, etc.) are integrated in the perception of distinct physical objects. Among topics pertaining to the spiritual order might be the Divine Ideas which serve as exemplars in God's creation of the natural world. Topping off the series of six courses, ethics would deal with the practical consequences of humanity's being created in the image of God. One possible tack might be keyed to the traditional Christian virtues, including the (theological) virtues of faith, hope, and charity. Another tack might focus on natural law and its practical consequences. These courses usually would be taught with the help of manuals, rather than by reading original authors such as Saint Thomas himself.

Taken as a whole, this course of studies amounted to a highly integrated system of thought. Courses taught to seniors were built on courses taught during the junior year, and those in the junior year on sophomore courses. Moreover, courses taught during the latter term of a given academic year presupposed those taught the term before. Thus general psychology followed logic, cosmology followed metaphysics, and ethics followed a study of mind and of practical reason. This all is in accord with the scholastic principle that the will is guided by reason (logic) to the ultimate Good, a study of which (ethics) is a study of God himself.

Another distinctive feature of this course of studies is that it purported to represent a system of knowledge that is essentially complete. Rather than engaging perennial philosophic issues to be considered on their own merits, ND undergraduates during this era were presented with a body of doctrine meticulously assembled centuries before they were born. When divergent views were presented, it would be to show respects in which these views "deviated from the truth." Generally speaking, this is the way theology was taught as well. Insofar as philosophy was assigned the role of theology's handmaid, and insofar as theology occupied the status of an established body of knowledge, philosophy's role required that it constitute an established body of knowledge itself. The curriculum provided an avenue for conveying this knowledge to fresh generations of students, for the supposed greater good of the individual and of the church at large.

With occasional exceptions like the shift from cosmology to philosophy of nature, ND's baccalaureate requirements in philosophy remained unchanged until the early 1950s. In 1954, the previous eighteen hours of credits required for graduation were reduced to twelve, with a standard sequence of logic, philosophy of nature, philosophy of man, and metaphysics. During the 1960s, as I recall, the department was experimenting with alternative curricula and devoted considerable time to discussion of curricular matters. This experimental period ended in 1970 with the adoption of a two-course (six-credit) requirement that has remained essentially unaltered up to the present.

From its beginning in 1930 and through the 1950s, the philosophy major program piggybacked on the standard undergraduate requirement. In addition to the six courses required of all BA candidates, philosophy majors in the 1930s took Greek philosophy, medieval philosophy, and (Thomistic) epistemology. In the late 1930s a course in theodicy was added, along with a seminar in special problems. The program was further expanded in 1960, with the addition of problems courses in ethics, metaphysics, psychology, and the natural sciences, and area courses in ancient, medieval, modern, and contemporary philosophy. A course in symbolic logic was added to the major requirement in 1966. Courses offered and required in the major program continued to alter during subsequent decades, in accord with proclivities of faculty members directing the program.

In contrast with a tightly organized undergraduate curriculum during the department's early years, its offerings on the graduate level exhibited little apparent order. For the most part, course titles during the 1930s seemed to reflect current interests of individual teachers and varied considerably from year to year. Fr. Leo Ward (about whom more later) offered courses covering then contemporary philosophers such as John Dewey, Ralph Barton Perry, and Roy Wood Sellars, as well as one dealing exclusively with David Hume. Other graduate offerings provided instruction in philosophy of religion, history of psychology, and various topics relating to Aristotle and Saint Thomas. It is unclear whom exactly these courses were intended to serve, inasmuch as *The University Bulletin* did not mention a graduate degree in philosophy until the end of that decade.

When a PhD degree program was officially announced in 1938, however, it adhered generally to the same scholastic line as its undergraduate counterpart. The only two topics available for PhD theses, according to that year's *Bulletin,* were an analytical study of Saint Thomas and a historical study of the texts of the twelfth and early thirteenth centuries. In 1940, although courses were taught in American philosophy and French positivism, all other graduate courses mentioned in the *Bulletin* dealt with Aristotle or Saint Thomas. By this time, moreover, it had become apparent whom the graduate curriculum was designed to serve. Of seventeen graduate philosophy students listed in the 1940 *Bulletin,* all but three were members of religious orders; and of those, eight were nuns, five were CSCs in training, and one apparently a diocesan priest.

Interestingly enough, only one of this group of seventeen went on to earn a Notre Dame PhD. This was Sr. Mary Alice Donovan, CSC, whose dissertation title was "The Henological Argument for the Existence of God in the Works of St. Thomas." Sr. Donovan's degree, conferred in 1946, was preceded by one PhD in 1934, one in 1940, three in 1941, three in 1942, and one each in 1944 and 1945. Most of these were probably in process before the official inauguration of the graduate program in 1939. Also interesting is the fact that nine of these earlier degrees, including Sr. Donovan's, are on record as being directed by Yves Simon, to whom we turn along with others in the following section.

PEOPLE AND PLACES

With a six-course philosophy requirement for all A&L degree candidates, the Philosophy Department in the late 1940s was one of the largest in the university (rivaled only by English). In 1950, there were thirty "regular" members, plus several CSCs brought in as temporary instructors. Of these thirty, thirteen were laymen, fourteen CSCs, and three priests with other allegiances. All but one of the laymen had PhDs, compared with only eight of the priests. Temporary appointments seldom had PhDs; their highest academic degree usually was an ND BA. For the most part, priests without PhDs had other responsibilities as dormitory rectors or university administrators.

Of the twenty-one PhDs held by regular members of the department, all but two were from Catholic institutions. Four each came from ND and from Catholic University, three each from Toronto and Louvain, two each from Laval and the Gregorian, and one from Ottawa. The two non-Catholic PhDs were from Munich and Chicago. This pattern of recruiting faculty primarily from Catholic universities in other countries continued well into the 1960s.

Judged by name, over half of the philosophy faculty in 1950 were of Irish background, five or six German, and most of the rest French,

Italian, or middle-European. All were Catholic and all were men. Upon arriving in 1958, I was the first non-Catholic in the department. Our first woman philosopher was Sheilah (O'Flynn) Brennan, who joined in 1971. The first African American was Laurence Thomas, who arrived in 1975. The department had no Jewish members until Milton Wachsberg came in 1979.

Behind these statistics, of course, were dozens of flesh-and-blood people, some of whom I remember as representing distinctive aspects of the early department. The lay professor of longest standing when I arrived was William Roemer, who joined the department in 1922 and retired in 1959. Bill Roemer was a gentle person with a twinkle in his eye who specialized in philosophy of law and ethics. He and I shared a cramped office with four other teachers, directly across from the department office in O'Shaughnessy Hall. This office arrangement prevented more than three or four of us from being there at the same time, and made confidential conversations with students impossible. Another memorable feature of that room was a small box on a wall which I assumed at first to be a part of an intercom system. A problem with that assumption was that the box was mounted close to the ceiling (beyond a normal person's reach) and that there were no controls to change its function from receiving to sending. My office mates made jokes about the chair, Fr. Herman Reith, using it to eavesdrop on our conversations. At least I thought they were jokes. But I remained suspicious of that box until I moved to more ample quarters in the Main Building a year or two later.

Bill Roemer was a vocal advocate of peace and justice with little time to spare for productive scholarship. His longest publication on record was a fifty-nine page pamphlet by the Paulist Press entitled "The Catholic Church and Peace Effort." It could be argued that his most substantial contributions to peace and justice came with the work of his children and grandchildren. One son, James, served ND as general counsel from 1972 to 1975, then as dean of students until 1984 and as director of community relations until he retired in 2002. Among Bill's grandchildren, the most widely known today is former U.S. congressman Tim Roemer. After retiring from twelve years in the U.S. House of Representatives, Tim served as a member of the 9/11 Commission and as president of the Center for National Policy. In 2009, he was appointed U.S. ambassador to India by President Obama.

The philosophy faculty at this time was not unique in having fewer offices than needed to go around. It was common practice in the university for lay faculty to work at home and to use public lounges and dining halls for student meetings. Unmarried faculty (priests and sometimes laymen) often had rooms in dormitories were they slept at night and held "office-hours" during the day. This lack of shared communal space gave the department an ephemeral quality. One knew that there were dozens of other people teaching classes in philosophy, but could go year after year without actually seeing them.

One colleague I never met was Fr. Thomas Joseph Brennan, who achieved legendary status as chaplain of the football team. Fr. Thomas Joseph ("Old Tom") should not be confused with Fr. Thomas James Brennan ("Young Tom"), whom I saw a number of times before he left in 1963. On game day, the elder Fr. Brennan would pray with the team, presumably requesting what it takes to "play like champions." On weekdays, he would teach them logic and metaphysics. When some exhausted player fell asleep in his class, the story goes, he would be awakened by a barrage of chalk. "Old Tom" also was an unusually skillful handball player, some still say the best ever in the university. Rumor had it that he would challenge each of his student-athletes to a handball game and that final grades were determined by success on the court. Beating the teacher (which seldom happened) earned an A, while less accomplished competitors got a B instead. In those days, B was an entirely respectable grade.

Judged by less parochial standards, however, the most outstanding athlete among ND philosophers of this era was Anton-Hermann Chroust. Tony Chroust was a university professor who taught in the History Department, the Political Science Department, and the Law School as well. But he was best known for his work in philosophy. His most notable publication was *Socrates, Man and Myth,*[7] arguing that Socrates was the creation of Xenophon and Plato. His other philosophic works include a book on Aristotle's lost dialogues, a reconstruction of Aristotle's *Protrepticus,* and a study of the meaning of time in the ancient world. Chroust was well versed in the doxography of (compilations of extracts from) ancient Greek philosophy, and had a working knowledge of ancient Greek profanity. Don't ask what Plato was called by his detractors, but a polite equivalent translates into *membrum virile*.

Tony Chroust's athletic fame rested on his accomplishments in water sports. He earned a gold medal as a member of Germany's winning water polo team in the 1924 Olympics. This was the Olympics immortalized by the movie *Chariots of Fire*. Tony's competitive edge had been tempered somewhat by the time he came to ND, but was still evident when he drove his own "chariot of fire" around campus— a low-slung, flame-red, Porsche convertible.

Chroust's presence in other departments illustrates another aspect of philosophy at ND which at first I found disconcerting. Several prominent philosophers in the university were only loosely connected with the department itself. Another was Otto Bird, founder of ND's General Program of Liberal Education (later the Program of Liberal Studies [PLS]), modeled after the University of Chicago's Great Books Program. Otto Bird wrote several books on philosophy, including *Syllogistic and Its Extensions* and *The Idea of Justice*. Ambiguous allegiance of another sort was exemplified by Fr. Gerald Phelan, who served terms both as director of the Medieval Institute and as chair of the Philosophy Department. Professional dispersion of this sort continues in ND today, with well-known philosophers in German (Vittorio Hösle), Political Science (Catherine Zuckert), the Medieval Institute (Stephen Gersh), the PLS (Gretchen Reydams-Schils), and the Law School (John Finnis).

My late colleague John James FitzGerald provided memories of a rather different sort. In contrast with philosophers located in other departments, and philosophers in my own department I never met, there was a core group of department members who enjoyed spending social time together. By the time I arrived at ND, the center of this group was the dignified but cordial John James FitzGerald.

John James joined the department in 1937. He is not to be confused with John Joseph FitzGerald, who came in 1957. Both being modest men with a sense of humor, they allowed others to refer to them as "John Senior" and "John Junior." John Senior's PhD was from Louvain, to which he returned in 1974 to do research in the philosophy of science. He also studied briefly at Cambridge and Harvard. From 1942 to 1946, he served in the Navy, rising to the rank of lieutenant commander. In the late 1940s, he was asked to put together a new philosophy program expressly for physics majors. This program was a major influence on developments in the Philosophy Department during the mid-1950s, in ways we shall examine presently. In 1966, he became the first director of graduate studies in the Philosophy Department, and then served as director of ND's Center for the Study of Man from 1971 to 1973. He was appointed assistant vice-president for graduate instruction in 1973, and served in that role until his retirement in 1977. His main scholarly contribution, before he got so heavily involved in administration, was a translation of Jacques Maritain's *The Person and the Common Good* (1947).[8]

While John was still active in the department, he went out of his way to make new faculty members feel welcome. He and his wife, Patricia, frequently gave parties to which only younger members of the department were invited. I have distinct memories of drinking eggnog with John in full view of a beautifully decorated Christmas tree. On these occasions John would sit back, loosen his tie, and regale us with stories about the "Old Notre Dame." John and Pat stood as godparents for the third of my four sons.

John James FitzGerald was fastidious both in habit and in dress. More than once I saw him gardening in coat and tie, and he was always impeccably attired when he appeared on campus. The last I saw John, in a nursing home not long before his death in February 2003, he was lying on his bed in a suit and well-shined shoes. His mind by that time had started to drift, but he took care to thank me for the visit before I left.

The most prominent member of the department in the 1940s was Yves Simon. Recruited in 1938 specifically to teach graduate courses in the tradition of Aristotle and Saint Thomas, Simon was well versed in contemporary political and social thought as well. After ten years he left ND to join the Committee on Social Thought at the University of Chicago. Simon directed ten of the twelve PhD theses completed in the department during that decade. This average number of theses directed per year by a single member of the department has remained a record up to the present.

Born in Cherbourg, France, in 1903, Yves Simon had a difficult adolescence. At age twelve he contracted tuberculosis of the bone, which left him lame for the rest of his life.[9] At age eighteen he was attending the Sorbonne and the Catholic University of Paris simultaneously. At the Sorbonne, he studied thinkers like Pierre-Joseph Proudhon, which fueled his future interest in humanistic social thought. At Catholic University he concentrated on the scholastic tradition, primarily as represented by Aristotle and Saint Thomas. It was at Catholic University that he became personally acquainted with Jacques Maritain, whom he came later to count as mentor and friend. He completed his doctoral dissertation at Paris's Catholic University in 1934.

Yves Simon came to ND initially as a visiting professor, with a salary of $3,500. When his return to France was blocked by the spread of World War II, however, ND offered him a regular professorial position. Reflecting back on this happenstance, Fr. Leo Ward described the addition of Simon to the department as "the greatest benefaction Notre Dame has ever had in philosophy."[10]

Simon soon became part of ND's fabled coterie that met in the house of political theorist Waldemar Gurian, which included James Corbett of History, Frank O'Malley of English, and occasional visitors from outside the university (e.g., Irish poet and politician Desmond Fitzgerald and University of Chicago Law School's Mortimer Adler). Less frequent visitors whom Simon met at Gurian's included such notables as British economist Barbara Ward, political thinker Hannah Arendt, and nuclear physicist Leo Szilard. Gurian was founding editor of ND's *The Review of Politics* in 1939. A piece by Simon appeared in its first issue.

Yves and his wife, Paule, frequently entertained guests in their own home as well. Fr. Ward tells of one party featuring lively singing, describing how, "late at night . . . all there including Simon, a crippled man," leapt "up and down in an Apache song."[11] If "all there" is to be taken literally, then Waldemar Gurian must not have been present, for

Gurian was a man of great girth who had difficulty even getting out of a chair.

Although Simon was hired primarily to teach and direct theses on Saint Thomas, the holocaust underway in Europe turned his attention increasingly to political thought and social commentary. Of the dozen or so books published during his lifetime, only three or four would normally count as works of philosophy.[12] The remainder were treatises and tracts dealing with issues raised by the social upheavals of his time. An oft-repeated anecdote highlighting Simon's preoccupation with real-life issues refers to a leaflet dropped over France the day before the Allied invasion in 1944, praising Simon's efforts supporting the Free-French cause in the United States. For this, he came to be known as "the philosopher of the fighting French" (possibly echoing "the fighting Irish" of ND?).

In 1946, Simon began teaching occasional courses at the University of Chicago, in both the Department of Political Science and the Committee on Social Thought. In 1948 he became a full-time member of the latter, a position he occupied for the rest of his active career. While teaching at Chicago, however, he maintained his home in South Bend, where his family continued to live. His wife taught at St. Mary's College (across the highway from ND), and their son Anthony went through the South Bend school system. Yves would leave for Chicago Tuesday morning on the South Shore Railroad (which then had trains leaving and returning on the hour) and return to South Bend late Thursday evening. This schedule enabled him to continue working with ND graduate students. In point of fact, four ND PhD theses under his direction were completed after he went to Chicago.

This schedule also enabled Simon to keep in touch with his ND friends and to lecture now and then at his former university. My only personal encounter with Simon was at a lecture he gave in 1959 on the philosophy of mathematics, which happened to be the topic of my first published paper in 1962. I remember being favorably impressed by his response to a question I asked after the lecture. Although courteous to a fault, his response left me with the sense that this man knew a great deal more than I about the humanistic import of mathematics.

Yves Simon was diagnosed with thyroid cancer in 1960. At this point he stopped traveling regularly to Chicago but continued tutoring students from the Committee on Social Thought in his home at South Bend. According to Anthony Simon, Yves's last three days were spent in South Bend's Memorial Hospital. He died on May 11, 1961, at the age of fifty-eight.

DISTINGUISHED VISITORS

Among ND philosophers of this early period, Yves Simon was the only one with an international reputation. Not until the late 1950s was the department home to philosophers destined to become well known outside the United States. This lack of prominence among its regular members in the 1930s and 1940s, however, was at least partially offset by a steady stream of high-profile visitors. The best known of these were Étienne Gilson and Jacques Maritain.

Étienne Gilson was born in Paris on June 13, 1884, attended Lycée Henri IV, and graduated from the Sorbonne in 1907. Among his teachers at the latter were Lucien Lévy-Bruhl, Henri Bergson, and Émile Durkheim. He completed a doctoral thesis on Descartes at the Sorbonne in 1913, and began a wide-ranging study of the medieval philosophy against which Descartes was reacting. He soon came to see more merit in Descartes's medieval background than in Descartes's philosophy itself.

From 1913 to 1921 Gilson taught at the Universities of Lille and of Strasbourg, with time out for several years of military service, including two as a prisoner of war. After the end of World War I, he began teaching the history of medieval philosophy at the Sorbonne, remaining there from 1921 to 1932. In 1932 he became professor of medieval philosophy at the Collège de France, where he remained on the faculty until 1951. In the meanwhile, he had spent 1927 as a visiting professor at Harvard, had founded the Institute of Mediaeval Studies at Toronto in 1929, and had delivered the Gifford Lectures at Aberdeen in 1931 and 1932. He returned to Harvard to deliver the William James Lectures in 1935. From 1929 to 1951, he divided his time between Toronto and Paris, and then moved to Toronto, where he remained until retirement in 1968. He died on September 19, 1978.

Gilson was a prolific author, having published well over a dozen books by the time he left the Collège de France in 1951. His Gifford Lectures were published as *L'espirit de la philosophie médiévale* (1932, translated as *The Spirit of Medieval Philosophy*). Other well-known books include *Saint Thomas d'Aquin* (1925), *Introduction à l'étude de Saint Augustin* (1929), and *La philosophie de saint Bonaventure* (1953). His *Moral Values and the Moral Life: The System of St. Thomas Aquinas* (1931) was translated by ND's Fr. Leo R. Ward.

Gilson's first lecture at ND, entitled "The Concept of Christian Philosophy," was delivered in 1931 to an "unusually large audience" in Washington Hall.[13] He returned the next year for two lectures in the same venue. According to one source, he also lectured at ND in 1934 and 1935.[14] Through visits such as these, along with other connections, Gilson became well acquainted not only with members of the Philosophy Department, such as Leo Ward, but also with scholars from other parts of the university. Significant among these for the anecdote that follows were James Corbett of History and Waldemar Gurian of Political Science.

The occasion of Gilson's last visit to ND was a series of lectures on Duns Scotus given in 1950. In the course of the lectures, for which he was paid $600, Gilson had been lavishly feted by Fr. Gerald Phelan, then chair of the Philosophy Department and former director of the Mediaeval Institute at Toronto, which Gilson had founded, and by ND President Fr. John J. Cavanaugh.[15] After the last lecture, there was a reception at Yves Simon's home in the late afternoon, followed by dinner at the home of history professor James Corbett. During the evening, Gilson reiterated his view, which he previously had made public in Paris, that France should remain neutral in the current stand-off between Russia and the United States. Corbett passed word of this to Waldemar Gurian, who was not at the dinner. Despite his Russian roots, Gurian had assimilated the democratic values of his adopted country and was furious to hear that Gilson did not back the United States over Russia as a more suitable ally for France. He penned an outspoken letter that soon appeared in *Commonweal,* portraying Gilson as a traitor to his native country.

Gilson was deeply irate in turn. It so happened he had just recently informed the Collège de France of his intention to retire, and had requested the honorary status that would enable him to receive a pension. When news of Gurian's denouncement reached Paris, however, Gilson's colleagues refused to grant him the status requested. He thus returned to teaching at Toronto without the anticipated retirement income.

Messy as the whole affair had been, it turned out to have an amicable ending. Colleagues at the Collège de France eventually reversed themselves and granted Gilson a pension. Remorseful at having wronged an old friend, Gurian signed a letter of apology that Yves Simon had drafted. The apology was gratefully accepted. And Gilson, ever more devout as he aged, had masses offered on the occasion of Gurian's death in 1954. But he never set foot on ND's campus again.

Jacques Maritain was born in Paris on November 18, 1882. Like Gilson, he was educated at the Lycée Henri IV and the Sorbonne. He was initially attracted to the works of Spinoza, but then at the Sorbonne fell under the spell of Henri Bergson. Maritain and his wife-to-be, Raïssa Oumansoff, whom he met in 1901, had fallen into seemingly genuine despair over the sterility of French intellectual life, and later credited Bergson with diverting them from suicidal tendencies. They were married in 1904 and both converted to Catholicism in 1906.

After two years in Heidelberg studying natural science, Jacques returned with his wife to Paris in 1908. At this point, he explicitly disavowed Bergsonian philosophy and began an intensive study of Thomas Aquinas. After two years at the Lycée Stanislaus (1912–14), he moved to the Institut Catholique de Paris as an assistant professor. He became full professor at the Institut in 1921, and then served as chair of logic and cosmology from 1921 to 1939. While on a lecture tour in the United States in early 1940, Jacques and Raïssa were advised by friends not to return to France, which fell to the Nazis a few months later. For the next twenty years they resided primarily on this side of the Atlantic.

Maritain's first teaching appointments in the United States were at Princeton (1941–42) and Columbia (1941–44). After the liberation of France in 1944, he spent most of the next two years in Rome as French ambassador to the Vatican. In 1948 he returned to Princeton as full professor, taking up residence in a house near the university.[16] During the period between 1948 and 1960, Maritain was busy writing and giving lectures, both in France and in other American and Canadian universities.

Maritain's first lectures at ND were delivered in 1934.[17] The circumstances leading up to this visit were described by Fr. Leo Ward in his article "Meeting Jacques Maritain."[18] Maritain had been scheduled to give some public talks in Chicago, and contacted Fr. Ward through his agent saying that he would be pleased to give a series of seven lectures (presumably duplicating those in Chicago) to a ND audience for $500. When ND's President O'Hara was informed of the offer, his immediate response was, "Yes, but make it $700; $500 is too little."

When the eminent man arrived on campus (accompanied by his wife and her sister, Vera), it soon became evident that the fledgling university was not fully prepared for a visitor of his stature. By their own choice, the Maritain entourage was housed in the infirmary for the duration of their stay.[19] One problem was that the person assigned to escort them from the infirmary to the dining hall spoke no French, while the visitors (including Jacques) had yet to gain fluency in English. Another was that both Jacques and Raïssa had dietary requirements that ND's dining hall could not easily satisfy. A further breach of professional courtesy occurred when the distinguished visitor's lecture was introduced by an undergraduate priest who seemed unaware of the speaker's importance. The chill that followed the introduction was broken by a hearty cheer from Irish poet and politician Desmond FitzGerald, a friend of Maritain's who happened to be in the audience. After that, the lecture apparently went smoothly. This was the beginning of an annual series of lectures that continued with few interruptions through the next two decades.

Maritain's last lecture at ND was in 1959. I was in the audience and recall a similarly egregious gaffe in the circumstances of his introduction. This time around, Maritain was close to seventy-six years old. His lecture was in the rather small auditorium of the newly built Moreau Seminary. Although the room was too warm for comfort, Maritain was dressed in a dark suit with a scarf around his neck. The introduction was made this time by a middle-aged CSC priest who happened then to be chair of the Philosophy Department. Having completed the introduction, this goodly priest took a seat on stage and promptly fell asleep. As I recall, he was finally awakened by the applause at the end of the talk.

The year after this final ND appearance, Maritain and his wife left the United States to spend the rest of their days in France. Raïssa (who had been sickly most of her life) died only months after their return, and Jacques moved to Toulouse to live in the monastery of the Little Brothers of Jesus. While with the Little Brothers, he wrote his controversial book *Le Paysan de la Garonne* (1967), one of the several books by prominent Catholic authors reflecting on the aftermath of the Second Vatican Council. Maritain officially joined the Little Brothers in 1970, and died on April 28, 1973.

Maritain's legacy of written work is extensive. He wrote many volumes for a general audience, typically examining social and political issues of the day from a Catholic perspective. He also wrote approximately two dozen for an academic audience, covering topics ranging from metaphysics and epistemology to political philosophy and the philosophy of art. Translations from this latter group have appeared in some twenty different languages. By the time of his death, Maritain arguably was the best known Catholic philosopher of the twentieth century.

Another famous visitor to the university during these years deserves a place in our story, even though he was not invited by the Philosophy Department. In the spring term of 1939, Kurt Gödel gave a graduate course on the axiomatization of set theory in ND's Department of Mathematics. Already famous for his incompleteness results published eight years earlier, Gödel had never held a regular university position. Although not targeted specifically by the Nazis (Gödel was not Jewish), he felt increasingly isolated as his friends in the Vienna Circle dispersed. And he needed extra income to support a newly wedded wife. So he was receptive to the suggestion of Karl Menger, an acquaintance from Vienna who recently had become chair of ND's Mathematics Department, that he might want to consider a stint at ND.

In addition to the course on set theory, Gödel teamed with Menger in teaching a second graduate course on elementary logic. This course covered the propositional calculus, including proof of the completeness and independence of the axioms grounding the system, and went on to treat the predicate calculus, the calculus of classes and relations, and Russell's theory of types. As Menger noted in an earlier letter to Gödel,[20] other logic classes at ND were "completely dominated by the writings of Jacques Maritain and the philosophical school of Laval," which was "quite opposed to mathematical ('merely formal') logic."

Despite its novelty, the logic course apparently went quite well. Menger reported that about ten graduate students in mathematics attended, along with a comparable number of "older philosophers and logicians." In particular, Menger cited the involvement of "Professor Yves Simon, a student and friend of Maritain," who "made a special effort to take advantage of Gödel's presence."[21] Given that Simon was only thirty-six at the time, one wonders what "older philosophers and logicians" might have been in attendance.

During the fall before his semester at ND, Gödel had spent time at the Institute for Advanced Study in Princeton, New Jersey. When he left ND, he returned to Vienna for a few stressful months (this was immediately prior to Hitler's invasion of Poland), and then returned to take up permanent residence in Princeton. As it turned out, Gödel's house also was on Linden Lane, only a few blocks from that later occupied by Jacques Maritain. There is no evidence that Gödel and Maritain ever met.

EARLY SPECIALISTS

Perusing successive issues of the *University Bulletin,* one gets the sense that the regular faculty (those who remained in the Philosophy Department for more than two or three years) taught a fairly wide variety of courses. Bill Roemer, for example, taught logic, philosophy of mind, general psychology, jurisprudence, and philosophy for engineers. And Fr. Leo Ward repeatedly taught philosophy of mind and philosophy of religion, British philosophy, and cosmology, along with metaphysics.

There is no reason to think that faculty of this era were hired for special competence in any particular area. Apart from basic requirements of education and intelligence, it was enough to be a Thomist and a professed Catholic.

This began to change with the development of a genuine graduate program in the 1940s. Whereas undergraduates might learn the rudiments of logic or ethics from a novice as well as an expert, graduate students who themselves are training to be teachers require instruction at a higher level of competence. Considerations of this general sort must have motivated the notable round of hires that took place in the late 1940s and early 1950s.

The first of this group of specialists to arrive on the scene was James Francis Anderson, a PhD from Toronto, whose brief stay at ND extended from 1948 to 1955. During these seven years, Jim Anderson published three books on no-nonsense Thomistic metaphysics: *The Bond of Being* (1949), *The Cause of Being: The Philosophy of Creation in St. Thomas* (1952), and *An Introduction to the Metaphysics of St. Thomas* (1953). Three more on the same topic followed in the decade or so after he left ND. I mention these books to emphasize that Jim Anderson was an accomplished scholar. Although he had moved to Marquette by the time I arrived in 1958, Anderson left behind a reputation for being a person of considerable charity. According to one story, while waiting for his family to load into the car moments before their actual departure, he was busy watering the lawn for the convenience of the next tenant.

Next in order of arrival was Vincent E. Smith, who came in 1950 with a PhD from Catholic University. Vince's specialty was philosophy of nature, which he viewed as tantamount to philosophy of science from a Thomist perspective. Throughout his career, he published nine books on this topic, including three (*Philosophical Physics* [1950], *St. Thomas on the Object of Geometry* [1954], and *The General Science of Nature* [1958]) during his time at ND. For Vince, work in the philosophy of nature was more than a way of putting bread on the table. The importance he attached to this work is expressed in a quotation from one of his writings that appeared in the American Philosophical Association's brief notice of his death.[22] Referring to Saint Thomas's

Summa Theologica, he says that he is convinced that the paramount "vocation of philosophy today is to work toward a new *Summa* that will expand the wisdom of the past to embrace . . . the scientific achievements of the modern world." It is safe to surmise that Vince thought of his own work as contributing toward that goal.

Vince left ND in 1960 when he received an offer to found and to direct an Institute in the Philosophy of Science (the Thomist version) at St. John's University in New York. His stay at St. John's did not go well from the beginning, apparently because of turmoil in the Philosophy Department that had nothing to do with his coming. Things went from bad to worse when his wife, Virginia, died from a fall down the basement stairway of their home.[23] Vince left St. John's in 1966, subsequently doing brief stints at Columbia, Sarah Lawrence, and Queensborough Community College. The last time I saw him was in an office I occupied while a visiting scholar at Princeton during 1966–67. He was attending a seminar by Carl ("Peter") Hempel, then premier U.S. scholar in the philosophy of science (*not* the Thomist version), and had stopped by to reminisce about ND. Hempel, a logical empiricist once associated with the Vienna Circle, was a kind and compassionate human being. I am sure he made Vince's entry into a new way of thinking about the natural world as gentle as possible. Vince died in 1972 as the result of a hit-and-run traffic accident in New York City.

John Oesterle arrived in 1954 as a specialist in logic. Two years earlier he had published *Logic: The Art of Defining and Reasoning,* a book on the syllogism and the theory behind it written expressly for use in Catholic colleges. A second edition came out in 1963. One distinctive feature of this text was its inclusion of work sheets to be filled out and submitted for correction in class. As a result of this astute design, which ensured that used copies had no resale value, John built up a substantial nest egg over the years the book remained in print. Decades later a chair named for John and his wife was endowed by money deriving from sales of this book. The first and current John and Jean Oesterle Professor of Thomistic Studies is Alfred Freddoso, a specialist in Catholic metaphysics and ethics.

John also wrote a textbook on moral philosophy, translated Aquinas's *Treatise on Happiness* and *Treatise on the Virtues,* and with his wife, Jean, translated *On Evil: Disputed Questions,* also by Aquinas. In 1965, John became editor of *The New Scholasticism,* the journal of the American Catholic Philosophical Association (ACPA). As a result, the journal returned to ND, where it had been located previously while Vince Smith was editor. When John died in 1977, the job of editor was taken over by Ralph McInerny, with Jean Oesterle serving as associate editor. Jean continued in this role until 1989, when the journal was succeeded by the *American Catholic Philosophical Quarterly.*

During my first decade or so on campus, John and Jean were mainstays of the department's social life. Both were outgoing people who seemed to enjoy throwing parties at a moment's notice. A hallmark of parties at the Oesterles' was a concoction John claimed to have invented called an "Ivan Collins"—essentially several jiggers of vodka in a Tom Collins mix. From time to time, local philosophers would convene at about 4:00 in the afternoon in the Oesterles' living room for an "official" department meeting, a subterfuge eventually dropped in view of the fact that few coherent decisions were ever made. I clearly remember a party held sometime in the 1960s—when it had become common for the department to invite non-Thomists (including logical positivists) to campus for talks—at which Herbert Feigl gave an impromptu recital on the Oesterles' grand piano. Feigl was an excellent pianist and, although he had trouble walking at that point, his fingers were still very nimble. A few years later Feigl remarked to me that the Oesterles' party was one of the best he had ever attended.

John had converted to Catholicism in the 1930s (as had his wife), received his PhD from Laval in the 1940s (as had Jean), and taught at the University of St. Thomas before moving to ND. Having arrived at ND, both Oesterles remained here for the rest of their lives. According to his close friend Ralph McInerny, John's last words when he died in 1977 were, "Very soon I shall know all." Jean died in 2001, with few people left to share happy memories of department meetings over glasses of vodka beginning at 4 o'clock in the afternoon.

Another specialist recruited during this period was my old friend, Joe Bobik. He had received his PhD from ND in 1953 and was considered locally to be a promising young Thomistic metaphysician. After a year each at Marymount College (Los Angeles) and Marquette University, he returned to ND in 1956, the year after Jim Anderson left for Marquette.

Other faculty arriving in the late 1940s and early 1950s included Élie Denissoff and Joseph Evans, who apparently were not appointed for specific research interests. Count Élie (later Elias) Denissoff was born in St. Petersburg, Russia, on January 11, 1893. He descended from a line of Don Cossack counts with titles deriving from Catherine the Great. He served as secretary to the Russian prime minister from 1915 to 1917, a position terminated by the Russian Revolution. Escaping to Belgium, he made enough money in the hotel business to begin studying philosophy on the graduate level (previously he had studied law). He received an MA from the University of Paris in 1935 and a PhD the next year from the University of Louvain. In 1943, he received an Agrégé from Louvain for a thesis titled "Scholase D. Thomas Aquinatis Magistrum Cooptatum."

Denissoff came to ND in 1948 as associate professor and had been promoted to professor by the time he left in 1958. While at ND, he taught courses in Greek philosophy and modern philosophy, especially Descartes. His publications were limited to a few articles and the lengthy *Maxime le Grec et l'Occident* (1953). These are in addition to literally thousands of manuscript pages authored by him in Latin, Greek, Russian, French, and German, and deposited in the ND archives. He also managed to collect a large number of books pertaining to Descartes, which ND's Memorial Library acquired for $30,000 in 1966 (the Denissoff collection).

Denissoff's personal career at ND was not entirely transparent. He converted from Russian Orthodoxy to Roman Catholicism in 1924. This was also the year he married Marie A. Haot, with whom he had three children (to one of whom, Jacqueline, Jacques Maritain was godparent). Yet he spent ten years at ND without either his marital status or his religious affiliation becoming generally known. This anonymity is illustrated by a story Fr. Hesburgh told about himself while being interviewed by Fr. Ernan McMullin in 2003.

A few years after becoming president (probably in 1955), Fr. Hesburgh was summoned to Washington, DC, for a meeting with the apostolic delegate, Cardinal Amleto Cicognani. The cardinal informed Hesburgh that there was "an irregular situation" at ND and that people had been calling to make sure he knew about it. The problem was that a married priest was teaching in the Philosophy Department, a man Cicognani identified as Élie Denissoff. Hesburgh responded by saying that he knew the person in question quite well, and that Denissoff in fact was a member of the Russian Orthodox Church, which permits married clergy, but that no one at ND knew that Denissoff was married. When asked what he intended to do about it, Hesburgh said that he did not consider the situation problematic, and that since Denissoff planned to retire in a couple of years no action was needed. As far as Hesburgh was concerned, that was the end of the matter.

What Hesburgh apparently never knew is that Denissoff, already a Catholic, had been ordained a priest in the Melkite Rite in 1955. Since Melkites ordain married clergy despite being in communion with Rome, Denissoff in fact was a married priest from 1955 to his departure from ND in 1958. As far as his marital status was concerned, Hesburgh may have been close to right in stating that no one then at ND knew Denissoff was married. But this was not the case for all former ND faculty. As already noted, the Simons continued living in South Bend after Yves began teaching in Chicago. According to Anthony, the Simons frequently entertained Élie Denissoff with his wife and family.

Leaving ND, Denissoff moved to St. Procopius College in a suburb of Chicago, now known as Illinois Benedictine College. Before the year was out, he had become head of their Philosophy Department and had been raised to the rank of Monsignor. Elias died in 1971 and is buried in the cemetery of St. Procopius Abbey. After his death, Marie moved to Albuquerque to be near her daughter, Jacqueline. When she died in 1998, Marie's ashes were buried in the plot occupied by Elias's remains at St. Procopius. Her Albuquerque death notice mentions that she was preceded by her husband, Rt. Reverend Archimandrite Elias Denissoff.[24] In the Melkite rite, however, the honorific title "Archimandrite" is reserved for abbots of monasteries (which Elias was not) and for especially distinguished unmarried clergy.[25] Had the title been bestowed on Denissoff by some bishop who was unaware that he was married? For purposes of our story, it makes no difference.

Joseph W. Evans received an ND PhD in 1951, began teaching at ND the same year, and by the time of his death in 1979 had become a living legend among ND students. Joe was an unassuming man, both physically and socially, who walked with a shuffle and spoke in labored sentences. He conveyed the impression of being immersed in the flow of a slower time. One thing that kept Joe going was his love of teaching. Whereas most other lay faculty had wives and families to support, Joe was a bachelor who lived primarily for his students. He quickly came to know everyone in his classes by name, and had a way of asking "How-are-you?" that convinced the person asked that Joe really cared. Students generally liked Joe as much as he liked them, and often mimicked his mannerisms with no tinge of disrespect. A pivotal lesson of his metaphysics course was that being is primarily an act (be-ing, like walk-ing) and only secondarily a state, which students were known to rehearse by imitating Joe staring in astonishment at a tree caught in the act (of be-ing) just outside the classroom window.

The second thing that kept Joe going was his devotion to the work and witness of Jacques Maritain. The title of his ND PhD thesis was "Development of Thomistic Principles in Jacques Maritain's Notion of Society." His scholarly output consisted primarily of the book *Jacques Maritain: The Man and His Achievement* (1963) and three translations of Maritain's works. A very special moment in Joe's life was the founding of ND's Jacques Maritain Center in 1957, which he directed from its founding to shortly before he died in 1979. We return for a closer look at Joe Evans and the Maritain Center in a later chapter.

Other members of the Philosophy Department listed in the 1950 *Bulletin* (with source of PhD when applicable) were Herbert Johnston (Toronto), John Glanville (ND), Karl Kreilkamp (Catholic University), Fr. Charles C. Miltner, CSC, (Gregorian), Joseph P. Mullally (Columbia), Daniel C. O'Grady (Ottawa), Fr. Peter O'Reilly, and Richard Thompson (Toronto). To these may be added a number of auxiliary faculty without PhDs.[26]

THE STATUS QUO

Viewed synoptically, ND's Philosophy Department at mid-twentieth century was a group of teachers and scholars with a common mission. Among the regulars, at least, all were trained at reputable institutions, all were practicing Catholics, and all save one or two were loyal Thomists. This means that they were in basic agreement about the goals of philosophy and about how those goals should be pursued.

Philosophy in its original sense is a devotion to wisdom, and the typical Thomist of the time remained faithful to that original sense. According to Saint Thomas himself (*Summa Contra Gentiles*), the highest wisdom is an intellectual grasp of first principles and of what follows from these principles. This includes God as the principle of all being and the created world that God engenders. As Maritain puts it in his *An Introduction to Philosophy*,[27] it belongs to "wisdom to study the highest causes: sapientis est altissimas causas considerare." For Maritain, this leads to a succinct definition of philosophy—"Philosophy is the science which by the natural light of reason studies the first causes or highest principles of all things." Although different people might put it differently for different purposes, it is safe to assume that most of ND's Thomists in the early 1950s would have agreed with Maritain's definition.

From this common conception of their discipline among ND philosophers flowed a common understanding of their role as scholars and teachers. As scholars, their objective was to pursue progressively more adequate knowledge of ultimate principles. While it was standard practice to specialize in particular branches of inquiry (e.g., Anderson in metaphysics and Oesterle in logic), all saw themselves as contributing to the same unified and systematic body of truth. As teachers, on the other hand, their responsibility was to introduce young people to the pursuit of wisdom and to acquaint them with truths accessible by natural reason. (Truths of revelation were left to theology.) Students with talent for advanced work could be treated accordingly, but all should learn the rudiments of philosophic truth.

One purpose for which *Aeterni Patris* prescribes the study of Saint Thomas, we recall, is to nourish young minds in Catholic seminaries and colleges. The fact that ND philosophy remained solidly Thomist seventy years after the encyclical was issued is ample testimony that Leo XIII's prescription was taken seriously. A further indication of Thomism's hegemony among Catholic schools in North America is that scores of colleges relied on philosophy textbooks authored by Notre Dame faculty. Prime examples are John Oesterle's *Logic: The Art of Defining and Reasoning,* Vince Smith's *The Science of Nature: An Introduction,* and Jim Anderson's *An Introduction to the Metaphysics of St. Thomas.* Joe Bobik was only one among hundreds of American philosophers who owed their Thomistic orientations to *Aeterni Patris.*

But what about the other purpose Leo XIII had in mind when he urged Catholic philosophers to study Saint Thomas? That other purpose was to combat heresies and errors inculcated by other philosophies. The problem on this front was that Christian soldiers have little chance of victory when they march forth to engage an unknown adversary.

Disconcerting as some may find it in retrospect, Catholic philosophers during the half-century or so after *Aeterni Patris* had almost completely lost track of what was current in philosophy outside of Thomist circles. Pragmatic empiricism was challenging the mind's ability to know nonempirical truths, emotivism was discrediting the claims of absolute moral norms, logical positivism was denying the very possibility of metaphysics, and Wittgenstein was casting doubt on the legitimacy of systematic philosophy itself. Yet Thomist philosophers made little effort to keep abreast of these developments. Not only were they failing to mount effective counterattacks against these probable threats, but they remained largely uninformed about the nature of the threats themselves. It was as if Catholic philosophy had not yet joined the twentieth century.

Whatever one might think about the combative role assigned Thomism by *Aeterni Patris,* ignoring twentieth-century philosophy was counterproductive for the cause in question. The Philosophy Department took major steps to bring ND philosophy into the twentieth century by adding new faculty in the mid- and late 1950s. As a prelude to discussing these corrective measures in the following chapter, however, we should consider a catalyst for change already active in the earlier department.

THE "CAMPUS MAVERICK"

The catalyst in question described himself as a "campus maverick," but was referred to by others as Fr. Leo "Rational" Ward. (Fr. Leo R.—hence "Rational"—Ward is not to be confused with his good friend Fr. Leo L. Ward, who taught literature—hence Leo "Literature" Ward—during the same period.) Fr. Leo R. Ward, CSC, first came to ND as a seminarian in 1914, spent several years after seminary earning a PhD from Catholic University, and returned in 1928 to begin teaching in the Philosophy Department. A prolific author, he published seventeen books and over seven dozen articles. Among his books are three volumes of poetry, several on Catholic life and education, and five that would be considered scholarly by today's standards. One of his most influential works is *Blueprint for a Catholic University,* which Fr. Hesburgh says influenced him extensively when he began his efforts to turn ND into a major center of higher education.[28] Leo Ward gives ample exposition of his own experiences as student and teacher in his monograph *My Fifty Years at Notre Dame,* from which all following quotations in this section are taken.

Fr. Ward had full credentials as a Thomist philosopher. From novitiate onward, he was educated in Catholic institutions. The first was ND's Moreau Seminary, which he literally helped build, followed by Holy Cross College (Washington, DC), where he studied theology, and then by Catholic University, where he received his PhD. When he returned to ND as a faculty member, he taught the usual round of Thomistic courses (metaphysics, cosmology, ethics, etc.). He translated Gilson's *Moral Values and the Moral Life: The System of St. Thomas Aquinas* (1931). And he was enthusiastically instrumental in bringing Maritain to ND for his first lectures in 1934. What made Leo Ward a "maverick" was not a deviation from standard Thomism, but his conviction that standard Thomism was not enough.

Two or three years into his teaching career, Leo Ward spent a year in Oxford, working with H. H. Joachim and J. A. Smith on the texts of Aristotle. He got to know W. D. Ross, Fr. Martin D'Arcy, and C. S. Lewis (whom he didn't particularly like). He also attended meetings of the Oxford Philosophical Society. The following year he spent in Louvain, where he met Auguste Mansion, Hans von Balthasar, and Albert Dondeyne. Turned off by what he described as a "labored sterility" at Louvain, he seems to have benefited more from his time at Oxford.

Fr. Ward's main research interest was contemporary value theory. His *Philosophy of Value: An Essay in Constructive Criticism* came out in 1930, followed by *Values and Reality* in 1935. Of particular interest was the philosophy of Ralph Barton Perry, which he sometimes treated in graduate courses along with works by John Dewey and Roy Wood Sellars. He spoke of Sellars as a personal friend.

Because of his interest in American philosophy, it was natural for Leo Ward to join the American Philosophical Association. He was the first from ND to join that organization, and for a decade after the death of Virgil Michel in 1938 was the only Catholic priest among its membership.[29] Fr. Ward participated regularly in the Midwest Division meetings, reading papers, commenting, and serving on committees. Among the many friends he made at these meetings was Paul Holmer of Minnesota, who later encouraged Ralph McInerny to join the ND Department because then he would get to know "the good philosopher Leo R. Ward."

In his monograph about his fifty years at ND Fr. Ward discussed various reasons why he thought Thomism was "not enough." Despite getting high marks in philosophy during his novitiate, he declared summarily that "the seminarian's philosophy in Latin is dead." One "Roman-trained teacher" he cited knew nothing of "Plato, Aristotle, Aquinas, or Kant" and had no inkling that "philosophy proceeds by way of inquiry and challenge." Regarding his theological studies in Washington, he remarked that the "Catholic Church in America . . . then lived as if outside history" and would remain thus "isolated until the days of John F. Kennedy." Of his course work in particular, he recalled that he was taught from textbooks that were "thoroughly dead manuals" and that the theology they contained was "stiff and corpse-like" as well.

Fr. Ward's conviction that philosophy proceeds by inquiry and challenge led him to a definition of philosophy quite different from that of Maritain previously quoted. The reason philosophy and theology had been "unreal" to him while training to be a priest, he said, was that this training relied on textbooks and professors teaching from them. But philosophy "does not begin with books or professors." Philosophy instead "begins where we are," which is to say that it begins with individuals in real-life circumstances. Past philosophers like Kierkegaard, Kant, and Aquinas can help, but only if we view their inquiries as "immersed in the basic problems of their times." Doing philosophy is an enterprise of a living person or, as he put it, an enterprise of "a modern man." Summing up his discontent with the way philosophy was then taught in Catholic seminaries and colleges, he avowed that "the catechetical method of answers that are no answers to questions that are no questions" deserves the wrath of everyone who is subjected to the process.

Fr. Ward repeated this basic message in an address he gave by invitation to the ACPA in 1966 on the fortieth anniversary of its founding. According to a eulogy delivered by Fr. Ernan McMullin two days after Fr. Ward's death on September 8, 1984, the elderly priest used this occasion to chide the group for being "a closed society," out of touch with the real "problems of man." The genuine philosopher, he insisted, approaches problems "given by his time," by its hopes and sufferings, its opportunities and challenges. And he addresses those problems as "a living modern man," aided but not co-opted by philosophers of the past.

In the foregoing discussion of *Aeterni Patris* and its aftermath, we saw that ND's Philosophy Department in the 1940s was ill equipped to bring Thomism to bear on issues occupying philosophers at non-Catholic institutions. Basic changes were needed before the department and its members could enter into fruitful interchange with their secular counterparts. The example set by Fr. Ward's maverick vision prepared the way for those necessary changes, to which we turn in the following chapter.

CHAPTER 2

Breaching the Ramparts

EARLY STEPS IN THE PURSUIT OF EXCELLENCE

Maverick that he was, Fr. Leo Ward did not play a major role in changing the academic profile of the department. There is nothing in the records of the time to suggest that his dissatisfaction with textbook Thomism had much influence on how his colleagues taught their courses. Nor did his regular attendance of APA meetings inspire other ND philosophers to follow suit.

The initiative that dislodged Thomism from its dominant role in departmental affairs originated in the upper administration rather than in the department itself. This initiative was an integral part of the "pursuit of excellence" effort that emerged in the early years of Fr. Theodore M. Hesburgh's presidency. The present chapter shows how the pursuit of excellence played out in the Philosophy Department and how it contributed to the displacement of Thomism as the cornerstone of ND's undergraduate education.

Although the slogan "pursuit of excellence" is usually associated with the Hesburgh administration, vigorous efforts to improve the academic quality of the university were already underway when Hesburgh took office in 1952. Before Hesburgh came Presidents John Cavanaugh (1946–52) and J. Hugh O'Donnell (1940–46), and before them President John O'Hara (1934–40).[1] Unlikely as it may seem to someone familiar with O'Hara, the tides of reform that swept the university in the 1950s had begun to stir under his leadership in the 1930s.

Described as "an energetic prude" by ND historian Philip Gleason,[2] President O'Hara is distinguished in ND lore as a tireless crusader for pious causes. As prefect of religion (1918–34), he encouraged students to participate daily in Holy Communion and made consecrated hosts available in every chapel, where students could receive them cafeteria-style without waiting for Mass. He kept track of correlations between numbers of daily communicants and victories on the football field. And he organized novenas for intentions dear to his heart, including religious vocations, spiritual purity, and gridiron success.[3] Perhaps the most widely known illustration of O'Hara's ingrained piety was his personal removal of books he deemed morally pernicious from the library shelves.[4] No one seems sure what became of these books, but rumor has it that he burned them in his fireplace.

Religious zeal aside, Fr. O'Hara was a moving force behind the university's emerging graduate program. Before his presidency, ND already had PhD programs in chemistry, biology, and metallurgy. While president, O'Hara added programs in physics, mathematics, politics, and philosophy. To staff these programs, he traveled to Europe looking for scientists and scholars seeking escape from fascist oppression. Among outstanding faculty gained in this fashion were mathematician Karl Menger and political scientist Waldemar Gurian, both mentioned in the previous chapter.

While O'Hara provided administrative support, however, design of these advanced degree programs was left largely to Philip S. Moore, CSC. Moore was a medievalist and paleographer who had obtained his doctorate from Catholic University and had spent several years at the École des Chartes in Paris. Fr. Moore occasionally taught in the Philosophy Department and worked closely with Fr. Ward in setting up the philosophy PhD program. He also launched a program in medieval studies that led to the establishment of ND's Medieval Institute in 1946. Fr. Moore was appointed ND's first academic vice-president by Fr. Hesburgh in 1952.

Fr. J. Hugh O'Donnell's presidency (not to be confused with that of Fr. Charles L. O'Donnell, president during 1928–34) bracketed the

Second World War. Most of ND's student body during this period were officer-candidates training in the Navy's V-12 program. By Fr. Hesburgh's account,[5] President O'Donnell would stride about campus swinging his cape in a manner that signaled his authority as local "commander-in-chief." Backed by ND's increasing visibility in scientific research, Fr. O'Donnell served with representatives from Cal Tech and MIT on the federally mandated Committee on Science and the Public Welfare, exploring how wartime developments in science could be put to industrial use through research efforts by private universities. This committee helped lay the groundwork for the National Science Foundation (NSF), which began awarding research grants in 1952. Fr. O'Donnell's involvement led to the appointment of ND biologist James A. Reyniers as a member of the first National Science Board. When Dr. Reyniers resigned a few years later, he was replaced by Fr. Theodore Hesburgh. As a consequence of Fr. O'Donnell's bringing ND's science program into national prominence, the university was represented on the top level of the NSF for the first eighteen years of its existence.

Fr. J. Hugh O'Donnell's immediate successor as president was Fr. John J. Cavanaugh (not to be confused with Fr. John W. Cavanaugh, president from 1905 to 1919). John J. Cavanaugh was a self-made man in the classic sense of the term. Born in Michigan on January 23, 1899, he was forced to leave high school early and take a job to help support his mother.[6] After a night-school course in business, he soon found a job as assistant to the private secretary of Henry Ford. He met ND's president John W. Cavanaugh while visiting a brother (Frank) then enrolled in Moreau Seminary, and agreed to serve as the president's private secretary for two years in exchange for a four-year college education. John J. graduated magna cum laude in 1923. He immediately went to work for South Bend's Studebaker Corporation, becoming assistant manager of advertising within little more than a year. Although engaged to be married, he soon changed course to follow his brother's lead and entered Moreau Seminary in 1925.

After ordination, Fr. John J. Cavanaugh occupied various administrative positions in the university, with increasing concentration on publicity and fund-raising. In the appreciative words of Fr. Hesburgh,[7] it was Fr. Cavanaugh's "personal magnetism, his business acumen, and his wide network of friends" that launched ND on its first major fund-raising venture. Among that wide network of friends were Joseph Kennedy and others of his family. Fr. Cavanaugh officiated at many Kennedy weddings, and was one of three priests officiating at John F. Kennedy's funeral.

Graduate studies and research were a priority during Fr. John J. Cavanaugh's administration. PhD programs were added in aeronautics, mechanical engineering, history, English, and medieval studies; and graduate enrollment in the university increased fivefold. The previously noted beginning of the Medieval Institute in 1946 was followed by the establishment the Lobund Laboratory in 1950. Major new construction included the Nieuwland Science Hall and the Hall of Liberal Arts (now O'Shaughnessy Hall), in which philosophy was housed for the next half century.

With due credit to earlier efforts, however, it was Fr. Hesburgh who elevated the achievement of excellence to a top university priority. "I want this to be a great university," he would say time and again in public addresses. "I want Notre Dame to be a great *Catholic* university, the greatest Catholic university in the world." He was still voicing this refrain a full fifty years later, although by then the goal was not far from accomplishment.

Backtracking a half century myself, I have clear memories of my first encounter with the "pursuit of excellence" slogan. In the early 1960s, I still considered myself a visitor to the university, biding time in a department chaired by someone who had told me to start looking for another job. Shortly after the new Memorial Library opened in the fall of 1963, I was walking through the library concourse, probably thinking of my next class, when presently I noticed several large colored banners displaying the words "Pursuit of Excellence." My immediate reaction, I confess, was a bit condescending. One would never see banners like that hanging in Widener Library at Harvard! Universities that are already on top don't make a public point of wanting to be better. By advertising its goal of self-improvement, I grumbled, ND was confirming its status as a second-rate institution.

True enough, the ND of the early 1960s was not yet a first-class university. But my initial reaction to the banners showed how little I knew about what was going on at ND at the time. Those "Pursuit of Excellence" displays, it turned out, were part of a major fund-raising campaign destined to transform ND into the great Catholic university its president envisaged. The campaign in question, I believe, was the first ND fund-raising effort to receive an official name. It was called "Challenge I" (first merely "Challenge"; the "I" was added later). It came about in the following manner.

In 1960 the Ford Foundation selected ND as one of five private universities to receive a matching grant of six million dollars (close to 44 million in 2010 dollars). To qualify, ND had to raise double that amount through its own efforts. By 1963, Challenge I had added $24.6 million to the university's coffers.[8] Most of this was spent constructing the new Memorial Library, then the largest university library building in the world. The "Pursuit of Excellence" banners were hung in the library to celebrate the successful completion of a record-setting fund-raising campaign.

During the Challenge I campaign, Hesburgh spent a disproportionate amount of his time traveling and talking to potential donors. But he had no illusion that achieving greatness would be a matter of money alone. Nor was it just a matter of enhanced classroom teaching, which has never made a university great.[9] To steer ND in a path toward academic excellence, it was clear that more demanding intellectual standards were required. With the rigors of a major fund-raising campaign behind him, Hesburgh finally could concentrate on matters of academic standards.

Fr. Hesburgh had been aware of the need for higher standards since his days as a Holy Cross seminarian. Seven years of theology out of Thomistic manuals had an influence on his intellectual formation that he later described as "deadening and regressive."[10] This negative attitude toward traditional scholastic training carried over into the early years of his presidency. In a controversial speech to the National Catholic Education Association in 1961, he stated bluntly that Catholic higher education would be impeded "if our philosophers and theologians continue to live among, work with, and speak to people long since dead and buried."[11] Bringing it down to particulars, he asked what future judges must think of us "if we live in the most exciting age of science ever known to mankind, and philosophize mainly about Aristotle's physics," or "theologize about the morality of war as though the spear had not been superseded by the ICBM."

The goals of excellence that motivated Fr. Hesburgh during his thirty-five years as president obviously applied to the university at large, and not just to a few departments. As these quotations show, however, the reforms he was intent on bringing about were keyed to changes in the Philosophy Department specifically. Let us take a closer look at the man who mandated these changes before turning to particular philosophers involved.

FR. HESBURGH TAKES CHARGE

Fr. Hesburgh had set for himself the goal of making ND the greatest Catholic university in the world. Although his predecessors had converted ND from a provincial college into a national university, there was still a long way to go before this goal could be met. According to Hesburgh's assessment, the only things great about ND when he took over were its football team and the school spirit that spurred the team to national championships.[12] As far as academic resources were concerned, the new president observed, "Our facilities were inadequate, our faculty quite ordinary . . . , our deans and department heads complacent, . . . and our graduates often lacking in intellectual curiosity" (65). To make matters worse, ND's "academic programs [were] encrusted with the accretions of decades" (65), and the graduate program was still in its infancy. As Hesburgh surely realized at the time, making the institution he now headed into a great Catholic university would be an undertaking of giant proportions.

But Theodore Hesburgh was a man of extraordinary means, both in his own professional accomplishments and in his leadership abilities. Regarding professional accomplishments, as is well known, he received more honorary degrees (150) than any other person to date on the face of the earth. While president of ND, he also served on the National Science Board and was a member of the governing boards of the Rockefeller Foundation and of the Carnegie Commission on Higher Education. He accepted an invitation from President Eisenhower to join the Civil Rights Commission, of which he became chair in 1969, and received (but declined) an offer from President Johnson in 1964 to take control of the country's fledgling space program.

In point of fact, Fr. Ted's involvement in the Rockefeller Foundation and his invitation to head the space program were both relevant to ND's pursuit of excellence. Immediately after Russia launched its Sputnik in 1957, the United States began a frantic effort to catch up in space. From the perspective of higher education, this amounted to a rapid upgrading of science and engineering curricula. Education in science must move from mediocre to truly excellent in minimum time. The Rockefeller Foundation responded to this need with a report in 1958 entitled *The Pursuit of Excellence*. And academic groups were quick to follow. The theme of the 1960 convention of the National Catholic Educational Association (NCEA), for instance, was "Emphasis on Excellence," with more than twenty Catholic scholars holding forth on the topic.[13] As a member of both the NCEA and the Rockefeller panel that issued the "excellence" report, Fr. Ted was in the midst of the ferment. His push for excellence at ND was not an isolated effort, but was reinforced by cooperation with other leaders in higher education with similar goals.

As to leadership, Hesburgh was both a visionary and a man of authority. These qualities engendered almost universal respect among his subordinates.[14] He also had an extensive range of personal contacts, which enabled him to get things done in days that otherwise might have taken years. All of these personal resources were necessary to change a place with "ordinary faculty" and "complacent administrators" into a place with a shot at becoming a great Catholic university.

In one ordinary sense of the term, a visionary is someone given to fanciful thoughts with little practical ability to get things done. But this was not the way of ND's president, who was one of the most practical university administrators of his generation. Apart from the ND venture itself, the best example of Theodore Hesburgh's kind of vision is the one he shared with Martin Luther King Jr. As already noted,

Fr. Hesburgh was appointed to the Civil Rights Commission by President Eisenhower in 1957. The work of that commission led to the Civil Rights Act of 1964, which outlawed discrimination on the basis of race or religion, provided for racially integrated schools, and facilitated equality in employment opportunities. Although their efforts were not coordinated in any regular way, there are few individuals who contributed more than Fr. Hesburgh to the realization of Dr. King's "Dream."

Fr. Hesburgh's brand of authority was a mixture of decisiveness, composure, and complete self-confidence. An illustration is his run-in with the legendary Frank Leahy when Hesburgh was first appointed vice-president under Fr. Cavanaugh in 1949. Fr. Ted was a newcomer only thirty-two years old, and Leahy was the most famous football coach in the world. President Cavanaugh had told Fr. Ted to reorganize the Athletic Department so that the football coach (then running that department) reported to an athletic director who reported to the vice-president in turn. Leahy was uncooperative from the start and tried to ignore Fr. Ted's directives. The showdown came when Leahy was informed that he could take only thirty-eight players to games away from home, which was the limit permitted under Big Ten Conference rules. Leahy was still planning to take 44 players the day before leaving for a big game at the University of Washington when Hesburgh told him that the extra players would not be given permission to miss class and would be dismissed from the school if they made the trip. The coach was furious, but cut the traveling team by six members at the last minute and went on to win the game. Reconciliation began soon after with Leahy complaining publicly about bad officiating and Hesburgh staunchly defending him against the adverse criticism that followed. Frank Leahy eventually turned to Fr. Ted as friend and confidant, and a new athletic director soon brought the Athletic Department under university control. The new director was the now legendary Ed "Moose" Krause, whose bronze facsimile, complete with cigar, is currently seated outside the Joyce Athletic and Convocation Center.

Another illustration of Hesburgh's great force of personality was his confrontation with Cardinal Alfredo Ottaviani, then head of the Congregation for the Doctrine of Faith. It so happened that Waldemar

Gurian and Matthew Fitzsimons, a history professor, had coedited a collection of essays to be published by the University of Notre Dame Press (hereafter UNDP). Titled *The Catholic Church in World Affairs,* the collection included a paper by Fr. John Courtney Murray upholding the right of Catholic scholars to disagree with current understandings of noninfallible church doctrine. Ottaviani had seen an advance copy, deemed the entry by Fr. Murray erroneous,[15] and instructed Fr. Christopher O'Toole, Superior General of the CSCs, to make sure the book did not reach the bookstores. Fr. O'Toole instructed Fr. Hesburgh to take care of the matter. Offended by both the tone and the content of this instruction, Fr. Ted told Fr. O'Toole that he would not suppress the volume. If O'Toole ordered him to do so, he would resign as ND's president. When the book actually appeared in local bookstores, Ottaviani was promptly notified. At this point the Cardinal called the Superior General of the Jesuits, who ordered Murray to buy all remaining copies from the press and to make sure no more were released to the public. When notified of this development, Fr. Ted acquired the remaining copies himself and stored them away for release after the controversy blew over. Fifty years after the incident, copies of the offending book can be purchased online.[16]

Fr. Ted's "networking" capacities were legendary. I have clear memories of presidential dinners, held for faculty and spouses at the end of the academic year, at which he would hold forth for over an hour about important meetings he had attended and influential people he had met. At the time, many faculty members thought talk of this sort was a form of bragging. I, for one, no longer view it in that light. Fr. Ted was giving us an annual update on a presidential activity that was essential to the way he ran the university.

Hesburgh's facility in making contacts was an enabling factor in the public arena as well. His role in establishing a working Peace Corps is a case in point. The Peace Corps originated with an executive order signed by President Kennedy in 1961. Within hours after the signing, Sargent Shriver (JFK's brother-in-law) contacted Hesburgh asking him to set up a pilot project. The next day Fr. Ted met with Latin American specialists at ND and put together a proposal for a project in Chile, which he rushed back to Shriver. The proposal languished in

Washington for a month and a half, after which Shriver informed him that people were worried because the whole thing seemed exclusively Catholic (JFK, Shriver, and Hesburgh were Catholic, and the proposal came from ND). Fr. Ted then got on the phone and within hours arranged to have the project sponsored by the Indiana Conference on Higher Education, which represented institutions of many religious denominations.

Shortly after the proposal was accepted, Hesburgh traveled to Chile with an assistant from Indiana University, only to find that no major Chilean educational institution was interested in joining the project. So Hesburgh contacted Fr. Mark McGrath, a fellow CSC and dean of theology at Catholic University in Santiago, who arranged a next-day meeting with Chile's extremely busy minister of education. This person was duly impressed and assured the U.S. contingent that President Alessandri of Chile would approve the undertaking. But the project needed the approval of the U.S. State Department as well. Returning to Indiana, Hesburgh contacted Harris Wofford, a Kennedy aide who had assisted Hesburgh on the Civil Rights Commission, and Wofford secured the necessary State Department signatures in a record-breaking two days. Hesburgh then cabled the Chilean government for final approval, which he received in a matter of hours. As a direct result of Hesburgh's multinational connections, the Peace Corps was up and running within a day after the State Department finally approved it.

Ted Hesburgh had vision, authority, and an enormous network of friends. He also had a taste for adventure. Of many venturesome episodes described in his autobiography, the most exciting had to do with flying. Most thrilling of all was a flight in an Air Force SR-71 that broke the world's speed record.

In 1976, the SR-71 had set a record of Mach 3.35, or about 2,200 mph. Fr. Ted was intrigued. In early 1979, Fr. Ted was speaking with President Jimmy Carter in the Oval Office about work done at ND in support of Carter's Vietnam-draft-evader amnesty program. When Carter asked what he could do to return the favor, Fr. Ted mentioned his persistent desire to fly in the "world's fastest airplane" (143). Shortly after, Hesburgh received a call from the Air Force chief of staff saying that he could serve as crew in an SR-71 if he could pass all the tests required of American astronauts. Although sixty-two years old, Hesburgh passed the tests and was cleared to fly in the world's reputedly fastest aircraft.

The day of the flight was Ash Wednesday of 1979. Both Hesburgh and the main pilot declined the traditional steak breakfast and climbed into the plane in their cumbersome space suits. The SR-71 accelerated down the runway, shot straight up like a rocket, and reached thirty thousand feet in a manner of seconds. At sixty thousand feet, the pilot explained the planned trajectory. They would dive to twenty-five thousand to reach Mach 1 (the speed of sound), and then head upward as fast as the craft would go. Fr. Ted watched the Machmeter as they shot higher and higher: Mach 2, Mach 3, Mach 3.5, and still accelerating. But Mach 3.35 was the record set three years previously. ND's president and the pilot in front of him had flown faster in an engine-driven aircraft than anyone else in human history.[17]

These are a few snippets from the personal life of the man who remade ND into a world-class university. Fr. Hesburgh's strategy for this endeavor was to find the best people he could for key positions. Upon becoming president in 1952, he lost no time in replacing a few deans and renovating a few departments. The first dean to go was Fr. Frank Cavanaugh of Arts and Letters, the brother of the previous president. Fr. Frank's replacement was Fr. Charles Sheedy, a close friend of Fr. Ted from seminary days. Fr. Sheedy was a theologian with ambiguous feelings about philosophy. As we shall see presently, he was a key factor in some of the troubles afflicting the Philosophy Department later in the decade. But his close relationship with Fr. Hesburgh endured to the end.[18]

The main departmental reshuffling mentioned in Hesburgh's autobiography took place in the Biology Department. With a certain amount of pride, he describes the conversion of Biology "from an old-fashioned taxonomic operation" to an experimentally oriented department with an "emphasis on molecular biology" (69). He seems equally proud that neither the Mathematics nor the Chemistry Department needed restoration. Mathematics was in good shape under the chairmanship of Arnold Ross, who succeeded Karl Menger in

1946. Regarding the sciences, Hesburgh says, "Chemistry had been our strongest department for many, many years, going back to Father Julius Nieuwland, the inventor of synthetic rubber" (69). It was for Fr. Nieuwland, of course, that Nieuwland Science Hall was named.[19]

The chair of the Philosophy Department when Hesburgh became president was Fr. Bernard Mullahy, newly appointed to replace Fr. Gerald Phelan, who had left the university mysteriously. Fr. Mullahy had been trained at Laval and was a dyed-in-the-wool Thomist. Mullahy was followed in 1955 by Fr. Herman Reith, also a Laval PhD. As already indicated, Fr. Hesburgh was uneasy about what was happening in the Philosophy Department and soon began looking for new leadership. His first choice for the role was Fr. Joseph M. Bochenski of Fribourg.

JOSEPH I. M. BOCHENSKI, OP, A FORCE OF NATURE

Fr. Ted had personal dealings with all US presidents and all Roman pontiffs in office during his time as ND president. He was arguably the most important Catholic priest in the United States during the second half of the twentieth century. What does such a man do when he wants to upgrade his philosophy department? He enlists the aid of Europe's most formidable Catholic philosopher. That is, he calls in Fr. Joseph I. M. (Innocent Maria) Bochenski, OP.[20]

Joseph Bochenski (1902–96) was born in a small village north of Kraków. His father was a landowner and industrialist with a doctorate in economics. His mother, née Countess Dunin-Borkowska, was known for her piety and published hagiographical writings on Saint Teresa of Avila and Saint John of the Cross. Bochenski's apparently comfortable early childhood was interrupted at the age of twelve by the outbreak of the First World War.

His gymnasium years were unsettled, as the family moved frequently to escape open hostilities. During these years, his main academic interests were mathematics and physics. After three of four subsequent years doing advanced work in law and economics, he became increasingly interested in logic and philosophy. His pursuit of philosophy as a career began around 1925 with a particular interest in Kant and a general skepticism about formal religion.

Despite his religious misgivings, the young Bochenski became convinced that the Catholic Church was the only institution that could save Polish society from chaos. Still an unbeliever, he entered the Catholic Seminary at Poznan in 1926. After studying the philosophy of Saint Thomas for a year, however, he disowned Kant, underwent a religious conversion, and joined the Dominican order in 1927. He went on to study philosophy at the University of Fribourg in Switzerland from 1928 to 1931, to become ordained in 1932, and to acquire a doctorate in theology from the Angelicum in Rome in 1934. He stayed at the Angelicum for another four years as a lecturer in logic. In the meanwhile he was working for a habilitation degree at the Jagiellonian University in Kraków, which he completed in 1938 with a dissertation on the history of modal logic.

Upon the invasion of Poland by the Nazis in 1939, Bochenski joined the Polish army as a chaplain. This was not his first military experience. After finishing gymnasium studies in 1920, he had joined a Polish cavalry unit that helped establish the borders of the Second Polish Republic in 1922. Although he was wounded during that campaign, the experience did not seriously interrupt his postgymnasium studies. His adventures as an army chaplain were considerably more harrowing. Within weeks after enlisting in 1939, Bochenski was wounded again and taken prisoner by the Nazis. He escaped prison camp through a latrine window and managed to find his way safely across several national borders to Rome.

Within months Bochenski was in uniform again, fighting with Polish forces in France. After France's defeat in 1940, he led a group of several hundred Polish soldiers to the Atlantic coast and eventually to England. Subsequently he spent time as an army chaplain in Scotland, during which he published extensively on religious themes and occasionally lectured at the University of Edinburgh. It was during this period that he started reading Hume and other British philosophers.

His last military action was in 1944–45, when he fought in the battle of Monte Cassino and lived through the aftermath of the Malta Conference, in which the Allies abandoned Poland to the Soviets. In recognition of his performance as chaplain through these episodes, Bochenski was decorated and promoted from captain to major. According to Guido Küng, his student and successor at Fribourg, Bochenski in later years described himself as a "soldat par goût et longue experience" (soldier by taste and long experience).[21] All this is worth noting as background to his adventuresome demeanor in the parts of the story that follow.

After leaving the army in 1945, Bochenski returned to Fribourg as ordinary professor for the history of modern and contemporary philosophy, a chair created for him personally. He served as dean of the philosophy faculty from 1950 to 1952, as rector of the university from 1964 to 1966, and as pro-rector from 1966 to 1968. He retired from Fribourg in 1972.[22]

Up to the beginning of his time at Fribourg, Bochenski thought of himself primarily as a Thomistic philosopher.[23] He took an active part in founding the Slavic Thomist Society and edited a Polish journal of Thomistic philosophy. Yet even during these early years, his philosophic orientation was considered unorthodox by his fellow Dominicans. As part of his habilitation work, Bochenski had studied Russell and Whitehead's *Principia Mathematica,* and had made a practice of incorporating mathematical logic into his courses at the Angelicum. His Thomist colleagues, however, considered the "new logic" to be positivist in orientation (for them a bad thing), and informed Bochenski that if he wanted to keep his job he should stay away from this deviant discipline.

After this brush with Thomistic orthodoxy, Bochenski shifted his teaching emphasis from mathematical logic to the history of logic generally. But mathematical logic remained at the heart of his research interests, and he became preoccupied with a project aimed at the renewal of theology with the tools of mathematical logic. In pursuit of this project, he teamed with other Polish logicians (including Boleslaw Sobocinski, who came to ND in 1957) in organizing the so-called Cracow Circle. Activities of this group brought him into frequent contact with members of the Vienna Circle, particularly Alfred Tarski, Carl Hempel, Rudolf Carnap, and Karl Menger (the mathematician who invited Kurt Gödel to ND). His major English publications during this second phase are *Ancient Formal Logic* (1951), *A Precis of Mathematical Logic* (1959), and *A History in Formal Logic* (1961).

In the mid-1950s, Bochenski's scholarly interests shifted once again to European philosophy and to Soviet thought in particular. His 1956 publication *Contemporary European Philosophy* was considered the best introduction to this subject at the time, and soon was translated into nine languages. As far as Soviet thought is concerned, Bochenski trained some of the world's best Sovietologists, including Nicholas Lobkowicz, who came to ND on his recommendation in 1960. His main English publications in this field were *Soviet Russian Dialectic Materialism* (1963) and *Guide to Marxist Philosophy* (1972). By the time the former had appeared, Bochenski had become one of the world's leading authorities on Soviet philosophy.

Toward the end of his tenure at Fribourg he entered a fourth and final phase. In deliberate contrast to his Thomistic past, Bochenski began describing himself as an analytic philosopher. With this self-description, he likened himself overtly to analytic philosophers such as Quine, Goodman, and Chisholm in the United States, and Austin, Ryle, and Strawson in the United Kingdom. One characteristic mark of analytic philosophy, as he conceived it, is that it begins with the concrete and proceeds to the abstract. In contrast with synthetic ("big picture") philosophies like his youthful Thomism, which are abstract from the beginning, analytic philosophy is rooted in the world of everyday experience. Another mark is that analytic philosophy employs the resources of formal logic. In Bochenski's view, the formalisms of logic are not human inventions but rather correspond to structures in the actual world. To do philosophy in an analytic manner is to engage in logical analyses of how things stand in the world.[24]

This is a brief profile of the Dominican priest Fr. Hesburgh brought to ND as a visiting professor of philosophy in 1955–56. During the first several years of his presidency, Hesburgh had conducted extensive tours of Europe looking for new faculty. On the trip during which he met Bochenski, he was looking for philosophers specifically. He had already visited Salamanca, Paris, Munich, and Louvain (where he recruited Ernan McMullin), and then descended on Fribourg to meet the great Bochenski. If the meeting had been adversarial, it would have been a case of irresistible force against immovable object. But Hesburgh came expecting to find a kindred spirit. He wanted Bochenski's help in rebuilding ND's Philosophy Department.

The best insight we have into that meeting comes from an interview with Fr. Hesburgh himself, conducted by Ernan McMullin almost fifty years later. As Hesburgh recalled, the first thing he noticed about Bochenski's office was that its walls were completely lined with books. Most were books on philosophy and theology, and several languages were represented. Bochenski pointed out fifteen books written by himself in languages including English, French, German, and Italian, as well as Polish. Hesburgh asked what he was working on currently. Bochenski said a history of formal logic, covering not only Europe, but China, Japan, and India as well. Hesburgh then asked about languages required for the necessary research, and about how many languages Bochenski had mastered. The answer was that Sanskrit was among the languages required, and that normally it would take two weeks or so for him to get the basics of a new language under his belt.

Intrigued by Bochenski's linguistic skills, Fr. Hesburgh asked whom he might find to translate the history of formal logic into English. Bochenski immediately named Fr. Ivo Thomas, a Dominican colleague in Oxford. The book in question came out a few years later, under the aforementioned title *A History in Formal Logic,* translated and edited by Ivo Thomas. Fr. Ivo came to ND in 1958, the same year I arrived.

It is not surprising that Hesburgh's fifty-year-old memories of Bochenski were dominated by the topic of books. An inveterate bibliophile, Hesburgh was responsible for the construction of ND's fourteen-story library that now bears his name. Another predilection Hesburgh shared with Bochenski was speed. In the interview with McMullin, Hesburgh described Bochenski as "a brilliant guy who had a thing about moving fast." He drove a high-powered sports car, Hesburgh said, "a Messerschmidt or something like that." On the Autobahn Bochenski would go full throttle, up to 100 kph faster than the nominal limit of 130. After they had known each other for a while, Hesburgh advised Bochenski to try an airplane because airplanes go faster. Acting on the advice of one who knew, the Dominican friar got his pilot's license at age sixty-eight and subsequently "flew all over Europe" and northern Africa as well.

Fr. Bochenski and Fr. McMullin both came to ND in 1955, with Bochenski slated to stay only one year. That year turned out to be the most disruptive time in the entire history of ND's Philosophy Department. As McMullin put it years later, Bochenski's radical view of philosophy hit the department like a whirlwind, and little remained of the old structure once the storm had cleared.

According to the *University Bulletin* for 1955–56, Bochenski taught a seminar on the history of late medieval logic and another on contemporary twentieth-century semantics. He conducted these seminars in an autocratic manner. He would not let latecomers enter the room; Vince Smith, a colleague in the department, once was denied entry for being tardy. And initially he would not let women attend, although he later relented when Jean Oesterle persisted. Despite his overbearing manner, McMullin recalls that Bochenski was a very effective teacher. Both seminars were well attended, including people from mathematics and science as well as philosophy.

In conjunction with his semantics seminar, Bochenski organized a conference on the problem of universals. The main speakers were Alonzo Church (under the title "Propositions and Sentences"), Nelson Goodman ("A World of Individuals"), and Bochenski himself ("The Problem of Universals"). Philosophers mentioned prominently in these talks include Frege, Russell, and Quine, who were total strangers to most of the local audience. Proceedings of that conference were published in 1956 by UNDP under the title *The Problem of Universals*.

Bochenski left in the spring of 1956 with a rather low opinion of the way philosophy was done at ND. His estimation of the department is summed up in an anecdote recounted years later in a 1986 interview with Jan Parys (*Entre la logique et la foi*).[25] Bochenski recalls that, after listening to an animated account of Aristotelian logic by a ND priest who taught the subject, he raised an objection. Pulling out a copy of Aristotle's *Analytics,* he asked the priest to look at it. The priest responded that he did not read Greek. Bochenski was stupefied, and gave the priest a lecture on why no one could understand Aristotle who did not read Greek. Feigning exasperation for the benefit of Parys, his interlocutor, Bochenski then remarks (idiomatically translated), "Such was the predicament I had fallen into at that university." Bochenski concludes this tirade with the conciliatory remark that ND had become (by the mid-1980s) not only one of the two good Catholic universities in the United States (the other being St. Louis), but also the country's primary center of mathematical logic.[26] This auspicious change in fortune, Bochenski goes on to say, is due to his having added Boleslaw Sobocinski and Ivo Thomas to ND's faculty.

Elsewhere in the same interview, Bochenski admits that he had been counting on the help of these two logicians in transforming the Philosophy Department. As he put it, the triumvirate "Aïvo, Sobo, and Bobo" (the last name he applied to himself) would wage war on the "traditional teaching of philosophy" at ND. The obvious allusion was to traditional Laval-style Thomism.[27]

Thinking back over the Bochenski episode fifty years later, McMullin recalled Fr. Bochenski's having told Fr. Hesburgh that the Philosophy Department was headed in the wrong direction and that it was too much committed to an archaic Thomism. An easily anticipated move on Fr. Hesburgh's part was to ask Bochenski whether he would be interested in taking over as department chair. When I arrived in 1958, there was a rumor to the effect that Bochenski's reason for declining was that Hesburgh refused to meet his demand that all present members of the department be terminated if he accepted. As things worked out, the department would have to wait another decade until it could make a new start with McMullin at the helm.

After leaving ND, and before retiring from his Fribourg professorship in 1972, Bochenski spent time at UCLA, Pittsburgh, the University of Kansas, Boston College, and Catholic University. After retirement, he held visiting appointments in Austria, Colombia, and Argentina. He returned to ND in 1966 to receive an honorary degree and in 1970 to deliver a series of Perspective lectures (see chap. 4, under "The Perspective Series"). The commendation accompanying the presentation of the honorary degree was written by Fr. McMullin, and contained lighthearted references to Bochenski's earlier stay at ND. Unaccustomed to levity on such portentous occasions, Bochenski accepted the certificate with visible displeasure. This reinforced Fr. Ernan's unabashed memory of Bochenski as a crotchety old man "with little feel for normal human relations."[28]

ERNAN MCMULLIN, A MAN OF MANY PARTS

Ernan McMullin was born in Ballybofey, County Donegal, on October 13, 1924. His father was a lawyer, and his mother a medical doctor. After the early deaths of his parents, he was raised under the care of adoring grandparents.[28] He received a bachelor's degree in physics from Maynooth College in 1945 and a bachelor's in divinity in 1948. He was ordained in 1949 as a priest in the Raphoe diocese, part of Donegal.

Fr. Ernan spent a year spanning 1949–50 at the newly established Dublin Institute for Advanced Studies. He was the only person without an advanced degree in science attending the Institute at the time. During this year he worked on a research project on cosmic ray energy-distribution and attended seminars given by Erwin Schrödinger. In 1950 he moved on to the Catholic University of Louvain, home of several leading Thomist scholars of the day, where he received a PhD in philosophy four years later. While working on his dissertation, "The Quantum Principle of Uncertainty," he returned to Dublin for further interaction with Schrödinger. Ernan McMullin was a physicist before he was a philosopher, and the physics he studied had nothing to do with Aristotle or Saint Thomas.

McMullin first met Fr. Hesburgh at Louvain in 1954, as part of Hesburgh's previously mentioned swing through Europe during which Bochenski had been recruited. Arrangements were made for Ernan to begin teaching at ND the following fall. Arrangements in this case involved negotiations with his bishop in Ireland. It turned out that the bishop had plans for Ernan to teach mathematics and Greek in a Gaelic-speaking diocesan school. (Ernan himself had learned Gaelic in high school.) As Fr. Hesburgh recalls, the bishop had no problem with delaying those plans for two or three years. So Ernan was cleared for a brief stint at the University of Notre Dame, beginning in 1955 as a part-time visiting instructor with joint duties in philosophy and physics.

His duties in the Physics Department were to teach logic and philosophy of science in John FitzGerald's highly successful philosophy sequence for physics majors. These courses went well, and Ernan's relations with the physicists were congenial from the beginning. He was assigned a single office in newly opened Nieuwland Science Hall, avoiding the six-occupant cells in O'Shaughnessy allocated to philosophy professors.

Ernan's interaction with his colleagues in philosophy, on the other hand, was rocky from the beginning. For one thing, the department had not been consulted when he was appointed. While still at Louvain, moreover, he had given Vince Smith's 1950 book *Philosophical Physics* a scathing review that put a strain on their relationship when they later became colleagues. To make matters worse, he had been asked to teach a logic course for the department using John Oesterle's text (the one with the tear-out pages), but after a few trials had replaced it with Copi's *Introduction to Logic*. Vince Smith, John Oesterle, and Fr. Herman Reith were further alienated by Ernan's involvement in the circulation of unflattering assessments of courses they were teaching in the GPLE.[29] Pending further details, it is enough for now to note that these unfortunate incidents left Ernan persona non grata in the department until he left for Yale in 1957.

Ernan's initial visit to Yale was funded by the very first postdoctoral grant in the history and philosophy of science awarded by the NSF. NSF's program in this area had been initiated in 1956 at the urging of Fr. Hesburgh himself, who then was a member of the National Science Board. Once postdocs in this area had been officially approved, Fr. Hesburgh promptly encouraged Fr. Ernan to apply for a grant. Upon being notified that his application was successful, Ernan made plans to spend a year at Yale and then to report back to his bishop in Ireland. For the time being, at least, he left further thoughts of ND behind.

Ernan was excited by his interaction with philosophers at Yale, particularly John Smith, Paul Weiss, and Wilfrid Sellars. He managed to add a year to the time funded by the NSF by working part-time at the Catholic Chaplancy, still planning to leave for Ireland when his time at Yale was over. The next development in Ernan's saga was wholly unexpected. He received a call from Fr. Hesburgh, who was in New Haven on other business, asking Ernan to meet him at his hotel. The point of the meeting, it turned out, was to invite Ernan back to ND as chair of the Philosophy Department. Quite sensibly, Ernan declined, explaining that as persona non grata in the department he could scarcely expect to lead it effectively. Despite Hesburgh's persistence, the meeting ended with its mission unaccomplished and Ernan still expecting to return to Ireland.

A few months later Ernan received an official offer to rejoin ND's Philosophy Department on a tenure track as assistant professor. This time he was inclined to accept. Upon requesting further time away from his bishop, however, Ernan was informed that he was expected to begin teaching in the Gaelic-speaking high school the following fall. He left Yale for Ireland in the summer of 1959.

Once back in Ireland, however, he found to his great surprise that the bishop had reversed his stand and was now willing to let him return to ND for an indefinite period. Ernan eventually learned what had caused the bishop to change his mind. One factor was a meeting in Rome between Msgr. Louis de Raeymaeker, once Vice-Rector of Louvain, where Ernan took his PhD, and Msgr. Gerard Mitchell, president of Maynooth, where he received his BSc. During this meeting, Msgr. De Raeymaeker persuaded Msgr. Mitchell to put pressure on the bishop to let Ernan go.

Another factor behind the bishop's about-face involved a ND contact from a few years earlier. Jacques Maritain, during a visit to ND in 1956, had been assisted by McMullin as a translator, and the two men got on well together. When Maritain heard that Ernan's return to ND was in doubt, he wrote a strong letter to the bishop on Ernan's behalf. Maritain at that point was arguably the most prominent Catholic philosopher in the world. With his voice added to that of Mitchell and de Raeymaeker, the bishop saw fit to relent. Ernan McMullin returned to ND for a stay that lasted almost five decades, and the Philosophy Department began its transition into a new identity.

Ernan returned with the resolve to put ND philosophy on the map. Despite his modest rank of assistant professor, he began to act on that resolve within months of arrival. His first major project was bold to the point of audacity. With the financial backing of Fr. Hesburgh, and drawing on a wide range of contacts he had made at Yale and Louvain, Ernan organized an ambitious conference on the concept of matter that convened in the fall of 1961. Distinguished presenters from the United States and abroad included Herbert Feigl (Minnesota), Mary Hesse (Cambridge), Norwood Hanson (Indiana), Wilfrid Sellars (Yale), Richard McKeon (Chicago), and Joseph Owens (Pontifical Institute, Toronto), along with a dozen or so others. By all accounts, the conference was a great success, resulting in the publication of *The Concept of Matter* (UNDP) in 1963. We return with more details on this conference in chapter 4.

As his success in bringing off this conference illustrates, Ernan was already highly accomplished in the social skill known as "networking." Perhaps more than any other single factor, Fr. Ernan's personal contacts with many of the world's most influential philosophers enabled ND's march to the forefront of American philosophy. As an indirect beneficiary of these contacts, I have sometimes paused to recall how I first met this or that prominent person in the profession. More often than not, the answer has been that I was introduced to that person by Ernan McMullin. His personality was such that he could make friends for life in the course of a brief conversation. Chalk it up to Irish charm if you will, but there was something about his person that was almost mesmerizing. An obituary on his undergraduate college website recalls that "Father McMullin's formidable intellect and erudition were transcended by the warmth of his personality. From the remotest rows of a lecture hall or from a hundred yards across a campus quadrangle, a humorous twinkle in his eyes would often be strikingly visible."[30]

Ernan spent the year 1964–65 at the University of Minnesota as a replacement for Grover Maxwell, then director of Minnesota's philosophy of science program. By his own confession, this was a landmark year in his career. He lectured on the relation between science and religion and led discussions at the local Newman Center on the significance of the ongoing Second Vatican Council. Friendships made during this year lasted until the end of his life. When he sold his house in South Bend, after a reluctant departure from ND in 2006, he retired to St. Paul, Minnesota, to be near some of these old friends.

To commemorate Galileo's birth in February of 1564, Ernan convened a "world conference" (as he described it) on Galileo in the spring of 1964, a few months before going to Minnesota. First editions of many of Galileo's works went on display (running up a large insurance bill), and topflight Galileo scholars read papers to large audiences. Most of these papers were published in *Galileo: Man of Science*,[31] which also included a complete bibliography of Galileo's works. Fr. Hesburgh distributed copies of this six-hundred-page volume to all faculty members of the Science College.

Ernan received tenure in 1965, was made chair of the Philosophy Department the same year, and was promoted to professor in 1967. During the academic year 1966–67, he inaugurated the renowned Philosophical Perspective Series which brought several dozen of the world's top philosophers to ND's campus. In 1968 he organized and directed the first installment of the Carnegie Summer Institute, which over the course of five years played host to two hundred or so teachers from small Catholic colleges while introducing them to trends in contemporary philosophy. These ventures are described more fully in chapter 4.

Ernan served as president of the ACPA in 1966–67, of the Metaphysical Society of America in 1973–74, of the Philosophy of Science Association in 1980–82, and of the Western Division of the APA in 1983–84. He was awarded the Aquinas Medal by the ACPA in 1981. He was appointed to ND's John Cardinal O'Hara Chair in 1984.

His five honorary degrees are from Loyola University in Chicago (1969), the National University of Ireland (1990), Maynooth College (1995), Stonehill College (2001), and ND itself (2001). In 1986, he was elected Fellow of the American Academy of Arts and Sciences. After retirement in 1994, he continued to teach occasional graduate courses until 2003. We remain attuned to the career of this extraordinary person up to the concluding paragraphs of the present story.

THOMISM ON THE WANE

Theodore Hesburgh's overarching ambition when he became president in 1952 was to transform ND into a topflight university. If a particular philosophic tradition seemed to be blocking that goal, then that tradition would have to be pushed aside. Joseph I. M. Bochenski was a historian of logic with a lively interest in analytic philosophy. During his single year with ND's Philosophy Department, he convinced Fr. Hesburgh that progress toward excellence in the department would require breaking free from its Thomistic moorings. Ernan McMullin was a physicist and philosopher of science for whom Thomism held little intrinsic interest. When charged by Fr. Hesburgh with making philosophy a first-rate department, he was ready to proceed without deference to its Thomistic heritage.

These three strong-minded priests set the stage for the gradual decline of Thomism at ND. As Catholic clergymen, they were surely aware of the papal mandate establishing Thomism as the philosophy of choice in Catholic higher education. Before beginning to trace the steps of Thomism's descent, we should retrace the history of this papal mandate.

Speaking for the church in his encyclical *Aeterni Patris,* we recall, Leo XIII commanded Catholic teachers and scholars to follow the lead of Saint Thomas in defending the faith. Thirty-five years later (1914), Pius X issued the document *Doctoris Angelici,* warning philosophers and theologians that the slightest deviation from the Angelic Doctor involves the risk of serious error. Benedict XV's *Code of Canon Law* (1917) required all professors of philosophy and theology to teach the method and the doctrine of the Angelic Doctor. Pius XI followed with *Studiorum Ducem* (1923), saying that the church has adopted the philosophy of Saint Thomas for her very own. This series of edicts is topped off by Pius XII's *Humani Generis* (1950), informing the faithful that "the church demands that future priests be instructed in philosophy 'according to the method, doctrine, and principles of the Angelic Doctor.'"

Although *Humani Generis* came out in 1950, it had little apparent effect on department hiring at ND during the ensuing decade. The department continued to hire Thomists, of course. Notable examples include Joe Evans in 1951, John Oesterle in 1954, and both Ralph McInerny and Joe Bobik in 1956. But starting with Ernan McMullin, a majority of subsequent hires during that decade were of people with no particular allegiance to the Thomistic approach. This at least appears to have run counter to papal edict. Moreover, papal edict aside, it was a major deviation from the department's long-standing Thomistic orientation. Let us focus on what was happening at ND during this critical decade to bring about such a dramatic change in direction.

In the early 1950s, when Fr. Hesburgh became president, department policy was guided by a fairly robust conception of the role philosophy was supposed to play in Catholic liberal education. This conception was based on three assumptions: (1) that the goal of Catholic liberal education is the acquisition of wisdom, (2) that the highest wisdom lies in the revealed truths studied by theology, and (3) that philosophy prepares the student for the study of theology. If philosophy fails to do its job, then so will theology. And if theology fails to convey the requisite wisdom, then Catholic liberal education falls short of its goal.[32]

Within months of taking office, Fr. Hesburgh asked Fr. Sheedy, his newly appointed dean of the College of Arts and Letters, to organize a self-study of how well A&L was fulfilling its mission. In effect, Fr. Sheedy was to assess philosophy's success in supporting theology and theology's success in transmitting wisdom to its students. The committee overseeing the self-study was chaired by Dean Sheedy, with membership including three senior faculty from theology, four from philosophy, and one each from the General Program of Liberal Education and the Program for Administrators (subsequently College of Business Administration). This oversight committee elected three of its members to a research group that did most of the actual work. The smaller group was headed by Vincent Smith of philosophy, with Edward O'Connor, CSC, of theology and Herbert Johnston of philosophy as other members.

Fr. Hesburgh's reason for mandating this study, boiled down to essentials, was his awareness of widespread dissatisfaction among A&L students with the courses they were required to take in philosophy and theology. According to data compiled by the study group,[33] about three-fourths of the students sampled felt that their philosophy courses failed to bring the subject to life, while about two-thirds felt the same about their courses in theology. With regard to the philosophy offerings themselves, over one-half felt that there was too much emphasis on memory and too little on understanding, and about two-fifths thought there was too much reliance on Saint Thomas in ways disconnected from their other courses and from concerns of daily life. Given these results, it was evident that philosophy was contributing very little to the process of imparting Christian wisdom to the average student.

The study group's recommendations for correcting these shortcomings were very interesting. The group raised no questions about philosophy's "handmaid" role in supporting theology or about theology's mission of imparting Christian wisdom. Instead it focused on reasons why these traditional objectives were not being met. The answers it came up with were that undergraduate courses in other departments were not closely tied in with philosophy and that philosophy courses were not set up to provide the best support for theology. The problem at hand, as the study group saw it, concerned the structure of the undergraduate curriculum rather than the mission it was supposed to accomplish.

Given this analysis of the problem, the group's response was predictable. If other courses are unconnected with what is taught in philosophy, then these other courses should be altered to remove that deficiency. For example, social science (economics and sociology) should be "subordinate to moral science" (249), and physical science should be continuous with philosophy of nature (209). These recommendations followed the group's conviction that every "discipline has its place in the order of learning" and that each "must be grafted in its proper place" (48).

To enable philosophy to support theology optimally, the group recommended a sequence of courses following the "Thomistic order of learning" (135). First comes logic, "the instrument of the sciences," which enables the mind to reason correctly. Next comes the philosophy of nature, which studies "the causes and reasons of mobile being." Third is ethics, "the science of right conduct," which provides a basis for moral theology. And last comes metaphysics, "the science of being as being," aiding theology in the "handmaid" role of making theology's arguments perspicuous (146). Such a curriculum, the study group urged, would serve effectively in the "transmission of Christian wisdom" (136), which was taken to be the aim of a Catholic liberal education.

When the study group's recommendations were implemented the following year, philosophical psychology (philosophy of man) was substituted for ethics, which in turn was moved to theology. The sequence of logic, philosophy of nature, philosophy of man, and metaphysics remained a standard part of the A&L curriculum until Vince Smith left in 1959. As might be anticipated, minor curricular changes like these would not alleviate philosophy's poor reputation among undergraduate students.

The next systematic indication of student discontent came with the previously noted questionnaire administered to seniors of the GPLE during the spring of 1957. GPLE was chaired by Otto Bird, its founder, who had worked closely with Mortimer Adler's Great Books Program in Chicago. The purpose of the questionnaire was to discover how that department's newly introduced Great Books curriculum was faring in comparison with other programs. Students were asked about their required courses generally, including the four-course philosophy sequence. Although the Great Books component of GPLE received a generally favorable response, results for the four philosophy courses were uniformly negative.

When Fr. Hesburgh caught wind of these results, as already indicated, he asked Fr. McMullin to write a summary report of details pertaining to those four courses in particular. With the philosophy chair's approval, Fr. McMullin submitted his report to Fr. Hesburgh shortly before leaving for summer break. Over the summer, Fr. Hesburgh sent a copy to Fr. Sheedy of A&L. For reasons no one now can reconstruct, Dean Sheedy sent copies to implicated members of the Philosophy Department. Particularly affected were John Oesterle, who taught

Aristotelian logic, Fr. Reith (chair), who taught philosophical psychology, and Vince Smith, who taught philosophy of nature and was the primary author of the four-course requirement. When Ernan returned from summer break, the senior members of the Philosophy Department were up in arms.

Ernan left for Yale a few days later, leaving behind a group of very angry colleagues. Subsequent events in his career were summarized in the previous section. What should be added at this point is that the very group of philosophers who were upset with Ernan over his report had completely lost credibility in the eyes of Fr. Hesburgh's administration. Thomism as taught at ND had suffered a blow from which it never recovered.

What had fallen from grace, it should be noted, was not Saint Thomas himself, but the way Thomism was being taught as an academic subject. If the works of any single philosopher had to be chosen as the basis for an entire Catholic-oriented curriculum, those of Thomas Aquinas arguably provide the best candidate available. The problem was that his philosophy was being taught on a "production line" basis. Given the thousands of students taking courses on Saint Thomas's thought, a high degree of standardization was unavoidable. This resulted in the "thoroughly dead manuals" to which Fr. Leo Ward had so strenuously objected.

Let us look at this phenomenon of mass instruction at ND more closely. During the mid-1950s, approximately 2,400 ND undergraduates were taking philosophy courses in a given semester.[34] Few of these students had either aptitude for or interest in the kind of abstract reasoning needed to benefit from a study of systematic Thomism. As Fr. McMullin reported from his own experience at the time, the typical American undergraduate was "an average sort of fellow" with "little experience of, or taste for, abstract thinking."[35] Students at ND were no exception.

Similar hazards were encountered on the other side of the lectern. Large numbers of teachers were required to teach so many students, and these teachers were not uniformly well prepared. As detailed in chapter 1 (see "People and Places"), close to three dozen people were teaching philosophy at ND moving into the 1950s, and a sizable number of these had no graduate training. Many were teaching courses they had taken as undergraduates only a few years earlier. With poorly prepared teachers holding forth before uninterested students, required courses in Thomism were hard to justify in the growing competition for curricular slots.

As one might surmise, the plight of Thomism at ND was repeated in other Catholic colleges and universities across the country. Addressing the issue at large, historian Philip Gleason observes that, whereas most Catholic philosophy departments were quite sanguine about Thomism in 1950, "openly expressed dissatisfaction [with Thomism] had become widespread by the end of the decade."[36] Moving ahead a few years, we find that by the mid 1960s a full one-quarter of Catholic departments in the country were made up with a majority of non-Thomist members.[37] In some cases, the rejection of Thomism as a dominant influence was quite emphatic. In 1964, for instance, the department at Chicago's DePaul University made *Time* magazine when its chair, Professor Gerald F. Kreyche, publicly derided "closed-system Thomists who still shadowbox the ghosts of the 13th century."[38] The *Time* article goes on to say that "Kreyche has received dozens of inquiries and letters of congratulations from Catholic educators across the U.S.," praising "DePaul's new philosophy program" that emerged under his leadership.

Interestingly enough, several prominent Catholic philosophers of that era singled out yet another reason for rejecting Thomism as an "official" Catholic philosophy. Fr. McMullin explained this reason in a suitably restrained manner. Alluding to the insistence of successive popes that Thomism should hold sway in Catholic institutions, he remarked that legislating "a philosophy that should be freely and intelligently chosen is to do it a grave injustice." Not only will such legislation "transform a worthwhile philosophy into a mere ideology," but it will also "alienate many who might otherwise have been led to accept it."[39]

Continuing the same line of criticism, Fr. W. Norris Clarke, SJ, was more emphatic in suggesting that papal backing of Thomism had created a "deadly aura of authoritarianism and official orthodoxy" that then surrounded "the name . . . of Thomism for so many of the younger generation of teachers and their students. . . ." The common effect, said Fr. Clarke, was to block them "from nourishing their thoughts with the great central ideas of St. Thomas."[40] Even more outspoken was Dominican Fr. James A. Weisheipl of Toronto, describing the times before Pope John's Vatican II as "days of suspicion, fear, and denunciation," and comparing the authoritarian approach of previous pontiffs with "methods employed by the German Gestapo during the Third Reich." As matters stood, he avowed, "Thomism as presented in the twentieth century rightly seems to many to be completely irrelevant."[41]

These point-blank statements are symptomatic of a growing discontent with Thomistic orthodoxy heading into the 1960s. Fr. Norris Clarke, in the article quoted previously, spoke of "a massive flight from Thomism all over the country."[42] Another Jesuit philosopher, Fr. Gerald A. McCool, referred to Thomism's being "forced to surrender the position of leadership which it had once enjoyed in Catholic philosophy and theology."[43] And Ernan McMullin, in his 1967 presidential address to the ACPA, described what he saw as a "massive failure of confidence . . . over the past decade" among Thomists who taught from textbooks in American Catholic colleges.[44]

ND's Philip Gleason, professor emeritus of History, summed it up by speaking of a "collapse" in the late 1950s of the hegemonic position that "Thomism had hitherto occupied in American Catholic Higher Education."[45] The way that collapse played out in ND's Philosophy Department is the topic of the following chapter.

CHAPTER 3

The Gates Swing Open

RALPH MCINERNY, KIERKEGAARD SCHOLAR

Fr. Hesburgh was convinced that the Philosophy Department's text-book version of Thomism stood in the way of the university's pursuit of excellence. This conviction motivated his persistent and ultimately successful effort to bring Ernan McMullin back to ND. Ernan returned in 1961, became chair in 1965, and within a few years had replaced Thomism with a vibrant pluralism. Energetically implemented by McMullin, Hesburgh's vision charted the future of the department.

Unaware that their days in the sun were numbered, the department's senior Thomists had been working in the early 1950s on a strategy for strengthening their ties with the past. In 1879, lest we forget, Pope Leo XIII had issued the encyclical *Aeterni Patris,* in which he ordered Catholic philosophers to follow the lead of Saint Thomas in defending the faith. Subsequent papal proclamations repeated this instruction with increasing insistence, up through Pius XII's *Humani Generis,* issued in 1950. Aware that Thomism in fact was losing support in American Catholic colleges and universities at the time, ND's Thomists considered themselves obligated to find a more effective way of implementing this repeated papal mandate.

The strategy they came up with is described in a charming lecture given by Ralph McInerny in 1992 entitled "Notre Dame and Dame Philosophy."[1] As we shall soon see, Ralph McInerny was probably the most committed and certainly the most outspoken Thomist in the history of the department. This notwithstanding, he had become familiar with Søren Kierkegaard, the Danish Christian existentialist, on his way to a PhD at Laval. He had done an MA thesis on Kierkegaard at the University of Minnesota, and his PhD dissertation at Laval had also dealt with this distinctly non-Thomistic philosopher. Ralph quite literally was a fighting Thomist with serious exposure to another philosophic tradition as well.

"Notre Dame and Dame Philosophy" relates the circumstances of Ralph's arrival at ND roughly thirty-five years prior to the lecture. After debating its mission in the early 1950s, Ralph recalls, the department decided that *Aeterni Patris* charged Catholic philosophers with two distinct tasks. One was to assimilate and to propagate the philosophic patrimony of Catholicism, in which Saint Thomas is the paramount figure. The other was to bring this patrimony to bear on issues of our contemporary era.[2] Quite sensibly, this twofold mission was interpreted as mandating the department to hire Thomists who were also trained in contemporary philosophy. Given his background in both Saint Thomas and Kierkegaard (who died in 1855!), Ralph considered himself to be the first person at ND hired under this dual requirement.

Ralph also suggests in the lecture that this dual-purpose hiring policy inadvertently moved the department along the path of "secularization," by which he meant philosophy pursued without Saint Thomas as a guide. However one views it, what happened is that expertise in contemporary philosophy soon took precedence in hiring over allegiance to Thomism, and that Thomists eventually became a minority in the department. The present chapter tells the story of how the Thomism that previously had prevailed in the department was replaced by other philosophic allegiances.

Ralph McInerny was born in Minneapolis on February 24, 1929. He attended Nazareth Hall Preparatory Seminary from 1942 to 1946, endured a year or so in the Marine Corps, and returned to Nazareth to graduate in 1949. He then went to St. Paul Seminary, where he spent another two years before leaving with a BA degree in 1951. Roughly eight years as a seminarian and one as a marine had convinced Ralph that he was not cut out for the celibate life. After so many years preparing for the priesthood, however, he continued to think of himself as having some special commitment to that role. It was not entirely in jest, I gather, that the third chapter of his autobiographical *I Alone Have Escaped to Tell You* is entitled "Spoiled Priest."[3]

Ralph met Constance Kunert within a year after leaving the seminary. He was working toward an MA in philosophy at the University of Minnesota, where she currently was a third-year undergraduate. As Connie recalled later, Ralph started talking marriage from the very beginning of their relationship. After receiving his MA in 1952, Ralph moved to Quebec to begin work on a PhD at Laval, but only after promising to come back for her when he found a place to stay. Ralph and Connie were married in January of 1953, scarcely eight months after they met. Their first son, Michael, was born in December of that year. Connie never finished her undergraduate degree.

Ralph received a PhL from Laval the summer after he and Connie were married and a PhD the following spring. With his PhD near completion, Ralph had sent a letter of inquiry to Fr. Bernard Mullahy, then chair of the ND Philosophy Department, but received a lukewarm response. His first full-time position was at Creighton University, a Jesuit school in Omaha, Nebraska, where he taught for the academic year 1954–55. During that year there was an exchange of letters between Charles De Koninck, Ralph's thesis director at Laval, and Fr. Heman Reith, incoming chair of philosophy at ND, who had been on friendly terms since Fr. Reith received a Laval PhD in 1945. Ralph began his teaching duties at ND in the fall of 1955. He stayed at ND until formal retirement in 2009.

Michael McInerny died of a brain tumor in February 1957, at the age of four, only a year and a half after the family moved to South Bend. By this time, two daughters had joined the brood. With four mouths to feed and medical bills coming due from Michael's illness, Ralph was in difficult straits financially. Fr. Reith described the family's predicament to Fr. Hesburgh, who then got in touch with Vice-President of Academic Affairs Fr. Philip Moore. Fr. Moore informed Ralph that the university would take care of all medical expenses not covered by Blue Cross. ND also gave Ralph money to cover the down payment on a house, enabling the family to leave their cramped quarters in Vetville, the graduate student housing complex.

The house Ralph and Connie bought was on Rexford Drive, a quiet street in South Bend's McKinley Terrace within shouting distance of the place I moved into a few years later. Our families spent a good deal of time together, time enlivened by Connie's gift for friendship and Ralph's ready wit. I vividly remember one Easter day in April when my three sons and the four older McInerny children had an Easter egg hunt in my backyard with at least five inches of snow on the ground. I also remember Ralph's wake on January 31, 2010, when his two oldest daughters, then in their fifties, mentioned their fond memories of hunting Easter eggs hidden under a deep layer of snow. In 1963 the family moved into a much larger house on Portage Avenue, closer to where Michael was buried.

Ralph had a dual career as a philosopher and a novelist, neither aspect of which can be adequately described without resorting to superlatives. Among literary figures, none I can think of comes close to matching Ralph's scholarly output. He wrote eighteen or so philosophy books (there are judgment calls here), including *The Logic of Analogy: An Interpretation of St. Thomas* (1961), *Boethius and Aquinas* (1990), and the 841-page *Thomas Aquinas,* issued in 1998 by Penguin Classics. He edited a substantial number of scholarly books (around eight) and published well over one hundred articles in professional journals and encyclopedias. Recognition for professional accomplishments such as these came in the form of seven honorary degrees (all from Catholic colleges) and six medals for achievements in Catholic philosophy. Over his career, he held sixteen visiting professorships in six countries.

Looking at his accomplishments from the other angle, I venture to say that no academic philosopher has ever come close to Ralph in literary output. An obituary published in the London-based *Times Online* credited him with eighty-one novels, including twenty-eight featuring Father Dowling. This legendary priest, needless to say, is the hero of the Father Dowling Mysteries series that appeared on television between 1987 and 1991. His first novel (*Jolly Rogerson*)[4] was published in 1969, and his last while alive (*The Letter Killeth*) in 2006, a span of thirty-seven years. This averages out to more than two novels a year. Ralph also published a textbook of Latin, a book of poetry, and hundreds of short stories and opinion pieces. Of recent note is his memoir, previously cited, which makes lively reading even for McInerny non-enthusiasts.

It would be a stretch to say that Ralph was the wittiest person in the world, but he certainly was wittier than anyone else I ever met. His propensity to pun peeps through even some of his academic writing—consider the title of *First Glance at Thomas Aquinas: Handbook for Peeping Thomists*. But in writing fiction, his wit was unrestrained. One novelist he might be compared with is Max Beerbohm, who also wrote clever stories about implausible events in academic settings. Like Beerbohm, Ralph had a penchant for drawing sketches. While other people were taking notes at faculty meetings, Ralph would draw elegant pictures of people taking notes. Another suggestive comparison is with Oscar Wilde, who was just as witty in person as in his writing. On his deathbed, Wilde is reputed to have quipped, "I am dying beyond my means." And Ralph, when told he probably had only six months to live after being diagnosed with esophageal cancer, is rumored to have responded, "That's scarcely time to learn to play the harp."

To be sure, Ralph's fondness for punning may have interfered with his development as a literary artist. One gets the sense that he would first hit on a clever title and then write a book to go with it. During his last decade of writing he published ten mysteries with an ND setting, each with a pun in the title. Consider *On this Rockne* (1997), *Lack of the Irish* (1998), *Irish Tenure* (2000), and *Book of Kills* (2000). An earlier title was *Getting a Way with Murder* (1992). This punning with word-spacing brings to mind his first novel, *Jolly Rogerson,* in which Rogerson pointedly omits a space in the aphorism "The pen is mightier than the sword." While Ralph's academic writings are suitably sedate, his early novels tend to be rather racy. I clearly remember an occasion right after a new novel came out when I was talking with Ralph in his living room and Connie came storming down the stairs—book in hand—proclaiming, "Ralph, this is a dirty book." The book in question may have been *Rogerson at Bay,* which is only slightly less raunchy than the first Rogerson book.

One might ask how Ralph found time to write all these books. The answer centers on Constance, his wife. Connie was one of those women, not uncommon in the 1950s and 1960s, whose self-chosen career was raising a family. As Ralph saw it in his memoir, ND wives at the time were happy to be known as "helpmates to their husbands."[5] Connie cooked the meals, cleaned the house, took care of the yard, raised the children, and generally kept the family on an even keel. Ralph's job, of course, was at the university, where he taught his classes and managed his sundry affairs. After dinner, he would help put the kids to bed and then retire to the basement to work on his fiction.

I remember visiting Ralph once in his basement den, with his typewriter on a workbench illuminated by a bare bulb overhead. He told me that his work habits called for a certain number of pages (I think he said five) written before he retired around 2:00 a.m. Once he hit his stride as a fiction writer, it seems he seldom rewrote the pages he filed away before going to bed. If some of his later novels are not as well written as *Jolly Rogerson,* the reason may have been that things came out of his word processor more quickly in later years.

During his first decade or so with the department, Ralph was a model junior colleague. He taught his classes conscientiously, attended faculty discussion meetings, and was as active as anyone in routine department affairs. Between 1955 and 1960, he published more than a dozen scholarly articles. His first book, *The Logic of Analogy,* came out in 1961, followed by volume 1 of his *History of Western Philosophy* in 1963. Although he had been toying with fiction writing since graduate-student days, most of his writing efforts during this first decade were academically oriented.

During these early years, moreover, Ralph showed no concern about the department moving in what he later termed a "secular" direction. Although a majority of the faculty being added to the department in the late 1950s were not Thomists, all (myself excepted) at least were Catholic. As far as Ralph was concerned, the future of Thomism in the department could be left to his older colleagues. He was content to let things run their course without raising objections.

This cooperative attitude on his part continued through the mid-1960s. In response to Vatican II's call for *aggiornamento* ("bringing up to date"), Ralph went so far as to organize a conference held at ND in September 1966 called "Philosophy in an Age of Christian Renewal." Papers from the conference were published in the volume *New Themes in Christian Philosophy* (UNDP, 1968) which he edited. Six ND philosophers contributed to this volume, only one of whom was a traditional Thomist. In his introduction, Ralph expressed thanks to "the wisdom of Pope John XXIII" and the forces of "renewal" it set in motion. He saluted the "virtue of variety" among contemporary strains of Christian philosophy and acknowledged that "different styles of Thomism" were necessary if Thomism itself was to survive. He also remarked that ND philosophers as a group had "no grand vision of what philosophy . . . ought to be." Particularly interesting is Ralph's "special tribute" to Fr. Ernan McMullin, whose "fine Hibernian hand" guided the conference from its inception to its conclusion. These are not remarks that Ralph himself would endorse a few years later.

Several things happened during the late 1960s to budge Ralph from this accommodating stance. One was the conference held in June 1967 on ND's property at Land O'Lakes, Wisconsin, convened by Fr. Hesburgh in his capacity as president of the International Federation of Catholic Universities. Presidents of several major Catholic universities attended, along with two bishops and several laymen. Their purpose was to discuss the role of Catholic universities in the renewal of the church sparked by Vatican II. More specifically, their concern was to devise means of pursuing their shared vision of academic excellence while preserving the Catholic identity of the institutions they represented.

Participants agreed from the outset that academic excellence requires academic freedom. This in turn requires institutional autonomy, including independence from bishops and religious superiors.[6] As far as Catholic identity was concerned, this was to be maintained by the presence of strong theology departments and by prominent roles assigned to priests in campus life. In ND's case, the charter required that the president of the university be a CSC priest. As seen by ND historian Philip Gleason, the Land O'Lakes statement was a "declaration of independence from the [Catholic] hierarchy."[7] Understandably, this outcome made budding conservatives like Ralph uncomfortable.

Another factor in Ralph's conservative migration was the aftermath of Vatican II itself.[8] As indicated by his involvement in the 1966

"Christian Renewal" conference, Ralph at first seemed to take the Council in stride. By the end of that decade, however, his attitude toward Vatican II began to change dramatically. A distinctly negative attitude prevails in his *What Went Wrong with Vatican II: The Catholic Crisis Explained.*[9] The second chapter of this little tract is entitled "1968: The Year the Church Fell Apart." This chapter deals with the impact of Paul VI's *Humane Vitae,* which upheld the church's traditional teaching on contraception. Ralph here attributes the rancor following that encyclical to a widespread disrespect for papal authority set up by Vatican II. The parties he sees as primarily guilty of disrespect are mostly young theologians who defy the magisterium in asserting their own right to interpret the church's sacred teaching.

A more immediate source of alienation on Ralph's part during the late 1960s was disagreement about the role of Thomism in the department under the new administration of Fr. Ernan McMullin. When he became chair in 1965, McMullin unveiled his plan for a pluralist department in which Thomism would take its place as one philosophy to be taught on an equal basis among many others. Ralph's view, on the other hand, was that Thomism should remain the department's dominant focus, with other approaches playing secondary roles. This disagreement between Ralph and Ernan was never resolved. In my several interviews with Ernan the year before his death, he repeatedly expressed disappointment that Ralph had been unwilling to represent Thomism in the department as one philosophy among many.

Following these discouraging events, the 1970s constituted a transitional period during which Ralph gradually withdrew from departmental affairs. He continued to teach graduate courses and to direct PhD theses. In point of fact, a full one dozen theses under his direction were accepted between 1970 and 1980. But his scholarly publications fell off substantially, with only two relatively unsuccessful books and a few articles in professional philosophic journals. His literary output, on the other hand, continued unabated. This was the decade of *The Priest,* far and away his best work of fiction, along with *Rogerson at Bay* and close to one dozen less-distinguished novels. During this decade he also was president of the ACPA (1971–72) and was granted his first honorary degree (from Benedictine College, Kansas, in 1978). None of these activities, however, involved much interaction with other members of ND's Philosophy Department.

Ralph's academic fortunes took a turn for the better during the final years of this transitional decade. In 1978 he was appointed Director of ND's Medieval Institute, which gave him an academic home beyond the confines of the regular department. With this appointment came the Michael P. Grace Professorship of Medieval Studies, a garnishment he retained for the remainder of his academic career. For various reasons, his leadership of the Medieval Institute was not well received, leading to his forced resignation from that role in 1985. In 1979, however, while his credibility as an administrator was still undiminished, Ralph had also been appointed Director of the Maritain Center. When he took charge, the Maritain Center was severely dysfunctional, with no residual staff to impede his plans to convert it into a center for Thomistic scholarship. By the early 1980s this center was well on its way to being the premier institute for Thomistic studies in the country. We return in chapter 5 to Ralph's involvement in these two enterprises.

Prior to moving into the Maritain Center, Ralph had a modest reputation as a fiction writer but little name-recognition as a Catholic intellectual. The latter began to change in 1982, when he teamed up with Michael Novak to publish a monthly journal, aimed at conservative lay Catholics, originally entitled *Catholicism in Crisis*. This publishing venture is another topic for later consideration. For the moment, it is enough to observe that Novak was a member of the American Enterprise Institute (AEI) and had good connections with various well-heeled conservative funding sources. As a result of this joint project with Novak, supporters of the AEI were soon pouring money into the coffers of the Maritain Center as well.

As the Maritain Center became more affluent, Ralph's personal finances also took a turn for the better. *The Priest* was on its way to becoming a best seller, approaching the mark of one million copies sold. Even more lucrative, presumably, was sale of the television rights to his Father Dowling mystery stories. By the end of the 1980s, he had published about thirty novels, proceeds from which had also added to his personal income.

With his growing prominence as a spokesman for conservative causes, Ralph spent less and less time at the university. From the mid-1990s onward, his standard teaching load was an easy two courses per year along with a few directed readings. He also spent substantially less time directing graduate theses. The last PhD thesis written under his sole supervision in the Philosophy Department was completed in 2000. All in all, he probably spent more time working with young Thomists from outside the university than with students enrolled in ND's own PhD program. A case in point was his work with the Thomistic Institute, financed by the Saint Gerard Foundation and the Strake Foundation, which convened each summer under Ralph's directorship for well over a decade.[10] Participants spent a week together in campus housing, attended daily Mass along with morning and evening prayers, and spent most of their time discussing Saint Thomas and the life of the church.

A new vista in public education opened up for Ralph in the mid-1990s when he founded the online International Catholic University (ICU). As explained on its website, Ralph's idea in founding ICU was to embody "the ideal of the Catholic university as set forth in Pope John Paul's apostolic letter *Ex Corde Ecclesiae*."[11] ICU provides forty courses of taped lectures, several of which Ralph recorded himself. In cooperation with Holy Apostles College and Seminary in Connecticut, ICU currently offers MA degrees in both philosophy and theology.

Ralph's health began to slip after Connie's death in 2002. In 2004 he experienced a series of heart problems, which might have been related to the open-heart surgery he underwent in 1996. Yet he continued to write at what for most would be a furious pace. Between 2000 and 2007, he published twenty novels, seven works of philosophy (including his Gifford Lectures), a book of poetry, and thirty-seven articles and occasional pieces. His autobiographical *I Alone Have Escaped to Tell You* was published in 2006.

In 2005, Ralph moved from the large house in the exclusive suburb of Knollwood, which he had shared with Connie in their later years, to a villa in the assisted-living community operated by Holy Cross College across from ND. The following year, friends and former students founded the McInerny Center for Thomistic Studies (MCTS), which offers classes taught live in Washington, DC. MCTS's program consists of six courses over a three-year period, each course meeting for twelve hours in two-hour sessions. According to its website, this seventy-two hour program is "intended for generally educated citizens who wish to develop a deeper grounding in Philosophy."[12] MCTS celebrates its accomplishments each year with a McInerny Banquet, a gala event to which we return in the final chapter.

Ralph died on January 29, 2010, roughly a year before Ernan McMullin. The last time I spoke with him was at Dujarie House, Holy Cross's intensive care unit. His last words to me were to the effect that he would fight to the end to see Thomism restored to its rightful place in ND's philosophy curriculum.

BOCHENSKI'S LOGICIANS

In his published interview *Entre la logique et la foi,* cited previously, Fr. Joseph I. M. Bochenski ("Bobo") mentions the mission he shared with "Sobo" and "Aïvo" in the 1950s of changing the way philosophy was taught at ND. It is unclear how much influence this triumvirate had on the teaching of philosophy at ND generally, but they certainly revolutionized the teaching of logic. By the time of Sobo's retirement in 1977, ND had become one of the foremost centers of mathematical logic in the world.

Boleslaw Sobocinski (Sobo) was born on June 28, 1906, of Polish parents in St. Petersburg, then capital of Russia. He attended Polish schools in St. Petersburg until the Bolshevik revolution in 1917, after which he was tutored privately until his family moved to Warsaw in the mid-1920s. At the University of Warsaw he worked with Jan Łukasiewicz and Stanisław Leśniewski, receiving his PhD in 1936. At the time, Warsaw was considered the world's premier school of formal logic.

Sobocinski served as dozent of logic at Warsaw from 1939 to 1945, when he accepted a professorial appointment at the University of Lodz. Before leaving for Lodz, however, he learned that he was wanted by the Russian secret police. While teaching at Warsaw, he had been active in the Polish underground, which was resisting both Russian oc-cupiers from the east and German invaders from the west. After several months in hiding and two unsuccessful attempts to escape, he finally managed to cross the border into Belgium with his wife-to-be, Ewa.[13]

After a few years in Belgium, Sobocinski immigrated to the United States in 1949. His first appointment, arranged by Bochenski, was at St. Thomas College in St. Paul, Minnesota. Since he lacked fluency in English, his single term at St. Thomas was an unmitigated disaster. In 1952 he founded *The Journal of Computing Systems,* published in St. Paul by his Institute of Applied Logic, which served as an outlet for his technical writings. Both the institute and the journal apparently went defunct when he left St. Paul for ND in 1956. It is unclear where money came from during this period, but the fact that Ewa was a skilled applied mathematician may have enabled the institute to turn a modest profit.

Sobocinski came to ND as a research associate, but within five years had been promoted to full professor. This promotion followed his founding of the *Notre Dame Journal of Formal Logic (NDJFL),* the first issue of which came out in 1960. Sobo taught a considerable range of graduate courses in formal logic and the foundations of mathematics. Among courses offered during his first three years were mereology (the logical study of parts and wholes) prototheric (first principles of the logical foundations of mathematics) modal logic, calculus of relations, advanced logic of names, and introduction to metalogic. During his twenty years of teaching before retirement in 1977, Sobo directed fifteen PhD students in the departments of philosophy and mathematics, more than any other person in the Philosophy Depart-ment during that interval. His graduate students remember him as an unusually effective and caring teacher.

His management of *NDJFL* was another matter. One irregularity was that Sobo refereed all submissions to the journal himself, rather than engaging outside readers. The journal even lacked an editorial board until Jack Canty was appointed managing editor in 1969. This appointment was insisted on by Ernan McMullin, who was chair of the Philosophy Department at the time. McMullin also arranged university space for an office staff, whereas the journal previously had been run out of Sobo's home study.

Another problem concerned the criteria Sobo used for accepting papers. He would divide submissions into three categories—"true" (logically sound) and interesting, true but uninteresting, and "false" (logically unsound). False papers were rejected summarily, true and interesting papers were promptly published, and papers in the remaining category would languish in Sobo's desk drawer indefinitely.[14] The fact that authors of "true but uninteresting" papers would go for years without learning the fate of their submissions turned out to be the biggest problem with Sobo's editorial style. Stacks of these papers accumulated in his desk, waiting to serve as fillers for issues short on true and interesting entries. As McMullin observed later, two extra-large issues of *NDJFL* relieved the backlog of "uninteresting" papers soon after Jack Canty took over as managing editor. I have not checked the issues involved, preferring to remain ignorant of the authors represented.

By the time I got to know Sobocinski in 1958, his days as an underground partisan were at least a decade and a half behind him. The man I knew at ND was hard to picture as posing a danger to either Russians or Nazis. For one thing, he walked with a shuffle and seemed considerably older than his fifty-two years. For another, he was uncomfortable around machines. As far as I know he never learned how to drive a car, relying on Ewa to transport him when he couldn't take a bus. For all that, he had an intimidating visage. In our twenty-two years as colleagues, I never once saw Sobo smile.

Another memorable fact about Sobo is that he smoked incessantly. His smoking routine was intriguing. He would take a cigarette from his box, break it in half, somehow manage to light one half from the stub still in his holder, and smoke it down to the hilt until it was time to light the other half. About the only time you could count on Sobo's not smoking was when he was expounding on logic in public. I never heard him read a paper of his own. But when he attended a talk by someone else, he would always ask the first question. His opening question would sometimes occupy twenty or thirty minutes, being prefaced by an elaboration of his own views on the topic at hand.

These are mostly personal memories. As far as the university was concerned, Sobocinski was a famous logician, master of the so-called Polish notation (which uses position of variables and operators instead of parentheses or dots for punctuation), founder of the prestigious *NDJFL,* author of ninety-one "true and interesting" articles (many published in the *NDJFL*), and prolific mentor of accomplished logicians and mathematicians. He was the first of a distinguished line of ND logicians, predecessor of Penelope Maddy, Michael Kremer, and Michael Detlefsen (editor of the *NDJFL* as of 2010).

Boleslaw Sobocinski died on November 2, 1980. Several men not associated with either logic or ND attended his funeral. In the hushed conversation after the Mass in Sacred Heart Church, it was whispered about that these were men with whom he had shared experience in the Polish underground decades earlier (South Bend has a large Polish community). Rumor had it that they were preparing to fire a military salute at his interment. I do not know whether this actually happened. Perhaps the sight of a troop of old men with rifles approaching ND's Cedar Grove cemetery was enough to elicit preventive action by the local constabulary.

The "Aïvo" of Bochenski's triumvirate was Ivo Thomas, born Herbert Christopher Thomas in Kensington on January 17, 1912. He converted to Catholicism in 1930, completed his Greats (Oxford's classics course) in 1935 at Queen's College, Oxford, and entered the Dominican Order of Preachers that same year. He took the name "Ivo" upon entering the order, presumably in memory of St. Ivo (St. Ives) of Cornwall. He studied philosophy at Hawkesyard Priory from 1936 to 1938 and theology at Blackfriars, Oxford, from 1938 to 1942. He was ordained in 1940, spent time in Edinburgh from 1942 to 1944, and served as professor of philosophy at Hawkesyard from 1944 to 1954. He then was professor of dogmatic theology at Blackfriars until he left for ND in 1958.

Ivo's first assignment at ND, following Bochenski's recommendation, was as visiting professor of philosophy (1958–60). During this time, he helped Sobocinski found the *NDJFL*. When this initial appointment ran out, he taught NSF summer programs for teachers and gifted students of mathematics at ND and at Ohio State University.

In 1963, he joined the GPLE under Otto Bird, becoming a full professor in 1970. Otto Bird remained one of Ivo's closest friends, and wrote the "In Memoriam" from which much of the above information was taken.[15]

Most of Ivo's publications before he came to ND are book reviews and notices, many appearing in *Blackfriars* and *Dominican Studies*. During the time he was helping to establish the *NDJFL*, he published numerous articles and reviews in the *Journal of Formal Logic*. Of the roughly eighty articles published between 1960 and his death in 1978, almost half are in the *NDJFL*. He also published a few encyclopedia articles and, as already noted, a translation of Bochenski's *A History of Formal Logic*.

Ivo was an imposing man with a distinguished face and aristocratic bearing. His self-assured movements were accentuated by his white Dominican habit, which he always wore in public. For all that, he was neither aloof nor reserved in manner. I clearly remember a trip he took with my family to pick apples at a farm across the Michigan border. After watching my boys climb an old apple tree, he hitched up his cassock and followed suit. Another memory of Ivo in a family setting has him reading *The Hobbit* to my boys as a bedtime story. It was from Ivo, in fact, that I first heard of J. R. R. Tolkien. They had been personal friends from Ivo's time at Blackfriars, where Tolkien would occasionally go to Sunday Mass.

Ivo became thoroughly Americanized during his time at ND. He developed a special interest in the history of the American frontier. My last distinct memory of Ivo dates around 1969 or 1970. He was standing in the lobby of Memorial Library, engaged in earnest conversation with three equally imposing Indian chiefs. He was attired as always in his white Dominican robe, and they in colorful headdresses and other regalia of their calling. It turned out that he had organized a conference on Native American religions, by way of comparing them with the religion he had joined some forty years earlier. Somehow, I was reminded of the then current movie *A Man Called Horse,* featuring another Englishman who had been captivated by Native American culture.

In 1972, Ivo Thomas was laicized and married Deirdre La Porte, a colleague in the GPLE. By then, he had left South Bend and taken up residence in Niles, Michigan. I never saw him again after his marriage. He died on February 2, 1976.

THE FRIBOURG ARISTOCRATS

The next group of European philosophers sponsored by Bochenski all studied with him in Fribourg. Nikolaus Lobkowicz arrived in 1960, only two years after Ivo Thomas. Lobkowicz was followed by Guido Küng in 1962 and Karl Ballestrem in 1967. These all were philosophers with fairly broad interests, inclined toward the humanities rather than formal logic. Lobkowicz and Ballestrem both belonged to European nobility. Given the phonetic resemblance between "Küng" and "König," the group might be described whimsically as the Fribourg aristocrats.

Nikolaus Lobkowicz was born July 9, 1931, in Prague. He left Czechoslovakia in 1948 after the communist coup d'état and finished high school in Switzerland. In 1953, he married Countess Josephine von Waldburg zu Zeil und Trauchburg.[16] We called them Nick and Osy. Nick studied philosophy at the Universities of Erlangen, Germany, and Fribourg, Switzerland, receiving his PhD from the latter in 1958. He came to ND in 1960 as an Associate Professor, retaining that rank until he left in 1967. While at ND he taught courses on Saint Thomas, metaphysics of knowledge, natural theology, Soviet philosophy, and Marxism. He also published two of his nine books during this period: *Marxismus-Leninismus in der CSR: Die Tschechoslowakische Philosophie seit 1945* (1962); and *Theory and Practice: History of a Concept from Aristotle to Marx* (1967). Bochenski, in his aforementioned interview with Jan Parys (45), describes Lobkowicz as one of the best Marx scholars Europe had ever produced.

Nick and Osy lived in a modestly upscale house on Kessler Boulevard, not far south of the university. The house was large enough for a growing brood of children and a nanny who had accompanied them from Germany. They had five children in all, the youngest of whom was born in South Bend and baptized by Fr. Ernan McMullin. Nick and Osy spoke mostly English at home and sent their older children to public schools. When the parents returned to Germany in 1972, they took with them a family of acculturated Hoosiers. The nanny stayed on in South Bend, married a local man, and later became victim in a gruesome murder incident.

Although their social life in South Bend was not extensive, Nick and Osy struck up a close friendship with Joe and Teresa Bobik. The two couples occasionally would drive to Chicago together. I remember hearing of one occasion when they stopped at a liquor store a few hundred feet from the Indiana border on the way back. As they proceeded into Indiana with their purchases, they were pulled over by a patrolman and arrested for smuggling alcohol over a state line. This brush with the law apparently did not stand in the way of Lobkowicz's successful application for U.S. citizenship in 1966. He subsequently regained Czech citizenship with the formal creation of the Czech Republic in 1993.

Leaving ND, Lobkowicz moved into a series of administrative roles at the University of Munich. He was chair of the Department of Political Theory and Philosophy from 1967 to 1970, then dean of the faculty of philosophy in 1970–71. In fall of 1971, he was appointed the 507th rector of the university, changing title in 1975 to become its first president. In 1984, he moved on to become president of Eichstätt University. All this while he was lecturing extensively in Europe, Asia, and South America. In 1981, he returned to ND to receive an honorary doctorate, one of six honorary degrees he had received to that date.

Herr Dr. Lobkowicz is a knight of the Order of the Golden Fleece, membership of which is limited to Catholic nobility. He is also a knight of the Sovereign Order of Malta, and a knight of the pontifical Order of St. Gregory. He has been admitted to the Order of Merit of Bavaria, the Order of Merit of the German Federal Republic, and the Mrsaryk Order of the Czech Republic. All of these orders recognize outstanding contributions, in one way or another, to humanity, to democracy, and to human rights.

Guido Küng was born in Switzerland on October 5, 1933. Between 1953 and 1962, he studied at the universities of Barcelona,

Fribourg, Münster, Amsterdam, Kraków, and Pennsylvania (in the United States). He received his PhD from Fribourg under Joseph I. M. Bochenski in 1962. Guido came to ND as an instructor in 1962, then was promoted to assistant professor in 1963 and to associate professor in 1969.[17] Guido's first residence in South Bend was a rented apartment on LaSalle Street, in the same house occupied by Thomas and Christine De Koninck.[18] He later bought a house in the Bercliff Estates, a few blocks from the residence of Mike Loux (of whom we will hear more later).

Guido began teaching at ND only a few months before Hans Küng's much-publicized lecture tour in the United States during early 1963. Fr. Hans Küng is an outspoken critic of papal infallibility, widely known for his *Infallible? An Inquiry* (1971). It so happens that Guido and Hans are cousins. During his tour, Hans lectured to large crowds in several Catholic universities, including Boston College, St. Louis University (where he received an honorary degree), and ND.[19] According to Ernan McMullin, Guido was a member of the ND audience, his face registering visible disapproval of what his cousin was saying.

As I remember, Guido had a long face (not unlike his cousin's), a pronounced jaw, and a somewhat labored smile. He was reserved in manner and spoke in a nasal voice stemming from a chronic asthmatic condition. He always wore a coat and tie when appearing in public, including classes, department meetings, and group discussions. The only time I remember seeing him in casual attire was once when I dropped by his house to deliver a toy my children had outgrown. He and his wife, Elisabeth, at that time had two children, who were South Bend natives. When they left, I remember regretting I had not gotten to know them better.

Guido left ND in 1973 and returned to Fribourg as Bochenski's replacement. He held the position of ordinary professor for the history of modern and contemporary philosophy at Fribourg from 1973 to 2000. During his distinguished career, he served as visiting professor at Laval (1969), Washington University (1972), the Pontifica Universidade de Rio de Janeiro (1979), and Shanghai's Fudan University (1987–88). From 1979 to 1981, he was president of the Swiss Philosophical Association.

Karl G. Ballestrem was born July 2, 1939, in Dresden, to Karl Wolfgang Graf von Ballestrem and Princess Therese zu Löwenstein-Wertheim-Rosenberg. Only after he left ND did I realize that the initial in his name stands for 'Graf,' meaning "Count" in English. As I found out later, Karl Ballestrem in fact was Osy Lobkowicz's first cousin, and more distantly related to Nikolaus himself. After studying a year (1959–60) at the Gregorian University in Rome, Karl received his PhD under Bochenski at Fribourg in 1965. Soon thereafter he left for the United States, spending a year at Rosary College in Chicago before coming to ND as assistant professor in 1967. Karl was back in Germany most of the year 1968–69, dealing with immigration issues. Given his final departure in 1971, he may have taught at ND for a total of only three years. While here, he taught classes in metaphysics, Marxism, and political philosophy. In philosophic discussion, he gave the impression of being a generalist rather than a specialist like Guido.

A year before arriving at ND, Karl married Maria del Consuelo Reichsfrein von Gegern. We knew them simply as Karl and Consuelo. Befitting their upbringing as European aristocrats, the Ballestrems were charming people and seemingly sociable by nature. Perhaps because of their relatively short time here, however, their circle of friends did not include the entire department. I do not remember ever interacting with them socially, and even Ernan McMullin (chair during their entire stay) could not recall ever visiting their local residence. They were particularly close to Ralph and Connie McInerny. It was probably through their wives that Ralph and Karl became friends initially. Karl shared Connie's ingrained empathy with other people, while Ralph shared with Consuelo a deep-seated religious conservatism.

After leaving ND, Karl served as a research assistant at the Political Science Institute at Munich, receiving certification as a specialist in Soviet Studies in 1976. Following certification, he taught in that institute until 1984. In 1984, he moved to Eichstätt as a chaired professor of political science. This was the same year Lobkowicz took over as president. While at Eichstätt, Karl also spent time teaching at the Gregorian University in Rome. Ballestrem authored six books, edited one, and wrote numerous substantial reviews and articles. Notable among the books are *Naturrecht und Politik* (1993), *Adam Smith* (2001), and *Politische Denken* (2004).

Karl Ballestrem retired from Eichstätt in 2003. Between then and his sudden death in 2007, he and Consuelo were very active in the World Youth Alliance, a pro-life organization sponsored by the United Nations. During his last year, he was a member of the Alliance's executive board. Like Lobkowicz, Ballestrem was a Knight of Malta.

ANALYTIC PHILOSOPHY ENTERS THE SCENE

Joseph I. M. Bochenski, as already mentioned, began classifying himself as an analytic philosopher in the early 1970s. In doing so, he explicitly associated himself with major American philosophers such as Quine, Goodman, and Chisholm, and with Ryle, Strawson, and Austin among English luminaries. This classification also served to distance him from phenomenologists like Husserl, existentialists like Heidegger, and philosophers given to grand syntheses like Hegel and Whitehead. In the opinion of Bochenski, at least, the analytic approach is the way of genuine philosophy (la "veritable philosophie").[20]

As I recall, the term "analytic philosophy" was not used much at Harvard during my graduate student days. But most of us there studied Ryle, Strawson, and Austin, along with Quine, Chisholm, and Goodman. And most of us were trained to be wary of Hegel, Husserl, and especially Heidegger. So I counted willy-nilly as an analytic philosopher when I arrived at ND in 1958.

Milton Fisk and Harry Nielsen had arrived a year earlier. With PhDs from Yale and Nebraska, respectively, Milton and Harry had received roughly the same kind of graduate training as I had. Scarcely aware of what the description meant, the three of us were received into the department as its first contingent of analytic philosophers.

Then as now, analytic philosophy was a *way* of dealing with philosophic issues rather than a branch of philosophy like ethics or epistemology. One aspect of this approach, for the three of us at least, was an interest in the methodology of empirical science. My first book-length publication (other than an edited volume) was *Recognition: A Study in the Philosophy of Artificial Intelligence*.[21] Harry's first was *Methods of Natural Science*.[22] And Milton followed with *Nature and Necessity: An Essay in Physical Ontology* a few years later.[23]

Another common concern was that each of us was preoccupied in some way with precision in argument. Milton had studied for a year with Bochenski in Fribourg, which paved the way for his first book, *A Modern Formal Logic*.[24] I had taken courses with Quine at Harvard, including his advanced mathematical logic. And Harry had acquired from his teacher O. K. Bouwsma at Nebraska an uncanny ability for unmasking flaws in everyday reasoning. Although relations with our Thomistic colleagues were almost always congenial, this tendency of ours to be picky with arguments occasionally resulted in intramural friction.

Yet another thing setting us apart from our Thomistic colleagues was an ingrained suspicion of "big picture" philosophy. Thomism, as then conceived, was a comprehensive system of thought, with an answer for most major questions pertaining to human existence. Our typical focus, by contrast, was on particular issues. We had learned philosophy by reading Ryle and Strawson, Quine and Goodman— Bochenski's heroes of analytic philosophy—instead of synthetic thinkers like Hegel and Saint Thomas Aquinas.

Not by coincidence, perhaps, this brief characterization of analytic philosophy is a fair match for that promulgated by the *Philosophical Gourmet Report* in 2011. Analytic philosophers, as there described, "aim for argumentative clarity and precision; draw freely on the tools of logic; and often identify, professionally and intellectually, more closely with the sciences and mathematics, than with the humanities."[25] When Harry, Milton, and I first joined the department, we were not aware of being representatives of a particular approach to philosophy. But we were aware of doing philosophy differently from our colleagues who had been trained at Catholic universities.

Harry Nielsen was born on February 21, 1924, in Bridgeport, Connecticut. After serving in the army from 1943 to 1946, he received a BA from Rutgers in 1949, an MA in English from the University of

Connecticut in 1952, and a PhD from the University of Nebraska in 1955. He then taught for a year each at Pennsylvania State and the University of Illinois, coming to ND in 1957.

Harry and I spent lots of time together, at department functions and elsewhere. We seemed to be particularly at ease with each other. Yet there was something ethereal about him that made one wonder whether he was entirely present. His mind always seemed preoccupied with other things. Ernan McMullin, another colleague at the time, remembers Harry as afflicted with a "deep internal sadness," born perhaps of being more scrupulous than the academy allows. Harry's wife, Donna, was a practical woman who helped keep him in touch with reality. Harry and Donna had four children, the oldest of whom (Mary Krista) died before they left ND.

The first Nielsen residence in South Bend was a good hour's walk from the university. A winter or two after I arrived, the area was hit with a major blizzard—bad enough to force the university to cancel classes. Instead of phoning the ND operator for information, Harry put on his heavy galoshes and battled the storm all the way to his empty classroom. After finding out that everything was shut down, he could only turn around and trudge a long hour against the wind in the opposite direction.

Another memory dates from November 11, 1960. Harry and I had made arrangements for me to pick him up at the polling place after he voted, hoping to take advantage of the rest of the afternoon by going fishing. I knew from a previous conversation that he had been undecided whether to vote for John F. Kennedy or Richard Nixon, so when he got in the car I asked him whom he had finally voted for. Harry remained silent for perhaps half a minute, and then replied in a sheepish voice, "I can't remember."

These anecdotes provide background for an account of Harry's brief time as department chairman. Fr. Herman Reith, who had been chair when both Harry and I arrived, was fed up with the job and wanted to resign as soon as a replacement could be found. Perhaps encouraged by Harry's nonconfrontational manner, Dean Sheedy decided to move him into the job. After a term of utter confusion in the department office, it became apparent that another chairperson was urgently needed. In the meanwhile, Harry had checked into the hospital with nervous exhaustion. Never one to waste time mulling over consequences, Fr. Sheedy visited Harry at the hospital and informed him that he would no longer be in charge of the department after the spring term ended. When Harry was finally discharged from the hospital, he cleaned out his desk in the department office. Occasionally he would wander in with a forlorn look on his face to sign official documents. The department ran on autopilot for the rest of the term, and Fr. McMullin took over in the fall of 1965.

Ralph McInerny remembers Harry's time as department chair in his 1992 lecture "Notre Dame and Dame Philosophy." Describing Harry as "a Wittgensteinian Kierkegaardian, one of the best standup philosophers" he has known, Ralph goes on to say that "as an administrator, he made Father Reith look like Henry Ford." Ralph was also bemused at Harry's "fairly radical redefinition of the department's traditional task, aimed directly at difficulties with faith generated by university study."[26]

What Ralph meant by his comment about Harry being such a good "standup philosopher," I gather, is that when he was talking philosophy, his remarks were always entertaining. They also typically were very provocative. Harry knew Wittgenstein's *Philosophical Investigations* almost by heart. When discussion took a turn suggesting that common ways of speaking were being overlooked, Harry would retrieve some aphorism from the *Investigations* and adapt it to the occasion at hand. The usual result was that some of us were both amused and edified, while others felt that their contributions were not being taken seriously.

In 1968, Harry left ND for the University of Windsor, Canada, where he spent the rest of his career. Although one of his sons subsequently earned an ND BA, none of us in the department ever saw him again. He died on February 16, 2003.

Milton Fisk was born in February 1932, son of the American Modernist painter Edward Fisk. Two of his uncles went to ND, a cousin was an ND football player, and a great uncle received ND's

Laetare medal in 1928. Milton followed family tradition by enrolling with the class of 1953. After his BS in chemistry, he joined the philosophy PhD program at Yale on a Woodrow Wilson scholarship. While at Yale, he was approached by ND with an offer of a faculty position, on condition that he spent a year at Fribourg learning Thomism. At Fribourg, he studied Saint Thomas with Fr. Norbert Luytens, OP, and Quine with Fr. Joseph I. M. Bochenski. He came to ND as an instructor in 1957, a year before receiving his Yale PhD.

During his first year in South Bend, Milton lived with Yves and Paule Simon. He taught undergraduate courses in logic (using Quine instead of Oesterle), philosophy of science (in John FitzGerald's physics program), and philosophy of nature. He also taught logic on the graduate level, along with semantic analysis and the later Wittgenstein. From 1959 to 1963, he was assistant editor of ND's *Natural Law Forum,* perhaps because of friendship with editor Robert E. Rodes of the Law School.

Milton spent only six years at ND, leaving in 1963. The circumstances of his leaving are an integral part of our story. During his last few months as chairman, Fr. Reith visited Milton in his home, bearing news of his impending dismissal. Milton's wife, Ruth, whom he married in 1960, was also present. As Milton recalls, Fr. Reith said something about "things getting stacked up" in the department and about his not being able to see Milton as part of its future. As it happened, Milton had just received an offer from Yale, which he wanted to accept in spite of his longtime loyalty to ND. Rather than inform the chairman of this offer, which he thought might seem like bargaining, Milton told Fr. Reith that he understood the problem and was not upset at having to leave the university. Fr. Reith must have wondered why the Fisks were so cheerful as he left their doorstep.

The interesting question here is what had happened during the previous six years to bring about Milton's severance from the university. He had graduated in 1953 with "favored son" status, received a PhD from one of America's premier universities, and spent a year at Europe's top Catholic university supposedly gaining familiarity with Thomistic philosophy. Moreover, he had a book that was about to appear (*A Modern Formal Logic*) and had already published six substantial articles in good journals totaling about 180 pages. Nor were there problems of any sort about his departmental contributions. He was a better-than-average teacher and an excellent colleague.

Milton's falling-out with the department administration began in Fribourg. He had been sent to study Thomism at ND's expense. But what had happened, by his own recollection, was that he "had fierce arguments" with Fr. Luytens in the Saint Thomas course and that he spent most of his effort studying Quine with Fr. Bochenski. Most of the classes he taught at ND were on analytic topics, with only an occasional offering (philosophy of nature, Aristotelian logic) that fit the standard curriculum. And none of his publications, either books or articles, had anything to do with the Thomistic tradition. With the department's self-image still anchored in its Thomistic past, Fr. Reith was speaking frankly when he said that Milton showed little promise of moving ahead in the department.

After spending three years at Yale, Milton moved on to Indiana University in 1966. His *Nature and Necessity: An Essay in Physical Ontology* was published in 1973 by Indiana University Press. And between 1964 and 1974, he published more than a dozen further articles on analytic topics. Since 1975, however, almost all of his writing has been on issues of social philosophy and political morality. Five books of his appeared between 1975 and 2009, along with two books edited and over seventy articles.

Milton retired from full time teaching in 1997. Recent blogs describe him as having been involved for a long time in the labor movement and in the movement for health care reform. He is also known as an interpreter of Marxist philosophy. A brief biography of his own posting notes that he "is currently working on a living-wage campaign in Bloomington," where he lives, that his "favorite activity is mountain walking," and that his most difficult task "is remembering the birthdays of his eight grandchildren."[27] He also mentions his role as manager of a sizable collection of his father's artwork.

I myself was born in Scottsbluff, Nebraska, on August 13, 1928, and grew up in western Nebraska, eastern Wyoming, and northern Colorado. At age thirteen, I worked on a dairy farm, read James Jean's *The Mysterious Universe* with its opening passage from Plato, and resolved to be a philosopher when I grew up. This resolve was strengthened in high school when I encountered Emerson and William James in a class on American literature.

After two years in the U.S. Navy following high school, I went to Grinnell College in Iowa and received a joint BA in philosophy and mathematics in 1952. From there I went to Harvard University, where I served as assistant dean of the graduate school from 1953 to 1956, received an MA in 1954, and decided in 1955 that I didn't want to be a philosopher after all. This decision followed my first experience at a philosophy conference (a "smoker" of the Eastern Division APA was held that year in Harvard's Memorial Hall). I have been averse to such conferences ever since.

Having decided to leave the field, I nonetheless saw clearly that I should complete my PhD. Needing financial support, I took a job in late 1956 at MIT's Lincoln Laboratory. At Lincoln, I worked on computer simulation, learned to play GO (the ancient oriental board game), and spent lunch hours with my office mate (Ed Fredkin, inventor of the Fredkin gate) discussing ways of making contact with aliens from outer space. This was the beginning of my interest in artificial intelligence.

Harvard granted me a PhD in philosophy in June 1958. A few months earlier, I had received the visit from Fr. Herman Reith, mentioned in the prologue, that led to my receiving an offer to teach at ND. It took a while to decide whether to accept the offer. Against accepting was the fact that I already had a good job with MIT and that I was disaffected by the very thought of "professional philosophy." In favor was the fact that I was engaged to be married to a practicing Catholic, along with the expectation that philosophy at a Catholic institution would be different from what I had experienced at the APA.

As it turned out, the pro side won. Lucille and I were married in August and shortly after set out for ND. We rented a house in a place known as Sleepy Hollow. Our first two sons (Gregory and Christopher) were born while we lived there, and this was where we entertained friends such as the Bobiks and Fr. Ivo Thomas. After three years there, we (barely) managed to finance a larger house in the neighborhood called McKinley Terrace. A third son (Jeffrey) joined the family in this location, which also was where my sons hunted Easter eggs in the snow with the McInerny children.

As far as I can recall, the only courses I taught during my first three or four years were in logic and the philosophy of science. I taught four courses each term for several years running. For logic, I used *Methods of Logic* by Quine, one of my most appreciated teachers at Harvard. I experimented with several texts for the other course, settling on *The Philosophy of Science* by Stephen Toulmin and *Patterns of Discovery* by Norwood "Russ" Hanson. Edward "Monk" Malloy was a student in one of these courses, roughly thirty years before becoming the sixteenth president of ND. A few more years into my stay, I started teaching theory of knowledge (epistemology) to some exceptionally talented students in the Arts and Letters Mathematics Program, along with a beefed-up treatment of *Methods of Logic*. I remember relishing the occasion of teaching Quine's book to one of his nephews with the same surname.

This brief description should make it clear that my courses did not fit neatly into the traditional Thomist-inspired curriculum. One bleak day in the spring of 1963 I was summoned to a meeting with Fr. Reith, who was in his final year as department chair. The department was growing too large, he said, and I had no secure place in it. Perhaps I should start looking for another job. I remember responding, in effect, with a shrug of the shoulders. For the past several years, I had been thinking of leaving. Much as Lucille and I had come to like ND, I simply could not support my family on the salary I was getting (then $6,500). During the summers, I had found temporary jobs around Boston in the electronics industry, and I had seriously considered returning to Lincoln Laboratory. But it was unpleasant to hear that my services were no longer valued by the very person who had invited me to ND.

As things worked out, Harry Nielsen promoted me to associate professor the following year when he took over as chair from Fr. Reith. And the financial problem was more or less resolved by some grants from the NSF to do research in artificial intelligence. This led to the founding of the Philosophic Institute for Artificial Intelligence (PIAI), in collaboration with my good friend Frederick Crosson. Most of my early publications were in this area, and a few are still quoted in contemporary work on AI. We return to the PIAI in chapter 5.

My interest in Plato began with repeated readings of the *Theaetetus* in my early epistemology courses. I began learning Greek at age forty, and my first book on Plato (*Plato's Analytic Method*) came out in 1969.[28] Since then, I have published four more books on Plato, along with some dozen and a half articles. The books are *Plato's Late Ontology: A Riddle Resolved, Plato's Literary Garden: How to Read a Platonic Dialogue, Parmenides' Lesson: Translation and Explication of Plato's* Parmenides, and *Metaphysics and Method in Plato's* Statesman.[29] Prior to the present writing, I had published eighteen books in all along with about fifty articles.

Lucille died in an auto accident in 1980. Sacred Heart Church (not yet a basilica) was filled to overflowing for her funeral, at which I read an encomium. In 1983, I married Patti White, who received her PhD in philosophy from ND in 1987. Patti started teaching at St. Mary's College in 1987, after two years at St. Olaf's in Minnesota. In 1993, I was received into the Catholic Church. Patti and I have one son, Michael, born in 1994. Like me, Patti is averse to professional philosophy meetings.

THOMISM EXITS UNDER A CLOUD

Following Fr. Bochenski's visit in 1955–56, the department's new hiring practice began auspiciously with the appointment of Ralph McInerny, a Thomist with expertise in Kierkegaardian philosophy. But next came Sobocinski and Ivo Thomas in formal logic, and Harry Nielsen, Milton Fisk, and I in analytic philosophy. All five of us had training in contemporary philosophy, but were relatively unversed in traditional Thomism. Then came Lobkowicz, Küng, and Ballestrem in continental philosophy. Although acquainted with Thomism through their early training, these three had little affinity with the Thomism still espoused in the department when they arrived. So much by way of review.

Largely as a result of these eight new hires between 1957 and 1967, the department began to head in a different direction. Whereas in 1950 Caponigri was the only non-Thomist in a thirty-man department, by 1970 the proportion of Thomists had dropped below 50 percent. When Fr. McMullin became chair in 1965, the department effectively was no longer Thomist and had become committed to pluralism instead. We return to this shift to pluralism in the next chapter. For the moment, let us briefly consider how the eight hires in question contributed to this change in identity.

The arrival of Bochenski's logicians had little impact at first on the daily business of the department. Sobocinski spent more time with mathematicians than with philosophers, and Ivo Thomas taught only a few courses before joining the GPLE in 1963. By the end of the 1960s, however, the role of logic in the curriculum had changed significantly. Before Bochenski, logic had seldom been taught on the graduate level. Practically speaking, Aristotelian logic was not a research topic. But when Sobocinski became available as mentor, graduate students were soon cranking out highly professional theses on formal logic. At least six of Sobo's philosophy PhDs (Jack Canty, Charles Quinn, Tom Scharle, Charles Davis, James Kowalski, Jack Boudreaux) went on to distinguished careers employing their logical skills.

Changes on the college level were more subtle but no less significant. During the 1950s and 1960s, John Oesterle's *Logic* was standard undergraduate fare in Catholic colleges and was used regularly in courses at ND. This text was not limited to syllogistic reasoning, which it referred to as the third act of the intellect. Preliminary to the third were the first and second acts of the intellect, dealing with what today would fall under philosophy of language, philosophy of mind, and perhaps ontology. When specific courses on these latter topics began to appear in ND's undergraduate curriculum, they were taught by newcomers (Milton Fisk, Guido Küng, myself) who had no interest in the scholastic approach. After traditional logic was phased out of the curriculum in the early 1970s, the three acts of the intellect were no longer taught at ND.

The arrival of the analytic philosophers, unlike that of the logicians, must have struck some traditional members of the department as a threat from the beginning. Despite his year at Fribourg, Milton was soon teaching courses featuring Alonzo Church, Paul Ziff, and Ludwig Wittgenstein. Harry was intent on making doctrine palatable to students rather than on defending it. Even more problematic from the traditional perspective, perhaps, was the epistemology I began teaching in the early 1960s. My epistemology course in 1963–64 was the first graduate course in theory of knowledge taught at ND. And then in 1965–66, I began teaching a yearly undergraduate course in theory of knowledge. Although no one seemed to realize it at the time (myself included), these courses posed an implicit threat to Thomist orthodoxy by calling into question the nature and the extent of human knowledge.

Stated simply, the problem is that most Thomists are committed to a realist epistemology. This is the view that the human intellect can know things in the world as they actually exist apart from human awareness. As exemplary Thomist Jacques Maritain put it, the "truth of knowledge consists in the conformity of the mind with the things,"[30] where "conformity" means correspondence or agreement with reality. Fr. Frederick Copleston puts it another way, saying that Thomists agree in rejecting "skepticism, positivism, subjective idealism and the pragmatic account of truth," and in accepting "realism and the mind's ability to attain truth and certainty."[31] Putting it yet more starkly, Jude Dougherty contends that the "basic principle" of Catholic thought asserts that "we are able to achieve objective truth."[32] Pope John Paul II tops it off in his *Fides et Ratio* (sec. 82), stating that "objective truth" can be reached by the *adaequatio rei et intellectus* (conformity of intellect to thing) maintained by Saint Thomas.

The issue here boils down to a question of the relative priority of epistemology and metaphysics. As Dougherty observes disapprovingly, but correctly, philosophy following Descartes puts epistemology first. Thus before setting out to discover objective metaphysical truth, the post-Cartesian epistemologist insists, one should have good reason for thinking that reason is up to the task. Most epistemologists after Kant have concluded that it is not. So much the worse for metaphysical realism. This was the view I brought from Harvard, presumably unknown by Fr. Reith when he recruited me in 1957.

The position of Dougherty and other Thomistic realists, on the other hand, is that the powers of reason cannot be assessed until we know the nature of reason itself. And discovering the nature of reason is a metaphysical enterprise. To get metaphysics underway, however, we have to assume that it is capable of grasping the truths it is looking for. Thus, metaphysics is prior to epistemology. So much the worse for philosophies that call metaphysical realism into question. This was the view (at least approximately) that my Thomist colleagues brought from places like Toronto and Laval.

I have no memory of the tension between these opposing views ever erupting into open controversy within the department. With the new age of pluralism dawning in the late 1960s, moreover, the presence of opposing views like these in the department was no longer considered problematic. But the fact remains that the advent of post-Cartesian epistemology in the curriculum did not contribute to a continuation of the department's Thomistic identity.

A more immediate challenge to the department's Thomistic orthodoxy came with the faculty imported from Bochenski's Fribourg. Lobkowicz, Küng, and Ballestrem were all committed Catholics, but none was a Thomist in the ND sense. Popes from Leo XIII to Pius XII had instructed Catholic philosophers to espouse the teachings of Thomas Aquinas. As far as traditionalists like Ralph McInerny and Herman Reith were concerned, being a Catholic philosopher was tantamount to being a Thomist. Yet here was a group of European newcomers who went to Mass regularly and raised their families by Catholic principles, but who showed no signs of being Thomists in a recognizable sense. Here, in brief, was a group of Catholic philosophers who seemed to disregard the authoritative teaching of multiple popes. The traditionalists could not be blamed if they found this bewildering.

In Ralph's case, the bewilderment must have been accompanied by a sense of betrayal. Although hired ostensibly for his knowledge of Kierkegaard, Ralph came to ND as a dyed-in-the-wool Thomist. Reflecting back on these early days in his 1979 address "Fides Quaerens Intellectum," delivered as part of his inauguration to the Grace Chair of Medieval Studies, he refers unabashedly to his docile acceptance of Saint Thomas as his philosophic mentor. The popes had spoken and Ralph obeyed. Obedience to ecclesiastical authority was ingrained in his very nature.[33] What could Ralph make of Catholic philosophers who obviously knew of repeated papal instructions to teach Saint Thomas, but who taught Karl Marx, Roman Ingarden, or Adam Smith instead?

Ralph and Connie were close friends with Karl and Consuelo Ballestrem, as noted previously. Karl was the last of Bochenski's humanists to join the department, arriving in 1967. This was also the year of the Land O'Lakes conference, where Fr. Hesburgh joined the heads of several other Catholic universities in proclaiming freedom from popes and bishops in matters academic. Ralph might be forgiven if he viewed Karl's divergence from Thomism as symptomatic of the kind of deviance supposedly authorized by the Land O'Lakes statement.

These are some of the forces within the department that were loosening the grip of traditional Thomism. Changes to the same effect were underway in the A&L College at large. In 1953 the college had completed a self-study, discussed previously, that recommended a college-wide curriculum organized to comply with a Thomistic understanding of philosophy and theology. While this recommendation received a lukewarm response at best on the college level, the Philosophy Department responded by establishing a strict four-course sequence (logic, philosophy of nature, philosophy of man, metaphysics) that remained intact for the rest of the decade.

In 1961 the A&L College initiated a second self-study, whose purpose was "to suggest ways for improving the intellectual substance of the college."[34] Uncertain what this meant, the five-person committee decided to evaluate the effects of the 1953 proposals and solicited faculty reactions to the college requirements resulting from them. These responses showed that a preponderance of the faculty favored greater departmental autonomy and opposed a curriculum dominated by the special interests of philosophy and theology. Although the committee was dissolved before it could issue a final report, this faculty response amounted to an unambiguous rejection of a curriculum organized around Thomistic principles.

Ralph himself was a member of this committee. When its work revealed a general disavowal of Thomistic principles as a practical guide to Catholic college education, he must have realized that Thomism was a lost cause in the college at large. Thomism's only chance of survival at ND depended on the individual efforts of a few committed adherents like himself. By the end of the 1960s, Ralph had adopted the reinvigoration of Thomism as a personal mission. Despite his last words in my presence, he must have realized in his final years that restoring Thomism to a position of dominance at ND was a lost cause.

CHAPTER 4

Pluralism

PLURALISM IN THE OFFING

Ernan McMullin became department chair in 1965, during the final throes of American Thomism described in the last two chapters. In the words of ND historian Philip Gleason, whereas Thomism had "reached its high point in this country in the 1950s . . ., the ideal of a 'Thomistic synthesis' had sunk far below the horizon of live options in American Catholic higher education" by the mid-1960s.[1] Being more concerned with the causes of Thomism's demise than with its aftermath, Gleason's account leaves unanswered such questions as whether Thomism simply disappeared from Catholic college curricula, whether former teachers of Thomism went back to graduate school for retraining, and whether a new orthodoxy arose to take its place.

In point of fact, these questions and others like them are answered by McMullin himself in his presidential address to the 1967 meeting of the ACPA.[2] Regarding the persistence of Thomism after its time in the sun, McMullin reported that about 60 percent of Catholic philosophy teachers were still classified as Thomists in 1966. But most of these were so classified because they taught from Thomistic textbooks, rather than on the basis of professional commitment. Only a small fraction of the 60 percent had anything approaching a scholarly competence in Thomism as a systematic body of thought.

As courses on Thomism declined in number, philosophers in Catholic schools were called upon to teach courses in other areas. As might be expected, however, this did not result in an appreciable number of teachers returning to graduate school for retooling. Instead, those affected began teaching in other areas they had studied during previous graduate training. According to McMullin's figures, one-quarter of the faculty in question had PhDs from European universities, where many of them would have studied phenomenologists like Merleau-Ponty and existentialists like Heidegger. This fits in nicely with McMullin's general finding that about 20 percent of the departments surveyed counted themselves as primarily existentialist or phenomenological in orientation. An even closer fit is seen between the 10 percent of faculty who got their PhDs from American secular universities and the 10 percent of departments surveyed that classified themselves as primarily analytic.

Obviously enough, a department's dominant philosophic orientation is influenced by factors other than the sources of its faculty's PhDs. In the case of existentialism and phenomenology in particular, McMullin suggests that these continental approaches accord well with the "categories of subjectivity" emphasized in Christian thought. Another factor revealed in his survey is that all major departments with nuns on their faculty stressed the importance of existentialism, regardless of other emphases (such as Thomism) they also considered important. This compares with 87 percent for departments without nuns. McMullin concludes from these figures that there appears to be "a correspondence between the feminine temperament and existentialism."[3] Whatever the reasons involved, a fair number of Catholic departments emerged from the 1960s with enduring reputations as places to study continental philosophy. Notable examples are Loyola (Chicago), Duquesne, Villanova, and Fordham.

ND's response to the demise of Thomism, on the other hand, was one of a kind: a pluralism tailor-made by the department's enterprising young chairman. In McMullin's view of the profession at the time, there were several reasons for setting the compass of ND's department in a pluralist direction. One was that pluralism was already making a stand against what some saw as the excesses of logical positivism. At this point, positivism in English-speaking countries was commonly associated with what came to be known simply as analytic philosophy, in that both seemed largely insensitive to the human dimensions of the discipline. During the 1960s, Yale in particular was known as a leading pluralistic department that encouraged approaches to philosophy other than analysis and positivism. Stalwart defenders of pluralism at Yale included Paul Weiss and John Smith, both of whom were among McMullin's mentors during his stay at Yale in 1957–59. His initial enthusiasm for philosophic pluralism undoubtedly stemmed from this time at Yale.

In McMullin's own estimation, however, Yale-style pluralism needed to be improved by rigor of a sort provided by a sensible admixture of sober analytic philosophy. As noted in his presidential address, "the relation of language to the philosophic act" was "under scrutiny [then] as it never [had] been before."[4] Traditional philosophy would be enhanced by such scrutiny, and the time might have come for members of his audience "to seek allies" among "contemporary Anglo-American philosopher(s)" who were sympathetic with traditional concerns. Analytic philosophers such as Harry Nielsen, Milton Fisk, and I had been part of ND's department for almost a decade; and in McMullin's view, at least, the department had been improved by our involvement.

A further factor in McMullin's espousal of pluralism emerged during several lengthy conversations we had during the year before his death. As will become clear presently, Ernan wanted to establish a two-way bridge between the Catholic philosophy of the past and the mostly secular philosophies of the twentieth century. Although other forward-looking Catholic philosophers before him had shared the same goal (ND's Leo Ward was an example), the Thomism of the pre-Vatican II popes had proven too rigid for a fruitful interchange between past and present. By making traditional Thomism one approach among many in his pluralistic department, Ernan was setting the stage for a renewed attempt to bring the two traditions together.

Ernan's vision for bringing Catholic philosophy up to date, it now seems clear, was inspired by Vatican II's vision of *aggiornamento* for the church at large. The literal meaning of this Italian term is "bringing up to date." Vatican II closed with a final session in December of 1965.

Ernan took over as department chair in July of the same year, bent on bringing philosophy at ND up to date with the help of a pluralist agenda.

PRIESTS IN THE DEPARTMENT FROM 1960 ONWARD

The backbone of McMullin's pluralistic department was a group of young philosophers hired between 1965 and 1969. In order of hiring, these were Fr. David Burrell, CSC (1965), Vaughn McKim (1966), Cornelius Delaney (1967), Michael Loux and David Solomon (1968), and Gary Gutting (1969). Before slots for these new hires became available, however, several faculty from previous decades had to work their way through the system. Most of these were Thomists, many were priests, and several were CSC priests in particular.

As observed several times already, ND's Philosophy Department in 1950 was composed almost exclusively of Thomist philosophers. Despite the initial influx of non-Thomists discussed in chapter 3, the faculty remained roughly 70 percent Thomist through the mid-1960s.[5] By 1970, however, the proportion of Thomists in the department had dropped below 30 percent. From that point onward, only a small proportion of faculty in the department could be classified as Thomists.

This drop from 70 to 30 percent in Thomist membership between 1950 and 1970 is accompanied by other interesting statistics. One has to do with the declining ratio of priests to laymen among regular faculty. In 1950, the ratio was close to 50 percent. By 1960 it had dropped to 40 percent, by 1965 to 35 percent, and by 1970 to 25 percent. Within twenty years, the proportion of priests to laymen teaching philosophy had been cut in half.

A related trend is the decreasing number of CSC priests with full-time appointments in the department. Whenever feasible, for financial as well as other reasons, the CSC order likes to place its members in regular academic positions. In 1950, 14 CSCs were teaching philosophy courses, only half of whom had PhDs. The number of CSCs had decreased to 11 in 1960, and to 9 in 1965. Of this last number, 6 had PhDs. By 1970 the number had dropped to 6, all but 1 with a

PhD degree. This is a decline by more than half of CSC department-membership over a twenty-year period. Of particular interest is the fact that only a single CSC was appointed as a regular member between 1970 and 2010. Fr. John Jenkins, CSC, joined the department in 1990, but soon was moved into a series of key administrative positions. He became president of the university in 2005.

Apart from Fr. Jenkins, only four CSC priests were brought into the department under its own initiative during my time at the university.[6] Fr. Charles Weiher came in 1959 and taught until becoming ill in 2001. Next to join were Fr. James Doig, who stayed from 1963 to 1968, and Fr. William Hund, who remained from 1965 to 1971. Last to arrive was Fr. David Burrell, who came in 1965 and played a prominent role in department affairs until he retired in 2006. As far as I can make out, Fr. Weiher holds the record among CSCs for length of time spent teaching in ND's Philosophy Department. Let us pause for a closer look at this long-serving priest, before turning to the remaining three.

Charles F. Weiher was born on February 18, 1923, in Wapakoneta, Ohio. He entered ND in 1941 and graduated in 1945 with an undergraduate degree in physics. After a very brief stint in the army, he returned to ND and entered Moreau Seminary in 1946. For the next two years he studied philosophy and other courses required for graduate work in theology. He spent 1950–53 studying theology at Holy Cross College in Washington, DC, and was ordained in June 1953. Shortly after ordination he was sent to Fribourg to study with Fr. Bochenski, but returned within months to begin working toward a philosophy PhD at ND. He wrote an MA thesis entitled "Motion and the Categories according to the Principles of Saint Thomas Aquinas" in 1955. His PhD thesis, directed by Vincent Smith, was titled "Foundations of an Abstractionist Theory of Natural Number" and approved for a degree in 1960.[7]

Fr. Weiher began teaching that fall and soon was promoted to assistant professor with tenure, a rank he retained for the rest of his career. He was refused promotion to associate professor in 1972. I was on the Committee on Appointments and Promotions (CAP) that year, and recall that the reason was his lack of publications. Although both his MA and his PhD theses had been issued by UNDP, he published little after that. With the exception of a year (1961–62) at the University of Portland, Fr. Weiher spent the rest of his career at ND. He was a gentle presence around the department, and seemed to enjoy going to departmental events. He retired in 1993 but continued teaching as emeritus until he fell seriously ill in 2001. He then moved to Holy Cross House, the CSC's extended care facility, where he died on April 13, 2005.

James C. Doig was born on June 22, 1929, in Washington, DC. Jim was on the department roster as a CSC priest from 1963 to 1968 and served as assistant chair under Harry Nielsen in 1964–65. Jim came to ND with an STL (Licentiate in Sacred Theology) from the Gregorian and a PhD in philosophy from Louvain. He was at Yale on sabbatical in 1967–68. After leaving ND, he was laicized in 1970 and began teaching at Clayton Junior College (later Clayton State College) in Atlanta. During his time at Clayton, he published three books dealing with commentaries by Saint Thomas on Aristotle. He married Ann Hardesty in 1979. Their daughter, Margaret, was a student of mine in 2001, did distinguished undergraduate work in philosophy and mathematics, and went on to earn a PhD in mathematics from Princeton. Jim Doig retired from Clayton State in 1993.

William B. Hund was born in Missouri on August 15, 1932. He enrolled in ND's College of Business Administration in 1950. Upon graduation in 1954, he spent two years in the novitiate in Jordan, Minnesota, then came back to take graduate courses in philosophy as a seminarian in Moreau. He studied theology at Holy Cross College in Washington, returned to ND during the summers for more graduate work in philosophy, and was ordained in May 1960. After a year teaching metaphysics at ND from a textbook by Fr. Reith, he was sent to Fribourg for a PhD under Fr. Bochenski. He completed his PhD in 1964 with a thesis on G. E. Moore.

Having earned a PhD, Fr. Hund returned to teach philosophy at ND from 1964 to 1970. After leaving ND he enjoyed a sabbatical in Paris and began teaching at the University of Portland in 1971. During his thirty-some years at Portland, he taught courses in Asian philosophy, aesthetics, and philosophy of religion, along with more standard offerings in metaphysics and medieval philosophy. Bill Hund retired from teaching in 2002.

David B. Burrell was born in Akron, Ohio, on March 1, 1933. He spent his undergraduate years at ND in the newly formed General Program of Liberal Education, receiving his BA in 1954. Having been attracted to the priesthood as an undergraduate, he joined the CSCs as a novice in 1955. The following year he was sent to study theology at the Gregorian University in Rome, where he fell under the spell of renowned Jesuit theologian Bernard J. F. Lonergan. He received his STL degree from the Gregorian in 1960 and was ordained the same year. David worked under Lonergan's influence for the next two decades, producing an edition of Lonergan's *Verbum: Word and Idea in Aquinas* (UNDP) in 1967.

David taught a course at ND after returning from Rome in 1960, close to the time that Ernan McMullin also returned after his two years at Yale. At Ernan's prompting, David asked his superiors for permission to study for a Yale PhD. Permission was granted with the stipulation that he would first spend a year at Laval studying Saint Thomas. When he got to Yale, the director of graduate studies (Wilfrid Sellars) officially recognized his year's work at Laval, enabling him to begin his thesis after only one year of additional course work. When he completed his PhD in 1965, he returned to ND as a full-time member of the Philosophy Department.

David Burrell soon began teaching theology as well, splitting time between the two departments. In 1971, he was appointed chair of theology, a position he retained until 1980. During that period he continued to teach and to direct theses in philosophy, but spent enough time in his chairperson role to bring the Theology Department into national prominence. His leadership in Theology was marked by a broad ecumenism, corresponding to the pluralism being developed by McMullin in Philosophy. Among prominent non-Catholic scholars in David's Theology Department were Stanley Hauerwas, Robert Wilkins, and John Howard Yoder. In 1975, David left ND for several months to spend a term teaching in Bangladesh and to interact with Jewish and Islamic scholars at Tantur in Jerusalem.[8]

After his time as chair of Theology, David returned to Tantur as interim director for the year 1980–81. This second stay at Tantur was

a major turning point in his career. As the 1980s progressed, he became increasingly engaged with Islamic thought, learned Arabic to do
research on primary texts, and developed an ever-widening circle of
friends and associates from Islamic and Jewish communities. At the
same time, his scholarly interests shifted from philosophy to theology
and cross-cultural religious thought.[9]

David's time at Tantur affected not only his scholarly orientation
but his sense of personal identity as well. Building on his experience in
Rome as a seminarian, his stay in and around Jerusalem transformed
him into what he described later as a "Mediterranean person."[10] He
became fascinated with the region's "different languages and practices,
different skin hues and dress, different ways of approaching and understanding reality." When he returned to Tantur in 1997 for its
twenty-fifth-anniversary celebration, he had a "truly overpowering"
realization that he was returning home. Shortly thereafter, he was reassigned to Tantur part-time to help integrate its program into one of
the nearby universities. He spent the next five years shuttling between
two homes, Jerusalem in the spring and ND in the fall.[11]

This cosmopolitan mode of life continued after he retired from
ND in 2006 and became professor of ethics and development at
Uganda Martyrs University, Nkozi, Uganda. A few years later he
moved to Tangaza College in Nairobi, Kenya, as professor of compara-
tive theology. While his friends at ND see him almost as frequently as
before retirement, the main difference is that he now books return
flights to equatorial Africa rather than to Northern Indiana.

David Burrell is one of the reasons I found ND so engaging during my early years here. We played squash together frequently, often
had lunch with colleagues from other colleges, and shared thoughts on
the relative merits of marriage and celibacy. David became close friends
with my wife, Lucille, as a matter of course. He visited our house frequently, played games with my children, and accompanied us to the
beach on family outings. Particularly memorable was his involvement
in a plan we were developing in the late 1970s to form a cooperative
living community.[12] When Lucille died in 1980, he was the first person
I contacted, other than family, and he delivered the eulogy at her
standing-room-only funeral in Sacred Heart Church.

David and I saw less of each other after he went to Tantur, but there were two memorable occasions on which our fellowship quickened to its previous level. My second wife and I were married in the chapel of Zahm Hall, where two of my older sons were still living as students. Patti and I found middle ground between our diverse religious practices by arranging to be married by Dean Robert Bizzaro of South Bend's Episcopal St. James Cathedral. David, in a gesture of ecumenism, had agreed to give the homily and was still seated in front of the congregation when Dean Bizzaro began the consecration. To the amazement of wedding party and congregation alike, Fr. Burrell rose from his seat, strode up to the altar, and proceeded to concelebrate with the Episcopalian priest. Patti and I still look back on it as the best wedding gift David could possibly have given us.

The other occasion of note was eleven years later. My youngest son, Michael, was born in 1994, about a year after my decades-long commitment to the Catholic Church was made official. Patti and I invited Fr. David Burrell and Sr. Elena Malits to stand as godparents. David and Elena had been close friends before joining their respective orders and now had a godchild to dote over together.

THE "WITTGENSTEIN READING GROUP"

In the fall of 1960, Harry Nielsen, Milton Fisk, and I organized a faculty discussion group which Ernan McMullin said decades later provided the strongest impetus toward pluralism the department ever received. The general idea was that the group would meet every other week at a faculty member's home to discuss major works of contemporary philosophy. Beer and soft drinks would be provided by the host, along with potato chips, pretzels, and maybe peanuts. We would convene promptly at 8:00 p.m. and adjourn around 10:00. Often cake or cookies would be served by the host's wife (or the host himself, if unmarried), and all visitors would be gone by 10:30.

As a rule, participants would take turns leading the discussion. Passages to be covered would be announced in advance, and members counted on each other to have read them carefully; we had too much invested in the occasion to let it degenerate into an erudite "bull session." Our purpose was to work through the details of specific texts and to help each other assimilate them. Some of us would have more experience with a given text than others, but everyone present was expected to participate.

The group began that fall reading Wittgenstein's *Philosophical Investigations* (*PI*).[13] Harry Nielsen had studied Wittgenstein at Nebraska with O. K. (Oets Kolk) Bouwsma, who had spent time with Wittgenstein at Oxford and Cornell,[14] so it was natural that he led the first few meetings to get us started. Other participants that first year, as best I can recall, were Fred Crosson (then of the GPLE), Ralph McInerny, Ernan McMullin, John FitzGerald (the younger), Milton Fisk, Edward Manier, and Nikolaus Lobkowicz, as well as myself. Otto Bird of the GPLE was also involved, along with his friend Ivo Thomas. Most of us had taken a turn as leader before the year ended.

We covered most of part 1 of *PI* during the first year, reading at a pace of about twenty pages a meeting. The next year we finished part 1 and moved on to part 2. I seem to remember reaching the famous "duck/rabbit" drawing (*PI* IIxi) before the year ended. We then spent several months working on Wittgenstein's *The Blue and Brown Books*. By this time, we were sufficiently accustomed to discussing Wittgenstein together that we permanently dubbed our gathering the "Wittgenstein group." Later on, when reading Strawson, for example, notices would go out announcing that the Wittgenstein group would meet to discuss chapter so-and-so of Strawson's *Individuals*.

Strawson's book, in fact, may have been the next thing we read—either that or Merleau-Ponty's *Phenomenology of Perception*. Fred Crosson led off with Merleau-Ponty, having studied with him in Paris. *Phenomenology of Perception* went over fairly well, and was followed by *The Structure of Behavior* by the same author. Other readings during this first decade were Edmund Husserl's *Logical Investigations,* Gottlob Frege's *Philosophical Writings,* and Sartre's *The Emotions.*

By mid-decade, Milton Fisk and John FitzGerald (junior) had left the university, and a few others had stopped attending regularly. Despite departures, membership of the group held steady with the addition of Stanley Hauerwas of Theology, Harold Moore of the GPLE, and five new members of the Philosophy Department coming between 1966 and 1969. This previously mentioned contingent included Vaughn McKim, Cornelius Delaney, Michael Loux, David Solomon, and Gary Gutting, who subsequently came to be known as the "Sellarsians."

I look back at the first decade of the Wittgenstein group as one of the most rewarding of my career at ND. Other members of the original group I have spoken with recently have similar memories. Although most of us were fresh from graduate school at the time, our collaborative concentration on a few major texts was a learning experience unlike anything available during graduate training. While most of us had come from good graduate schools (Yale, St. Louis, Fribourg, Chicago, Harvard), these schools represented quite different approaches to philosophy.

Our exercise of bringing all these approaches together turned out to be both more challenging and more illuminating than more familiar approaches confined to a single perspective. For my part, at any rate, bumping heads with talented colleagues from other institutions taught me considerably more than discussions with other graduate students at Harvard.

As Ernan noted in retrospect, it was apparent that the cross-fertilization provided by these faculty discussions contributed significantly to the development of pluralism in the department. People trained in empiricism (like myself) became familiar with phenomenology, people trained in phenomenology (like Crosson) became familiar with philosophy of science, and people trained in philosophy of science (like Gutting) became familiar with history of philosophy (represented by Delaney, for instance). In the sense of "pluralism" relevant to ND in the 1960s, a department encouraging interchanges like this is by definition a pluralistic department.

It so happened that all authors read by the Wittgenstein group before the late 1960s were European. From then on, as I recall, most of our discussions focused on American authors. Prompted by the arrival of the Sellarsians, we spent a year reading Sellars's *Science, Perception, and Reality*. This was followed by his *Science and Metaphysics: Variations on Kantian Themes*. I believe we also read Sellars's famous article

"Empiricism and the Philosophy of Mind," in which he attacks the foundationalism represented by (among others) C. I. Lewis, one of my most revered teachers at Harvard. After a few years with Sellars, we turned to W. V. O. Quine's *Word and Object*. Quine also had been one of my teachers, and I remember how disconcerting it was to encounter his views colored by my colleagues' Sellarsian lenses.

The original Wittgenstein group went into decline as interest in Sellars began to peak. The stage for this decline was set with the departure of three key members. Harry Nielsen left ND for Waterloo in 1968, and Fred Crosson became dean of the A&L College (replacing Fr. Sheedy) the year following. David Burrell then was appointed chair of the Theology Department in 1971, which precluded further regular attendance on his part. Loss of these stalwarts was a serious blow to the group. At this point, the rising interest in Sellars also came into play. About the time when the main group moved from Sellars to Quine, the subgroup with a Sellarsian slant decided to write a collection of essays on Sellars's thought. (The collection appeared in 1977 as *The Synoptic Vision: Essays on the Philosophy of Wilfrid Sellars,* authored by Delaney, Loux, Solomon, and Gutting, published by UNDP.) As they began working on this project in earnest, the Sellarsians gradually stopped attending meetings of the regular group and started meeting on their own. Another factor in the group's impending demise may have been a scarcity of recent philosophers whom all members considered worthy of careful study.

Whatever the reasons, the last meeting of the Wittgenstein group took place in late spring of 1974. It was held in my home, and we were slated to read something by J. L. Austin.[15] The only other person who came that evening was Biswambhar Pahi, a Yale-trained expert in propositional logic who soon after returned to India. Pahi and I chatted awkwardly for a while, and then agreed unanimously to close the book on ND's first philosophy discussion group.

This, of course, was not the end of philosophy faculty discussions at ND. I remember one well-attended meeting at Neil Delaney's house on Peter Unger's recently published *Ignorance: A Case for Skepticism.* But faculty discussions from the 1980s onward tended to be conversations among specialists on specialized topics. One of the last

I remember attending was in 1978 on the topic of epistemic foundationalism. It occurred while I was busy building my solar house. A
constant distraction I encountered during this meeting was the nag-
ging thought of foundations composed, not of incorrigible statements,
but of iron bars and hard concrete.

FRIDAY COLLOQUIA

From start to finish, the Wittgenstein group was sustained by the initiative of individual faculty members. Also initiated in 1960 was the
Friday afternoon colloquium series, which operated largely under departmental supervision. Departmental supervision in this case meant
that department officials appointed series coordinators, reserved meeting rooms, and made sure no classes were scheduled after 3:00 on Friday afternoons. This colloquium series is the only departmental practice of that vintage to be retained through the first decade of the
twenty-first century.

The first Friday colloquium on record was held in the spring of
1960,[16] and took place in the Faculty Clubhouse on Bulla Road. The
paper on this occasion was my "Gasking on Arithmetical Incorrigibility,"[17] subsequently published in *Mind* (my first publication). My
commentator was Thoralf Skolem, a Norwegian mathematician who
established the existence of nonstandard models of arithmetic (models
containing elements beyond the standard natural numbers) and who
lent his name to the Löwenheim-Skolem theorem.[18] The general impression conveyed by his comments was that there was little overlap
between my interest in alternative arithmetics and his in nonstandard
number theory. Skolem was seventy-three at the time, and I barely
thirty-two.

Friday colloquia continued to meet on Bulla Road until we moved
to the lounge of the newly completed Memorial Library sometime in
the mid-1960s. My memory of these early meetings is spotty, but I do
recall that they generally were well attended. The next available documentation of the series is in the Philosophy Newsletter (the department's informal news bulletin) for 1968, the second year of its publi-

cation. The paper in this case was by Alvin Plantinga, under the title "De Re and De Dicto." In 1968 Plantinga was still at Calvin College, indicating that the series at that point included presentations by people outside the ND department.

By the early 1970s the Friday colloquium series had evolved into the form it would maintain for roughly the next two decades. In the Philosophy Newsletter for 1972, colloquium presentations were listed separately from lectures by visiting philosophers. All colloquia that year were led by ND faculty, and all but one took place on Friday. Colloquia readers included Mike Loux, Gary Gutting, Neil Delaney, Vaughn McKim, Ralph McInerny, Ernan McMullin, and myself, along with several others who subsequently left the department after three years or less. Commentators were involved, but were not listed in the newsletter. I was coordinator of the series that year and remember the work involved in recruiting suitable commentators.

More important than the series' structure at that point is the role it played in departmental life. Faculty members looked forward to the colloquia as occasions to find out what their colleagues were working on and to discuss stimulating topics. Active members of the department attended regularly, and most were ready to present papers when slots were available. For younger members in particular, reading a paper at colloquium provided valuable training for professional appearances away from home. Mike Loux tells me that he found reading a colloquium paper more nerve-wracking than reading at an APA meeting.

Graduate students were expected to attend as an integral part of their professional training. The presumption was that they could learn the "give and take" of the profession by watching their more seasoned teachers in action. For the most part, however, their only active role was to arrange for refreshments (with a department budget) and to clean up when the session was over. Students were asked to volunteer for the job, and since only women generally would volunteer, the early colloquia were catered by female graduate students.

Many graduate students during this era, as I was to learn subsequently, looked upon faculty demeanor at colloquia as great theater. Fr. McMullin would sit in an overstuffed chair at the side, appear to doze off shortly after the session began, but then usually ask the first question when time came for discussion. Invariably, his questions were right on target. Fred Crosson would fiddle with his pipe and keep his eyes closed when the paper was being read, occasionally nodding in sage agreement. Then he typically would offer some comment during discussion about the relevance of the paper to the Western Literary Tradition. Harry Nielsen would begin his comments by leaning forward in his chair, raise his arms as if framing the topic, and give a deadpan analysis of odd locutions employed in the paper. And I, according to some informants at least, would tilt my head, stroke my chin, clear my throat loudly, and then ask the presenter what he thought his paper contributed to the topic at hand. Other questioners would follow suit until those of us with families had to go home for dinner. Graduate students (those without cleanup assignments) then would go off on their own to share stories about the antics they had just witnessed.

Both the format of the colloquia and graduate student involvement remained relatively unchanged throughout the 1970s. From the student perspective, the first major change came when the women graduate students refused en masse to be solely responsible for refreshments. An agreement was worked out whereby the entire first-year class would be responsible for procurement and cleanup, and jobs would be distributed equally among all members of that group.

Other changes were soon made to encourage graduate students to participate more actively in the discussion itself. Faculty were asked to defer their comments until students had raised questions, and most faculty had the will power to comply. A more substantial change in the early 1980s was the reservation of a few colloquium slots in which advanced graduate students could present their own papers. Although faculty attendance began to fall off at that point, the inclusion of student papers in the colloquium series continued for at least another decade. Later on, around the turn of the century, graduate students set up their own "colloquia series" to share results of their thesis research projects.

In the meantime, further changes were taking place in the colloquium format that may not have been entirely auspicious. Whereas colloquium slots in the 1070s had been reserved for members of our own faculty, by the mid-1990s they were available not only to our graduate students but to visiting lecturers as well. As the millennium rolled to its end, Friday afternoon slots were also being used for talks by visiting job candidates—by graduate students, that is, from other institutions. Papers by our own faculty by this time had become a rarity. Since talks by visitors tended to be rather specialized, local faculty became more selective in their attendance.

By this time the Friday colloquium series had vacated its previous role of keeping ND philosophers abreast of each other's interests. In this role, it had contributed much to the broadly pluralistic department of the 1960s and 1970s. As its format changed to one encouraging specialized papers by visiting philosophers, however, it became part of the department's transition from pluralism into a department overtly dedicated to professional philosophy. We return to this transition in subsequent chapters.

MCMULLIN'S CONFERENCE ON THE CONCEPT OF MATTER

The first deliberate move in the direction of pluralism was initiated by Fr. McMullin shortly after returning from his NSF year at Yale. The move in question, previously mentioned in chapter 2, was a four-day conference on the concept of matter held in the Main Building during the fall of 1961. This, of course, was the year McMullin returned to ND as a full-time member of the Philosophy Department. Funding was provided by Fr. Hesburgh, likely as part of a package of inducements by which McMullin had been persuaded to return.

The aim of the conference was to trace the roles played by various concepts of matter in early Greek thought, where science had yet to diverge from philosophy, through the medieval period with its predominantly Aristotelian understanding of science, and then on to the modern period when science and philosophy became definitively separated. As a result of this separation, the concept developed differently in the two domains. In the philosophic tradition, following Descartes, matter tends to be equated with extension, whereas in science it tends to merge with mass and momentum. McMullin's twofold intent in organizing the conference, he told me later,[19] was to broaden the perspectives of ND philosophers and to impress outsiders with the quality of ND's younger faculty.

All papers presented at the conference were invited by the organizer. Full papers were circulated among participants in advance, and actual presentations were limited to summaries. Presentations were followed by formal comments, also prepared in advance. After commentary, time usually remained for open discussion. All in all, the conference was well planned, well conducted, and uniquely memorable to many participants. Proceedings, including papers, comments, and occasional discussion, were edited by McMullin and published as *The Concept of Matter* (UNDP, 1963). After further editing, the material was divided and reissued under the titles *The Concept of Matter in Greek and Medieval Philosophy* (1965) and *The Concept of Matter in Modern Philosophy* (1978).

For present purposes, however, the roster of people attending the conference is more interesting than its proceedings. Nine of the twenty-eight invited presenters were from ND.[20] In order of seniority (time at ND), these were Bob Caponigri, Ernan McMullin, Joe Bobik, Harry Nielsen, Milton Fisk, myself, Ed Manier, Cecil Mast (mathematics), and Nikolaus Lobkowicz. Only Caponigri was more than forty years old, and most of us were in our early thirties. Most of the visitors, in marked contrast, were well advanced in their careers. For a few examples, consider Richard McKeon from Chicago, Joseph Owens from Toronto, Herbert Feigl and Grover Maxwell from Minnesota, and Wilfrid Sellars from Yale. This was an early illustration of a benefit worth repeated mention: Ernan's ND was a great place for young philosophers to meet leading scholars in their discipline.

Another interesting statistic is that relatively few of the visitors came from Catholic universities. Adding these few to the nine ND participants leaves the group evenly split between Catholic and non-Catholic institutions. Among philosophers from Catholic schools, moreover, only two among active participants (Fr. Joseph Owens from Toronto and Joe Bobik from ND) would count as spokesmen for traditional Thomism. This may well have been the first large-scale philosophy conference at an American Catholic university not dominated by issues from the scholastic tradition.

Most of the visitors were people McMullin had met at Yale or at events connected with the NSF. Wilfrid Sellars was teaching at Yale when McMullin arrived with an NSF fellowship in 1957, and they soon found common ground in their approaches to philosophy of science. McMullin also met Richard Rorty, a younger participant, via his Yale connections. Rorty had written his Yale PhD under Paul Weiss's direction before moving to Princeton.[21] Ernan met Grover Maxwell on an NSF panel in the early 1960s and subsequently was invited by Maxwell to give a talk at Minnesota's Center for the Philosophy of Science. Herbert Feigl was then head of that center. By Ernan's own account, he and Feigl got along well together, which led to his being asked to fill in for Feigl while the latter was on leave in 1964–65. Sellars, Maxwell, and Feigl were key outside participants in the conference.

My most vivid memories of the conference involved Norwood Russell ("Russ") Hanson. I had been using his *Patterns of Discovery* in my course on philosophy of science for engineers, and was eager to meet him. Russ Hanson was a musician (he once played trumpet in Carnegie Hall), a Golden Gloves boxer, and an ace fighter pilot during World War II. He received advanced degrees from both Oxford and Cambridge, developing a British accent that persisted when he returned to the United States. He founded the Department of History and Philosophy of Science at Indiana University, Bloomington, in 1957 and remained its chair until 1963.

Hanson traveled from Bloomington to ND on his very large Harley-Davidson motorcycle. I remember his roaring down Notre Dame Avenue just minutes before the conference was to begin, hopping off his Harley with the motor still running, and urgently asking where he could find a "necessarium." He regaled the meetings with his witty comments until the final day, when he read his paper "The Dematerialization of Matter." The paper was forcefully rebutted by Feigl in his formal comments and in subsequent discussion by McMullin and McKeon. It was not included in the volume published in 1978, focusing on the modern period.

Russ Hanson moved from Indiana University to Yale in 1963. While at Yale, he gave air shows under the moniker "The Flying Professor," and would do aerobatics over Yale Bowl during football games.

He died in 1967 when his Grumman F8F-2 Bearcat crashed into a fog-covered mountain top en route to a lecture engagement at Cornell University.

THE CARNEGIE SUMMER INSTITUTE

Almost without exception, outside participants in the concept of matter conference came from well-known research universities. One of the conference's main accomplishments was to bring ND's relatively young philosophy faculty into fruitful contact with senior members of their profession. We now move on to the Carnegie Summer Institute in Philosophy, with a sharply contrasting purpose serving an entirely different clientele.

Shortly after becoming chair, Fr. McMullin obtained a $200,000 grant from the Carnegie Foundation for a program aimed at familiarizing teachers in small Catholic colleges with major trends in contemporary philosophy. The program was to extend over five consecutive years, occupying a full six weeks each year during summer vacation. Philosophers from Catholic colleges in the United States and Canada were invited to apply, and between forty and forty-five applicants were chosen each year. In a typical year, there were roughly twice as many applicants as acceptances.

The first session was held during the summer of 1968. Its general theme was contemporary analytic philosophy. Each day of the week was divided between morning and afternoon meetings. There were two morning lectures by "expert" staff, which were attended by all outside participants. In the afternoon, the participants were divided into three working subgroups. These subgroups, each with its own discussion leader, retained the same membership throughout the six weeks. Various social gatherings were arranged from time to time, during which lecturers and participants could get together informally and exchange impressions. As Fr. McMullin recalls, such exchanges were often complicated by the presence of participants' families, who had come along for a vacation with no interest in philosophic discussion.

Morning lecturers during the first year included four philosophers from ND and four from other universities. Those from ND were

Harry Nielsen (his last year here), Guido Küng, Fred Crosson, and myself. Harry lectured to the group on Wittgenstein and Kierkegaard, Guido on Roman Ingarden, Fred on phenomenology, and I on the methodology of artificial intelligence. Lecturers from outside were Richard Bernstein (Haverford), Milton Fisk (then of Indiana), Richard Rorty (Princeton), and Jerome Shaffer (Swarthmore). Working group leaders that summer were Ernan McMullin, Vaughn McKim, and David Burrell, all of ND.

Fr. McMullin was in Cambridge during the academic year 1968–69, funded by a grant from the NSF. In his absence, the 1969 session of the Carnegie Summer Institute was organized by Fr. David Burrell. It followed the same general format as in 1968. The topic this year was the philosophy of religion, pursued in a manner indicative of David's interest in Wittgenstein and Lonergan. This year there was only one ND lecturer, Fr. John Dunne, CSC, of the Theology Department. Lecturers from outside included Harry Nielsen (then of Windsor), Donald Evans (Toronto), Victor Preller (Princeton, Department of Religion), John Smith (Yale), David Tracy (Catholic University), and Michael Novak (Stanford). Nielsen, Evans, and Preller were all influenced by ordinary language philosophy (Wittgenstein, Ryle, Austin), David Tracy by Lonergan, and John Smith by American pragmatism. Michael Novak is an intriguing case, having studied under Lonergan with Burrell in the late 1950s but destined to collaborate with McInerny in founding *Crisis* magazine in the early 1980s. We return to Novak in the following chapter.

Documents pertaining to the remaining three summers are less informative. We know that McMullin was back in charge, that fewer ND faculty were involved, and that there still were far more applicants than could be accommodated. The topic of the third summer was history of philosophy, that of the fourth philosophy of science, and that of the fifth ethics. Notable visiting lecturers during these later sessions included Wilfrid Sellars, Carl Hempel, Thomas Kuhn, Mary Hesse, Michael Scriven, Philippa Foot, Stanley Hauerwas, and R. M. Hare. As we shall see presently, several of these returned to ND later as lecturers in the Perspective Series.

A significant fact about the people giving morning lectures in this five-summer Carnegie program is that no Thomists were included. Among invited participants, on the other hand, a majority most likely had Thomistic leanings.[22] This disparity in Thomistic representation between lecturers and participants was deliberate on Ernan's part. As already noted, his hope at that point was to invigorate a flagging Thomistic movement with infusions of contemporary ideas from other traditions. Shortly before he died, Ernan told me regretfully that this particular hope for the Carnegie series went unfulfilled. But he insisted that the non-Thomistic orientation of the lectures was intended to strengthen Thomism rather than to undermine it.

THE PERSPECTIVE SERIES

Another McMullin initiative was the annual Perspective Series, intended both to broaden the acquaintance of ND people with contemporary trends in philosophy and (not incidentally) to impress outsiders with the quality of our department.[23] The general plan of the series called for weeklong visits by four (occasionally five) preeminent representatives of a given area of philosophy each year. Two would usually come in the fall and two in the spring. While here, each visitor would give three evening lectures, would participate in graduate seminars, would have lunches with graduate students and dinner with faculty, and would attend at least one major social gathering at a faculty member's home. Meals and lodging were provided at university expense, and each visitor would receive a $1,000 honorarium (worth about six times that amount in 2010 dollars) for his or her week's effort.

The series began in the academic year 1966–67, under the direction of Joe Bobik. Its topic, chosen by faculty vote, was the nature of philosophy. The first fall visitor was Stephan Körner of Bristol University, followed by A. J. Ayer of Oxford. Speakers in the spring were Stephen Pepper from Berkeley, Martin Versfeld from Cape Town, and O. K. Bouwsma from Nebraska.

During that year, I was at Princeton and so have no personal memories of these visits. Newly arrived Vaughn McKim, however, retains sharp memories of both Ayer and Bouwsma. Ayer lectured to a near-capacity audience in Washington Hall, which then had a stage with a wooden floor. He was a chain-smoker and delivered his lecture while pacing back and forth with a burning cigarette. Vaughn recalls being more concerned with the length of the ashes than with what Ayer was saying, and suspects that was true of the audience generally. Bouwsma, as noted previously, was a student of Wittgenstein and a teacher of Harry Nielsen. Vaughn has no memories of Bouwsma's formal lectures, but recalls an awkward dinner at the Morris Inn when no one could get a conversation going because of Bouwsma's persistent questioning of what people meant to say.

The 1967–68 round was organized by Ralph McInerny on the topic of ethics. Josef Pieper (a Thomist from Münster) and Charles L. Stevenson (Michigan) came in the fall, followed by Abraham Edel (City College, New York) and Brand Blanshard (Yale, emeritus) in the spring.

Neither Vaughn nor I remember much about Pieper or Edel, but I retain a strong impression of Blanshard voicing defiant opposition to all forms of positivism and empiricism in ethics. Stevenson, of course, was one of those he opposed. Being disengaged from issues of professional ethics, I found interaction with Stevenson quite congenial and remember a pleasant dinner with him talking about mutual acquaintances at Harvard.

Visitors in 1968–69 were James Collins (St. Louis), Walter Kaufmann (Princeton), Albert Levi (Washington University), and Guido Calogero (Rome). The topic that year was the historiography of philosophy, and the director, I believe, was A. Robert Caponigri. I had a special tie of sorts with Walter Kaufmann, having once visited his house in Princeton while it was being occupied for a year by David Pears and his wife, Anne. Kaufmann had an astounding library covering the history of philosophy, including numerous first editions. He was also deeply engaged in photography. We spent a relaxed evening in the Faculty Club discussing a book he was planning that would contain photographs he had taken of people in Israel.

By general agreement of those who attended regularly, 1969–70 was one of the two most successful years of the Perspective Series.

Speakers in the fall of 1969 were Roderick Firth (my thesis director at Harvard) and Wilfrid Sellars (Pittsburgh); those in the spring, Roderick Chisholm (Brown) and Willard Van Orman Quine (Harvard). The topic that year was epistemology, and I served as director. Firth and Sellars accepted promptly when asked, but Chisholm was more hesitant. He was willing enough to come, but made a firm point about his lectures being "more successful if given during the day instead of the evening." Fortunately, we were able to schedule his lectures at 4:00 in the afternoon. It turned out that from cocktail time onward on any given day, Chisholm's ability to talk philosophy diminished progressively. Quine, on the other hand, at first was reluctant to come at all. He finally accepted after I told him that his *Word and Object* had received an enthusiastic reading in our faculty discussion group and that he would not be expected to lecture to undergraduates. I still have copies in my files of his handwritten lecture notes. Of the four sets of lectures that year, his drew the largest audience and was the most enthusiastically received.

The second especially successful Perspective year was 1980–81. Ernan McMullin was the director, on the topic of philosophy of science. Speakers were Carl Hempel (Pittsburgh), Thomas Kuhn (MIT), Wesley Salmon (Arizona), and Ian Hacking (Stanford). Despite his reputation as a standard-bearer for logical positivism, Hempel's talks were clear and intelligible to a wide audience. In social gatherings, he proved to be easily approachable by faculty and graduate students alike. Hempel left the impression of being an excellent philosopher who was also a kind and gracious human being. Thomas Kuhn was legendary for his 1962 publication *The Structure of Scientific Revolutions,* and conducted himself accordingly. Wes Salmon gave some interesting talks on various senses of probability, and Ian Hacking filled out the year with some remarks on Ernan McMullin's favorite cause of scientific realism.

Quite apart from the unusual merits of 1969–70 and 1980–81, Perspective speakers for the years in between (with a few exceptions) constitute a veritable *Who's Who* of philosophers during the 1970s. These speakers are worth naming as an indication of the stellar quality of the department's visitors during that period. The following list identifies speakers, their institutions, and the topics addressed.

(1970–71) J. I. M. Bochenski (Fribourg), Victor Preller (Princeton), John Smith (Yale), Paul Ricoeur (Paris), on philosophy of religion;

(1971–72) Alasdair MacIntyre (Brandeis), Joel Feinburg (Rockefeller), Sheldon Wolin (UC Santa Cruz), Stuart Hampshire (Oxford), on political philosophy;

(1972–73) Max Black (Cornell), Donald Davidson (Rockefeller), John Searle (Berkeley), Jerrold Katz (MIT), on philosophy of language;

(1973–74) Wilfrid Sellars (Pittsburgh), Stephan Körner (Bristol), Donald Williams (Harvard), Anthony Quinton (Oxford), on metaphysics;

(1974–75) Bernard Williams (Cambridge), Richard Brandt (Michigan), Alasdair MacIntyre (Boston University), Alan Gewirth (Chicago), on contemporary ethics;

(1975–76) Stephen Toulmin (Chicago), Arthur Danto (Columbia), Adolf Grünbaum (Pittsburgh), Richard Bernstein (Haverford), on science and rationality;

(1976–77) Nicholas Rescher (Pittsburgh), Israel Scheffler (Harvard), Murray Murphy (Pennsylvania), Wilfrid Sellars (Pittsburgh), on C. S. Peirce;

(1977–78) Alasdair MacIntyre (Boston University), Richard Wasserstrom (UCLA), John Hospers (USC), Kurt Baier (Pittsburgh), on justice;

(1978–79) Norman Malcolm (Cornell), Richard Rorty (Princeton), K. M. Sayre (ND), Jerry Fodor (MIT), on philosophy of mind;

(1979–80) David Kaplan (UCLA), Saul Kripke (Princeton), Hilary Putnam (Harvard), Robert Stalnaker (Cornell), on philosophical logic.

It will be noted that Alasdair MacIntyre gave three Perspective lectures, in 1971–72, 1974–75, and 1977–78. But Wilfrid Sellars takes the prize with a total of four. In addition to other ND appearances, Sellars gave Perspective lectures in 1969–70, 1973–74, 1976–77, and 1986–87.

After almost two decades of exemplary service, the old format started to break down in the mid-1980s. The number of speakers was reduced to three in 1985–86, when David Kaplan (UCLA), John Perry

(Stanford), and Saul Kripke (Princeton) were invited to speak on the philosophy of language. Another change this year was the reduction in time each visitor spent on campus from five days to just three (Wednesday, Thursday, and Friday).

A more radical change occurred in 1994–95, when the series took on the format of three miniconferences. Three main speakers were invited each year as before, along with a panel of three commentators for each. Panelists for Bas van Fraassen (Princeton) that year were Arthur Fine, Gary Gutting, and Ernan McMullin; those for Daniel Dennett (Tufts) were David Chalmers, Christopher Hill, and Leopold Stubenberg; and those for Bernard Williams (Cambridge) were Simon Blackburn, Alasdair MacIntyre, and Lynn Joy. The lead speaker would hold forth in the Friday afternoon colloquium spot, and the commentators would respond on Saturday morning. Discussion would follow the individual commentaries, and then the visitors would depart after less than two days on campus. Whereas Perspective lectures once were held in large meeting halls, these miniconferences took place in small seminar rooms. Another innovation this year was a change in title to "Ernan McMullin Perspective Series in Philosophy," effected by then department chair Gary Gutting.

This pattern held until 1998–99, when Richard Foley (then of Rutgers) spoke under the title "Intellectual Trust in Oneself and Others." In 1999–2000, Robert Nozick (Harvard) spoke on truth and relativism, and John McDowell (Pittsburgh) on naturalism and the philosophy of mind. No commentators were invited for these two years. The last four perspective speakers were Fred Dretske (Stanford) and Michael Friedman (Indiana), speaking in 2000–2001, Robert Adams (Yale) in 2001–2, and Terence Parsons (UCLA) in 2002–3. The Ernan McMullin Perspective Series in Philosophy then disappeared from the scene, to be followed all too soon by the man it commemorated.

THE COMMITTEE ON APPOINTMENTS AND PROMOTIONS

An administrative component of McMullin's legacy that has remained essentially unchanged through the years is the Committee on Appointments and Promotions (CAP). Here is how it came about. Before Fr. McMullin became chair in 1965, major decisions regarding department policy and personnel were made by the upper administration. In many cases, they were made by President Hesburgh himself. Hesburgh's decision to bring McMullin back from Yale in 1959, for instance, was made without department input, as was A&L Dean Sheedy's decision to make Harry Nielsen chair in 1964. Hand in hand with the department's lack of self-determination in these matters was its lack of internal procedures for reviewing colleagues seeking promotion or tenure.

One of McMullin's first steps after becoming chair was to constitute an informal group of faculty advisers. As he recalled more than forty years later, the group consisted of John FitzGerald (Sr.), John Oesterle, and Joe Bobik (all Thomists). In 1967, this ad hoc arrangement was replaced by an elected Committee on Appointments and Promotions (CAP). The committee consisted of six tenured faculty elected by the department, with the department chair ex officio as a seventh member. Elected members were restricted to three-year terms, with reelection possible after a year in absentia, whereas the chair was a member as long as he remained in office.

Ernan was justifiably proud of this committee, the idea behind which he had brought from Yale. Although initially resisted by Dean Sheedy, philosophy's CAP worked so well that it was soon copied by most other departments in the college. The first person to be voted down in the Philosophy Department was a CSC priest, which may have had something to do with Fr. Sheedy's disapproval.

Elected to the CAP for its first year were FitzGerald, Oesterle, and Bobik, all members of the previous ad hoc committee, along with Ralph McInerny, Herb Johnston, and Bob Caponigri. In 1968–69, McMullin was on leave in Cambridge and John FitzGerald took over as acting chair. Elected members that year were McInerny, Johnston, Bobik, and Caponigri, carried over from the previous year, with Sobocinski and myself newly elected. McMullin returned to head the committee in 1969–70, with the same elected members as 1968–69 save FitzGerald in place of Sobocinski.

Composition of the CAP interacted with the changing membership of the department in two important ways. As membership in the department changed, so did the pool of tenured professors eligible for election to the committee. Even more importantly, the CAP had a critical voice in selecting new members of the department. For these reasons, it is germane to have a membership list of the CAP at hand. Such a list is provided in appendix B.

Compared with the roster of regular faculty in appendix A, appendix B gives a useful overview of political life in the department. Between 1955 and 2010, sixty-two faculty joined the department who eventually achieved tenure. Of these, thirty-eight served at one time or another on the CAP. The most active person in this role was Neil Delaney, who was reelected every time he became eligible after his ex officio term as chair from 1972 to 1982. Between 1972 and 2010, Delaney served thirty-one annual terms on the CAP. McInerny served every eligible year from 1967, when the committee began, to the end of his term in 1980. In 1979 he had been appointed Director of the Maritain Center, after which he withdrew his name from CAP elections. I served regularly from 1968 to 1990, after which I also withheld my name from subsequent elections. This action coincided with changes in the department discussed in chapter 6.

For purposes of anticipating subsequent developments in the department, the most revealing aspect of the list in appendix B may be the growing proportion of non-Catholics on the committee. I was the first non-Catholic member of the CAP, having been elected during the second year of its existence. Next came Ameriks in 1979–80, McKim in 1981–82, and Foley in 1982–83. In 1989–90, four of the six elected members (Ameriks, Detlefsen, Plantinga, and Solomon— Ameriks and Solomon serving only one term each) were non-Catholics, as was ex officio member Richard Foley himself. This adds up to a committee in which non-Catholics outnumbered Catholics four to three. By 2007–8, after committee membership had been increased to eight, six elected members out of seven were either Protestant or self-proclaimed atheist. Such facts and figures provide background for understanding several of the more salient changes in the department discussed in the chapters following.

THE SELLARSIANS

Having gained substantial control through the CAP over the makeup of his faculty, McMullin began assembling his version of a pluralistic department. As already mentioned, his main acquisitions for this purpose were Vaughn McKim from Yale (hired in 1966), Cornelius Delaney and Gary Gutting from St. Louis (hired in 1967 and 1969, respectively), along with David Solomon from Texas and Michael Loux from Chicago (both hired in 1968). As it turned out, these five were also the main members of a group that came to be known as the "Sellarsians," which played an influential role in the department during the 1970s. Quite remarkably, all five remained in the department for more than forty years. Let us pause for a closer look at these department mainstays.

Vaughn McKim received his BA from Oberlin College in 1962. One of his teachers at Oberlin was Bruce Aune, author of Sellars-inspired *Knowledge, Mind, and Nature*. Sellars himself was still at Yale when Vaughn arrived as a graduate student. His thesis director at Yale was Milton Fisk, just recently arrived from ND. Vaughn was awarded his PhD in 1966, the year he came to ND.

I first met Vaughn while a member of ND's interviewing committee at the 1965 meeting of the APA in New York. We were also considering another highly rated candidate from Yale that year, but Vaughn's interview convinced us that he was the man for the job. When Vaughn and his wife, Carole, first arrived, they occupied our house on Whitehall Drive while my family and I spent the year at Princeton. Vaughn and Carole McKim are among the most considerate and orderly people I have known. Our house was in better shape when we returned than when we left it.

Vaughn had a distinguished career at ND before retiring in 2009. His most memorable traits as a colleague were solidity and integrity. He was an active participant in every constructive aspect of departmental affairs. Especially notable were his skills as an administrator. Shortly after coming, he became director of undergraduate studies

(1967–74), then moved on to serve as director of graduate studies from 1974 to 1981. From an organizational point of view, at least, this period was the heyday of the department's graduate program. Later on, he shifted his efforts to the Graduate Program in History and Philosophy of Science. Ernan McMullin, who founded that program in the mid-1980s, credits Vaughn with holding it together while it was first getting started. An important appointment for Vaughn outside the department was his directorship of the Reilly Center for Science, Technology, and Values, during several years from the mid-1990s onward.

Although capable of high-quality original work,[24] Vaughn's most outstanding scholarly contributions came in the form of unusually clear and insightful expositions of diverse philosophic positions. This made him a paradigmatic member of ND's pluralistic department during its early development. He was a frequent commentator at Friday colloquia, often making a more persuasive case for the views being presented than the main paper itself. Vaughn was a solid citizen of the department in every good sense of the term. It was the department's loss that he never served as its chair.

Cornelius ("Neil") Delaney joined the department in 1967, having just received his PhD from St. Louis University under historian of philosophy James Collins. Soon after, his thesis was published as *Mind and Nature: A Study of the Naturalistic Philosophies of Cohen, Woodbridge, and Sellars* (UNDP, 1969). The Sellars of the title was Wilfrid's father, Roy Wood, then at the University of Michigan. By his own account, Neil became interested in the philosophy of Wilfrid Sellars after realizing it was similar to that of his father, albeit in updated terminology. Neil's voluminous correspondence with Roy Wood Sellars is still in his possession.

One of Neil's proudest moments at ND must have been in 1970 when he brought the elder Sellars and his son to campus together. After nostalgic recollections by Roy Wood himself, Wilfrid, Neil, and Andrew Reck of Tulane offered appreciative comments. At the end of the event, Roy Wood presented to the department an original painting by French postimpressionist Robert Genicot (1890–1981) titled *Leav-*

ing Church. It is still on display in one of the department's administrative offices.

Neil is a superb teacher, a brilliant administrator, and an outstanding historian of philosophy. He has won almost every teaching award available to A&L faculty, including the Madden Award in 1974, the Sheedy Award in 1987, and the Kaneb Award in 2001. On the occasion of the Sheedy Award, he received not only $1,000 but also two tickets to the Wimbledon Championships. This latter was a fitting bonus for someone who was unquestionably the best amateur tennis player ever to teach at ND. Neil was still hard to beat when he turned seventy in 2008.

His main administrative appointments in the Philosophy Department were as director of graduate studies (1971–72), as chair during 1972–82 (following McMullin), and as acting chair in 1984–85. Outside the department, he has served for over twenty years (since 1990) as codirector of the Glynn Family Honors Program in the A&L and Science Colleges. Despite persistent urgings from several quarters, Neil has declined consideration for higher-level administrative positions in the university.

In addition to *Mind and Nature,* Neil has published *The Synoptic Vision: Essays on the Philosophy of Wilfrid Sellars* (UNDP, 1977), which he coauthored with fellow Sellarsians, and *Science, Knowledge, and Mind: A Study in the Philosophy of C. S. Peirce* (UNDP, 1993). He currently is preparing *Philosophy in America in the Twentieth Century* for Cambridge University Press. Neil has edited or coedited five other volumes as well, including *The Problems of Philosophy: Classical and Contemporary Sources* (UNDP, 1976).

Michael Loux received his PhD from Chicago in 1968 under Manley Thompson. Like Neil Delaney, Mike not only has excelled in teaching and research but has done distinguished work as an administrator as well. Mike's teaching style is a mix of erudition and showmanship. A born performer, he tends toward flamboyance in both voice and behavior. He can wave his arms dramatically with his feet in the air. I remember once seeing him step (accidentally?) into an exposed wastebasket, and then kick it toward a row of astonished students. And

I have been told of another occasion when he actually fell through an open window, continuing to lecture on Ockham while crawling back inside. Regardless of such histrionics, Mike was known as an unusually effective teacher. An introductory course under his tutelage was an unbeatable preparation for a philosophy major. Mike received a Sheedy Award in 1974, a Madden Award in 1979, and a Kaneb Award for Excellence in Teaching twenty years later.

As far as research is concerned, Mike published about fifty articles before retiring in 2010, including two in *The Synoptic Vision: Essays in the Philosophy of Wilfrid Sellars.* He also wrote four books, edited four others, and translated Ockham's *Theory of Terms.* Especially notable among his authored books are *Primary Ousia: An Essay on Aristotle's Metaphysics Z and H* (Cornell University Press, 1991), *Metaphysics* (Routledge, 1997), and *Nature, Norm and Psyche: Explorations in Aristotle's Philosophical Psychology* (Scuola Normale Superiore, Pisa, 2004).[25] Although one's scholarly propensities tend to shrivel with time spent in administration, all these books were published after Mike's time as A&L dean.

Mike Loux was in the Dean's Office from 1983 to 1991, after having served eight years (1974–82) as Philosophy's director of undergraduate studies, one year (1979–80) as acting chair while Delaney was on leave, and then one year (1982–83) as chair in his own right. Even while dean, it should be mentioned, Mike continued to work conscientiously with his graduate students in philosophy. One graduate student earning a PhD under his guidance during this period was Patricia Ann White Sayre.

David Solomon received a BA from Baylor University in 1964 and a PhD from the University of Texas in 1972. He served as assistant professor in ND's Philosophy Department from 1968 to 1975 and as associate professor from 1977 onward. In 1975 he had been denied tenure because of insufficient publications. For the next two years, he was at Boston University as a Milbank Research Associate, studying with Alasdair MacIntyre. In 1976 he was brought up for tenure at ND again, on the basis of a strong recommendation from MacIntyre citing important work about to be published. I was on the A&P committee that year and remember unanimous agreement that life in the department was better with David Solomon than without. In David's case, at least, contagious affability proved more important than words in print.

Since rejoining the department with tenure in 1977, nonetheless, David's scholarly contributions have been impressive. He has read roughly five dozen papers pertaining to general ethics, and to medical ethics in particular. A good portion of these have been delivered in foreign countries, including England, Scotland, Austria, and Germany, as well as Italy, Slovakia, the Netherlands, and China. Comparably numerous are his popular presentations on topics of current interest, such as bioethics, abortion, and managed health care. David's published volumes to date are *The Synoptic Vision,* mentioned previously as coauthored with Loux, Delaney, and Gutting, and *Abortion: New Directions for Policy Studies* (UNDP, 1977), coedited with Edward Manier and William Liu. In addition, he has published close to twenty scholarly articles. David Solomon not only is a delightful conversationalist; by now he is also a seasoned scholar.

In 1999, David founded Notre Dame's Center for Ethics and Culture, of which he was still W. P. and H. B. White Director in 2010. We return to this center in chapter 8, along with further episodes in David's engrossing career.

Gary Gutting was the last member of the Sellars group to join the department. Gary received his PhD from St. Louis University in 1968 under philosopher and historian of science Richard Blackwell. After a year at Louvain as a Fulbright Fellow, he came to ND as an assistant professor in 1969. He was promoted to associate professor in 1975, and to professor in 1982. From 1990 to 1996, he served as chair of the Philosophy Department. In 2004, he was elevated to a Notre Dame endowed chair in philosophy, in recognition of the highly successful online *Notre Dame Philosophical Review,* which he founded in 2002 and to which we will return.

Since his time at Louvain, Gary's research interests have been divided among continental philosophy, philosophy of science, and philosophy of religion. More than half of his published work has been on twentieth-century European philosophy, of which he is an exceptionally articulate expositor. His *Michel Foucault's Archeology of Scientific Reason* (Cambridge, 1989) is exemplary in that regard.[26] Among numerous other works in philosophy of science are his entry on Sellars's philosophy of science in *The Synoptic Vision* and his contribution to *Science and Reality: Essays in Honor of Ernan McMullin* (UNDP, 1984), which he edited with Neil Delaney and James Cushing. A major contribution to philosophy of religion is his *Religious Belief and Religious Skepticism* (UNDP, 1982). Throughout the decades, he has offered graduate students an alternative to the analytic approach championed by other members of ND's Center for Philosophy of Religion. Between 1981 and 1987, Gary directed five theses in that category.

In all, Gary has authored six books, edited three, and coedited two others. He also has authored about four dozen articles in encyclopedias and scholarly journals. He has given numerous talks and presented numerous papers in the United States and abroad. In 1971, a symposium on his work was held at the University of Utrecht in the Netherlands. Like Neil Delaney and Mike Loux, Gary is an award-winning teacher, receiving a Kaneb Teaching Award in 2004 and the Madden Award in 2007. His teaching prowess was recognized by an appointment as Faculty Fellow of the Kaneb Center in 2005–6.

In retrospect, the coalescence of these five young philosophers into a group of self-described "Sellarsians" seems somewhat anomalous. Only McKim and Delaney had known much about Wilfrid Sellars before coming to ND. When the other three accepted their invitations to join the department, taking Sellars as a mentor surely was far from their minds. Although Ernan had come to know Sellars during his time at Yale, there is no reason to think that his intent in hiring these five was to foster an enclave of Sellarsian scholarship.

Anomalous or not, the Sellarsian initiative was the consequence of several easily discernible factors. In the background was the realization following Vatican II that Thomism had lost its status as "official" philosophy of the church.[27] The retreat of Thomism had left room for other philosophic initiatives, and Sellarsianism impressed some people as a viable contender. A more immediate factor was that key works by Sellars were being read by the Wittgenstein discussion group. McKim and Delaney were already Sellars fans, and their enthusiastic advocacy piqued the interest of other participants. Yet another factor was Mc-

Mullin's sympathy with Sellars's panoramic approach to philosophy (the "synoptic vision" of the title), leading him to encourage this growing interest in Sellars's thought among his new recruits.[28]

These were enabling factors at best. The driving force behind the Sellars initiative was the undertaking that culminated in the publication of *The Synoptic Vision* in the mid-1970s. This volume contains essays by Delaney on theory of knowledge, Loux on metaphysics, Solomon on ethical theory, and Gutting on philosophy of science. And the main source of inspiration behind that undertaking, in turn, was Vaughn McKim, who curiously was not represented in the collection. In their preface, the coauthors acknowledge "the contributions of Dr. Vaughn McKim, who was not only the moving force" in the project's early stages, but also "an invaluable critic of the work as it progressed." Vaughn had intended to contribute a chapter on Sellars's philosophy of mind, but because of time pressures was unable to complete this essay to his own satisfaction. The section on philosophy of mind in *The Synoptic Vision* was written by Loux and Gutting instead. As a matter of almost palpable irony, the person primarily responsible for the Sellarsian venture that dominated the department during the 1970s was not represented in the volume that constituted its main achievement.

After publication of *The Synoptic Vision,* the Sellars group began to disband. By the end of 1977, McKim had shifted his administrative skills to the fledgling Graduate Program in the History and Philosophy of Science, Solomon had returned from Boston University with a distinctly non-Sellarsian interest in the thought of Alasdair MacIntyre, and Delaney was busy running the department as McMullin's handpicked successor. Loux, in turn, had become engrossed in Aristotle and possible-worlds ontology, while Gutting was increasingly preoccupied with continental philosophy.

In the meanwhile, Wilfrid Sellars was approaching the age of seventy and showing signs of decreased vitality. His last visit to ND that I can recall was in 1987, scarcely two years before his death. The department had long since relinquished any thought of becoming a bastion of Sellarsianism, having directed its energies toward the development of a robust pluralism instead.

PLURALISM, PROS AND CONS

The philosophic pluralism that prevailed at ND during the 1970s was a reaction to the monolithic Thomism of the previous era. Prior to 1960, the vast majority of courses taught in philosophy were dominated by a Thomistic perspective. By the end of the 1960s, Thomism was only one approach among many in a department seeking to evolve its own pluralistic identity.

In one rather anemic sense, a philosophy department is pluralistic if its faculty represents a diversity of philosophic viewpoints. ND's department had become pluralistic in this nominal sense before McMullin took over as chairman. This was assured by the presence of philosophers as diverse as Lobkowicz (Marxism), Küng (phenomenology), Fisk (analytic), McInerny (Thomism), and of course McMullin himself. In this watered-down sense, ND's Philosophy Department has remained pluralistic up to the present.

During its heyday under McMullin, however, the department exhibited a pluralism of a more robust sort. Although most of us arriving between the late 1950s and the early 1970s had been trained in some specific philosophic tradition, we shared a confidence that significant philosophic insight could be found in traditions other than our own. Philosophic inquiry, we tended to think, is a cooperative enterprise, fruitfully undertaken by people trained in different approaches. Philosophic understanding is not the prerogative of isolated "isms," but is best pursued in the confluence of diverse traditions.

As already noted, McMullin later confided in me that the pluralism he advocated was epitomized by the Wittgenstein discussion group. What made that group pluralistic in the robust sense was that we read works from different philosophic traditions and that we made a sustained effort not only to understand these works but to incorporate their insights into our own philosophic thinking. This made participation in the Wittgenstein group unusually rewarding, especially for young philosophers fresh from graduate work focused on specialized areas.

The thing that made McMullin's department pluralistic in the robust sense, I hasten to add, was not just that it contained individual philosophers with a strong pluralistic bent. Philosophers with such proclivities were still active in the department some thirty or forty years later. The difference between then and now is that McMullin's department actively encouraged these pluralist inclinations, whereas today they are tolerated at best. Among forms of tangible encouragement received by the pluralistic group that put together *The Synoptic Vision* was departmental funding for Sellars's visits to campus which led to publication of that volume.

Beyond embracing diverse philosophic traditions, this early pluralism was attentive to interdependencies among different branches of philosophy. By branches of philosophy I mean subdisciplines such as ethics, metaphysics, and epistemology. Previously mentioned was the view of traditional Thomists that metaphysics is prior to epistemology, resulting in their engrained metaphysical realism. Another example is the opposing view (which I advocated) that questions of epistemology are prior to those of metaphysics. Apart from matters of priority, moreover, both parties agreed that moral philosophy is premised on assumptions of both metaphysical and epistemological character. If this latter view is correct, then work in ethics can proceed securely only with a background in these other more fundamental disciplines.

Respect for interdependencies like these was a major factor in the design of the written comprehensive examinations ("comps" or "candidacies") introduced into the graduate program during McMullin's chairmanship. One portion of these exams covered the history of philosophy, broken down into ancient, medieval, and modern. Another covered what we then called the "systematic" areas of epistemology, ethics, and metaphysics. A major purpose of these examinations was to ensure that candidates had a broad acquaintance with major branches of the discipline before beginning to write their PhD theses.

A related purpose of the candidacies was to prepare candidates for careers in college teaching. College philosophy programs during that period typically offered a relatively large number of courses (often enough to sustain a major) taught by a relatively small faculty. Under such circumstances, every faculty member normally is expected to teach a variety of different courses. To be competitive in the job market, accordingly, applicants had to be qualified to teach in several areas. In point of fact, most of ND's philosophy PhDs during the 1960s and 1970s went on to teach in colleges and universities without graduate programs in philosophy. And our placement rate during those years (jobs in both colleges and universities included) was one of the best in the country. Requiring its PhD candidates to pass comprehensive examinations in basic areas of philosophy was the department's way of certifying that they were ready for this job market.

But robust pluralism had its downside as well. It so happened that ND's graduate program in philosophy underwent its first external review in 1975, about a decade after the department had taken its pluralistic turn. External reviewers on this occasion were Louis White Beck of Rochester and Manley Thompson of Chicago. The review process itself consisted mainly of a description of the department's graduate program submitted by the director of graduate studies (Vaughn McKim), followed by a short visit by the external evaluators, and then a lengthy report by the visitors and a response by the graduate director. The external review was overseen by a ND committee, appointed by the Graduate School, consisting of psychologist Fr. William Botzum, CSC, and Professor Thomas Werge of the English Department.[29]

As I recall, it came as a surprise to find that the reviewers directed most of their negative criticism toward the pluralistic aspect of the program. In their opinion, "the requirements of pluralism [interfered] with the requirements of advanced research" by the students. The reviewers were particularly concerned about what they perceived as an excessive burden placed on graduate students by the written comprehensives, and recommended that these examinations be discontinued. Apart from the "often traumatic" experience of undergoing the examinations themselves, they observed, the main price paid by the student was "to shorten the time available for concentrated work in [his or her] field of specialization."

Other problems of pluralism pointed out by the reviewers concerned recruitment and retention of appropriate faculty. One such problem stems from the obvious prerequisite that members of a good philosophy department be outstanding scholars in their respective fields. In most cases, being a leading scholar in a given area requires frequent interaction with other people working in the same area. A reasonable consequence foreseen by the reviewers was that prominent members of the department will advocate recruitment and retention of "other philosophers of the same commitment," which, as they noted, supports specialization rather than pluralism.

A related problem is that as individuals advance in their own specialized fields, they are likely to receive "offers they cannot resist from other departments less concerned about pluralism." Pluralist departments, the reviewers concluded, thus are subject to continuing change in personnel. Further advancement by individuals who remain in the department, on the other hand, requires spending more time on their own specialties and less time talking with each other. When this happens, the reviewers warned (citing Yale as an example), a department that "strives for pluralism may do so at the cost of becoming a fragmented department."

Yet another problem mentioned by the reviewers is that good philosophers with the right temperament for a pluralistic department are hard to find. As they described it, this is a temperament "that leads one constantly to seek meaningful dialogue with others committed to philosophies which one cannot accept." Within the ranks of seasoned philosophers, this temperament is "extremely rare" and "hard to discern on the basis of published work, lectures, . . . casual encounters and interviews." The expedient recommended by the reviewers in this regard was to focus on the recruitment of junior faculty, who can be acculturated into pluralism once they join the department.

Not surprisingly, given its circumstances, the department found these criticisms to be of mixed value. For one thing, the reviewers' advice that graduate students be relieved of comprehensive exams so they can move more quickly to specialization was perceived as a recommendation to dismantle the most successful part of the graduate program. Philosophy departments where our PhDs found jobs during that era tended to prefer teachers with broad training rather than specialized researchers.

Equally unimpressive was the reviewers' argument that pluralistic programs are subject to constant change in personnel. Although a few people hired during the 1970s moved on to better academic positions (notably Dick Foley and Penny Maddy), most who left the department did so for tenure-related reasons. In point of fact, the five Sellarsians hired by Fr. McMullin remained at ND for an average of over forty years per person. And as far as fragmentation is concerned, I remember the 1970s as the period of most extensive cooperation among faculty in department history. Collegiality and camaraderie did not begin to break down until the middle of the following decade.

On the other hand, the reviewers were certainly right in pointing out that up-and-coming scholars tend to advocate hiring and retention of others who share their scholarly interests, which encourages development away from pluralism toward specialization. And they were also right in advising that philosophers well suited for a pluralistic program are hard to find. Indeed, these were among the problems ND's department began to encounter by the end of the 1970s.

On balance, the department's general reaction to its first external review was that Professors Beck and Thompson had paid too little attention to ways in which philosophy at ND differed from the practices of their own research-oriented departments. As phrased in its own official response, the department remained "unconvinced that the potential problems cited in the [external] report are all matters of serious concern at the present time." Members of the Graduate School's oversight committee (Fr. Botzum and Professor Werge) summed up their report by saying that the reviewers' "misgivings on pluralism were appreciated but bypassed by the Philosophy Department."

The "chickens" of pluralism, as the saying goes, did not "come home to roost" until pluralism yielded to professionalism in the 1980s. All in all, the external reviewers of 1975 represented a view of professional philosophy that did not overtake ND's department until well into the subsequent decade. The eventual downfall of pluralism at ND during the 1980s is among topics treated in the second part of this volume.

Fr. Leo Ward, CSC.
Courtesy of University of Notre Dame Archives.

Fr. I. M. Bochenski, OP.
Photo © Fribourg State University Library (Switzerland).

Ralph McInerny.
Courtesy of University of Notre Dame Archives.

Fr. Ernan McMullin.
Courtesy of University of Notre Dame Archives.

Alvin Plantinga.
Courtesy of University of Notre Dame Archives.

Philip Quinn.
Courtesy of University of Notre Dame Archives.

Alasdair MacIntyre.
Courtesy of University of Notre Dame Archives.

Fr. John Jenkins, CSC.
Courtesy of University of Notre Dame Archives.

PART II

From Pluralism to Professionalism

CHAPTER 5

Centers and Institutes

PHILOSOPHERS AT THE HELM OF THE MEDIEVAL INSTITUTE

A major factor in ND's growing reputation as a research university has been its increasing number of centers and institutes for specialized study. Taken as a group, these organizations both enhance the university's visibility and bring in money to help defray faculty expenses. The first such organization at ND to receive substantial outside funding was the Medieval Institute, which was formally established in 1946.

Although not a branch of the Philosophy Department, the Medieval Institute (MI) is part of our story for two more than ample reasons. One is that philosopher Ralph McInerny was director of the MI from 1978 to 1985, a critical time in its development. Second is that the two people most directly involved in its founding were members of the Philosophy Department as well. This pair, in fact, served back-to-back terms as department chairmen. Fr. Philip S. Moore, CSC, who served as chair from 1942 to 1949, had initiated a program in medieval studies in the early 1930s that received official status as the Medieval Institute in 1946. And Fr. Gerald B. Phelan, who succeeded him as chair, was brought in that year as the MI's first director.

Fr. Philip Moore, later to become ND's first academic vice-president, had a degree in medieval studies from the École des Chartes in Paris and had begun teaching courses in that area at ND in 1933. In 1935 he submitted plans to expand these courses and to provide them an academic home modeled after Toronto's Pontifical Institute for Mediaeval Studies, but these plans were shelved for lack of funds and of adequate staff. The staffing shortage was alleviated in the mid-1940s by several departmental appointments of faculty with competence in medieval thought, including Anton-Hermann Chroust and Yves Simon in philosophy. In 1946, ND president Hugh O'Donnell decided it was time to go ahead with Fr. Moore's proposal and provided start-up funds from the university's own coffers. Since Fr. Moore then was chair of the Philosophy Department, O'Donnell looked outside the university for suitable leadership. The first director of ND's MI was Fr. Gerald Phelan, brought in from Toronto to fill that role.

Fr. Phelan's time with the MI began auspiciously. Space was made available in the library by the lake. Generous funding was provided by the Michael P. Grace Foundation (an initial $20,000 in 1947).[1] Distinguished visitors were brought in from other countries, including Étienne Gilson and Jacques Maritain from France and Canon Astrik Gabriel from Hungary. And an endowment to build up the library was obtained from university Trustee William J. Corbett of Chicago. A full-time librarian was hired in 1948; and by the mid-1950s the MI was spending more money on books than was being spent on behalf of several regular academic departments.

In 1949, ND president John J. Cavanaugh prevailed upon Fr. Phelan to take on additional duties as chair of the Philosophy Department, presumably to free Fr. Moore for other administrative assignments. Phelan served as department chair until 1952. But the double burden of running both the Medieval Institute and the Philosophy Department proved more than he could bear. He vacated both roles before the end of the 1952–53 academic year and unceremoniously left the university.[2] Phelan was succeeded as department chair by Fr. Bernard Mullahy, CSC, and as director of the MI by Canon Astrik Gabriel.

Rt. Rev. Canon Dr. Astrik L. Gabriel, O.Praem., was born in 1907, was ordained in 1931, and received his PhD from the University of Budapest in 1936. In 1938 he founded the Premonstratensian French College in Gondolo (near Budapest), which he directed until the communist takeover of Hungary. Escaping from Hungary in 1947, he first went to Toronto's Pontifical Institute of Mediaeval Studies. While he was there, Maritain recommended him for a position at ND. He was on the staff of ND's Medieval Institute from 1948 to 1952, at which point he replaced Gerald Phelan as its director. He remained in that position until 1975, and then stayed on as professor emeritus until he died on May 16, 2005.[3]

Canon Gabriel was a scholar of undoubted renown. Over one hundred entries are listed under his name in the ND library catalog, with publication dates ranging from 1935 to 1998. In the context of Medieval Institute history, he is best known for the additions he brought to its collections. One holding (the Astrik L. Gabriel Universities Collection) comprises over two thousand microfilms of original documents and out-of-print books pertaining to the history of universities in the Middle Ages. Even more notable is the "Ambrosiana" collection of microfilms he had assembled of medieval and Renaissance manuscripts and works of art held in the Biblioteca Ambrosiana and Monza Archives in and near Milan.[4] Within a decade after filming began, this collection contained microfilms of over ten thousand originals.

Astrik Gabriel gained a distinctive place in ND lore. He was an "unmistakable presence" who spoke English with a "thick Hungarian accent, a booming voice and the imperious tone of an extinguished aristocracy," and who moreover loved "good food, fine wine, and talkative companionship."[5] A more intimate anecdote is recounted by librarian Marina Smyth, who apparently heard the story from Gabriel himself. On one particularly hot evening in the old library (not air conditioned), Canon Gabriel and a male assistant were working late, stripped to their underwear. Presently a timorous knock sounded at the door. On opening the door, Gabriel encountered a nun who needed help exiting the locked building. According to Ms. Smyth, the nun's consternation at being greeted by a stout priest in his underwear was matched by the canon's great glee in retelling the story.[6]

Gabriel was compelled to retire in 1975. His replacement was Jeffrey B. Russell, who remained in the position for only two years. Russell received a PhD from Emory in 1960, spent a year with Harvard's

Society of Junior Fellows, and moved to the University of California at Riverside. He came to ND in 1975 as the first holder of the Michael P. Grace Chair of Medieval Studies. Explanations for his short stay at ND vary. Ralph McInerny, his successor in the Grace Chair, thought he had problems getting along with Professor Emeritus Gabriel. But according to Tim O'Meara, the provost responsible for appointing his successor, Russell left because his wife could not tolerate ND's cultural isolation and cold winters. Whatever the reason, Russell returned to California in the spring of 1977, clearing the way for Ralph to enter the picture.

The search committee to find Russell's replacement comprised Thomas Werge of English, Fr. Marvin O'Connell of history, and Michael Loux of philosophy.[7] The leading candidate at first was Bernard McGinn of Chicago's Divinity School, who had an STL from the Gregorian in Rome and was already a prominent historian of Christian thought. McGinn's candidacy, however, was opposed by two senior members of the History Department, who objected to a younger historian from the outside receiving an endowed chair before they did. (Both remained chairless until retirement.) When McGinn indicated that he could not accept the chair under such inauspicious circumstances, the committee turned its attention to other candidates. One was James J. John, a protégé of Canon Gabriel, but his name was soon withdrawn because of doubts about his qualifications. A more promising candidate was Elizabeth T. Kennan, then professor of medieval history at Catholic University. Her candidacy was soon terminated, however, when it was learned that she was about to return to Mount Holyoke College (her alma mater) as its sixteenth president.

Ralph McInerny had been kept abreast of these developments and had been encouraged by some to consider himself a reasonable candidate. Ralph was quite open about his interest in the position. As we have seen, Thomism had been replaced by pluralism as the department's dominant orientation, and Ralph himself had been sidelined by the rising influence of the newly arrived Sellarsians. In the words of then department chair Neil Delaney, Ralph thought that if only he "could get a department of his own," he might still have a chance to counter the secularism he saw engulfing the regular department in the wake of Vatican II.[8]

After some lobbying by Marvin O'Connell, Ralph's longtime friend, the other committee members overcame their initial reluctance to back an internal candidate and sent a letter to Provost O'Meara unanimously recommending Ralph for the position. O'Meara, it turned out, had reservations of his own. After several months of inaction on the matter, however, O'Meara finally called Ralph into his office, unceremoniously handed over the medal designating the Michael P. Grace Professor of Medieval Studies, and publicly announced that Ralph would take office in the fall of 1978. After over a year in administrative limbo, the MI at last had a new director.

Ralph remained in this position for seven years. By the time terms for his resignation had been negotiated in 1985, friends and detractors alike agreed that his stint as director had been singularly unsuccessful. As Ralph himself acknowledged,[9] "not everyone was enthralled by my direction of the Medieval Institute." One problem had to do with details of routine administration, such as budgeting, scheduling, and keeping books. Reflecting on Ralph's ineptitude in this regard, then dean Mike Loux recalls the aftermath of Ralph's previous stint as director of graduate studies in the Philosophy Department. That office in the department had been so poorly managed that it took the next graduate director (Vaughn McKim) a year or more to put it back in order. According to John Van Engen of the History Department, who was appointed Ralph's successor in 1985, essentially the same thing happened at the MI. In a twist of phrase that Ralph himself might have relished, his performance as administrator was a tough act to follow.

Like other universities, however, ND routinely gets by with poorly qualified administrators. What really did Ralph in was his attempt to reconfigure medieval studies into a study of Thomistic philosophy exclusively. Over the years since its founding, the Medieval Institute had fostered scholarship in medieval theology, history, and other humane disciplines. Staff had been added to pursue this broad range of interests, including Canon Gabriel's specialty of medieval universities.

When it became evident that Ralph was concerned only with medieval philosophy, and with a single branch of medieval philosophy at that, complaints began to surface within the MI itself. As the complaints became more vocal, Dean Loux had Ralph circulate a questionnaire among the staff to bring some of the problems to the surface. But Ralph seemed blind to the results, and the unrest continued.

Realizing the situation was beyond repair, Dean Loux took a list of Ralph's administrative lapses to Provost O'Meara, with the recommendation that Ralph be relieved of his MI responsibilities. After receiving approval from Fr. Hesburgh, O'Meara informed Ralph that he had been fired.[10] It so happened that Ralph at that time was Director of the Maritain Center as well. By way of severance package, Fr. Hesburgh let Ralph retain both the Maritain Center position and his chair as Grace Professor of Medieval Studies. Within weeks, John Van Engen had been appointed the new Director of the Medieval Institute. But Van Engen did not receive an endowed chair until several years later, when he became Andrew V. Tackes Professor of Medieval History.

RALPH TAKES COMMAND OF THE MARITAIN CENTER

The Jacques Maritain Center (JMC) was founded in 1957, a result of the joint efforts of Joe Evans, Fr. Leo Ward, and graduate student Frank Keegan (who was writing a thesis on Maritain under Ward's direction). Joe Evans was director of the JMC from its inauguration in 1957 to shortly before his death in 1979. Maritain himself was present at its inauguration. The center was located in the old library by the lake until 1964, when it moved to more spacious quarters on the seventh floor of the new Memorial Library.[11]

The original purpose of the JMC was to serve as an archive for Maritain's papers and letters. After France entered the war in 1939, Maritain spent most of his time in the United States, making it reasonable that his literary output during this period should remain on this side of the Atlantic. This purpose was still active when the Maritains returned to France in 1960.

As things turned out, however, Raïssa died within months after their return to France; Jacques moved to Toulouse, where he took up residence with the Little Brothers of Jesus; and his literary artifacts were stored in an outbuilding of a chateau owned by a close friend in Kolbsheim. The initial plan was to keep them there until they could be shipped to ND for permanent storage. But as the time approached for moving these materials to the United States, the French government intervened, declared them a national treasure, and prohibited their leaving the country. The remodeled outbuilding at Kolbsheim is now home of the Cercle d'Études Jacques et Raïssa Maritain, and contains most of his papers as well as sundry personal memorabilia.[12]

Thwarted in its expectation of these materials from France, ND's Maritain Center started building up its holdings from other sources. It acquired original editions of works by both Jacques and Raïssa, English translations of their works, and works by other authors with close Maritain connections. Important in this regard were numerous works by Maritain that had still to be translated from the French. Joe Evans's main scholarly activity during the decade or so before Maritain's death in 1973 had been the translation and publication of a few previously untranslated books. There is reason to think that Maritain in some way oversaw this work and considered Joe Evans an "official" translator.

There is also reason to think that Maritain was not completely satisfied with Joe Evans's work. For one thing, Joe was not a prolific translator. He had published translations of only two relatively short studies (*Art and Scholasticism* and *The Frontiers of Poetry,* both in one volume) before Maritain died, leaving dozens yet to be rendered in English. There were problems with the quality of Joe's work as well. In the estimation of Bernard Doering, professor emeritus of ND's Romance Language and Literature Department, Joe's translations were "overly literal and stodgy." Having caught wind of a general dissatisfaction with his work, Joe sent Maritain a letter pleading to be retained as translator. According to Doering, who has seen the letter, its gist was that Joe had dedicated his life to the translation project and hoped Maritain would take this into consideration. By this time, however, it seems that Maritain was preoccupied with his affairs in France and saw no reason to interfere with what was going on at ND.

After Maritain died in 1973, Joe's scholarly activity came to a halt and his administration of the JMC became erratic. According to Neil Delaney, Philosophy chair during most of the 1970s, Joe began thinking of the JMC as an autonomous academic entity and resisted administrative guidance by the Philosophy Department. A more serious issue concerned Joe's treatment of center visitors. He began accusing visiting scholars of various misdemeanors, including stealing books from the center's shelves. Delaney recalls several instances in which high-level university administrators had to smooth the ruffled feathers of important people who had been offended while visiting the JMC.

Troubles of this sort led to Joe's dismissal as director of the center he had helped establish. On July 25, 1979, the university announced that Ralph McInerny had been appointed new director of the JMC, effective on the first of August. Joe was devastated by this development. As his friend Bernard Doering put it, his "heart was broken." Classes were scheduled to begin in a matter of weeks. But Joe never again would be seen in a classroom. When concerned authorities finally broke into his quarters, this lonely man had been dead for several days. As reported in the September 14, 1979, *Notre Dame Scholastic,* it was estimated that he died on August 24, 1979, roughly three weeks after Ralph took over as director. A severe diabetic,[13] Joe had neglected to take the medications needed to sustain a viable blood sugar level. Shortly after his death, an elaborate fountain was constructed in his memory just west of the Nieuwland Science Hall. After the fountain was dismantled a decade or so later, a modest memorial plaque inscribed to Joe was mounted on a lectern-shaped pedestal near newly constructed Malloy Hall.

Between Maritain's death and his own, Joe Evans had fallen into a pattern of spending most of his time with students while at ND and of traveling in Europe during the summers. It is not unfair, I believe, to surmise that he used his director's office mostly as a place to meet his devoted undergraduate students. Alice Osberger, Ralph's longtime administrative assistant in both the MI and the JMC, recalls that the rooms of the latter were usually dark when Joe was not in the office.

By her account, the JMC sometimes served as a trysting place for en-amored graduate students who had access to a key.

The fact that little scholarly activity was going on in the Maritain Center may explain the administration's willingness to replace Joe with someone already busily occupied as leader of a bustling research insti-tute. Ralph had been director of the Medieval Institute for only a year after Joe died, and his administrative shortcomings had yet to become evident. In the spring of 1978, Ralph's main role on campus had been that of a dissident philosophy professor. By the fall of 1979, he had become director of ND's two most prominent organizations for the study of medieval philosophy.[14]

According to a brochure written some years later, Ralph's original intent for the JMC was to make it a repository for documents bearing on the response in North America to *Aeterni Patris* and to other papal encyclicals fostering study of Thomistic thought. To that end, plans were set in motion to augment the center's incomplete Maritain col-lection with works of other leading Thomists and of budding Thomis-tic scholars. Before long, facsimiles of Yves Simon's manuscripts and correspondence had been added to the collection, followed by micro-films of Charles De Koninck's works from archives at Laval. Accom-panying the latter were copies of some one hundred doctoral disser-tations written under De Koninck's influence. These acquisitions provided the foundation of a collection of works contributing to what Ralph considered the "Golden Years of Thomism," which subse-quently has grown into the most extensive collection of this sort found anywhere in the world.

Ralph's primary goal in taking over the Maritain Center, however, was not to become an archivist for documents related to Thomism. His underlying intent was to combat the progressive secularization of Catholic intellectual culture. The JMC was to become the staging ground for a venture reaching beyond the academy to American Ca-tholicism at large. Here is where Michael Novak comes back into the story.

Michael Novak first came to ND as a Holy Cross seminarian in the late 1940s. He graduated from Stonehill College in 1956 with a BA in philosophy and English, and then earned a BA in theology from the Gregorian in 1958. He continued studying theology at Catholic University, and moved on to receive an MA in history and philosophy of religion from Harvard in 1966. He taught at Stanford from 1963 to 1968, at SUNY, Old Westbury, from 1969 to 1972, at the Rockefeller Foundation in 1973–74, and then at Syracuse in 1976–78. In the spring of 1978 he joined the American Enterprise Institute (AEI), where he remains currently as the George Frederick Jewett Chair of Religion, Philosophy, and Public Policy.[15]

Ralph McInerny and Michael Novak had much in common. Both were former seminarians who had abandoned their clerical aspirations to get married. Both were professionally involved in teaching, with a special interest in Saint Thomas. And most importantly, both were appalled by progressive currents within the American Catholic Church that had surfaced in the aftermath of Vatican II. When Novak approached Ralph in the early 1980s for help in finding ways of combating these baleful tendencies, it was only a matter of time before a new journal was born.

The first issue of *Catholicism in Crisis* came out in November 1982. Ralph McInerny was identified on the masthead as editor and publisher, with Michael Novak as executive editor and Alice Osberger as editorial assistant. The journal, slated to appear monthly, was described as "a publication of the Jacques Maritain Center" at ND. Authors featured in the first issue include Michal Novak, Jude Dougherty, and neoconservative Catholic theologian George Weigel. With its newly initiated sponsorship of *Catholicism in Crisis,* the Maritain Center was transformed overnight from an obscure ghetto on the seventh floor of Hesburgh Library into a breeding ground for conservative political activism.[16]

Scarcely a month passed before people with close ties to the JMC began to voice their disapproval. The sitting president of the American Maritain Association (Donald A. Gallagher) issued a disavowal of any connection between his organization and "the new journal of Catholic opinion, *Catholicism in Crisis.*"[17] Madame Antoinette Grunelius, a close friend and goddaughter of the Maritains, and then supervisor of the Cercle D'Études Jacques et Raïssa Maritain in Kolbsheim, France, remarked in a letter to Fr. Hesburgh that, while she previously had enjoyed good relations with Prof. McInerny, Maritain himself would not have allowed his name to be associated with such a politically contentious publication. Maritain himself, the letter added, always avoided partisan politics, whereas the offending journal took positions that "ignore absolument ce que Jacques Maritain en aurait pense" (completely ignore what Jacques Maritain would have thought).

These complaints and similar objections from ND faculty were enough for Fr. Hesburgh to insist that the name of the Jacques Maritain Center be removed from the masthead. Often whimsical in the face of opposition, Ralph devised the term "Quodlibetal Publications, Inc." for the magazine's place of origin and continued publishing as usual. Camouflaging the magazine's relation with the JMC in this way, however, was not enough to keep it out of trouble with the university administration. In March 1985, Fr. Hesburgh received a letter from Msgr. George G. Higgins of Catholic University, a prominent labor advocate, a recent recipient of the U.S. Medal of Freedom, a subsequent recipient of ND's Laetare Medal, and a personal friend of Fr. Hesburgh himself. Its contents were not to be ignored.

Higgins was outraged by two articles in the most recent issue of *Catholicism in Crisis*. One was an outspoken criticism of Chicago's Archbishop Cardinal Joseph Bernardin by Ralph McInerny for the cardinal's aligning himself publicly with local Democratic opposition to President Reagan's Strategic Defense Initiative (the quixotic "Star Wars" venture). The other was a denouncement by another author (Robert Royal) of Maryknoll's Orbis Press for publishing a series of "politically naïve" books on social justice. Higgins described these articles as "arrogantly pompous," "patronizing," and "outrageously superficial."

Within a year after Higgins's letter to Hesburgh, the magazine's title was changed from *Catholicism in Crisis* to simply *Crisis,* Ralph's role as editor was transferred to Philip F. Lawler (subsequently of the Heritage Foundation), and Dinesh D'Souza (of AEI) was brought aboard as Washington editor. Ralph was now listed as publisher, and Novak was named innocuously as cofounder. More significantly from the university's perspective, editorial operations were moved from the Maritain Center to the local La Salle Hotel. At this point, the publisher was identified as the Brownson Institute, Inc., an entity founded by Ralph with an ND address.

A more convincing separation from the Maritain Center occurred in 1988 when the editorial offices were moved to Washington, DC. Then in 1995, the whole operation was turned over to Deal Hudson, who founded the Morley Publishing Group, Inc., to replace the Brownson Institute as publisher. Hudson was forced to resign as editor and publisher in 2004.[18] Sustained for a few more years by Morley Publishing, the magazine itself went out of business in 2007. Funding during this last period was provided by the John M. Olin Foundation, Inc., and the Lynde and Harry Bradley Foundation, Inc.

Ralph's extended involvement with Novak and *Crisis* magazine had compromised the good repute of the JMC both inside and outside the university. As noted previously, however, it also had made the center a major beneficiary of conservative funding agencies. Particularly generous from the mid-1980s onward were the Bradley Foundation and the Olin Foundation, the same agencies that kept *Crisis* magazine afloat after its move to Washington. According to Alice Osberger, these foundations "heard about Ralph, liked what he wrote, and approached him with offers of money." This money often was not earmarked for specific purposes, but was given for "whatever Ralph wanted to do with it."[19]

With the *Crisis*-crisis more or less behind him, Ralph could now attend to the primary mission set for the JMC when he took over in 1979. This mission, as noted previously, was to stem the tide of secularism Ralph saw spreading through Catholic higher education. One means toward that end, he thought, was to augment the ranks of young scholars with Thomistic commitments. An obvious place to begin was with his own graduate students.[20] Before he moved into the JMC, a strong majority (20 of 23) of theses directed by Ralph bore titles unrelated to Thomistic thought. After *Crisis* moved from ND to Washington, however, almost all subsequent theses under his direction (7 of 8) had an explicit Thomistic orientation. Several of these were by authors who went on to prominent positions in Catholic colleges and universities.

Another faith-building activity of Ralph's Maritain Center was a series of evening seminars devoted to the sixteen conciliar documents of Vatican II, along with some of the more celebrated encyclicals of John Paul II. Intended as a corrective to what Ralph perceived as a lack of attention to "magisterial documents" in theology courses, these seminars eventually were turned into directed reading courses and accepted as such by both the Theology and the Philosophy Departments. As Ralph admitted in his *I Alone Have Escaped to Tell You* (157), these "seminars became the most heartening experience of [his] twilight years at Notre Dame."

Unlike the Medieval Institute, the Jacques Maritain Center has never been a degree-granting branch of the university, and does not list courses that can be taken for credit. All Ralph's courses were listed by the Philosophy Department, and all his PhD students relied on departmental listings to fulfill their course requirements. From the departmental point of view, Ralph was but one among dozens of professors who guided students toward philosophy PhDs. With respect to administrative aspects of graduate training, the JMC was parasitic on the Philosophy Department.

In other respects, however, Ralph's PhD students were in a class by themselves. Unlike other PhD candidates in the department, who were assigned carrels in the library measuring roughly two yards square, Ralph's students could count on workspace at comfortable tables in the midst of an ample research library. Unlike other candidates, who had to compete with all comers for financial aid, Ralph's students often could take advantage of generous fellowships tailored to their specific needs.[21] In case of special needs, according to Alice Osberger, Ralph sometimes would provide additional support with substantial gifts from his own bank account. His PhD students, moreover, did not have to rely on APA meetings to meet established scholars in their particular fields of interest. When other institutions went on the market for well-trained Thomists, Ralph's students would be among the first to hear about it.

Let us summarize. By the late 1970s Ralph had realized that he would be in a better position to combat secularism if (to quote Delaney once again) he had "a department of his own." After the Medieval

Institute was withdrawn from his command, he founded his "alternative department" in the JMC. Ralph was director of this center for twenty-seven years, during which time he did more to advance the cause of Thomistic philosophy in the United States than probably anyone else of his generation. I recall again the last words of our parting conversation a few weeks before he died, to the effect that he would never give up on the fight to see Thomism restored to its rightful place in ND's philosophy curriculum.

In 2006, John O'Callaghan replaced Ralph as director of the Maritain Center.[22] John was one of the last ND graduate students to receive a PhD (in 1996) under Ralph's direction. Continuity was assured by Alice Osberger, who stayed on as administrative assistant. In addition to being a prominent Thomist, John is well versed in several areas of contemporary philosophy. This bodes well for the future of the JMC.

THE GLORY DAYS OF THE PHILOSOPHIC INSTITUTE

My move from MIT's Lincoln Laboratory to ND in 1958 resulted in a 50 percent cut in salary. Like other faculty with families at the time, I found that making ends meet required additional employment. Some colleagues worked in shoe stores, some drove taxis, and others did copyediting for academic presses. Beginning in 1962, I did sponsored research on artificial intelligence (AI). Although not the first philosopher to take notice of this arcane discipline,[23] I may have been the first to get involved on the level of actual research.

The general idea was that I would teach my regular courses during fall and spring terms, and then concentrate on AI during the summer. Between 1962 and 1972, this summer work was supported by an uninterrupted series of grants from the NSF. The first grant came under the title "Simulation of Mental Processes." Its objective was to compare current mechanical pattern recognition strategies with traditional philosophic accounts of human pattern recognition. This initial work resulted in the publication of my "Human and Mechanical Recognition" (1962); of "Pattern Recognition Mechanisms and St. Thomas'

Theory of Abstraction" (1963), coauthored with Joe Bobik; and of *The Modeling of Mind: Computers and Intelligence* (1963), coedited with Fred Crosson.[24]

When the grant was renewed at a higher level of funding in 1963, negotiations began with the university to establish a center for AI research with its own budget and office space. By 1965, the Philosophic Institute for Artificial Intelligence (PIAI) had been incorporated as a part of George Shuster's Center for the Study of Man in Contemporary Society, and housed in a five-room suite (with a window) on the eleventh floor of Memorial Library. This office space was intended to accommodate me (as director), Fred Crosson (as associate director), our part-time secretary, and a growing contingent of participating faculty. Other participants at this early stage were Fr. David Burrell of Philosophy and James Massey of Electrical Engineering. In later years, Jim Massey went on to become a world-class authority on information theory. The four of us collaborated in writing *Philosophy and Cybernetics,* which was published by UNDP in 1967.

In the meanwhile, we had been working on a computer program for recognizing handwritten letters. Results were promising enough to be presented in a demonstration to the Arts and Letters Advisory Council in late 1965. As I recall, their response was surprisingly enthusiastic. At long last, they seemed to be saying, the Arts and Letters College is doing something to attract attention outside the traditional circle of Catholic Universities. Another development in 1965 was the publication by UNDP of my *Recognition: A Study in the Philosophy of Artificial Intelligence.*

Although initial results of the recognition project were encouraging, considerable improvement was needed before it could be considered successful. A yet larger grant was forthcoming in 1966 for continuation of the project under the title "Pattern Recognition and Formation by Machine." In addition to continued work on the program itself, this grant was to support theoretical work aimed at explaining certain phenomena of Gestalt psychology on a quantitative basis and at exploring the potential of information theory as a tool for resolving long-standing problems in theory of perception. By way of preparation, Fred and I had completed formal courses in information theory with Jim Massey and in recursion theory with Thoralf Skolem. During the summer of 1967, we also held a conference on information theory and psychology with invited speakers from outside the university.

From this point onwards, our work in AI proceeded along two parallel paths. During the school year, Fred and I (taking advantage of reduced teaching loads enabled by the NSF) were involved in book-length studies fulfilling the theoretical requirements of the grant. Results were my *Consciousness: A Philosophic Study of Minds and Machines* (Random House, 1969) and Fred's edited volume *Human and Artificial Intelligence* (Appleton-Century-Crofts, 1970). Fred's active participation in the PIAI ended in 1969, when he became dean of the College of Arts and Letters.

During the summers, work continued on the letter recognition program. With the renewed grant, our staff of programmers had been expanded to include four philosophy graduate students (Kerry Koller, Charles Davis, Michael Crowley, and James Heffernan) along with Vaughn McKim as supervisor. By 1968, the program was able to identify individual letters from previously segmented cursive lines with about 90 percent accuracy. But the process of segmenting a cursive line mechanically remained problematic. We were faced with what subsequently became known in automated handwriting-recognition literature as "Sayre's Paradox":[25] a letter cannot be recognized before being segmented and cannot be segmented before being recognized. This is an adaptation of the "learner's paradox" in Plato's *Meno*: you must learn something in order to know it, and you must know something in order to learn it (know it in a way that enables you to recognize what you set out to learn when you actually find it). Plato's problem was solved with his "theory of recollection"; ours required a more practical solution.

Our practical expedient at this point was to enlist the help of Celso Souza, another information theorist from the Electrical Engineering Department, and to arrange yet another grant from the NSF (entitled "Completion of Program for the Mechanical Recognition of Handwritten Sentences"). Souza's approach to the segmentation problem was to develop a "statistical filter" that would break up the cursive line into all combinations of possible letter symbols and then eliminate combinations that never occur in the relevant language (English). After many adjustments to the program, and several trial runs, the finished product was ready for testing in late 1971. In the final test, 84 handwritten words were presented to the program for identification. Of these, 66 were correctly identified, giving a success rate of 79 percent. This not only exceeded the success rate of comparable programs then being developed elsewhere, but did so under more demanding conditions. (In competing systems, letters were humanly segmented before being fed into the program.) After a decade of sustained work, we had produced the most successful handwriting recognition program then available. The final report of the project was published in the technical journal *Pattern Recognition* in 1973 under the title "Machine Recognition of Handwritten Words: A Project Report."

The four NSF grants supporting this research between 1962 and 1972 totaled $112,800, easily the largest amount that had been brought into the Arts and Letters College by a single research project at the time. Beyond that, our project involved the first systematic use of computers (we used the university's UNIVAC 1107) in research by Arts and Letters faculty. Another first, as I recall, is that it involved interdisciplinary cooperation with faculty from another college (Jim Massey and Celso Souza were electrical engineers). Probably most significant in the long run, however, was the publicity it afforded the department within the profession at large. In that regard, I remember being introduced by a colleague to Thomas Kuhn, the renowned expositor of paradigm shifts. Upon hearing my name, Kuhn immediately asked, "How are things with the Institute for Artificial Intelligence?"

With the successful completion of the handwriting project, members of the PIAI felt that time was ripe for a change in direction. The late 1960s and early 1970s were years of social unrest, in the nation at large and on college campuses especially. Largely in response to U.S. involvement in the Vietnam War, student protests brought normal educational activities of several major universities to a standstill. By dint of Fr. Hesburgh's firm leadership, however, protests at ND never crossed the line into physical violence. As newly appointed chairman of the Theology Department, David Burrell was personally involved in the university's response to this predicament. Fr. David was also associate director of the PIAI, having replaced Fred Crosson when he became dean in 1968. With David's help, we came to realize that automated pattern recognition had little social significance at the time and that we should turn our attention to more relevant issues.

In 1973, we submitted a proposal to the NSF Office of Exploratory Research entitled "Decision-Making in the Power Industry." The underlying premise of this proposal was that the social unrest of that troubled era could be traced, at least in part, to disparities between values driving technologically oriented industry (self-serving values) and values underlying an equitable society (other-directed values). Its specific objectives were (1) to analyze conflicts between commercial, environmental, and ethical values in power industry decision-making, (2) to develop normative guidelines for resolving such conflicts, and (3) to work with decision makers in applying these guidelines. Organizations that had agreed to cooperate with this study were Commonwealth Edison (ComEd) of Chicago and Northern Indiana Public Service Company (NIPSCO). NSF provided $149,100 to fund the study, which was to extend from 1973 to 1976.

Ten ND faculty members were enlisted to conduct the inquiry. Participants from philosophy included myself (principal director), Vaughn McKim, and Kenneth Goodpaster. Also from Arts and Letters were David Burrell (theology) and Kenneth Jameson (economics). Participants from engineering were Neil Schilmoeller (nuclear engineer, coprincipal director) and William Biles (industrial engineer). Michael McIntire (environmental law) came from the Law School, Robert McIntosh (ecology) from the College of Science, and John Kennedy (marketing) from the Business School. All five major academic units of the university thus were represented. Joining from outside the university were Alasdair MacIntyre (philosophy, Boston University), Ellen Maher (sociology, Indiana University at South Bend), and Mary Trainor (mathematics, Valparaiso University).[26]

Research tasks were divided between two sections. The Corporate Division Section, supervised by Neil Schilmoeller, was responsible

(1) for devising a description of factual circumstances that influence policy decisions in the industry and (2) for determining the value presuppositions underlying these decisions. Data for both purposes were gathered through questionnaires administered to upper-level decision makers at ComEd and through personal interviews with the ComEd executives and their counterparts at NIPSCO. The questionnaires were designed primarily by Ellen Maher. Most members of the group were involved at some stage of the interviews.

The Value Theory Section, which I supervised, was responsible for (1) articulating potentially conflicting values involved in company decision-making in a manner enabling decision makers to weigh them against each other and (2) exploring possible ways of resolving such conflicts. To this end, we drew extensively upon major normative traditions pertaining to contemporary culture, particularly utilitarianism, Kantianism, and Judeo-Christian morality. The efforts of Alasdair MacIntyre, Vaughn McKim, and Kenneth Goodpaster were central to this undertaking.

Major results forthcoming from the power company study were (1) that company decision-making is dominated by an implicit utilitarian moral outlook, leading to a disregard for groups (e.g., future generations) outside the company's customer base, (2) that in cost-benefit analysis of new plant siting it is always assumed that additional generating capacity is needed (no-growth in this regard is not a live option), (3) that growth is equated with progress in company thinking, and (4) that in practice the relevant regulatory agency serves as company conscience ("if the regulators let us do it, it must be okay").

These results are elaborated and documented in the volume *Values in the Electric Power Industry* (UNDP, 1977), which I edited, containing essays by McKim, Goodpaster, MacIntyre, Maher, Jameson, and myself. Also included is an essay by Charles Murdock, who was slated to participate in the project before leaving ND to become dean of Loyola's Law School. As the results may suggest, this volume was not uniformly well received by company executives. Another volume resulting from this project is *Ethics and Problems of the 21st Century* (UNDP, 1979), edited by Goodpaster and myself and containing essays by Goodpaster and MacIntyre as well as other moral philosophers not directly associated with the study (W. K. Frankena, R. M. Hare, Kurt Baier, Peter Singer, et al.).

In view of result (4) above, a natural next step was to look at the value orientations of power company regulators. In 1977, we received a grant of $83,000 from NSF's EVIST (Ethical and Human Values Implications of Science and Technology) section under the title "Values and Electric Power Industry Regulation." Members of the Illinois Commerce Commission (ICC) had agreed in advance to cooperate with this study. Its stated purpose was to determine the values these regulators brought to bear in dealing with companies like ComEd, and then to assess the extent to which these values served the public interest.

Four members of the previous group stayed on to help with this new study: Goodpaster and myself from ND, MacIntyre from Boston University, and Maher from Indiana University at South Bend. Additional participants were Peri Arnold (government), James Stewart (economics), John Lucey (engineering), and Robert Rodes (law) from ND, along with Mark Lipsey from Claremont Graduate School. Maher was primarily responsible for questionnaires used in this study (Allport's *Study of Values,* Rokeach's *Value Survey,* and one of her own design). Rodes and Lucey handled technical aspects of the study, and I assisted Goodpaster in matters of value assessment. All ND members of the group participated in interviews.

Value orientations of individual regulators were tested by questionnaires and interviews, much in the manner of the previous study. As research progressed, it became clear that the main moral issue in question had to do with the extent to which regulatory commissions become "captured" by (aligned with) the industries they regulate. To probe a common conclusion of academic literature on regulation that "capture" is widespread, we undertook to test three hypotheses: (1) that most regulators on the ICC are *not* aligned with the industries they regulate, (2) that aligned and nonaligned ICC regulators hold significantly different personal values, and (3) that aligned and nonaligned regulators are guided by significantly different ethical principles.

Results of this study are reported in *Regulation, Values, and the Public Interest* (UNDP, 1980), coauthored by Sayre, Maher, Arnold, Goodpaster, Rodes, and Stewart. Regarding the three hypotheses, we found the first to be strongly confirmed. Contrary to the common perception of utility regulators as being aligned with the industries they regulate, most members of the ICC (in the late 1970s) were aware of the dangers of "capture" and had succeeded in avoiding it. The second and third hypotheses, however, were disconfirmed. Both aligned and nonaligned members of the ICC were similar in value orientation to the populace at large (in the 1970s), as measured by the Allport and the Rokeach tests. And both classes of regulators showed general agreement in their conception of the public interest and in the utilitarian principles that governed their decision making.

Pleased with these results, which they found in keeping with their own self-conceptions, several members of the ICC suggested that the study be extended to regulatory commissions in other parts of the country. By way of preparation, we submitted a proposal for a more general study under the title "An Ethical Analysis of State Regulatory Agencies." In the meanwhile, however, the National Association of Regulatory Utility Commissioners had officially declined to cooperate with the project. The proposal for continuation was withdrawn accordingly.

By this time, the research group had begun to break up. Ken Goodpaster, who had been slated to succeed me as director of the PIAI, was denied tenure and moved on to a teaching position in Harvard's Business School. Ken Jameson and Jim Stewart also left for other institutions. David Burrell decided to devote most of his research time to Islamic studies. And I became more deeply engrossed in my work on Plato (*Plato's Late Ontology* came out in 1983). From 1980 onward, no further applications for support of interdisciplinary research were forthcoming from the Philosophic Institute.[27]

During its heyday between 1965 and 1980, the Philosophic Institute received approximately $350,000 in grants from the NSF (well over $1.6 million in 2010 dollars), about one-fourth of the research money brought into the A&L College during that period.[28] This money funded research by a total of twenty-five academic professionals.[29] Of these, eleven were philosophers (including four graduate students), and twenty-one were ND personnel at the time. As already noted, all five colleges of the university were represented.

After we stopped doing sponsored research, the Philosophic Institute slipped into a sort of shadow existence. I continued to occupy a reduced suite of offices on the eleventh floor of Hesburgh Library until the space was given over to bookshelves in the mid-1980s. After that, I moved into a generic office in newly opened Decio Faculty Hall. The name "Philosophic Institute" was kept alive as the designation of a desk used by my undergraduate assistant in nearby office-space occupied jointly with the Center for the Philosophy of Religion. In addition to an antiquated computer, my assistant's desk had a telephone listed under "Philosophic Institute" in ND's telephone directory. The listing has been retained in the directory each successive year up to the present. But if you call the number (631-7346), no one will answer. The telephone was removed in 2005.

ND'S CELEBRATED CENTER FOR PHILOSOPHY OF RELIGION

According to its current website,[30] ND's Center for Philosophy of Religion (CPR) was established to promote scholarly work on such topics as the problem of evil, the nature of religious language, and the rationality of Christian belief. Although these topics obviously can be addressed from other perspectives, the approach of the CPR is explicitly Christian. To borrow a phrase from Alvin Plantinga, its best known member, the perspective of the CPR is that shared by "Catholics and other Christians" (read with due emphasis on "other Christians").

One thing the website does not mention is that the CPR was the brainchild of Neil Delaney. Neil had succeeded Ernan McMullin as chairman in the fall of 1972 and, like Ernan, was committed to increasing the department's national visibility. Setting up a center for Christian philosophy of religion seemed a natural way of advertising one of the department's main strengths.

But Neil had less publicity-oriented goals in mind as well. For one, there was the matter of getting Fred Crosson to join the department.

Fred was scheduled to leave the A&L Dean's Office in 1975. Before becoming dean, Fred had been chair of the General Program of Liberal Education. An expeditious way of moving him into the Philosophy Department would be to appoint him director of a center under the department's umbrella. The project of founding a center for this purpose, it may be added, was one that enjoyed then dean Michael Loux's full cooperation.

A more long-term goal was to entice Alvin Plantinga to leave Calvin College and to join the ND department as a permanent member. Al had begun teaching graduate courses at ND as a visitor in 1975, driving down once a week from Grand Rapids, Michigan. It was generally agreed that making him a full-time member would strengthen the department. Neil's expectation was that Al would find ND more attractive if it had an ongoing program in the philosophy of religion with which he could join forces.

True to plan, Fred Crosson moved to the Philosophy Department in 1976 as the first director of the CPR. As part of the move, he was appointed the John Cardinal O'Hara Professor of Philosophy. This made Fred the first member of the department to hold an endowed chair. He retained the O'Hara Chair until he left the department in 1984, when he returned to the PLS as the John J. Cavanaugh Professor of Humanities.

Fred Crosson (Director, 1976–84)

Frederick J. Crosson was born on April 27, 1926, in Belmar, New Jersey. His BA and MA were from Catholic University, granted in 1949 and 1950, respectively. In 1951–52 he studied at Paris University, where he attended lectures by Maurice Merleau-Ponty. Also studying in Paris at the time was Mary Patricia Burns, whom Fred married in 1953.

Fred and Pat moved to ND that same year, where he became an instructor in the General Program of Liberal Education (after 1980 the Program of Liberal Studies, or PLS). He was promoted to assistant professor in 1956, after receiving his PhD from ND that year under the direction of A. Robert Caponigri. Promotion to associate professor came six years later. He then became chair of GPLE in 1964, at which time he was advanced to professor. While chair of GPLE, Fred also served as associate director of the PIAI from 1965 to 1969, after which he moved into the Dean's Office of the A&L College. The first lay dean of A&L, he stepped down in 1975 just before becoming director of the CPR.

During his first six years (1976–82) as director of the CPR, Fred also served as editor of ND's *Review of Politics*. During these years, he was active in the National Phi Beta Kappa (PBK) Society as well.[31] He served as philosophy and religion reviewer for PBK's *The Key Reporter* from 1973 to 1997. Between 1977 and 1991 he was on its National Committee on Qualifications, acting as chairman of that committee from 1982 to 1991. Then he became a PBK senator in 1992, vice-president in 1994, and in 1997 president of the national society. He remained PBK president until 2000, two years after his official retirement from ND.

Among other contributions to the academic profession, Fred was active in the North Central Association of Schools and Colleges from 1984 to 1998. In 1990–91, he was president of the American Catholic Philosophical Association. His publication list included six academic books which he edited or coedited and (by his count) about four dozen articles.

Fred Crosson was an unusually effective teacher, the kind students learn a lot from without feeling overworked. He won the Sheedy award in 1997. He was also an uncommonly congenial colleague. Everyone on the faculty knew who he was, and most held him in high esteem. As an administrator, by contrast, he received mixed reviews. He was much appreciated as chair of GPLE, exercising a firm hand in smoothing ruffled feathers in that sometime fractious program. As dean of the A&L College, however, according to subsequent dean Mike Loux, Fred ruffled a few feathers himself because of his suspected bias in favor of teaching over research.

The character of Fred's personal life was also ambiguous. Beyond the confines of a tightly structured academic context, he was reticent and inclined to keep his feelings to himself. Even his family, I fear, sometimes found him reclusive. When the workday was over, there were relatively few he could count as close personal friends. I considered myself fortunate to be among those few. Perhaps because of our frequently being seen in each other's company, as well as our similarity in appearance, Fred and I became accustomed to being called by each other's name. As with Cebes and Simmias in Plato's *Phaedo,* the sight of one of us would remind people of the other. We would work on AI programs together during the day, run together in the late afternoon, and play GO together during spare time in the evening. During rare moments of reflection on our own relationship, however, we both tended to be restrained. On the evening of my first wife's funeral, after other friends had left with their empty pie plates and casserole dishes, Fred stayed for another two hours, just sitting there with me without saying a word.

Fred himself died on December 9, 2009, almost two years after suffering a brain-damaging fall while wintering in Florida. His final residence was a terminal-care nursing home in South Bend, where I would visit him fortnightly. My usual approach during these visits was to ask questions about how he was being treated and what he was watching on television. These questions were obviously frustrating because he had lost the ability to reply in coherent sentences. On what turned out to be my last visit, I stopped asking questions and began telling him stories about people we had known and things we had done together. Fred loosened his grip on his wheelchair and began to smile. His last words in my presence were "Thank you, Ken."

Alvin Plantinga (Director, 1984–2002)

Al Plantinga is a member of the Christian Reformed Church (CRC), and easily the most prominent non-Catholic in the history of ND's Philosophy Department. The CRC is an offshoot of the Dutch Reformed Church inspired by Zwingli and Calvin, from which a small group seceded in the early 1800s and immigrated to Michigan.[32] Another secession in 1857 resulted in the CRC, which was joined by Plantinga's progenitors when they came to the United States in the late nineteenth and early twentieth centuries. Retained through these schisms was an emphasis on Bible reading, preaching, and simple piety. CRC congregations today number around one-quarter million people, roughly 1/10,000th of the world's total Christian population. Catholics, by contrast, are 5,000 times more numerous. This contrast in denominational size is worth bearing in mind as we consider the substantial impact Alvin Plantinga had on philosophy of religion at ND.

Alvin Carl Plantinga was born on November 15, 1932, in Ann Arbor, Michigan. His father (Cornelius), who was born in the Dutch province of Friesland, held a PhD in philosophy from Duke University. One brother (Leon) is a retired professor of musicology at Yale, and another (Cornelius, Jr.) until recently was president of the Calvin Theological Seminary. Al and his wife, Kathleen (de Boer), whom he married in 1955, have two sons, both professors at Calvin College, and two daughters, both active in Christian ministry.

Al enrolled in Calvin College in 1950, received a scholarship from Harvard, where he studied for a year, and then returned to Calvin to receive a BA in 1954. His most venerated teacher at Calvin was Harry Jellema. He received an MA from Michigan in 1955, having worked there with William Alston, William Frankena, and Richard Cartwright. He then transferred to Yale University, where he received a PhD under Paul Weiss in 1958.

His first teaching job after Yale was at Wayne State University, where he was a colleague of George Nakhnikian, Hector Castañeda, and Edmund Gettier. Al's time at Wayne State was critical for his development as a philosopher. Speaking in his "Spiritual Autobiography," Al said, "My colleagues were people I loved and for whom I had enormous respect; there was among us a close and happy camaraderie unmatched in my experience of philosophy departments."[33] It was at Wayne State that he refined the tightly reasoned style of argument that marks his later work. Al returned to Calvin in 1963, was promoted to professor in 1964, and remained there until coming to ND in 1982.

Al has served as president of the APA Western Division (1981–82) and as president of the Society of Christian Philosophers (1983–86). He has held numerous fellowships, including a Guggenheim in 1971–72. In 1975, he was elected a Fellow of the American Academy of Arts and Sciences. *Time* magazine, in its issue of April 5, 1980, described him as "America's leading orthodox Protestant philosopher of God." He delivered one set of Gifford Lectures at Aberdeen in 1987 and another at St. Andrew's in 2005. According to records I have seen, the only other person to give two separate courses of Gifford Lectures was British idealist James Ward (in 1896 at Aberdeen and in 1907 at St. Andrews). Al has honorary degrees from Glasgow University (1982), Calvin College (1982), North Park College (1994), Free University of Amsterdam (1995), Brigham Young University (1996), University of the West in Timisoara, Romania (1998), and Valparaiso University (1999). He has published eight books, edited three others, and been the featured subject in sixteen volumes written or edited by other people. As of 2009, he had published a total of 133 articles.

With these credentials, it is not surprising that Al received job offers from many other institutions. His remaining at Calvin College for eighteen years was due to his commitment to the CRC. As he recalls, his decision finally to leave Calvin for ND was based on a combination of factors. One was the fact that he had been teaching at ND part time since 1974. Save for a year at Oxford (1975–76), he would drive down from Grand Rapids once a week to teach a graduate course on his current research interest. He continued teaching at ND as a visitor during his semester at Arizona (fall 1980), when he would fly up from Tucson to conduct a seminar every other week. This time at Arizona worked to ND's benefit, convincing Al that his ties to Calvin were not as binding as once appeared.

For someone of Al's scholarly bent, teaching graduate students at ND had obvious advantages over teaching undergraduates. Another factor in ND's favor was that it could offer Al a teaching load of a single graduate course each year. As he sees it in retrospect, however, the main factor behind Al's decision to come to ND was its situation as a Christian university. Having taught here several years part-time, he was well aware of Fr. Hesburgh's efforts to remake ND into a great Catholic university. In Al's estimation at the time, ND's "opening up" to the secular world had gone a bit too far.[34] With the resolve of a Calvinist reformer, Al thought he might be able to nudge the university back into a more traditional posture. In a conversation shortly after his retirement, Al expressed regrets to me that he had not been able to do more in that regard.

As the above account shows, Al's professional accomplishments are not hard to describe. What he is like personally is another matter. My own impressions of Al changed significantly as I got to know him better. In later years we stopped viewing each other as antagonists and became rather good friends. Our earlier encounters, however, were mostly adversarial. During the 1970s, the philosophy departments of Calvin and ND participated in a series of miniconferences involving our taking turns driving to each other's campus, exchanging papers and comments, and talking philosophy well into the evening. In 1975 or 1976, I believe it was, ND was at Calvin listening to Al read an early version of his "Boethian Compromise."[35] Mike Loux made some hard-hitting criticisms in his comments, which Al managed to ignore. I sided with Mike during discussion and was caught up in a blow-by-blow interchange with Al that ended in my being severely trounced. Stung by the apparent indignity, I was so upset that I started for home along the limited-access expressway in the wrong direction. After driving north for twenty or thirty minutes, I was finally able to turn around and head back for South Bend. Outrage eventually gave way to quiet amusement, and I now think of this as one of the funniest episodes in my early career.

I cannot recall ever having seen Al being bested in philosophic argument.[36] And I have seen him in action with dozens of fine philosophers, including several in our own department. As far as outside adversaries are concerned, an encounter with Saul Kripke is particularly memorable. Kripke (one of the world's smartest—and most idiosyncratic—philosophers at the time) was on campus as part of the Perspective Series in 1986. He was defending the thesis that some contingent truths (not true a priori) nonetheless are necessary. Expert on necessity that he was (his *The Nature of Necessity* came out in 1974), Al took exception and an extended interchange of dialectical salvos ensued. An impartial judge would probably hold that the interchange ended in a draw. Al may not have won, but he plainly was not defeated either.

A stereotype of the CRC faith championed by Al might portray it as heavy on rational underpinning and light on personal religious experience. Applied to Al specifically, the stereotype would suggest that his personal religious involvement boils down to complex rebuttals of standard objections to a simple faith accepted docilely from his CRC forebears. Militating against this stereotype is the fact that Al's "simple faith" was severely challenged during his year at Harvard. As acknowledged in his "Spiritual Autobiography," there were so many "intelligent and accomplished people" at Harvard who had "little but contempt for what [he] believed" that he doubts whether he "would have remained a Christian at all" if he had not returned to Calvin at the end of the year.

Sustaining him during his second semester at Harvard, moreover, was an event that might be described as a "mystical experience." Al's poetic description of this event in the "Spiritual Autobiography" is worth quoting in itself. When returning to his room one "gloomy evening" that was "dark, windy, rainy, nasty," he writes, "suddenly it was as if the heavens opened; I heard, so it seemed, music of overwhelming power and grandeur and sweetness; there was light of unimaginable splendor and beauty; it seemed I could see into heaven itself; and I suddenly saw or perhaps felt with great clarity and persuasion and conviction that the Lord was really there and was all I had thought." The effects of this experience, Al recalls, convinced him that "arguments for the existence of God" are "merely academic," much like arguments whether "there has really been a past."[37]

The "Spiritual Autobiography" goes on to describe another occasion on which he "felt the presence of God with [comparable] immediacy and strength. That was when [he] once foolishly went hiking alone off-trail in really rugged county south of Mt. Shuksan in the North Cascades, getting lost when rain, snow and fog obscured all the peaks and landmarks. That night, while shivering under a stunted tree in a cold mixture of snow and rain, [he] felt as close to God as [he] ever [had], before or since." In addition to these two overpowering experiences, Al refers to "many other occasions" on which he "felt the presence of God . . . in the mountains, . . . in church, . . . reading the Bible," to name a few. These are not the words of someone whose belief in God is supported primarily by an exercise of reason.[38]

Anyone who knows anything about Alvin Plantinga has heard of what he describes as his "lifelong love affair with mountains." In his

"Spiritual Autobiography," once again, he mentions having climbed "many of the main ranges of the United States . . . concentrating on the Tetons and the Cascades and the Sierras" as well as the Matterhorn and Mont Blanc in Europe. But as the years wore on, he admits, his "obsession with the mountains . . . gradually dissipated." In the last decade or so, he has "turned more to rock climbing, which is less prodigal of time and energy than mountaineering."[39]

Putting these facets of Al's persona together, we have a picture of a man who has become an icon unto himself. With rational powers approaching those he thinks order the universe, his quick wit is seldom matched among contemporary philosophers. Being able to see God while lost on a mountain side, he has spiritual fortitude worthy of a desert father. And possessing a physical frame with the solidity of a mountain ridge, he is ready to joust with any infidel who steps forward to challenge him.[40] Add to that a visage reminiscent of Abraham Lincoln, and we have a man ready to reinvent philosophy at ND.

Al's full-time appointment to ND had no sooner been announced than students began arriving to study with him specifically. A majority came from good evangelical colleges like Wheaton in Illinois, Calvin in Michigan, and Huntington in Indiana. Between 1985 and his retirement in 2010, Al directed (or codirected) the PhD theses of twenty graduate students in philosophy. In terms of theses-per-year, this level of productivity was exceeded only by Yves Simon during his decade at ND between 1938 and 1948. Of these twenty PhD recipients, about half went on to church-affiliated schools, and several found positions in research departments, although a handful seem never to have taken academic jobs.

Al also had a decisive impact on department hiring after he came in 1982. In several cases, he took a leading role in deciding what candidates would be offered jobs. Key appointments expedited by his formidable support include those of Thomas Flint, William Ramsey (another rock climber), Eleonore Stump, Dean Zimmerman, Peter van Inwagen, Ted Warfield, and Michael Rea. Flint and Rea, as we shall see, succeeded Plantinga as directors of the CPR. And van Inwagen, who came in 1995, was soon to join Plantinga both as a Gifford lecturer (in 2003) and as a member of the American Academy of Arts and Sciences (as of 2005).

Plantinga's most far-reaching impact on ND philosophy, however, was to build the CPR into the world's foremost center for the study of philosophy of religion. This enhanced the visibility both of the Philosophy Department and of the university itself. Another consequence, perhaps less desirable from the university's standpoint, was that ND also became known as host to the world's foremost center for Calvinist studies, a reputation bolstered by the presence of other prominent CRC scholars and chair holders as well (Nathan Hatch, John Van Engen, George Marsden, and Mark Noll of history, and Michael Detlefsen of philosophy). This reputation was a cause of consternation to various members of the local Catholic community, including some in the Philosophy Department itself. A related source of malaise was that not everyone in the department was happy with the agonistic way philosophy of religion was pursued in the CPR when Al was in charge. The general perception seemed to be that you either supported Al's approach or rejected it, with no neutral ground in between. If CPR's stellar reputation was a silver lining, then a divided department served as the encompassing cloud.

A celebration of Al's retirement from ND was held in the spring of 2010. Funded by the John Templeton Foundation, the Society of Christian Philosophers, Calvin College, ND's Department of Philosophy, and the CPR itself, this celebration was attended by hundreds of Al's friends, colleagues, and former students. Delegates attended from as far away as Romania, Israel, and China. Within months of this event, Al had sold his local residence and returned with Kathy to Grand Rapids. Devoted as he was to ND, Al admitted that he was swayed by his wife's desire "to go back home."

Programs and Activities

Fred Crosson's stint as founding director got the CPR off to a good start. The first of many conferences under CPR auspices, entitled "Rationality and Religious Belief," was held the year Fred took charge

(1976). Other than Fred, ND participants were Ernan McMullin, Neil Delaney, Mike Loux, Joe Bobik, Bob Caponigri, Ralph McInerny, David Burrell, Gary Gutting, William Frerking, and myself. Notable among outside participants were G. E. M. Anscombe (Cambridge), Alvin Plantinga and Nicholas Wolterstorff (Calvin), John Smith (Yale), George Mavrodes (Michigan), Robert Adams (UCLA), John Post (Vanderbilt), and Langdon Gilkey (Chicago). An interesting statistic of this conference is that all ND participants other than myself were Catholic, whereas Anscombe was the only Catholic among visitors.[41] To engage Plantinga's hallmark phrase, the first philosophy of religion conference at ND was not Catholic but "Catholic and other Christian."

The 1979 conference was titled "Religion and the Notion of a 'Form of Life'" (a phrase reminiscent of Wittgenstein). The featured speaker was D. Z. Phillips (Wales), followed by me in the first regular session. Other visiting speakers were James Cameron (Toronto), Kai Nielsen (Calgary), Louis Mackey (Texas), William Alston (Illinois), Alan Donagan (Chicago), Harry Nielsen (Windsor), Stephen Evans (Wheaton), James Ross (Pennsylvania), and again Alvin Plantinga (Calvin). ND speakers besides me were Neil Delaney and Sheilah Brennan. Papers from this conference were edited by Fred Crosson and published by the UNDP in 1981 as *The Autonomy of Religious Belief.*

A third conference, organized by Thomas P. Flint and Alfred J. Freddoso, was held in 1981 on the topic "The Existence and Nature of God." Contributors included Nelson Pike (UC Irvine), Richard Swinburne (Keele), Philip Quinn (Brown), James Ross (Pennsylvania), Clement Dore (Vanderbilt), and Mark Jordan (Dallas), as well as the two organizers. Papers were edited by Fred Freddoso and published in 1983 as *The Existence and Nature of God* with the collaboration of the UNDP.

These three conferences under Crosson were the beginning of a highly successful series which continued under CPR sponsorship through the next several decades. When Crosson returned to the PLS in 1984, however, he left the material circumstances of the CPR in shaky condition. The center had yet to be assigned its own proper quarters, and it had yet to acquire a staff for clerical support. Further developments of this sort had to wait until after Al Plantinga took over as director. But we should not forget that when Plantinga took over, he had the advantage of a solid record of achievement left by the previous director.

The first conference with Plantinga in charge took place in 1986, under the title "Philosophy and the Christian Faith." Although there were several repeats among participants (Nick Wolterstorff, Robert Adams, George Mavrodes, Bill Alston, Eleonore Stump, Norman Kretzmann), there also were several prominent additions (Peter van Inwagen, Richard Swinburne, Linda Zagzebski), who would show up at later conferences as well. This 1986 conference was organized by Thomas V. Morris.

The next conference, organized by Plantinga and Thomas P. Flint, was called "Christian and Theistic Philosophy" and held in 1988.[42] With one exception, the main papers at this conference were presented by visiting philosophers, with ND people serving as commentators and chairpersons. Visitors presenting papers were Nick Wolterstorff (Calvin), Norman Kretzmann (Cornell), Christopher Menzel (Texas A&M), Alan Donagan (California Institute of Technology), Richard Purtill (Western Washington), Merold Westphal (Fordham), and Eleonore Stump (Virginia Polytechnic). The only ND philosopher (and only Catholic) reading a paper was Jorge Garcia, soon to leave for Georgetown University. Other ND participants were Fred Crosson, Thomas Morris, Alfred Freddoso, and Ralph McInerny. Prominent visitors who did not present papers included Nicholas Rescher (Pittsburgh), William Alston (Syracuse), Alvin Plantinga (Calvin), Philip Quinn (Brown), and Robert Audi (Nebraska). The last three would join the department later, in the order mentioned.

The 1990 conference, "Philosophical Theology and Biblical Exegesis," gained notoriety for its acerbic interchange between Michael Dummett (then Wykeham Professor of Logic, Oxford) and John J. Collins (then theology professor at ND). Dummett was well known as a conservative Catholic. The drift of his paper ("The Impact of Biblical Studies on the Substance of Catholic Belief") was that proponents of "higher criticism" in biblical studies have come up with interpretive views that are heretical and that threaten the faith of common believers. One such view, Dummett claimed, is that Jesus had no intention of founding a church. Collins's incensed response was that Dummett was attributing outrageous claims to the higher critics without supporting evidence. With the help of other sympathetic theologians, Collins put pressure on UNDP to renege on its contract to publish the papers.[43] Proceedings nonetheless were published in 1993 as *Hermes and Athena: Biblical Exegesis and Philosophical Theology*, edited by Tom Flint and Eleonore Stump.

To mention a few others, the conference in 1994 was organized by Robert Audi and William Hasker on the topic of philosophy of mind, and that in 1998 by Dean Zimmerman and Ted Warfield on the topic of dualism. None of these organizers was Catholic, and one probably not even a theist. Notable first-time participants during the 1990s were Lynne Rudder Baker (Massachusetts), Hugh McCann (Texas A&M), David Lewis (Princeton), Jaegwon Kim (Brown), Fred Dretske (Stanford), David Chalmers (California, Santa Cruz), and George Bealer (Colorado), few of whom were either Catholic or other Christian.

Another activity that helped put the CPR on the map was its program of postdoctoral fellowships. During Plantinga's first year as director the center hosted Richard Otte (California, Santa Cruz) and Charles Taliaferro (St. Olaf) as postdocs, each with a stipend of $30,000.[44] During the next ten years, the number of postdocs at the center averaged two per year. Over roughly the same time period, the center also welcomed a dozen or so visitors under the title "Distinguished Scholar."

Then in 2002, the center renamed its senior fellowships after its past and present directors. The first three Crosson Fellows were Tesur Aben (Theological College of Northern Nigeria, 2002–3), Balazs Mezei (Anselmians University, Hungary, 2003–4), and Oliver Crisp (St. Andrews, 2004–5). The first three Plantinga Fellows were Brian Leftow (Oxford, 2002–3), Michael J. Murray (Franklin and Marshall, 2003–4), and Hugh J. McCann (Texas A&M, 2004–5). In addition to offering named fellowships, the CPR continued to host visiting scholars under the designations "postdoctoral fellow" and simply "visitor." The category "Templeton Research Visitor" was added in 2008–9.[45]

Between 1984 and 2010, 161 visitors spent at least one term with the CPR. This averages more than six visitors a year. Of these, approximately 40 percent were senior people, including more than a dozen chaired professors. Roughly 50 percent were in mid-career, and 10 percent were graduate students. On the basis of personal acquaintance and of home institutions, I estimate that about 15 percent of the 161 are (or were when visiting) Catholic. Some were Jewish, some Muslim, and some atheists. But as Al was prone to put it, the great majority were "other Christians." As mentioned earlier, there have been grumblings now and then in the Philosophy Department about ND providing an academic home (with funding) for one of the world's most visible centers of conservative Protestant thought. But at the same time, few deny that much of the department's own visibility is due to the prominence of the CPR.

Al stepped down as director of the CPR in 2002, to be succeeded by Tom Flint, a Catholic whose 1980 ND PhD dissertation was directed by Al Plantinga and Mike Loux. Tom served until 2008, when Mike Rea took over. Mike received his ND PhD under Al's direction in 1996 and, like Al, is a member of the Christian Reformed Church.

THE REILLY CENTER FOR SCIENCE, TECHNOLOGY, AND VALUES

The John J. Reilly Center (named for its donor's father) is an umbrella organization comprising (1) ND's five-year A&L/Engineering (AL/ENG) sequence, (2) its undergraduate Science, Technology, and Values (STV) minor, and (3) its graduate History and Philosophy of Science (HPS) program. Each of these three had an identity of its own before being brought under Reilly Center auspices. This section tells the story of how they came together, featuring philosophers Ernan McMullin and Vaughn McKim, along with the donor John D. Reilly (known locally as "Jack").[46]

Early in the 1960s, the university initiated a five-year undergraduate program leading to dual degrees in Engineering and A&L. John D. Reilly was one of the first beneficiaries of that program, receiving a 1963 BA in art history and a 1964 BS in chemical engineering. Moving on to earn an MBA at Harvard, Reilly soon established himself as a highly successful executive in the mortgage business. Eventually he became chairman of the Reilly Mortgage Group, one of the largest commercial mortgage firms in the country, and after that, president of the Reilly Investment Corporation. By the mid-1980s, Jack was ready to show appreciation for his early training by underwriting a scholarship program for ND's AL/ENG sequence.

In the years immediately preceding Reilly's scholarship offer, McMullin and McKim had been trying to put together an undergraduate STV minor for the A&L College. Initially this program got by with courses the departments involved (primarily Philosophy and PLS) happened to offer during a given semester. To gain stability, however, it became apparent that the program had to provide a number of set courses that could be repeated with some regularity. For this purpose, it proved necessary to seek funding outside the university. A short time before Reilly's offer, McMullin had applied to the National Endowment for the Humanities (NEH) for a $75,000 grant in support of the STV program. Because of this application, ND's money raisers were aware of STV's funding needs.

When Reilly made his offer known, the Development Office promptly contacted A&L Dean Michael Loux. After consulting with McMullin and McKim, Loux came up with a counterproposal which he hoped would satisfy the donor and meet ND's preexisting needs as well. What Loux proposed was the founding of a center carrying the Reilly name that would fund and oversee both a scholarship program for AL/ENG and A&L's minor in STV. The arguing point of the proposal was that STV shared AL/ENG's goal of combining courses in science and technology with courses in the humanities, but would benefit a much larger group of students. Effectively put forward by Dean Loux and the Development Office, this modification of Reilly's original plan soon met with his approval. ND now had a viable undergraduate STV program and a John J. Reilly Center for Science, Technology, and Values to support it. Ernan McMullin was named the Reilly Center's first director, with Vaughn McKim as associate director.[47]

There was another component of ND's counterproposal, however, that Reilly at first found problematic. This involved efforts long underway to upgrade ND's offerings in history and philosophy of science. An MA program in the history of science had been established in 1974 by Michael Crowe and Phillip Sloan of GPLE. In 1977, courses in philosophy of science (taught by McMullin) were added, and the fledgling program became a freestanding entity independent of GPLE oversight. Its courses, offered during summer sessions, were taken mostly by high school teachers looking for graduate credits. But every so often a student would complete the MA requirements and move on to a PhD program in either history or philosophy.

In the late-1970s, A&L Dean Isabel Charles threatened to shut down the program unless it could attract larger numbers of regular students. Ernan McMullin negotiated a temporary reprieve and was asked to come up with a better plan. His resulting plan, in a nutshell, was (1) to combine the MA graduate courses in history of science taught by Crowe and Sloan in GPLE with PhD courses in philosophy of science taught in the Philosophy Department, and (2) to hold students to requirements comparable in rigor to those of the Philosophy PhD program. At the time there were only a handful of universities with PhD programs in history and philosophy of science, and Ernan was confident that ND could compete successfully.

The Dean's Office approved McMullin's plan in principle, but funds were lacking to put it into operation. Pressure for immediate action was removed when Loux took over as A&L dean in 1983, and the program limped on for several more years conferring an average of less than one MA degree per year. With the arrival of Reilly money on the scene, however, hopes were rekindled for an HPS program offering a PhD degree.

In 1985, soon after the Reilly Center had been established, factors began to converge that persuaded Jack Reilly to include a PhD-level HPS program under its umbrella. First was the hiring of a new historian. The NEH grant for which McMullin had applied came through, and the funds it provided helped bring in Christopher Hamlin from the University of Wisconsin's prestigious history of science program. The Reilly Center now included three highly competent historians of science (Crowe, Sloan, Hamlin), along with McMullin and McKim in philosophy of science. Another influential factor was a pair of conferences organized by McMullin that resulted in volumes published under Reilly Center auspices.[48] As Ernan recalled in recounting this part of the story, Jack Reilly was quite happy with these publications.

A further factor was the gentle pressure brought to bear by Provost Nathan Hatch through the university's Development Office. Hatch had been associate dean of A&L from 1983 to 1988, then acting dean a year later. As provost, he continued to support A&L projects he considered worthy. With Hatch's help, a PhD program in History and Philosophy of Science was included under the Reilly Center's umbrella in 1990.

The HPS program had been carefully thought out from the beginning. Part of the plan was that the program would be small, admitting only three or four students a year. To complete the degree, students were required to fulfill all requirements except dissertation in either philosophy or history, in addition to other requirements unique to HPS including the dissertation itself. Although this meant unusually heavy loads on aspiring PhDs, Ernan believed that a demanding program like this was the best way of placing its graduates in desirable academic jobs.[49]

In addition to providing graduate training, HPS has sponsored numerous conferences in conjunction with its encompassing center. Several of these have resulted in published proceedings.[50] Especially noteworthy is *The Church and Galileo* (UNDP, 2005), volume 6 of the series, edited by McMullin and stemming from a Reilly Center conference by that name in 2003.[51] The stage was set for this conference by the report of a commission charged by Pope John Paul II in 1979 to examine the church's handling of the Galileo affair. In the words of a reviewer of the 2005 book, that commission failed "to grasp the nettle" implicit in the situation.[52] As this reviewer suggests, the 2002 conference at ND was charged with taking a more careful look at the evidence available to John Paul's commission. Participants included historians, astronomers, and theologians who had written previously on the church's treatment of Galileo. Also present were various performing artists who had experience in roles dramatizing the interactions of the historical characters in question. Among nonscholarly events programmed into the agenda were a dinner for participants and local faculty (which I attended) and a live performance of Brecht's *Life of Galileo* (which I missed).[53]

Given the multifaceted character of the Galileo conference, it is understandable that more resources were needed to stage it than the Reilly Center itself could provide. Additional funding came from ND's College of Science, the Vatican Observatory, and the Templeton Foundation. Although the conference did not lay all the "nettlesome" aspects of the Galileo affair to rest, it marked a distinct advance in McMullin's efforts to gain international visibility for the Reilly Center and its constituent HPS program. Both continued to flourish as the decade progressed.

Augmenting its well-attended conferences, the Reilly Center has attracted a steady flow of individual visiting scholars. Since its founding, it has sponsored an average of roughly six outside lectures a year. It also has a visiting scholars program for outside researchers wanting to take advantage of its research facilities. Over the past decade or so, this program has hosted more than a dozen scholars from the United States and abroad.

Despite the important roles played by faculty from other departments since its founding,[54] the Reilly Center has always operated in especially close coordination with the Philosophy Department specifically. At critical junctures, its course has been set by the two philosophers who hammered out organizational details in the mid-1980s. During the 1990s, McKim and McMullin devoted more of their efforts to the Reilly Center than to any other endeavor of the Philosophy Department. In an interview with me shortly before his death, McMullin unequivocally credited McKim with bringing the administrative skills to bear that kept the center running. As we shall see subsequently, McMullin's role of keeping the center on target during its initial decade can be viewed as his last major leadership role in the department. He retired in 1994.

CHAPTER 6

Sea Change

KEEPING DIFFERENT COMPANY

The transition from Thomism to pluralism depicted in chapter 4 had little immediate effect on the general culture of the department. People were still cordial toward each other and interested in each other's work. There still were ample opportunities to interact socially with colleagues and their families. Most importantly, the department retained a sense of common purpose. We still thought of philosophy as a way of life, instead of just a way to make a living.

This sense of general affability began to diminish in the late 1970s. The shift itself was gradual and easily missed by someone not paying close attention, like myself at the time. As for long-term effects on the department, however, the transition underway was no less profound than that from Thomism to pluralism a decade or so earlier. The aim of the present chapter is to make the main outlines of this second transition apparent.

We begin with some statistics. During the decade 1950–59, 16 PhDs were hired into the department.[1] Of these, 11 were from Catholic universities, and 5 (Sobocinski, the younger FitzGerald, Nielsen, Fisk, and myself) from non-Catholic institutions. Corresponding figures from 1960–69 are 14 PhDs from Catholic schools and 6 from non-Catholic, for a total of 20 new hires at the PhD level. A total of 24 PhDs were recruited in1970–79, including 5 from Catholic and 19 from non-Catholic institutions. For the decade 1980–89, there were 3 new faculty from Catholic and 24 from non-Catholic programs, for a total of 27 new hires with PhDs.

Two significant trends appear in these figures. One pertains to rate of hiring. During 1950–59, 16 PhDs were newly hired into the department, at a rate of 1.6 per year. Corresponding rates are 2.0 per year for 1960–69, 2.4 for 1970–79, and 2.7 for 1980–89. These figures are consistent with a gradual growth in department size. But they also suggest an increasing rate of turnover in department personnel.

More significant for present purposes is the increasing proportion of new hires from non-Catholic institutions. During the 1950s, 31 percent of new faculty came from non-Catholic programs. Corresponding proportions subsequently are 30 percent for 1960–69, 79 percent for 1970–79, and 89 percent for 1980–89. Put otherwise, the proportion of PhDs recruited from Catholic institutions shrivels from roughly two-thirds in the 1950s to about one-tenth in the 1980s. And in that later decade, only one hire came from a Catholic university other than ND itself.[2] These statistics pertain to faculty entering the department. Equally striking are statistics regarding departures. Records show that 12 regular faculty (with PhDs, having stayed at least three years) left the department during the 1950s. Most of these either retired or moved to administrative positions. As far as I can tell, only 4 transferred to other academic positions, 3 of whom (Phelan, Glanville, and Denissoff) went to other Catholic institutions.

Twelve faculty also left during the 1960s. Four of these retired and 8 took other academic jobs. Five of these latter, or 62 percent, took jobs at Catholic universities.[3] Of 23 faculty departing during the 1970s, 9 left academic employment. Five of the remaining 14, or 36 percent, continued teaching in Catholic institutions. During the 1980s, finally, 25 tenure-track faculty left the department. Of these, 6 retired and 19 remained in the academic profession. Only 2 of these 19 (11 percent) went on to jobs in Catholic schools.

Converting these figures into relevant statistics, we find that during both the 1950s and the 1960s faculty left the department at a rate of 1.2 per year. The departure rate increased to 2.3 for the 1970s, and to 2.5 for the 1980s. This increasing departure rate follows the same curve as the increase in hiring rates from 1.6 in 1950–59 to 2.7 in 1980–89. Over the period between 1950 and 1990, however, the rate of hiring is consistently higher than the rate of departure, reflecting the gradual growth of the department over the interval in question.

As in the case of hiring, the most significant statistic here concerns the departure of personnel from ND to other Catholic institutions. During the 1950s, 75 percent of departing faculty who stayed in the academic profession went on to jobs in other Catholic schools. In 1960–69, the corresponding figure was 62 percent, in 1970–79 36 percent, and in 1980–89 a mere 11 percent. This decline is approximately as steep as that in percentage of hires from Catholic institutions, from 69 percent to 11 percent between 1950–59 and 1980–89.

To recapitulate, we see that ND's Philosophy Department during the 1950s hired most of its new faculty from other Catholic institutions, and that when faculty left for other academic jobs they most likely would move to another Catholic setting. During that decade, it seems accurate to say, the department functioned as part of what might be termed a "Catholic consortium" of philosophy programs. By the 1990s, however, it had withdrawn from that association to enter a new alliance with departments in predominantly secular institutions. With regard just to faculty arriving from and leaving for Catholic institutions, it would be hard to distinguish ND's department in the 1950s from departments at Catholic University, Fordham, and Boston College, and in the 1980s from those at Harvard, Yale, and University of Chicago.

Another relevant statistic concerns what might be called the "retention rate" of the department. Considered without regard to religious character of PhD-granting institutions, a substantial majority of faculty joining the department in the 1950s stayed until death or retirement. A careful count of comings and goings shows that about 62 percent of people taking tenure-track jobs during that decade stayed at ND until their careers were finished. In 1960–69, the retention rate drops to 35 percent, and in the two-decade period of 1970 to 1989 it holds around 27 percent. One way of reading these figures suggests that in the 1950s faculty tended to stay as long as they could, whereas in later years many stayed only until they could find more attractive jobs.

THE PRINCETON INCURSION

Of the many sources of PhDs involved in this shift from Catholic to secular company, three stand out as particularly noteworthy. Between the late 1950s and the early 1980s, 7 of the department's incoming faculty had PhDs from Yale University (Fisk, Burrell, McKim, Pahi, Ameriks, Garcia, and Plantinga). Through the 1970s and 1980s, 5 more came with PhDs from the University of Pittsburgh (Sterba, Garson, Blackburn, Quinn, and Kremer). Of the 12 newcomers from these two sources, we find 6 remaining in the department for at least 20 years.

Whereas the arrivals from Yale and Pittsburgh were spread over almost three decades, however, there was a surge of new faculty from Princeton who arrived in rapid sequence over four consecutive years. Penelope Maddy came in the fall of 1978, Milton Wachsberg in 1979, Phillip Bricker and Eileen O'Neill in 1980, and Aron Edidin in 1981. Although their sojourns at ND on the average were unusually brief, this group of freshly minted Princeton PhDs left an indelible mark on a curiously susceptible department.

Penelope Maddy received her PhD in 1979. She came to ND in 1978 to serve as managing editor of the *Notre Dame Journal of Formal Logic*. My second-wife-to-be, Patti White, served as Maddy's editorial assistant and took a graduate course with her in formal logic. In both contexts, I am assured, Maddy was exceptionally thorough, methodical, and conscientious. After leaving ND in 1983, she went to the University of Illinois at Chicago as associate professor. Then in 1987 she moved to the University of California at Irvine (UCI), where she was made professor in 1989. She was inducted into the American Academy of Arts and Sciences in 1998. In 2007, she became the Distinguished Professor of Logic and Philosophy of Science and Mathematics at Irvine. In addition to some forty articles, she is author of three books published by Oxford University Press. Penny Maddy is a clear example of someone who used ND as a stepping-stone to a distinguished career elsewhere.

I did not spend much time with Penny herself, but became fairly well acquainted with her husband, Steve. Steve was an artist who divided his time between studio work and duties around the house. He was an excellent cook, and spent significant time showing me how to prepare meals for my three teenage sons. Having a homemaking spouse clearly was a substantial boost to Penny's highly successful career.

My only distinct memory of Steve and Penny together goes back to a Halloween party they hosted the year before they left. This was the most "serious" Halloween party I ever attended. Friends from both art and philosophy were invited, and everyone was instructed to appear in costume. One guest (an artist) came in a suit made entirely from paper. Steve, I think, was the Tin Woodman from the Wizard of Oz, and Penny was Glinda, the Good Witch of the North. I came as a sandwich-sign with "The statement on the other side is false" written on both panels. None of the artists, as I recall, could figure out what it meant.

Milton Wachsberg joined the department as an instructor in ethics. One did not have to know him long to realize that ethical concerns were inseparable from his personal life. A deeply private person by nature, he was always ready to help other people put a positive spin on their own vicissitudes. I considered Milton a good friend during his five years in the department. He kept watch over my house during my first wife's funeral in 1980.

Although accommodating in his relations with other people, Milton imposed severe demands on himself. He was one of the first vegetarians I knew personally and made regular bicycle trips to the health-food store in Berrien Springs, Michigan, systematically peddling faster when he went up hills. Strenuous physical conditioning like this made him an excellent player of racquet sports. During his brief stay here, Milton was the best squash player in the university. I know, because at the time I was in the running for second best. Among regular partners, he was the only one I never beat.

Shortly after leaving ND for Cornell, Milton married Susan Sauvé Meyer, added her last name to his own, and followed her to the University of Pennsylvania. Susan Meyer received her PhD from Cornell in 1987, spent a six-year stint at Harvard, and moved to Penn in 1994. She recently has been chair of Penn's Philosophy Department, where Milton serves as lecturer in ethics and feminist philosophy. After his marriage, Milton joined a Reconstructionist Jewish congregation near Swarthmore.

Eileen O'Neill was the first single woman to join ND's Philosophy Department, and the third woman (after Sheilah Brennan in 1971 and Penny Maddy in 1978) overall. O'Neill's specialization leaving Princeton was the history of modern philosophy. In my estimation, her greatest hour at ND was a paper on Descartes she read at one of our Friday colloquia. Her commentator was recently retired Fr. Herman Reith. The contrast between the two was striking. She was attired in a stylish suit, he in black trousers and black shirt with a Roman collar. She was in her mid-twenties, he in his late sixties. Yet both seemed to be enjoying their roles enormously. I had known Fr. Reith for over two decades, and had never seen such a pleased look on his typically dour face. I learned later that Eileen and Hermie sometimes had dinner together. Eileen left ND in the spring of 1983 to spend eleven years at City University of New York. In 1994, she moved to the University of Massachusetts at Amherst. In the meanwhile, her interest in modern philosophy had become focused on woman philosophers of that period. A conference celebrating her work on the history of modern philosophy from a feminist perspective was held at Barnard College (her alma mater) in 2009.

Phillip Bricker arrived at ND the same year as O'Neill, but stayed only one year. He then spent nine years at Yale, after which he joined the faculty at UMass, Amherst, in 1990. Again a colleague of O'Neill's when she went to Amherst in 1994, he at one point was chair of its Philosophy Department. Bricker's main areas of interest are philosophy of language, philosophy of mathematics, and philosophy of science.

Maddy, Wachsberg, O'Neill, and Bricker stayed at ND for an average of just over three years each. Aron Edinin stayed almost as long as the other four combined. Aron arrived from Princeton in 1981 as a specialist in epistemology and philosophy of science. According to the

Philosophy Newsletter for 1983, he and his wife, Robin (whom I don't recall meeting), had a daughter, Rachel, in the fall of 1982.

By seemingly unanimous agreement within the department, Aron was a brilliant philosopher who never felt entirely at ease in a research university. He spent significant time with graduate students but produced only a few article-length publications. He nonetheless was promoted to associate professor with tenure in 1987. The only other entries regarding Aron in nonconfidential department records mention that he gave a colloquium paper in 1983, commented on another in 1987, and was present at several department meetings. He left without fanfare in 1992, returning to New College of Florida, his alma mater. New College values teaching over published research, and Aron has established himself as one of its most popular teachers. His recent course offerings include theory of knowledge, philosophy of music, and topics in feminist philosophy.

Yet another Princeton PhD joined and left the department while Edinin was still here. Christia Mercer was at ND from 1987 to 1989, then spent two years at the University of California, Irvine (with Penny Maddy), and moved on to Columbia, where she currently is the Gustave M. Berne Professor in the Department of Philosophy. Mercer has published two books and about thirty articles, dealing primarily with Leibniz and other philosophers of the modern period. She became a founding member of the Women in Philosophy Task Force in 2009. Mercer thus joined Wachsberg, O'Neill, and Edinin as the fourth of ND's first six PhDs from Princeton to enter the field of feminist philosophy.

ND's seventh Princeton philosopher was Anja Jauernig, who came in 2002 and left for Pittsburgh in 2011. Anja's research interests include history of modern philosophy (especially Kant), philosophy of science, and philosophy of art. In a recent online posting, she attributes her move from South Bend to Pittsburgh to a gradual realization that "it was time to move a little closer to civilization."[4] With Anja's departure the department's retention rate for unmarried women returned to an all-too-familiar 0 percent.

More recent hires with Princeton PhDs are Jeff Speaks, who came to ND from McGill as assistant professor in 2006, and Sean Kelsey, who came from UCLA as associate professor in 2009. Kelsey received his PhD in 1997, Speaks in 2003. Speaks currently is Rev. John A. O'Brien Associate Professor of Philosophy.

PHILIP QUINN AND THE APA

Phil Quinn did more than any other single person to secure the department's standing in the philosophic community at large. Ralph McInerny worked long and hard to maintain its leadership among departments in Catholic institutions, Ernan McMullin brought it prominence in philosophy of science, and Al Plantinga made it a landmark in the domain of Christian Evangelical philosophy. Apart from McMullin's presidency of the Western Division in 1983–84, however, none of these devoted much time to activities of the American Philosophical Association (APA) itself. Phil Quinn solidified ND's role in the philosophic community by bringing the department into lockstep with the policies of the APA.

Although he spent the last two decades of his life at ND, Phil's primary allegiance was always to the APA and to the professional community it represents. Paul Weithman put it aptly in his eulogy at Phil's funeral Mass (November 16, 2004), saying that Phil's "home was in the APA," and "his citizenship . . . in the republic of letters." It was largely due to Phil's dual residency at ND and in the APA that the department's image in the profession was changed from that of a Catholic outsider striving for recognition to that of a prominent department that just happens to be located in a Catholic university.

Phil served the APA in over four dozen different capacities.[5] Notable among these were employment ombudsman for all three divisions (1989–90), president of the Central Division (1994–95), chair of the National Board of Officers (1996–99), and chair of the Budget Committee (1996–99). In addition to the APA, Phil was a member of the American Academy of Religion, the Society of Christian Philosophers, the American Association for the Advancement of Science, and the Philosophy of Science Association. He was elected to the highly prestigious American Academy of Arts and Sciences (AAAS) in 2003.[6]

Reflecting trends in the profession at large, Phil's publication list is heavy on articles and light on books. As best I can tell from his CV, he wrote about one hundred article-length pieces for journals and encyclopedias, many of which have been reprinted in collections and anthologies. One collection of Phil's essays, edited by Christian Miller, has already been cited. Another collection of essays about Phil's work was edited after his death by Paul Weithman, namely *Liberal Faith: Essays in Honor of Philip Quinn* (UNDP, 2008). Phil himself edited two collections, *A Companion to Philosophy of Religion* (1997), with Charles Taliaferro, and *The Philosophical Challenge of Religious Diversity* (2000), with Kevin Meeker.[7] The only book-length work (166 pages) authored by Phil himself is *Divine Commands and Moral Requirements,* put out in 1978 by Oxford University Press. It is interesting to note that, whereas a majority of Phil's essays before 1985 were in philosophy of science, almost all of his publications after he came to ND pertain in one way or another to philosophy of religion.

Philip L. Quinn was born June 22, 1940, in Long Branch, New Jersey, to Joseph and Gertrude Quinn. His undergraduate work was at Georgetown University, yielding a philosophy BA in 1962. After a year at Louvain in Belgium, he spent three years at the University of Delaware, leading to an MS in physics in 1966. Three more years at the University of Pittsburgh resulted in a philosophy PhD granted in 1969.

ND tried to hire Phil right out of graduate school. I remember a pleasant breakfast with him at the Morris Inn on campus which left me with a strong impression of his talents and breadth of interests. Despite an offer from ND, however, Phil went to Brown as an assistant professor. He was promoted to associate professor in 1972 and to professor in 1978. He remained at the latter rank until 1982, when ND reentered the picture. At the instigation of department chair Neil Delaney, Phil came to ND as a visiting professor during the spring of that year. With a few exceptions, the department's reaction to his presence was highly positive. Following Delaney's lead, the CAP prevailed upon acting A&L dean Robert Burns and Provost Timothy O'Meara to rush through an offer of a full professorship with tenure to begin that very fall. The salary was to be $42,000 a year.

At this point, a bidding war between Brown and ND ensued, which Phil orchestrated with consummate skill. A month or two after receiving ND's offer, Phil sent a letter of rejection to O'Meara, signed over the title "William Herbert Perry Faunce Professor." During the brief period following ND's offer, Phil had persuaded Brown to counter with an endowed professorship. The ND department was unprepared for this development and delayed its response for over a year. The delay was due primarily to administrative changes in the department and in the Dean's Office. Mike Loux had replaced Neil Delaney as department chair in 1982, and then Dick Foley replaced Loux when the latter became dean in 1983. Acting quickly once lines of command had been stabilized, ND sent Quinn a letter dated October 20, 1984, offering him the title "John A. O'Brien Professor." This time the salary was increased by one-half to $65,000, plus $12,500 for travel and other expenses. In his letter of acceptance, dated January 16, 1985, Phil described this as "an offer I can not decline," which he scrupulously cited as his reason for accepting it. He started teaching at ND in the fall of 1985.

Despite the department's eagerness to bring him on board, and his seemingly wholehearted acceptance, Phil was never fully content during his almost twenty years at ND. The problem was not the department itself, which he found quite congenial. The problem, as he repeated on many occasions, was what he experienced as South Bend's cultural isolation, coupled with Northern Indiana's inclement winter weather.

My impression from conversations and personal correspondence is that if Phil had ever been offered a better job, he probably would have taken it. In 1990 he spent the spring term at Princeton in the Department of Religion, but returned without an offer of a regular position. In 1995 he told department chair Gary Gutting that he "had decided to look for a position elsewhere," but was keeping it quiet save from "a few close friends." Still restless, he told the next chair, Stephen Watson, in 1999, that he "was not willing to commit to staying" at ND past the next year. His best shot at actually finding a more suitable location, however, came in 2001 when he began negotiations with Yale aimed at his succeeding Nicholas Wolterstorff as the Noah Porter Professor of

Philosophical Theology. For a while, Phil spoke openly as if the job were in the bag, but then in January of 2002 he received a letter from Yale's Marilyn McCord Adams informing him that Yale was no longer interested in hiring another "senior analytic philosopher of religion."

With the failure of the Yale venture, Phil apparently gave up looking for better positions and started thinking of retirement. On March 22, 2004, he sent an open letter to philosophy faculty and graduate students saying that 2004–5 would be his last year full-time at ND. For the next two academic years he would be in residence only during the fall semesters. Other times during those years, the letter continued, he would be looking for a "permanent retirement home" in places that are "better than South Bend in terms of climate and culture." The search turned out to be unnecessary. Phil died of esophageal cancer on November 13, 2004.

In his eulogy, Paul Weithman refers approvingly to Phil's "obstinately contrarian spirit." A contrarian trait I found attractive was his aversion to modern technology. Although he owned a car in Providence, he did not bring it to South Bend. His apartment here was about a one-mile walk from campus, and he would shuffle back and forth in all kinds of weather. Sometimes colleagues would give him a ride when he needed transportation, but generally he would just call a cab.[8]

And then there was Phil's fabled refusal to have anything to do with computers. By the end of the 1990s, there were only three members of the department who did not use email—Phil Quinn, department chair Stephen Watson, and myself. Watson and I later relented, but Phil remained unaccepting of electronic media as long as he lived. Not surprisingly, he did not use computers for word processing either. He processed all his nonspoken public utterances by hand. Unlike me, he even avoided typewriters.

A less endearing personal trait was Phil's unfortunate addiction to nicotine. As part of his eulogy, Paul Weithman told a story about Phil's contrarian behavior in the Decio Hall coffee shop. In days when smoking was still permitted in ND buildings, tables in the coffee shop were segregated by the presence or absence of "No Smoking" signs. If Phil happened to find himself relegated to a "No Smoking" table, he would simply move the sign to another table (sometimes, Paul mentioned, to one where people were already smoking). It was Phil's incessant smoking, of course, that led to his death.

In places Phil frequented, the odor of smoke would permeate the walls, the rugs, and other furnishings. When he first joined the department, he was assigned a relatively spacious office across from the elevator on the third floor of Decio Hall. When the rest of the department moved from Decio to adjoining Malloy in 2001, Phil conspicuously was left behind. The official explanation was that there were no offices in the new building big enough to hold his freestanding bookshelves. But the real reason, as everyone knew, was that Phil's office had been so infused with smoke that it would have to be gutted and rebuilt before another occupant could move in. Paul Weithman took it upon himself to empty the space after Phil died, a heroic undertaking for a nonsmoker. As department chair, Paul couldn't conscientiously assign the task to anyone else.

Phil seemed actually to relish being at loggerheads with the university administration. In 2001, for instance, he was one of the main instigators behind the Faculty Senate's move to disband itself in protest against "being ignored" by President Edward Malloy. Although various points of contention were involved at the time, the one closest to Phil's heart was alleged university discrimination regarding sexual orientation. In the spring of 2001, Phil was being considered as a possible replacement of Steve Watson as department chair. According to a memo he addressed to the department dated May 10, 2001, Phil withdrew his name from consideration because issues were then being debated within the university that he felt duty-bound to address without dragging the department into the argument. To quote the memo, these issues concerned "the way in which Notre Dame treats gays and lesbians" and the university's refusal to "extend benefits to same-sex partners."[9]

A goad stimulating Phil's career-long campaign for gay and lesbian rights may have been the church's opposition to same-sex unions. One aspect of Phil's contrariness was his ingrained distrust of authority. Although serious about his membership in the Catholic Church, he objected to what he perceived as an excessively authoritarian posture of its all-male hierarchy. If the church says same-sex unions are wrong,

Phil took this as a challenge to defend their legitimacy. After learning of his inoperable cancer in early 2004, Phil began to attend Mass daily. Sunday was the only day he stayed away from church, for the simple reason that Sunday Mass is considered obligatory.

Phil received a healthy salary and had few expenses beyond food, lodging, and books. A consequence was his accumulation of considerable wealth. In our society, of course, wealthy people are expected to have wills. True to his contrarian nature, Phil had avoided taking legal steps to dispose of his assets after death. He did, however, have an accomplished lawyer among his circle of friends. Mary Lou Solomon, David's wife, had received a law degree from ND in 1981 and was practicing in the South Bend area. Mary Lou and Paul Weithman composed a will which Phil gratefully signed only a few weeks before he died. Paul and Mary Lou were named as executors.

The manner of Phil's passing was extraordinary. When it became clear that he could no longer live by himself in his apartment, Phil moved into Dujarie House, the intensive care unit of the Holy Cross retirement community just south of St. Mary's College. Instead of reacting to his approaching demise with dismay and apprehension, Phil seemed calmer and happier as the days went by. The last time I saw him alive, just before he moved into intensive care, his face was literally glowing. A few days before the end, he was moved to a hospital. Paul and Mary Lou visited him the day before he died. Here is Paul's description of that last visit from his funeral Mass eulogy: "When we were ready to go, we each gave him a hug. As we left Phil's room, he gave *us* a grin. It was not a cloying little smile. It was the kind of great big, open-mouthed, toothy grin that lights up a face and makes you feel like a million dollars." Paul's eulogy concludes by noting that the last look on Phil's face "was the look of somebody who could not have been happier."

Among other close friends who spent time with Phil during his final hours are Steffie Lewis (David Lewis's widow), Lizette Bolduc (Peter van Inwagen's wife), and former colleague Eleonore Stump. Eleonore has her own story about final leave-taking. Steffie and Eleonore were with Phil in what they thought was a comatose state. They were hugging and kissing his expressionless face. Suddenly, on a hunch,

Eleonore said loudly, "Phil—look at Steffie!" Phil's eyes popped open, and he looked directly in Steffie's direction. He died shortly thereafter, perhaps savoring the kisses of these two affectionate women.

Phil's last-minute will left the disposition of his estate to his executors. His only instructions were that the proceeds should go to non-profit, tax-exempt organizations, specifically excluding individual persons (he had several living relatives). Several million dollars were involved. Part went to the APA Quinn Prize, to be conferred "in recognition of service to philosophy and philosophers broadly construed." Part went to the Philip L. Quinn Fellowship in Philosophy, administered by the National Humanities Center, and another to the *Boston Review,* in which Phil had occasionally published. A very substantial portion went to Dujarie House to establish the Philip L. Quinn Memory Center for treatment of seniors with Alzheimer's disease and other memory impairments.

Yet other portions were set aside to advance certain interests in the A&L College. A three-year subvention of the Gender Studies Program enabled it to appoint its first full-time director. And then there was the endowment of an annual Philip Quinn Lecture, followed by a lavish banquet for members of the Philosophy Department and their guests. The inaugural lecture in 2009 was given by Phil's onetime colleague, Alasdair MacIntyre. The lecture in December 2010 was given by Adolph Grünbaugh, who was Phil's thesis director at Pittsburgh. The lecture in 2011 is slated to be given by Eleonore Stump, whose lavish kisses sent Phil to eternal rest.

GENDER AND RELATED MATTERS

Phil Quinn was a member of the APA's National Board of Officers from 1982 to 1990. In 1989 this body drafted a policy proposal stating that its jobs-listing service would not be available to departments that exclude candidates "for reasons of race, ethnicity, or gender." What this policy statement rules out might be referred to as "level-one discrimination." Discussion within the board ensued regarding other forms of discrimination that should be prohibited, notably regarding sexual orientation and gender identification. As a class, these might be labeled "level-two discrimination." The Statement on Nondiscrimination finally promulgated by the National Board in 1990 covers both levels. According to this statement, the APA "rejects as unethical all forms of discrimination based on race, color, religion, political convictions, national origin, sex, disability, sexual orientation, gender identification, or age."[10]

As far as level-one nondiscrimination is concerned, ND anticipated the APA by several decades. More than any other single person (except perhaps Martin Luther King Jr.), Fr. Hesburgh was responsible for the Civil Rights Act of 1964, which covered race and national origin. From the 1960s onward, ND not only avoided racial discrimination, but actively encouraged the recruitment of racial minorities. Largely because of problems of supply and demand, however, efforts by the Philosophy Department to recruit African Americans have never been more than moderately successful. Laurence Thomas was the first full-time African American member of the department, from 1975 to 1979, and Jorge Garcia the second, from 1980 to 1989. Jorge was an exemplary colleague in every way, receiving tenure in 1986. But he had been brought up in New York City and never became fully acclimated to South Bend. Jorge and his wife, Laura, a 1983 ND PhD, moved on to positions at Georgetown, then Rutgers, and subsequently Boston College.

More time was needed for ND to abandon its ingrained habits of discrimination against women. During the 1950s and before, the only women with regular business on campus were nuns, housekeepers, cooks, and secretaries. This continued until the mid-1960s, when the Theology Department hired Josephine Massingberd Ford, the university's first full-time lay woman faculty member. I have sharp memories from my early days here of a sign posted in the chancel of Sacred Heart Church reading, "No women permitted in the choir stalls." The sign remained until the church was renovated in 1968 to bring it in line with the liturgical reforms of Vatican II. An example of overt discrimination within the Philosophy Department itself came with a lecture by Peter Geach in 1960 or 1961. I met Geach at the Niles train station and was surprised to find that Elizabeth Anscombe (his wife) had come with him. Although Anscombe was already one of the most prominent women philosophers in the world, she had not been invited to speak at ND. While we male philosophers were listening patiently to Geach that evening in a dimly lighted classroom, Anscombe was giving a rousing talk to the women of St. Mary's across the road.

All this changed when the university went coeducational in 1972. ND's initial plan for going coed was to merge with St. Mary's, under a single administration with a single faculty. The intention to merge was made public in 1971. Within weeks of this premature announcement, however, it became clear to both parties that the plan was not going to work. ND saw difficulties of a financial nature, while St. Mary's was rightly apprehensive about losing its institutional identity. The merger was called off before classes began in the fall of 1972.

Fr. Hesburgh and his administration followed up by making ND coeducational itself. As he put it in his autobiography, *God, Country, Notre Dame,* ND had always been "in the business of educating students for leadership," and now it was time to broaden "that commitment to include the other half of the human race."[11] Fifteen hundred women were enrolled in the entering class of 1972, replacing fifteen hundred anonymous men who never knew why they were not admitted. Larger numbers were enrolled in subsequent years until women came to compose about 50 percent of ND's and St. Mary's combined enrollment. Almost everyone was pleased with the results. Not only did the presence of women undergraduates create a "much more normal and healthier atmosphere on campus,"[12] but it substantially boosted the average grade point average of the undergraduate student body.

With increasing numbers of female undergraduates, it seemed necessary to augment the previously all-male faculty with some female professors to serve as role models. The first woman to join the philosophy faculty was recruited by Fr. McMullin just before the projected merger with St. Mary's was announced. Sheilah Brennan had received her PhD from Laval in 1954,[13] spent a postdoctoral year at Oxford, and joined the St. Mary's department in 1956. She was preparing for a year's leave of absence from St. Mary's when McMullin made the job offer, and initially agreed to come only for the year

1971–72. Because of the turmoil caused at St. Mary's by the failed merger, however, she decided to remain at ND in a tenure-track position. She was granted tenure in 1978.

A few months after receiving tenure, Sheilah was diagnosed with breast cancer and underwent successive surgeries in 1978 and 1979. After a year of chemotherapy, she returned to teach half-time for the next five or six years. Then another surgery turned out to be necessary, after which she taught a reduced load until retirement in 1991. Despite medical problems stretching out over more than thirty years, Sheilah survived her husband, ND English professor Joseph X. Brennan, who died in 2010.

The second and third women to join the department were Princeton products Penny Maddy and Eileen O'Neill. Unlike Sheilah, neither Penny nor Eileen was preoccupied with raising a family. Penny had the additional advantage of a spouse who cooked meals and took care of the house. If Sheilah had been free from home duties like Penny, her career undoubtedly would have taken a different path.

Following O'Neill, the next three women hired into the department were Cindy Stern (1981), Bonnie Kent (1985), and Cristina Bicchieri (1986). Cindy Stern, who specialized in metaphysics and philosophy of language, and was an excellent piano player, remained at ND for three years before going to the University of Oklahoma. She subsequently received tenure at California State University, Northridge. Bonnie Kent, despite being Catholic with a specialty in medieval philosophy, was unhappy at ND and stayed only for one term. She returned to the New York area, spent time as assistant professor at Columbia (her PhD-granting institution), and eventually became professor of philosophy at University of California, Irvine. Cristina Bicchieri, who worked in game theory and rational decision-making, and who could stare down anyone in an argument (even Plantinga avoided her), also remained for just three years. She is now Carol and Michael Lowenstein Professor of Philosophy and Legal Studies at the University of Pennsylvania, colleague of mild-mannered Milton Wachsberg.

ND's seventh woman philosopher was Christia Mercer, previously noted as also having a Princeton PhD. Arriving in 1987 as a specialist in the history of early modern philosophy, Mercer stayed only two years. After Bicchieri and Mercer left the department in 1989, only two women remained in regular faculty positions.[14] One was Sheilah Brennan, due soon to retire in 1991. The other was Lynn Joy, who came in 1988 with a PhD from Harvard as a specialist in modern philosophy. ND's second philosophy PhD from Harvard, Lynn soon proved herself a formidable presence in the department. During her first few years here, she was prone to lace her conversation with statistics from professional athletics. This tendency subsided when she realized that most of her male colleagues were less interested in football and baseball than she seemed to be. Lynn had arrived with her husband, Alasdair MacIntyre, and left with him in 1995 when both received offers from Duke University. They returned to ND in 2000, when Lynn rejoined the Philosophy Department as Professor and Alasdair (then retired) took a titled position with ND's Center for Ethics and Culture.

Two other highly talented women joined the department in 1991. Eleonore Stump came as a specialist in medieval philosophy, having received her PhD from Cornell in 1975 under Norman Kretzmann. She previously had taught at Oberlin College and Georgia Tech. Although seemingly a natural fit for the department, she left after only two years for St. Louis University, where her husband also was able to secure a position. She currently is Robert J. Henle Professor of Philosophy at St. Louis.

Sun-Joo Shin came to ND directly after receiving her PhD from Stanford in 1991. Sun-Joo was another natural fit for the department. Specializing in logic and the philosophy of language, she moreover was a practicing Catholic. A problem on the horizon was that ND had no position for her husband, Henry E. Smith, a highly trained linguist. After making do for over a decade, Sun-Joo moved to Yale in 2003, where she now is a professor of philosophy. Henry in the meanwhile had given up linguistics, had graduated from Yale Law School in 1996, and in 2002 became a member of Yale's Law School faculty.

Patricia ("Paddy") Blanchette, a 1990 Stanford PhD, arrived in 1993 as assistant professor. Paddy specializes in the overlapping areas of philosophy of logic, philosophy of mathematics, and philosophy of language. She was promoted to associate professor with tenure in

2000. Unlike Eleonore's and Sun-Joo's time at ND, Paddy's stay here has not been interrupted by spousal problems. Her husband, Don Wheeler, whom she married in 2001, is owner of a local house-inspection business.

Kate Abramson arrived in 1997 with a Chicago PhD, and left for Indiana University, Bloomington, in 1999. The last three women to join the department before 2010 were Kristin Shrader-Frechette (1998), Anja Jauernig (2002), and Katherine Brading (2004). Shrader-Frechette had received a ND PhD in 1972 and returned as the O'Neill Family Professor of Philosophy and concurrent professor of biological science. Jauernig, a Princeton PhD as already noted, came to ND as an instructor, was promoted to assistant professor in 2004, and left in 2011 for a position at Pittsburgh at the rank of associate professor. Brading, a specialist in philosophy of science, came as an assistant professor with a DPhil from Oxford. She was promoted to associate professor with tenure in 2010, when she also received the title of William J. and Dorothy K. O'Neill Collegiate Professor of Philosophy.

Through the spring of 2011, a total of 15 women had been full-time members of the department. Of these, only 4 (Brennan, Kent, Shin, Shrader-Frechette) were Catholic while here (Stump converted later). During the 1980s and 1990s, the department contained an average of 3 women for any given year. During the next decade, that average increased to between 5 and 6. After the departure of Jauernig in 2011, 5 full-time women remained, all of whom are married. This compares with 34 full-time male faculty, comprising 87 percent of a 39-member department.

Some might say that a department with only 13 percent women among its full-time faculty is a department that discriminates against women. But that would be both inaccurate and uncharitable. If discrimination has been involved, it has been in behalf of women rather than against them. From the 1980s onward, ND's Philosophy Department has done all it can to recruit additional women faculty. As far as I can tell, two factors in particular have kept us from being more successful. One is well known and often noted. South Bend is a relatively drab environment for people accustomed to larger cities. This is true for unmarried women in particular. While South Bend actually is a fine place to raise a family, single people looking for a social life usually end up spending lots of time in Chicago. After Jauernig's departure in 2011, the department had only three unmarried members, all of them men.

The second factor is the spousal problem. A considerable number of people looking for academic jobs today have spouses who are also academics. Candidates with good credentials often hold out for positions at institutions that can offer employment to their spouses as well. This impediment can also apply in cases where one spouse is already employed by a given institution. ND lost both Eleonore Stump and Sun-Joo Shin because it could not find positions for their academic spouses.

There are other reasons, of course, why particular individuals might find teaching at ND unattractive. One is uneasiness with a de facto male-dominated department, a malaise that might be harbored by men as well as women. Another is what might be perceived as the university's continuing refusal to add second-level concerns such as sexual orientation to its nondiscrimination policy. This is a matter that continues to be debated within the university.[15] For the record, it should be clear that although ND's Philosophy Department has no nondiscrimination policy of its own, for all intents and purposes it abides with the policy of the APA with respect to both first- and second-level discrimination.

It is interesting to note, however, that ND's Philosophy Department has never had a Catholic nun on its faculty. Although nuns have taught in the Science College and Law School, as well as in the Theology Department, the only nuns officially associated with the Philosophy Department have been graduate students. Nuns in the graduate program, to be sure, were once quite common. Graduate School records indicate that eighteen nuns received PhDs through the Philosophy Department, beginning with Sr. Mary Frederick Eggelston, CSC, in 1934 (the first philosophy PhD on record) and ending with Sr. Gerald Mary O'Donnell in 1976 (a decade after Vatican II).[16] Some of these moved on to positions of considerable distinction, notably including both Kristin Shrader-Frechette, a current ND chair-holder, and Anita Pampusch, who was president of the College of St. Catherine in Minnesota from 1984 to 1997.

SPECIALIZATION TAKES OVER

In its heyday under McMullin's chairmanship, the department was a congenial place to do philosophy. One reason is that we spent considerable amounts of social time together. As a priest with an uncommonly active social life of his own, McMullin understood the value of time together over food and drink as a catalyst for congenial social interaction. The primary cause of congeniality in the department at the time, however, was probably the fact that faculty were recruited for "fit" rather than specialization. Whereas fit previously had been a matter of Thomistic training, under McMullin it changed to sympathy with pluralism in philosophy. Our hiring of Vaughn McKim provides a memorable illustration. McKim was one of the first hired into the department on the basis of an APA interview. I was a member of the interview team. McKim's specialty out of Yale was philosophy of social science, with an area of competence in analytic philosophy. In our discussion of his candidacy after the interview, however, little was said about his skills in these particular specialties. Our main concern was whether he would make a good colleague, a question soon answered in the affirmative.

McKim, of course, was one of the Sellars group discussed in chapter 4. Recruitment of other Sellarsians followed a similar pattern. Delaney was trained in history of philosophy, Solomon in ethics, Loux in metaphysics, and Gutting in philosophy of science. But Fr. Mc-Mullin, in making these hires, was not looking just for people with those particular specialties. He was looking for well-trained PhDs in tune with his own pluralistic view of philosophy. Which is to say that he was looking for young philosophers who fit in with his plans to build a pluralist department.

This practice of targeting recruits with broad philosophic vision continued under Neil Delaney, who became McMullin's hand-picked successor in 1972. Almost all outside appointments during Delaney's decade-long chairmanship came fresh from graduate school, making it easier to assimilate them into the department's pluralistic culture. With a few exceptions (logician Penny Maddy was one), field of specialization seemed not to be a major factor in their being hired. A consequence of this continued emphasis on pluralism in hiring was that by the mid-1970s ND's Philosophy Department had become a distinctly cohesive group of people. Most of us got along well together, respected each other's work, and enjoyed spending time in each other's company.

A personal anecdote may help put all this in focus. In the late winter of 1978 (the year of the legendary Great Blizzard) I bought a sizable property within walking distance of the university and set about building a solar house for my family. As it happened, this was a time of accelerated house-building activity in the area because mortgage rates were rising precipitously. Within months after taking out a construction loan, I became fearful that the house would not be finished in time to obtain a mortgage at a rate I could afford. Early one Saturday morning after my predicament became known, the entire department arrived on site and worked until dark. Think of three-dozen men hammering, sawing, painting, and mixing concrete. Ralph McInerny spent the day chipping mortar off old bricks, which Hal Moore and David Solomon then laid to compose an atrium floor. David Solomon came back the next day to help lay tiles in the main bathroom. Lots of work after that remained to be finished, but the boost in morale I received that day proved essential to the house being finished on time.

To continue the story, I have to introduce Lawrence Simon and Lynn Stevens, two muscular colleagues who joined the department in 1977 (the year ND won the national football championship under Dan Devine). Larry Simon studied at Oxford and Cambridge before receiving a PhD from Boston University. After leaving ND in 1987, he started teaching at Bowdoin College, where he now works in political philosophy and environmental ethics. As far as this story is concerned, the foremost thing about Larry was his size. In the fall of 1978, he must have weighed well in excess of two hundred fat-free pounds.

There usually was a twinkle in his eye and a smile on his face, but if push came to shove he was someone to avoid.

Lynn Stevens was even more imposing in stature. Lynn received a BA from Harvard in 1973 and a PhD from the University of Massachusetts in 1978. He taught at ND from 1977 to 1979, moving on to the University of Alabama. His main area of concentration is the philosophy of mind, particularly the nature of sensations. This concentration on mental phenomena stands in sharp contrast with his massive body. During his time at ND, Lynn was a ranking amateur weightlifter. In the spring An Tostal of 1978 (ND alumni will know what that means), Lynn won the beer-keg throwing event, besting several football players by about twenty feet. My guess is that he weighed more than three hundred pounds.

The story takes up again with the observation that I had obtained financing for the solar-house project by selling my previous house, which required putting most of my family's furniture in storage. A good portion had been taken to the residence of the main building contractor. By the time the new house was ready to occupy, relations with the contractor (not a small man himself) had taken a negative turn involving lawyers. Anticipating difficulty in recovering my furniture, I enlisted the help of some dozen colleagues and arrayed them on the back of a flatbed truck. Larry Simon and Lynn Stevens were prominent among them. When we arrived at the contractor's house, he opened the door, took one look at my companions, smiled feebly, and proceeded to help the rest of us load the furniture on the truck. This was the last I saw of that irascible person. Without the presence of my hefty colleagues, it might have been the last I saw of my furniture as well.

This exceptional collegiality at ND during the 1960s and 1970s is best understood in comparison with the ambience of other philosophy departments of the same era. During the academic year 1966–67, I was a visiting scholar at Princeton University. I had an office in 1878 Hall, and became fairly well acquainted with most of the philosophy faculty. It did not take long to realize that Princeton philosophers as a group had little interest in what their colleagues were doing, being focused instead on what was happening elsewhere in their specialized disciplines. Although most of them had offices in the same building, they were more involved with their disciplines than with colleagues in the department.[17]

Whereas Princeton had already succumbed to specialization in the mid-1960s, ND gave priority to collegiality over specialization at least through the late 1970s. I remember a conversation with Milton Wachsberg, fresh from Princeton in 1979, in which he remarked that ND was much more friendly than the place he had just left. Ironically for Milton and me, however, it was the incursion of Princeton philosophers that tipped ND priorities away from collegiality toward specialization. Princeton had trained Milton and the rest to fill specialized slots in other universities. The same emphasis on specialization prevailed at other major graduate programs in the country. By the time Wachsberg moved on in 1984, ND had begun to follow suit. From then onward, most new philosophy faculty arriving at ND were recruited for their expertise in specialized areas.

When O'Neill left in 1983, for example, her slot in modern philosophy was filled first by Christia Mercer and then by Lynn Joy. Penny Maddy, after her 1983 departure, was replaced promptly by Michael Detlefsen, who had received rigorous training in logic at Johns Hopkins University. Richard McClelland, who had come from Cambridge in 1981 as a specialist in ancient philosophy, was replaced by David O'Connor from Stanford in 1985. Joseph Mellon was hired specifically as a philosopher of mind from MIT in 1983, to be replaced in that area a few years later by Leopold Stubenberg from Arizona. And so it went. These people had been recruited for the specializations they brought with them, with only incidental thought of how they would fit in with the culture of the department.

By the end of the 1980s, ND's Philosophy Department was irrevocably committed to specialization in research and graduate teaching. The robust pluralism initiated by McMullin two decades previously had faded into the memories of its former participants. In its place was the "watered down" pluralism so characterized in the last section of chapter 4. According to a graduate bulletin distributed a decade later, the department then boasted strength in philosophy of science, philosophy of religion, medieval philosophy, ethics, and continental philosophy. Hires were made subsequently to beef up logic, metaphysics, epistemology, philosophy of mind, and ancient philosophy. By the end of the 1980s, to put it succinctly, ND's Philosophy Department had become a group of specialists.

RESHAPING THE GRADUATE PROGRAM

The centerpiece of our pluralistically inspired PhD program during the 1970s was a demanding set of comprehensive examinations that had to be passed before thesis work could begin. The definitive mark of the transition from pluralism to specialization was the dismantling of this comprehensive system in 1984. We turn now to an account of how that came about.

In their initial version, the written comprehensives consisted of three separate three-hour examinations in the fields of epistemology, metaphysics, and ethics, followed by a six-hour examination in the history of philosophy. The examinations were taken on different days over a two-week period, with the history section divided into two parts taken the same day. Although scheduling was subject to change, most students took these examinations at the end of their second year of classes. In addition to the written comps, PhD candidates had to pass a two-hour oral examination in an area of particular interest. They also had to pass a graduate level course in formal logic and had to exhibit reading skills in two foreign languages.

This system of comprehensive examinations originated during McMullin's chairmanship in the mid-1960s. As he remarked over four decades later, it was modeled after the candidacy system then in place at Yale. This is plausible, inasmuch as there were two Yale PhDs in the department at the time (Burrell and McKim). My own memory, however, is that the comps were modeled after Harvard's system of preliminary examinations which I had weathered in 1953.[18] Since all four of us had collaborated in the design of ND's system of comprehensives, Ernan's memory and my own may both be right.

As far as I could tell, most graduate students who took comps during the late 1960s and 1970s seemed content with the system.

Although preparation was time consuming, and although the weeks waiting for results were ridden by anxiety, students generally seemed to feel that the examinations were worth the effort. I recall several former students making a point of telling me later that taking the comps was the most valuable part of their graduate experience. Those who prepared conscientiously learned a great deal of philosophy in the process.

Grumblings of discontent, however, began to surface in the early 1980s. This coincided with the arrival of the young faculty from Princeton, who had been unencumbered with such requirements in their own graduate training. Whether this was more than coincidence remains uncertain. But ND's graduate students at the time must have come to realize that the philosophic breadth fostered by the comps was not essential to finding a good job. In the perception of some, it might even have appeared a hindrance.

Our story of the dismantling of the comprehensive system begins with Richard Foley's becoming department chair in the fall of 1983. Foley had joined the department only six years earlier, and was its first chair without personal memories of a Thomistically dominated period. He nonetheless was not a stranger to the South Bend area. Two decades earlier, he had been a student in the local John Adams High School, then reputed to be one of the best in the country. Foley went on to earn a BA from Miami University (Ohio) in 1969 and a PhD from Brown in 1975. Brown, like Princeton at the time, had a graduate program dedicated to preparing specialists. Dick Foley's specialty was epistemology.

Dick joined the department in 1976 as an assistant professor. At ND he came to be known not only as an effective administrator but also as an inspiring teacher. He received the Madden Award for Freshman teaching in 1984 and the Sheedy Award for A&L teaching in 1988. He chaired the Philosophy Department from 1983 to 1990, the year he received ND's Presidential Award for University Service.

Dick Foley left ND as a professor in 1990, when he moved on to chair the up-and-coming department at Rutgers University. At Rutgers he served as Philosophy Department chair from 1990 to 1992, as dean of the College of Arts and Sciences from 1992 to 1996, and next as dean of the Graduate School from 1996 to 2000. He then moved to

New York University, where he served as dean of the Faculty of Arts and Sciences until 2009, after which he became NYU's vice-chancellor for strategic planning. Along with about six dozen articles, Dick has published four substantial books on epistemology, one each with Harvard, Oxford, Cambridge, and Princeton University Presses. This is an extraordinary publication record for someone actively involved in administration for over twenty-five years.

Foley scheduled the department meeting fated to topple the comps for the late afternoon of April 18, 1984. According to minutes recorded by Montey Holloway, his administrative assistant,[19] the express purpose of the meeting was to discuss problems that had been mounting in the graduate program. The graduate students were complaining of being seriously overworked. In addition to course work and teaching assistant (TA) responsibilities, they were expected to attend weekly colloquia, to be present at Perspective Series talks, to take seminars on teaching, and—most burdensome of all—to study for the comprehensive exams they had to pass to remain in the program. All in all, they felt they "had no time for doing philosophy." What they thought "doing philosophy" amounted to was not specified in the minutes, but presumably it was more important than gaining a basic competence in the discipline.

Another bit of background is necessary before the story continues. When the written comps were initiated in the 1960s, it was unusual for PhD students to receive financial aid.[20] ND's first step toward student remuneration came when it received a number of NSF fellowships to support graduate work in logic (because of Sobocinski) and philosophy of science (because of McMullin). When those outside fellowships were terminated, the Graduate School continued to support a small number of philosophy students under its own budget. The next step was a broad program of tuition scholarships, which amounted to little more than not charging tuition to those who qualified. Recipients of these scholarships, however, still had to pay for food, housing, and other expenses out of their own pockets.

This remaining financial burden was largely removed in the late 1970s, when the university started paying graduate students for their work as TAs. After completion of two years of course work, TAs would serve as section leaders in large classes, where they were responsible for leading discussions and grading papers. Assisted by an ample number of TAs, seasoned faculty would teach "super section" courses of two hundred or more students. With this experience behind them, advanced graduate students could move on to teach their own introduction to philosophy courses. Use of graduate students in this role obviously worked to the university's advantage, since paying PhD students fixed salaries for such services was much cheaper than hiring their teaching equivalent in full-time faculty.

A consequence of this increasingly liberal program of support was that doing graduate work in philosophy began to look more and more like a salaried job. In the 1960s, completing a PhD program in philosophy was likely to result in a considerable debt, and most people would not undertake such a program without a serious commitment to philosophy itself. By the 1980s, however, there were monetary rewards for merely enrolling as a philosophy PhD student. Although most PhD candidates undoubtedly continued to be motivated primarily by the discipline itself, the program was also attractive to bright college graduates who needed income while still considering other career opportunities.

We now return to the story of the ill-fated comps. Following his report to the faculty in April 1984 that the graduate students felt "overworked," Foley instructed his graduate committee to develop a proposal for modifying the system of written comprehensives. The committee's proposal took shape during the following academic year, with regular input from the graduate students themselves. When the finished proposal was submitted for faculty vote on April 29, 1985, it was accompanied by a statement signed by thirty-one graduate students (roughly three-fourths of those currently in residence) indicating enthusiastic support. This statement conveyed the sense of a "job action" by salaried employees bargaining for better working conditions.

The committee's proposal retained a written examination in the history of philosophy. Examinations in the areas of epistemology, metaphysics, and ethics, however, were eliminated in favor of a single written examination in the area chosen by the student for dissertation research. Competence in the three areas eliminated from the comps was to be established by passing broad survey courses in those areas that would be developed specifically for this purpose.[21]

Discussion of the proposal began immediately after the faculty meeting was called to order at 7:40 in the evening. Main topics of discussion were whether the proposed system would help faculty evaluate a student's readiness to begin thesis work and whether it would contribute to a candidate's growth outside his or her area of specialization. The discussion at times was heated and went on for two hours with no sign of resolution. Then Foley called the question to a vote, remarking on the lateness of the hour. By secret ballot, the committee's proposal passed, twelve to seven. Although only half of the faculty were there to vote, the old system of written comps vanished with the setting sun.

Before the final vote was taken on this fateful date, the department had agreed that the new system would be "seriously reviewed" after a four-year trial period. The year before this review was due, it so happened that the department itself underwent its second external review. The reviewers in this case were Bas van Fraassen of Princeton, Norman Kretzmann of Cornell, and Ernest Sosa of Brown (one of Foley's graduate teachers). What the reviewers had in common, according to department minutes of March 20, 1989, was that all were from "unusually informal, small, and intensely research oriented" graduate philosophy programs.

In keeping with their research orientation, the reviewers recommended cutting back on formal graduate requirements even further. *All* written examinations, they thought, should be eliminated, and course requirements for PhD candidates should be substantially reduced. Free from impediments of this sort, candidates could move more quickly to the "cutting edge" of research in their chosen specialties. After all, this research-focused approach seemed to be working well in the reviewers' own departments. Despite the much larger size of the ND department, and its unique responsibility for teaching two required courses to all undergraduates (unheard of at Brown, Cornell, and Princeton), the reviewers saw no reason why this approach should not work at ND as well.

The external reviewers' report was delivered in March 1989, and department members were asked to submit recommendations for an appropriate response. Three recommendations were submitted for discussion at a department meeting held October 4, 1989. One was submitted by me on behalf of senior members of the department who wanted to see the written comprehensives restored to their original state. Another was prepared by a group of third-year graduate students who advocated adoption of the reviewers' recommendation that all written exams be eliminated.[22] The third was a proposal by Gary Gutting, on behalf of the graduate committee, which he then chaired, calling for retention of the written history comp with all other requirements to be met by course work instead.

A straw vote showed seven members in favor of returning to the old system, six in favor of eliminating written comprehensives completely, and eight in favor of the graduate committee's compromise proposal. Exercising his prerogative as chair, Foley interpreted this as a two to one majority against returning to the old system. Since the meeting was impinging on dinnertime, further discussion of the history comp was postponed to a subsequent occasion.

The final meeting on the issue was held November 1, 1989. One of two options on the table was a last-ditch attempt to reinstate the original system of comprehensives. The other was Gutting's proposal to confine written examinations to history of philosophy alone. Gutting's proposal carried by a vote of thirteen to six. The original comprehensive system was officially buried roughly twenty years after its inception. A few months later, Dick Foley left for Rutgers, another research-oriented department, and Gary Gutting took over as chair at ND.

Perhaps needless to say, this restructuring of the graduate program had numerous long-term ramifications. One was a major repositioning of the department with respect to other PhD programs it competes with for status. In its heyday of robust pluralism, ND was vying with Yale, Texas, and a few smaller institutions for recognition as the country's premier training program for college teachers. A case could be made for its being in front of the pack during the late 1970s and early

1980s. Once the department established itself as a training ground for specialists, however, it began competing for recognition with literally dozens of excellent PhD programs. And try as it may, ND has never succeeded in getting close to the front in this much more competitive race. Whether this change in status from "big fish in medium-sized pond" to "medium-sized fish in big pond" was good for the department remains a debatable question.

A more important consideration in sizing up this restructuring of the department's PhD program is its impact on the careers of graduate students involved. Given the shift in emphasis from training college teachers to training specialists for jobs in research universities, it seems reasonable to postulate that the proportion of PhDs finding university jobs would increase after the change in requirements took effect. Data are available to test this hypothesis.

Candidates who took the comprehensives in their original form began to get PhDs in the late 1960s. Those under the new system initiated in 1985 began to complete their degrees in the late 1980s. A total of 135 PhDs were granted during the period 1969–88 (the first group). This number is closely matched by the 139 PhDs completed during the period 1989–2008 (the second group). For purposes of comparison, these two groups are subdivided into (a) those who did not enter academic employment, (b) those who found jobs in PhD-granting universities, and (c) those who went to colleges and universities without philosophy PhD programs.[23]

Eleven of the first group were members of religious orders who found employment (academic or otherwise) without going on the open job market. Of the remaining 124, 90 (73 percent) found academic employment. Among those 90, 21 (23 percent) went to PhD-granting universities and 69 (77 percent) went to colleges and other institutions without philosophy PhD programs.

No recipients of PhDs during 1989–2008 belonged to religious orders. Of the 139 PhDs in this second group, 117 (84 percent) found academic employment. Among these, 33 (28 percent) found jobs in PhD-granting universities, while 84 (72 percent) went to colleges and universities without PhD programs in philosophy.

Comparing the two sets of data, we find that a significantly higher proportion of the second group (84 percent) than of the first (73 percent) found academic employment through the open market. This is due primarily to the absence of nuns and priests in the second group. We also find a slightly higher proportion of academicians with university employment in the second group (28 percent) than in the first (23 percent).

This difference is compatible with our foregoing hypothesis that a higher proportion of graduating PhDs would find jobs in research-oriented universities after the shift toward specialization in ND's graduate philosophy program. But the difference is not enough to strongly confirm this hypothesis. The only firm conclusion supported by these data as they stand is that the shift to specialization in the mid-1980s may have had some effect on where ND's philosophy PhDs found jobs, but if so the effect was minimal. We return for a more fine-grained examination of these data in the next chapter.

CORRELATIVE CHANGES IN THE UNDERGRADUATE PROGRAM

ND's undergraduate philosophy program had acquired a coherent structure by the late 1940s, had sustained some major changes around 1960, and had arrived at essentially its current form by 1970. The graduate program, by contrast, was relatively amorphous in the 1950s, achieved coherent structure with adoption of the system of written comprehensives in the mid-1960s, and reached its current form with the dismantling of this system in the mid-1980s. Despite this lag in structural development, however, there were significant interactions between the programs on these two levels. To help bring these interactions into view, let us return for a closer look at the growth of the undergraduate curriculum.

Since its beginning, as already noted in chapter 1, the Philosophy Department has played two distinct roles in the education of ND undergraduates. One is to teach the philosophy courses required by the Arts and Letters (A&L) College for a BA degree. This will be called the "A&L requirement." The other, the "major requirement," is to implement an undergraduate curriculum leading to a BA in philosophy specifically. Inasmuch as the major requirement has always included the courses required of all A&L undergraduates, we begin with a brief review of the A&L requirement.

The *University Bulletin* for 1950–51 lists six courses (eighteen credit hours) required for a BA degree: logic, introduction to philosophy, philosophical psychology, general metaphysics, ethics, and natural theology. These courses were to be taken in the order listed, beginning in the student's sophomore year. Since six courses in a given field then constituted a minor, every student graduating with an A&L degree had earned a minor in philosophy.

For the academic year 1954–55, the A&L requirement dropped to four courses: logic, philosophy of nature, ethics (or philosophy of man), and metaphysics. As noted previously, this sequence followed the "Thomistic order of learning." First came the study of "scientific reasoning" (Aristotelian logic), then the "causes of mobile being," followed by the "science of right conduct," and then the "science of being as being." Eccentricities aside, this is a carefully structured sequence of courses, purporting to impart "Catholic wisdom" to the minds of hapless undergraduates. Although intensely disliked by its intended beneficiaries, this sequence persisted through the 1960s.

A new era in ND undergraduate education began with the academic year 1970–71. Specific A&L course requirements were no longer listed in the *University Bulletin*. Taking their place was a general university requirement that students in all colleges must take two philosophy courses to qualify for an undergraduate degree. Despite repeated outcries of protest from other departments, this "two course requirement" has remained in effect up to the present. The first course typically has been some sort of introduction to philosophy, while the nature of the second has usually been left to the instructor's discretion.

We turn now to changes in the major requirement. As a general rule, from the 1940s onward, students majoring in philosophy took eight courses beyond those required of all undergraduates. In addition to the basic six required of all students in 1950, someone entering the major program that year was expected to take six specified courses and two open electives, totaling fourteen in all. By 1960, the total had dropped to twelve, including all four from the A&L list (previously reduced from six) plus four "problems" courses (natural science, psychology, ethics, metaphysics) and four in history of philosophy (ancient, medieval, origins of modern, contemporary). Several of these courses were still Thomistic in character.

A new approach to the majors curriculum emerged in 1965. Twelve courses in all were still required, including the four standard A&L requirements. But the remaining eight were selected from three particular categories. Majors chose three historical courses from a list of five (Presocratics and Plato; Aristotle; medieval; Descartes, Leibniz, and Kant; Locke, Berkeley, and Hume), three systematic courses from a list of four (philosophy of nature, metaphysics, ethics, epistemology), and two from a list of six special courses (philosophy of science, philosophy of politics and law, philosophy of God, contemporary philosophy, existentialism, aesthetics). By careful choice of course and instructor, a student could complete a major in philosophy without exposure to the thought of Saint Thomas Aquinas beyond that provided by the standard A&L requirements.

The majors sequence was further relaxed in 1968. Instead of choosing specific numbers of courses under particular categories, majors now select all eight of their electives from an open list of twelve: Plato, Aristotle, Aquinas, Kant, classical empiricism, classical rationalism, philosophy of nature, theory of knowledge, philosophical theology, American philosophy, phenomenology, and analytical philosophy. Although available electives varied in following years, this open-list approach continued when the A&L requirement was reduced to two courses in 1970. From this point onward, the number of philosophy courses required for an undergraduate major remained fixed at ten.[24]

With this summary background, we are ready to consider some of the main interactions between the undergraduate and graduate programs. One has to do with department size. Since the mid-twentieth century, ND's Philosophy Department has been known as one of the largest in the country.[25] More than any other single factor, the department's size has been determined by the number of undergraduate courses it teaches. As already observed, however, the number of required courses dropped to four in 1954, and even further to two in 1970. And yet the size of the philosophy faculty continued to grow. Holding more or less constant through 1960, it increased to thirty-two in 1970 and to thirty-four in 1980. What accounts for this continued growth in conjunction with decreasing course requirements?

One obvious factor is a growing undergraduate enrollment. During the thirty-five years of Hesburgh's presidency, total university enrollment almost doubled, and most of this increase was in the undergraduate sector. Another major factor is a reduction in faculty teaching loads. Whereas in 1950 the standard A&L teaching load was four courses per term, by the mid-1970s most regular faculty were down to four per year. The overarching consideration, however, is a shift in emphasis from undergraduate to graduate teaching. Whereas the range of courses in a standard undergraduate program remains relatively fixed, a competitive graduate program is under pressure to increase the specialized topics in which it offers instruction. With this comes pressure to increase the number of specialists on its faculty.

The way this dynamic has played out in the Philosophy Department is intriguing. From Delaney onward, the chair of the department has considered it a preordained duty to convince his dean that philosophy needs additional slots for faculty recruitment. For his or her own accounting purposes, the dean ties number of faculty slots in a given department to number of undergraduates for whom it provides instruction. The bargaining begins with the department chair presenting statistics showing a surplus of undergraduates awaiting course assignments, to which the dean has generally responded sympathetically.[26] If new faculty slots are granted, the chair promptly creates a new "super section" employing graduate student TAs to handle the undergraduates and proceeds to recruit new specialists for the graduate program. Although somewhat oversimplified, this scenario illustrates one way in which the graduate faculty is subsidized by the undergraduate program.

A second form of interaction between the undergraduate and graduate programs works directly to the detriment of the undergraduate program itself. As a result of the dynamic sketched above,

tenure-track faculty from the late 1970s to the present have been recruited almost exclusively for what they could contribute to the graduate program. This means that they have been recruited according to
area of specialization. The upshot, over the years, was that more and
more faculty were on hand who wanted to enhance their research
projects by teaching graduate courses. But the number of PhD students taking courses during a given year remained relatively constant.

The problem was aggravated by the fact that some graduate teachers were more in demand than others. When Plantinga joined the full-
time faculty in 1982, for example, an influx of graduate students from
evangelical colleges came to study with him personally. After mulling
over the problem for a year or so, the department's graduate committee
put forth a proposal for discussion in the faculty meeting of April 18,
1984. The proposal was that faculty members be limited to one graduate course every three terms, with exceptions when needed to "insure
proper balance in the graduate program" and "to meet special student
interests" (as in Plantinga's case).

Two alternatives to this proposal were considered at the meeting.
One (the "free market model") was to continue the then-current practice of allowing faculty to offer graduate courses as often as they
wanted, not knowing until registration whether a course would draw
enough students to be taught. The second was to split faculty into
graduate and undergraduate teachers, an alternative no one found attractive enough even to merit discussion. With no significant support
for either alternative, the rule of one graduate course in three terms
was accepted as department policy.

For faculty who viewed graduate courses as opportunities to pursue their research interests, this was not a welcome development. An
immediate consequence of the new policy was that research-oriented
faculty began teaching courses with graduate content on the undergraduate major level instead.[27] Most knowledgeable observers would
admit, I think, that specialized courses like this generally are not good
for the majors program. With the exception of a few highly motivated
students headed for graduate school, such courses are unsuitable for
even the brighter among undergraduate students. Graduate courses do
not fit naturally in an undergraduate program.

A more serious problem, perhaps, is the impact that specialized interests have had on the structure of the department's undergraduate program. We have already noted how the undergraduate major curriculum devolved from a tightly organized structure in the 1950s to a mere list of choices from 1968 onward. A modicum of structure was regained a decade or so later with the introduction of the two-course history survey normally taken during the sophomore year. But the vast majority of undergraduate majors take their remaining courses in random sequence. As often as not, a given undergraduate student has to cope with difficult material without skills normally developed in easier courses. A consequence is that there is little orderly development of philosophic expertise as the student moves through successive years of the program. A parallel consequence is that students often accumulate little knowledge of important figures who happened not to be treated in their two-course history survey. I remember several occasions during recent years when I was comparing the views of major figures (e.g., Spinoza with Wittgenstein, or Malebranche with Leibniz) and found that a majority of senior philosophy majors in the class had not even heard of the philosophers in question.

Problems of this sort were commonly recognized, and attempts were made now and then to do something about them. Any attempt to regain structure in the undergraduate program, however, would invariably be perceived as a threat to the faculty's privilege of teaching specialized undergraduate courses of their own choosing. After adoption of the rule allowing only one graduate course in three consecutive terms, this privilege has been carefully guarded. The upshot is that efforts to reorganize the undergraduate major curriculum along more rational lines have never got seriously underway.

The university's public relations organs have been relentless in promulgating ND's "vision of being a preeminent Catholic research university with an unsurpassed excellence in undergraduate education."[28] The vision is laudable. Unless the recent history of the Philosophy Department is viewed as anomalous, however, one might wonder whether preeminence in research and excellence in undergraduate education are fully compatible.

CHAPTER 7

Professional Philosophy

RANKINGS

Time was when aspiring philosophers had little help in choosing among graduate schools beyond advice from their undergraduate teachers. My own experience around 1950 is a case in point. Of my three main teachers at Grinnell, two (Hippocrates George Apostle and Paul Kuntz) had PhDs from Harvard, and one (Neal Klausner) a PhD from Yale. Having been accepted by the graduate programs of both institutions, I set about trying to evaluate their relative merits. But the only relevant information I could find was limited to faculty rosters and publication lists. Not knowing how to proceed from there, I finally deferred to the majority of my teachers and went to Harvard to begin my graduate training.

This dearth of information about graduate programs ended in the late 1980s with the advent of the Philosophical Gourmet Report (PGR).[1] PGR began as an impromptu list of twenty-five graduate programs in philosophy deemed by its founder, Brian Leiter, to be the best in the country. Leiter was a graduate student in philosophy at the University of Michigan at the time,[2] and his list initially was intended as an aid to Michigan undergraduates contemplating a career in philosophy. Updated regularly, Leiter's list soon became popular among graduate students as well, who passed it on to friends in other universities.

The first publicly available issue of PGR covered the academic year 1991–92. It divided top U.S. graduate programs into nine groups, without further ranking within particular groups. Group 1 contained Princeton exclusively, with Harvard, Pittsburgh, Michigan, and UCLA in the second group. ND shared the ninth group (twenty-second to twenty-seventh) with five other schools. The next report, for 1994–95, distinguished ten groups instead of nine. Princeton again was alone at the top, with Pittsburgh now the sole occupant of the second rank. And ND again was in the lowest group (twenty-fourth to thirty-first) along with seven other programs. This apparent demotion coincided with the departure from ND of Eleonore Stump (in 1993) and Alasdair MacIntyre (in 1995) and the retirement of Ernan McMullin (in 1994).

After this low point in 1994–95, ND began to gain ground with a series of key appointments. On the senior level, Peter van Inwagen came from Syracuse in 1995. Jaegwon Kim began sharing time with ND in 1999,[3] Alasdair MacIntyre returned from Duke in 2000, and Robert Audi shifted part of his gravitas to the Philosophy Department from ND's Business School in 2004. Junior appointments during that period included Leiter acolyte Ted Warfield in 1995 and highly touted ND graduate (and Harvard PhD) Tom Kelly in 2003. These appointments were enough to boost ND's Gourmet rank to a four-way tie for twelfth in 2004 (by which time ties had replaced groupings).[4] Within PGR's first dozen years of existence, ND had increased its rank by at least ten notches, a notable improvement to say the least.

In its initial form, Leiter's report was intended to help undergraduates locate programs for advanced training in philosophy. As it gained popularity in the 1990s, however, its influence spread to other aspects of the profession as well. For one thing, philosophy departments tend to hire new faculty from programs more prominent than themselves. All but one or two of the young PhDs hired by ND's department during the 1990s, for example, came from programs with higher rankings in the 1994–95 Leiter report. A consequence of this general tendency is that PhDs from highly ranked departments often have more choices when they go on the job market. High PGR rankings thus improve not only a given department's ability to attract good graduate students but also its ability to find good jobs for its own PhDs.

Desire to maintain or to improve its PGR rankings also affects a department's hiring of senior faculty. A department will usually show preference for senior people who are well known in the profession over others with perhaps comparable achievements but lower profiles. As I recall from faculty meetings, all senior professors brought to ND with tenure during the 1990s (Stump, van Inwagen, Howard, Shrader-Frechette) were vetted with an eye toward their impact on future rankings. These investments in high-profile personnel eventually paid off, as indicated by ND's improved rankings toward the end of that decade.

As lower-level administrators know all too well, moreover, a department's outside ranking is a major factor in determining resources it receives from the powers above. Highly ranked departments normally get more faculty slots, more ample budgets, and more student aid. Reasons for this favoritism toward highly rated departments will be examined in subsequent sections. In the meanwhile, it is enough to note that few aspects of a typical graduate program in philosophy today escape the sway of the Leiter report.

By the end of the 1990s, at any rate, observant members of the profession had come to realize that the fortunes of any given graduate program of philosophy were bound up with its success in the ratings game. Not everyone reacted favorably to this realization. On the national level, an open letter of complaint, signed by nearly two hundred philosophers and reported in the *Chronicle of Higher Education,* charged that the PGR and its author had come to exercise undue influence within the profession.[5] Several senior members of ND's department shared this view, concerned that scholarly inquiry in the field was being engulfed by a cult of personality.[6] From this perspective, it was unclear whether personal visibility had much to do either with cogent thought or with lasting contributions to the field of philosophy.

The dominant reaction in the department, however, was to view ND's already high standing as an incentive to compete for still higher rankings. In every practical respect, the goal of national prominence in the Leiter rankings became an end in itself. According to PGR's initial intent, a department's ranking depends upon the reputations of its individual members. Thus the department did what it could from the mid-1990s onward to help its members increase their visibility in the profession at large.

CVS AND OTHER FORMS OF SELF-PRESENTATION

Like score cards in golf, a curriculum vitae (CV) records one's accomplishments in a perspicuous format enabling comparison with the accomplishments of one's competitors. Primary among relevant accomplishments are scholarly publications, professional presentations, and academic honors, all of which contribute to one's professional reputation. Scholarly publications include books and articles, typically reporting results of specialized inquiry. Professional presentations include invited talks at other universities, papers read at conferences, and comments on papers by other participants. Notable honors include medals and prizes, offices held in professional associations, and elected membership in learned societies. Honors carrying particular prestige in philosophy include named lectureships (e.g., the Gifford Lectures) and membership in such groups as the American Academy of Arts and Sciences. As might be expected, ND's Philosophy Department is favored by some unusually voluminous CVs. Let me describe two notable examples, without impugning the merits of others that might also be mentioned.

Kristin Shrader-Frechette, the department's O'Neill Family Professor, has the longest CV I have ever seen. My copy, compiled in 2009, is thirty pages long, single-spaced in unusually small print, with roughly ten times as many words as Wittgenstein's *Tractatus*. It begins in standard fashion with a listing of her degrees and academic appointments.

Kristin received her BA in mathematics from Edgecliff College in 1967, and her PhD in philosophy from ND in 1972.[7] She taught at Edgecliff College from 1971 to 1973, and then went to the University of Louisville, where she earned the rank of professor before leaving for UC, Santa Barbara, in 1982. After two years at Santa Barbara, she moved east for a three-year stint at the University of Florida, Gaines-ville. Then in 1987 she became distinguished research professor at the University of South Florida (Tampa), a position she held until return-ing to ND in 1998.[8] She returned as an endowed-chair holder in Phi-losophy and as concurrent professor in ND's Department of Biology.

As for scholarship, Kristin has authored eight books put out by university presses, coauthored two more, and coedited yet another. She also has authored two lengthy studies published by U.S. government agencies and edited a volume for the World Council of Churches. She has published approximately 200 articles in professional journals and collections, along with about 150 reviews and other short pieces. As of 2009, her most recent volume is *Taking Action, Saving Lives: Our Duties to Protect Environmental and Public Health,* published in 2007 by Oxford University Press.

Shrader-Frechette's list of honors and awards is almost three dozen items long. Among the more unusual are serving as first woman presi-dent (a) of the Society for Philosophy and Technology (1985–87), (b) of the Risk Assessment and Policy Association (1997–99), and (c) of the International Society for Environmental Ethics (2000–2003). In 2004 she won the World Technology Award in Ethics, the third American to be so honored (following Daniel Callahan and Peter Singer). In 2007 she was named one of twelve "heroes for America" by the *Catholic Digest* for her work exemplifying Catholic teachings on social justice. She has been invited to address national academies of science in three different countries, and has served as ad-viser to both the United Nations and the World Health Organization.

Shortly after Kristin returned to ND in 1998, she was inducted as an Honorary Member of Phi Beta Kappa. I was asked to introduce her to the local chapter, which amounted to giving a twenty-minute sum-mary of her professional life and accomplishments. There was much left to say when my time ran out. Her professional accomplishments during the decade following that occasion are sufficient to fill a "nor-mal" CV by themselves.

Stellar academic record aside, Kristin is first and foremost a social activist. Her concern for social justice traces back to her mother, who was Kentucky's first white member of the NAACP. Kristin's advocacy for poor people who suffer from environmental pollution, which has gained her an international reputation, stems from her mother's death from environmentally induced cancer at age forty-five. A lion's share of Kristin's teaching and research at ND has dealt with issues of environmental justice. Her recently established Center for Environmental Justice and Children's Health supports students doing pro bono work in defense of the poor.[9]

Another weighty CV has been compiled by James P. Sterba, who came to ND with a PhD from Pittsburgh in 1973. Single-spaced in small print like Shrader-Frechette's, Sterba's document is a twenty-page synopsis of a remarkable career, recording his extensive list of publications, his professional honors, and his record of presentations both here and abroad. Jim has published seven books of his own and written four with coauthors. Most of these were issued by top publishers, including the presses of Oxford, Cambridge, and Cornell Universities. His most recent book (with Jan Narveson) is *Are Liberty and Equality Compatible?*, put out in 2010 by Cambridge University Press. In addition, his CV lists 169 contributions to journals and edited volumes, along with over thirty critical reviews of scholarly books.[10] Regarding honors, Jim has been president of the International Association for Philosophy of Law and Social Philosophy (1987–89), president of Concerned Philosophers for Peace (1990–91), and president of the North American Society for Social Philosophy (1990–95). More recently, he held the highly visible post of president of the Central Division of the APA (2007–8).

A particularly striking feature of Sterba's CV is a year-by-year account of places visited, papers read, and support provided. Leafing through his entries for 1979 to 2003, for example, we find that he made at least one trip each to thirteen countries during that period (Australia, China, Costa Rica, England, Germany, India, Italy, Japan, New Zealand, Poland, South Africa, Turkey, Yugoslavia), and more than one to each of Canada, Finland, Latvia, Russia, and Scotland. Almost all of the fellowships and grants listed on his CV have been for travel and faculty development.

Few issues of contemporary social and political philosophy have escaped Jim Sterba's probing attention. Topics he has addressed at length include feminism, abortion, and affirmative action, along with environmentalism, pacifism, and nuclear deterrence. Jim follows the lead of John Rawls in many of these issues. Like Rawls, he harbors an unwavering confidence in the power of reason to establish binding norms of social justice. His work is a testimony to the rationalist credo that reason can show that a thing is right if and only if in fact that thing is right.[11]

There are of course other modes of professional self-presentation beyond academic CVs. An entertaining illustration is provided by Thomas Victor ("TV") Morris, who made self-display into a veritable art form.

TV Morris was born in 1952, received his undergraduate degree from North Carolina in 1974, and went on to Yale for a 1980 PhD in philosophy and religious studies. He taught at ND from 1981 to 1996. Tom's career at ND got off to a seemingly normal start. He published two fairly standard professional books in the mid-1980s, *Understanding Identity Statements*[12] and *Anselmian Explorations: Essays in Philosophical Theology* (UNDP, 1987). In the late 1980s he also edited a few collections and published several articles.

It was in the classroom, however, that Tom's extraordinary public persona began to take shape. Within two or three years of arrival, he clearly was the most popular teacher in the Philosophy Department. His classes would draw hundreds of students and had to be held in large auditoriums, prompting some of his more staid colleagues to suspect that these classes had more to do with entertainment than with philosophy. On one occasion he rigged up a talking robot to make some point about solipsism. On another occasion he arranged to have the ND marching band perform in class to put his students in the right mood for an examination. Tom's reputation as a teacher reached its zenith in 1990 when he was named Indiana Professor of the Year by the Council for the Advancement and Support of Education.

An avid rock guitarist, Tom would inspire his students with motivational songs of his own composition. At one point he wrote a rousing march which he offered to the band as replacement of the world-famous "Notre Dame Fight Song." ("Cheer, cheer for Old Notre Dame . . .") Some cynics think that chagrin at the Athletic

Department's refusal to accept this offer had something to do with Tom's eventual departure from the university.

A more credible explanation of his leaving is that Tom had found a new vocation as a motivational speaker. He spent increasing portions of his time during the early 1990s giving inspirational talks to corporate leaders. Before long he was appearing on TV shows (*Regis Philbin, The Today Show* with Matt Lauer), and even in network TV commercials (publicizing Winnie the Pooh for Disney Studios). His books in print began to veer in the same direction. *The Bluffer's Guide to Philosophy* came out in 1989, then *True Success: A New Philosophy of Excellence* in 1994, *If Aristotle Ran General Motors: The New Soul of Business* in 1997, and *Philosophy for Dummies* in 1999. In 2006, he published *If Harry Potter Ran General Electric: Leadership Wisdom from the World of the Wizards.*

When TV Morris left ND, he founded the Morris Institute for Human Values, based in Wilmington, North Carolina. Recent offerings of this organization include a series of National Wisdom Retreats, where business leaders spend a weekend learning to "dig deep," to "broaden their vision," and to "resolve long-standing issues" at more than $1,000 a pop.[13] One of Tom's more intrepid entrepreneurial ventures is a spin-off of his 2009 publication *Twisdom* (Twitter Wisdom). His online vending company (TwisdomShop.com) features items such as clothing and coffee mugs, adorned with his picture or one of his quotes. Also available at his store are Twisdom stamps approved by the United States Postal Service.

While Tom Morris was a colleague, I was always impressed by his versatile and well-focused mind. But as his efforts at self-promotion intensified, his stature as a philosopher seemed to diminish. There was no apparent effect on the department's Gourmet rankings when he left in 1996.

THE BUSINESS OF ACADEMIC RESEARCH

CVs were likened previously to score cards in golf. An even more telling comparison is with résumés in business. Like a business résumé, an academic CV presents highlights of one's accomplishments to potential employers, and often figures in salary increases and professional promotions. In such circumstances, the competitive edge belongs to those with the most impressive CVs.

CVs thus add a further dimension of competition to professional philosophy. We have already seen how Leiter rankings put graduate departments in competition with each other. And we have seen how individual CVs tend to focus on accomplishments that bolster the Leiter rankings of the departments involved. In this respect, competition among department members interacts with competition on the level of departments themselves. There is yet another level of academic competition, however, that interacts with these two lower levels in turn. This is the competition among universities for funds and other resources to support their research activities.

When I arrived at ND in the late 1950s, competition was not a standard part of the university's culture. I was not hired because I had a better CV than other applicants. As far as I know, there were no other applicants; and I had few academic accomplishments at the time that would make compiling a CV worthwhile. I gather that this was also true of other newcomers to the department, extending at least through the 1960s. And some of us, needless to say, stayed longer than others. But the reasons for this, again, had little to do with accomplishments that would add heft to a typical CV today. If one of us had submitted a 1990s-style CV to the department chair in hopes of a favorable tenure decision, he wouldn't have known what to do with it. The kind of competition that made CVs relevant in the 1990s was absent from department life during this earlier period.

Similar remarks apply to competition (or lack thereof) on the department level. If a ranking system like PGR had been current in the 1950s and 1960s, ND's department would have considered it a mere curiosity. Regardless of how the department ranked, its members would have had trouble understanding the relevance of such rankings in the first place. The department's task was to provide good instruction to its students, and perhaps to enrich the philosophic lives of its members. Success in such undertakings had little to do with the department's reputation in the profession at large. There may have been some general perception of how our department stacked up against departments in various other institutions, but there was no sense that these departments were in competition with us. Viewed either from the perspective of individual members or from that of the department itself, philosophy at ND during the 1960s was not a competitive enterprise.

On the university level, however, a different story was already unfolding. As recounted in chapter 2, Fr. Hesburgh had embarked on a "pursuit of excellence" campaign soon after he became president in 1952. As a matter of course, when excellence is a goal (rather than an accomplished state) it is pursued in competition with others who share the same goal. Moreover, as we have seen, the kind of excellence Hesburgh had in mind was not excellence in undergraduate teaching. No university becomes "truly great" (one of his pet phrases) by superior teaching alone. Hesburgh's goal was excellence in specialized research, the kind that had propelled the United States ahead of Russia in the space race of the 1950s and that was sponsored subsequently by well-funded government agencies like the National Science Foundation.

It was Hesburgh's extensive involvement with the NSF, in fact, that initially fueled his campaign for excellence at ND. Naturally enough, his main focus at first was on research in departments such as biology and chemistry, which already were nationally known when Hesburgh took over. Next came physics, which with Hesburgh's help received a state-of-the-art accelerator from the NSF in 1955. His initial breakthrough outside of the Science College, however, came when he brought Ernan McMullin back to the university full-time in 1961 and made him chair of the Philosophy Department in 1965.[14] During his early years of interaction with the NSF, Ernan brought in substantial grants to strengthen research in the philosophy of science. Following Ernan's example, other faculties in the A&L College started soliciting outside funds for specialized research.[15] By the end of the 1970s, departments and colleges throughout the university had joined the race to gain prominence in research within their respective disciplines.

By the end of the 1970s, in effect, Hesburgh had changed ND from an institution devoted primarily to undergraduate teaching into a major contender for preeminence among research universities. And by the mid-1980s, ND was in direct competition with other major universities for top research faculty and for funds to support their operations. As universities begin to compete for top faculty, furthermore, senior faculty in turn begin to compete for positions at top universities. Playing an integral part in this competition were the CVs faculty compose to highlight their accomplishments as research specialists. Whereas research-oriented CVs were foreign to most teaching institutions of the 1950s and 1960s, in short, they now became an integral part of academic research endeavors in the 1980s.

By this time, a research university's quest for excellence had become directly tied to the prestige of its research-oriented departments. Competition among universities had devolved into competition among their research departments, and competitive success on the departmental level added up to success of the university in turn. Thus all three levels of competition became bound up with each other. In the case of philosophy departments specifically, Leiter rankings came to interact with strength of individual faculty CVs on the one hand and with national university reputations on the other. In return, universities tended to reward their most visible departments, and departments tended to reward their most visible members.

Well and good, one might want to say. But what does this have to do with the conduct of research universities as businesses? The answer boils down to the fact that specialized research is an expensive undertaking. In some fields it requires specialized equipment and specialized buildings. In any field, it requires specialized faculty who command high salaries. Whereas institutions devoted primarily to teaching often get by with income from tuition, investments, and alumni giving, research universities require additional income from granting agencies, supporting industries, and highly orchestrated fund-raising campaigns. Fund-raising at ND engages the services of Development Office personnel numbering in the hundreds, supported by several dozen public affairs specialists and staff. With the help of highly trained professionals like these, ND increased its average "annual giving" from about $1.5 million in the mid-1950s to roughly three hundred times this amount in the mid-1980s (see chap. 2, the first section and n. 8). A good portion of this additional income went to endowed chairs, laboratory equipment, and buildings serving the needs of specialized research operations.

Managing money already at hand is another expensive activity, requiring the services of many dozen investment officers, accountants, and legal experts. Almost without exception, money managers like these are specially trained professionals in their own right. In addition to professional salaries, these specialists require offices, parking spaces, and janitorial services. According to a rough count I made around 2005, whereas ND undergraduate enrollment had increased about 10 percent since the mid-1980s and faculty had expanded by about 50 percent, the size of the support staff (including nonacademic administrators) had more than doubled. By 2010, more than three hundred nonacademic positions were listed by title on ND's organization chart, including fourteen vice-presidents and fifteen associate vice-presidents.[16] And most of these titled positions supervise additional numbers of untitled support staff. Once located almost entirely in the Main Building, nonacademic staff now occupies an eleven-story high-rise and several former classroom facilities.

With a growing nonacademic superstructure like this, it was inevitable that at some point ND would begin to function like a corporate bureaucracy. This amounts to operating as an administrative system with a rigid hierarchy of authority, fixed job descriptions, and largely impersonal lines of communication. It was only a matter of time, that is to say, before ND began to operate in ways indistinguishable from those of other business enterprises.

From the perspective of rank-and-file faculty members, the first sign of an emerging business mentality may have been a subtle shift in their relationship to upper-level administrators. When I first came to ND, most administrators were drawn from either the CSC order or the teaching faculty, and most returned to those ranks after vacating their administrative roles. The prevailing conception at the time was that their function as administrators was to provide support for the rest of the faculty. They worked for us, not we for them. Beginning sometime in the late 1970s, however, increasing numbers of key administrators were recruited from the business world, bringing with them corporate attitudes and corporate practices. By the mid-1980s it was clear to all concerned that the faculty worked for the administration rather than the other way around.

A more tangible sign of growing corporate influence was a new name for what used to be a cheerfully accommodating Personnel Office. In 1987, I believe it was, Personnel disappeared and was replaced by the Office of Human Resources. One of the first changes made in Human Resources was to separate services that deal with employees paid by the hour from others dealing with employees (including faculty) paid by the month. By the 1990s, both classes of employees were being treated, along with buildings and physical property, as resources to be efficiently managed in pursuing the corporate goals of the university. Like most business offices at ND, Human Resources is currently located in Grace Hall, denizens of which are easily recognizable by their strict adherence to corporate dress codes.

Another change in business operations during the late 1980s was a reorganization of several university facilities that provide services for money. When I first came to ND, facilities such as dining areas, meeting venues, and duplicating offices were operated primarily for the convenience of university personnel. Although no documentation to this effect is available, it is evident that such facilities are now managed as little businesses operated to draw income from a customer base of university employees. One bizarre side effect has been a regular flow of advertising brochures circulated internally among the operations involved, sometimes including "special offers" to stimulate sales.

Other recent forms of commercialization include the "outsourcing" of ND Bookstore management, establishment of off-campus outlets for (patented) ND memorabilia, and financial cooperation with private industry to provide laboratories and funding for research by ND faculty. In 2008, ND teamed with the City of South Bend to found a research center on its property known as Innovation Park. An overtly commercial undertaking, its publicly announced purpose is to connect "innovators, market experts and capital providers to transform innovations into viable marketplace ventures."[17] In 2011, the university added an Office of Technology Transfer (OTT) to its preexisting Office of the Vice-President for Research. The mission of OTT is to help "university faculty, research staff, and students identify, protect, market, and license promising new technologies to industry."[18] Quartered in Grace Hall, OTT is obviously intended to provide university clout in converting the vision behind Innovation Park into profit-making businesses.[19]

The vision behind Innovation Park was the perception that, since "cutting-edge" research at ND often has commercial applications, the university has a legitimate interest in pursuing these applications to the point where they begin to show profit. Some readers may favor that vision and others not. My guess is that Fr. Hesburgh would side with the former. He was on the National Science Board in the mid-1950s, when it established policies to be pursued with NSF money. One aim that organization has been committed to from the start is to "stimulate knowledge transfer among academia and the public and private sectors."[20] In line with this NSF mandate, at any rate, part of the business of ND is to help businesses in the private sector make a profit.

ENDOWED CHAIRS

An endowed chair is an academic position with a salary paid from proceeds of a fund donated specifically for that purpose. In addition to salary, the person holding the chair typically is provided with a discretionary account intended to cover travel, research costs, and clerical assistance. When the endowment is not large enough for these several purposes, it may be augmented in various ways by other budgets in the university.

An endowed chair is one of those seemingly rare financial arrangements that work to the advantage of all parties involved. On the part of the individual occupant, being appointed to a chair is a significant academic honor, contributing substantially to the competitive punch of his or her CV. Moreover, academic protocol dictates that the chair holder incorporate the name of the chair into his or her professional title (not just "Professor Quinn" but "William Herbert Perry Faunce Professor Quinn"), so that the honor is reaffirmed whenever the title is used. This honorific benefit continues even after the chair is vacated.

Thus Ralph McInerny, for instance, was officially known after his retirement as the Michael P. Grace Professor of Medieval Studies Emeritus.

The chair's donor, in turn, gains name recognition among successive generations of students and alumni, many of whom are socially and financially well placed. Wealthy people have long been attentive to the prestige that comes with having one's name attached to prominent buildings.[21] Under auspicious circumstances, however, named professorships can command attention even longer than physical structures. The Lucasian Chair of Mathematics at Cambridge University, for instance, was founded in 1663, and has kept the name of its founder (Henry Lucas) before the public for 350 fame-filled years (an early occupant was Isaac Newton, a more recent Stephen Hawking). By contrast, the spraying fountain dedicated to Joe Evans near ND's Nieuwland Science Hall was demolished less than twenty years after its construction in 1980.

Whereas chair holders and donors receive boosts to their personal and public esteem, the departments concerned receive impersonal benefits as well. Almost as a matter of course, incoming chair holders are well known in the profession. This increases the likelihood of their bringing in capable graduate students and enterprising junior faculty. A previously noted example is Al Plantinga, who soon attracted a considerable number of talented graduate students from evangelical Christian colleges after he moved into the O'Brien Chair. Al's presence here, moreover, was also a drawing card for other accomplished scholars of analytic metaphysics (Dean Zimmerman, Peter van Inwagen, Michael Rea), forming a "critical mass" that made ND probably the best place in the world around the turn of the century to pursue that particular discipline.

There are also advantages for the university at large. Chair holders with high visibility are positioned to attract research grants from outside funding agencies, which can be used to finance not only their own research but also that of graduate students and young faculty members. Having prominent researchers on its faculty also tends to enhance the university's reputation in less tangible ways, such as making it easier for junior faculty to secure grants for themselves.

Endowed chairs are advantageous from a budgetary perspective as well. When chair holders are brought in from the outside, the local scholarly community benefits by adding a productive faculty member without depleting budget lines allotted to other faculty. And when a chair is given internally to a tenured faculty member, funds previously used for his or her salary can be given over to other purposes. It is unclear whether the community benefits more from chairs assigned to new or to veteran faculty. That issue notwithstanding, chairs made available to ND's Philosophy Department over the past three decades have been split almost evenly between the two categories.

With the appointment of Robert Audi in 2010, the department had used chairs seven times to bring people in from the outside:

Frederick Crosson, John Cardinal O'Hara Professor of Philosophy (1976)
Philip Quinn, Rev. John A. O'Brien Professor of Philosophy (1985)
Alasdair MacIntyre, McMahon-Hank Professor of Philosophy (1988)
Peter van Inwagen, John Cardinal O'Hara Professor of Philosophy (1995)
Kristin Shrader-Frechette, O'Neill Family Professor of Philosophy (1998)
Richard Cross, Rev. John A. O'Brien Professor of Philosophy (2007)
Robert Audi, Rev. John A. O'Brien Professor of Philosophy (2010)

These chairs were negotiated to move people into the department, as distinct from acknowledging accomplishments by present members. As of 2011, Crosson and Quinn were deceased and MacIntyre had retired.

Over the same period, nine chairs were awarded for outstanding accomplishment by people already in the department.[22]

Ralph McInerny, Michael P. Grace Chair of Medieval Studies (1978)
Alvin Plantinga, Rev. John A. O'Brien Professor of Philosophy (1983)
Ernan McMullin, John Cardinal O'Hara Professor of Philosophy (1984)
David Burrell, Hesburgh Professor of Philosophy (1989)
Michael Loux, George Shuster Professor of Philosophy (1994)
Karl Ameriks, McMahon-Hank Professor of Philosophy (1999)
Alfred Freddoso, John and Jean Oesterle Professor of Thomistic Studies (2003)

Gary Gutting, Notre Dame Chair in Philosophy (2004)
Michael Detlefsen, McMahon-Hank Professor of Philosophy (2008)

Of these, McInerny and McMullin are deceased, while Plantinga, Burrell, and Loux have gone emeritus. As of 2011, the Philosophy Department had eight active chair-holders from both categories combined. Although comparisons in such matters are often subjective, I believe that most people in a position to judge would consider Alasdair MacIntyre to be the most distinguished chair holder in department history to date.

Alasdair Chalmers MacIntyre was born to John and Emily (Chalmers) MacIntyre in Glasgow, Scotland, on January 12, 1929. He earned a BA in classics from Queen Mary College (University of London) in 1949 and began graduate work in philosophy at Manchester University the same year. He received an MA in 1951 and spent the next six years at Manchester as lecturer in philosophy of religion. From 1957 to 1959 he was lecturer in philosophy at Leeds University. He then went to Oxford for further study of philosophy, receiving an Oxonian MA in 1961. This is his highest academic degree.

During the 1960s MacIntyre made brief stands in England and abroad. He was research fellow at Nuffield College, Oxford, in 1961–62, spent a year at Princeton as senior fellow with the Council of the Humanities in 1962–63, and then returned to Oxford to serve three years as fellow of University College. From 1966 to 1970, he was professor of sociology at the University of Essex, with a side trip to University of Copenhagen as visiting lecturer in 1969. In 1970 he immigrated to the United States, to become Richard Koret Professor of History of Ideas at Brandeis University.

MacIntyre's very substantial list of publications began to proliferate even before he left Essex University. While still at Manchester, he published *Marxism: An Interpretation* (1953) and coedited *New Essays in Philosophical Theology* (1955) with Anthony Flew. Next came *The Unconscious: A Conceptual Analysis* (1958) and *Difficulties in Christian Belief* (1959). His landmark *A Short History of Ethics* appeared in 1966, followed by *Secularization and Moral Change* in 1967. *The Religious*

Significance of Atheism came out in 1969, and then *Herbert Marcuse: An Exposition and a Polemic* in 1970.[23]

As these titles indicate, MacIntyre's scholarship during this early period was preoccupied with two interconnected themes. One was Marxism as a theory of social action. During his first few years at Manchester, in fact, he had been an active member of the Communist Party.[24] Although he subsequently rejected Marxism as a philosophic theory, he continued to respect socialist ideology as a system of beliefs that could impart purpose to the lives of ordinary people. The other theme dominating his research was the role of Christianity and the Christian tradition in providing a social order in which a human life could be lived coherently. MacIntyre emerged from this period neither Marxist nor Christian, but was already working with concepts that would underlie his later thinking about institutions and traditions.[25]

MacIntyre's next major publication was *Against the Self-Images of the Age: Essays on Ideology and Philosophy* (1971),[26] which came out while he was still at Brandeis. In 1972, he left Brandeis for Boston University (BU), assuming the university professorship of philosophy and political science. He was soon made dean of the College of Liberal Arts by John Silber, who had become president of BU just the previous year. The collaboration with Silber went badly, and MacIntyre retreated to the Philosophy Department proper in 1973. He became chair of that department in 1976, a position he continued to occupy through 1979. In 1980, he moved a few miles north to Wellesley College, where he became the Henry B. Luce, Jr., Professor of Language, Mind and Culture. I had been vetted for that position, but Wellesley wisely chose McIntyre instead.

During his stay at BU, Alasdair had married Lynn Joy, then a graduate student at Harvard in history of science.[27] When Lynn received her PhD in 1982, he left Wellesley and the two of them took positions at Vanderbilt University. Alasdair thereby became the W. Alton Jones Distinguished Professor of Philosophy, while Lynn switched to philosophy from history of science to become assistant professor in the same department. They stayed at Vanderbilt for six years, until 1988.

In the meanwhile, Alasdair had been making overtures to ND. He had visited the Philosophy Department three times as Perspective lecturer in the 1970s, and each time had been very well received. Aware of his interest, the department invited him for another lecture in February 1986 and did everything in its power to make him feel welcome. After a year's delay, the university was ready to make him an offer.[28] In February 1988, Provost Timothy O'Meara offered Alasdair the McMahon-Hank Professorship of Philosophy, which he readily accepted. Lynn Joy came with him to ND as associate professor of philosophy with tenure. They stayed for six years, until the spring of 1995. During this time, Alasdair published *Whose Justice? Which Rationality?* (UNDP, 1988) and *Three Rival Versions of Moral Enquiry: Encyclopedia, Genealogy, Tradition* (UNDP, 1990), while Lynn published *Gassendi the Atomist, Advocate of History in an Age of Science.*[29]

Alasdair's departure to Duke University in 1995 was a matter of consternation for ND administrators. Knowing that he had converted to Catholicism early in the 1980s, A&L Dean Harold Attridge sent Alasdair a letter dated October 4, 1994, stressing the importance of his continued presence for ND's development into "a major Catholic University." He also offered Alasdair a contract exceeding Duke's offer in every respect involving money, as well as season tickets to home football games on the "30 yard line or better." His counteroffer to Lynn was even more attractive. If she stayed, she would be promoted to full professor, draw a salary almost $4,000 higher than Duke had offered, receive an annual "research fund" of $5,000, and be granted a full year leave of absence every four years. But to no avail. Alasdair was approaching an age when retirement seemed natural, while Lynn, already in her late thirties, was eager to get on with her own career. Thanking Dean Attridge for his generous offer, Lynn went to Duke as professor in the Philosophy Department and Alasdair accompanied her as arts and sciences professor of philosophy.

The coming of Joy and MacIntyre was much heralded by the Duke department. In the January 27, 1995, issue of *The Chronicle,* Duke's daily student newspaper, Alasdair reported that he came to Duke "because of the possibilities offered by the department," and Lynn explained her arrival by saying that her work could "complement the work of others" at that university. The article ended by quoting Owen Flanagan, then chair of the Duke department, as saying that he believed "that MacIntyre and Joy [were] prepared to stay at Duke . . . through retirement." As it turned out, Flanagan was right in the case of MacIntyre, who left Duke as arts and sciences professor emeritus in the year 2000. But after five years of "complementing the work of others," Joy was ready to return to active duty at ND. By the end of the 1990s, after all, Duke was a dozen or so notches below ND in the Gourmet rankings. And that seemed unlikely to change within the next decade.

Lynn Joy returned in 2000 as professor of philosophy and has remained at ND up to the present. Perhaps because of his emeritus status at Duke, Alasdair thought better of returning to the Philosophy Department itself. Instead he became senior research professor with ND's Center for Culture and Values. Although his salary was modest by his own request, he was assigned a substantial discretionary fund and taught only one or two undergraduate courses a year. After returning to ND, he published *Edith Stein: A Philosophical Prologue, 1913–1922* in 2006, and *God, Philosophy, Universities: A Selective History of the Catholic Philosophical Tradition* in 2009, both with Rowman & Littlefield in Lanham, Maryland (not a university press). In 2005, after the death of Phil Quinn, Alasdair's position in the Center for Culture and Values was upgraded to the O'Brien Senior Research Professor of Philosophy. He retired from that position in 2010, the year Al Plantinga vacated his own O'Brien Chair.

Alasdair's second stay at ND, from 2000–2010, was the longest in one place of his entire career. Desire to migrate prevailed again in 2010, when he joined the faculty of newly founded (and soon beleaguered) London Metropolitan University. Undaunted by the commuting this entails, he and Lynn maintained their primary residence in a suburb a few miles from ND. They also bought an apartment in Chicago.

Unlike Plantinga, MacIntyre did not attract other prominent scholars in his discipline to the university.[30] And relatively few graduate students came to ND to study with him specifically. But as already suggested, he probably attracted more favorable attention to the university than any other single member of the Philosophy Department. He was president of the American Philosophical Association, Eastern Division, in 1984. He was elected Fellow of the American Academy of Arts and Sciences (AAAS) in 1985, and gave the Gifford Lecture at the University of Edinburgh in 1988. He has received honorary degrees from Swarthmore College (1983), Queen's University of Belfast (1988), University of Essex (1990), Williams College (1993), New School of Social Research (1996), Marquette University (2000), St. Patrick's University, Maynooth (2002), and National University of Ireland (2009).

In addition to these and other professional honors, MacIntyre to date has authored or edited eighteen books (several previously mentioned) and published over 150 professional articles. To borrow a line from his friend and collaborator, theologian Stanley Hauerwas, few would "dispute that Alasdair MacIntyre is one of the most important philosophers of our time."[31]

THE MARKETING POWER OF PROFESSIONAL JOURNALS

Gourmet rankings of philosophy departments are keyed to the reputations of individual department members. Beyond gaining prominence for specialized research, there are other things an individual might do to enhance the visibility of his or her department. One is to edit a professional journal.

An obvious illustration is Cornell University's *Philosophical Review* (*PR*), edited by its philosophy department ("The Sage School of Philosophy"). Founded in 1892, *PR* has remained under Cornell editorship ever since. The preeminence it has gained in the meanwhile has contributed substantially to Cornell's high reputation as a center of philosophic research. Another example is *The Review of Metaphysics* (*RM*), founded by Paul Weiss when he first went to Yale in 1947. Although Weiss took the journal with him when he moved to Catholic University in the early 1970s (where it is now edited by Jude Dougherty), philosophers of my generation still tend to associate *RM* with its first academic home.

Similar publicity benefits can be ascribed retrospectively to *The New Scholasticism* (*NS*), the first philosophic journal edited by ND faculty. Founded in 1927 as the official organ of the American Catholic

Philosophical Association, *NS* came to ND when then Editor Vincent Smith arrived from Catholic University in 1950. Although Smith took it with him again when he went to St. John's in 1960, *NS* returned to ND in 1966 under the editorship of John Oesterle. After John's death in 1977, Ralph McInerny took over as editor with the help of Jean Oesterle (John's widow) as associate editor.[32] Fred Freddoso joined the team as assistant editor in 1984, remaining in that role until the journal moved to the University of Saint Thomas in 1990 and resumed publication as the *American Catholic Philosophical Quarterly*.

By the time it moved to ND in 1950, *NS* had become the world's premier outlet for scholarship in the Thomistic tradition. As Ralph remarked in his 1992 lecture "Notre Dame and Dame Philosophy," the transfer of *The New Scholasticism* to ND signaled acknowledgment of ND "as emerging leader in American Catholic Philosophy." During the heyday of its period under ND editorship (thirty-four years in all), *NS* contributed significantly to the growing prominence of both the department and the university.

Yale lost a bit of its luster among professional philosophy departments when *RM* moved to Catholic University, and ND suffered likewise when *NS* moved to Saint Thomas. In naming the first journal founded by members of its own Philosophy Department, ND found a way of ensuring that the publicity value of that journal would not be lost to another institution. The publication in question is the *Notre Dame Journal of Formal Logic* (*NDJFL*). One advantage of this eponymous title is that the journal would continue to broadcast the name of its founding institution even if moved elsewhere. Another is that it brings ND to the attention of many philosophers who are not logicians and would never look beyond the front cover itself.

As noted in an earlier chapter, the *NDJFL* was founded by Boleslaw Sobocinski in 1960. Sobocinski remained editor until two years before his death in 1980, although his erratic editorial practices had led to the appointment of Jack Canty as managing editor in 1969. Fred Rickey from mathematics was editor-in-chief during 1979–80, and continued to help manage the journal for several years later. The distribution of editorial responsibilities from 1981 onward was unusually complicated, with several categories of editor listed on the masthead and several individuals under each category.[33] With respect to day-by-day operations, Penny Maddy was main editor from 1981 until she left in 1983. Mathematician Mark Nadel kept things going in 1984 and continued to play an editorial role for several more years. Editorial stability returned in 1985 when Mic Detlefsen took over. Anand Pillay (mathematics) replaced Nadel as Detlefsen's coeditor in 1992, and then Peter Cholak (mathematics) replaced Pillay in 2000. Detlefsen and Cholak remain coeditors up to the present.

A second journal with ND's name in its title is *Notre Dame Philosophical Reviews* (*NDPR*), a free online publication devoted exclusively to relatively long (1,500–2,500 words) reviews. Founded by Gary Gutting in 2002, it aims to make reviews of books available within a year of publication. Reviews are requested and vetted by a carefully chosen editorial board consisting of some four dozen members. One advantage of this format is that reviews can be published within days after they become available. After *NDPR* got up to speed in 2003, it put out reviews at a rate of approximately one per day. Another attractive feature of the online format is its home site's front page, which displays arresting pictures of famous philosophers that alternate every few minutes.

NDPR has been well received, both inside and outside the profession. Brian Leiter (of Gourmet fame), speaking as a member of the 2007 editorial board, refers to it as "a wonderful resource, for which the whole profession is indebted to Gary Gutting who runs it so well."[34] And in 2009, a trendy blog known as "Film Studies for Free" treated its followers to "some links to high-quality, film studies-related, book reviews from that very worthy e-organ *Notre Dame Philosophical Reviews*."[35] For reasons including the prospect of good publicity like this, Gutting was elevated to a Notre Dame Chair in Philosophy in 2004.

Another online journal currently published under ND editorship is the *Journal of Philosophical Research* (*JPR*). This journal came to ND with a thirty-year history. It was first published in 1975 as *Philosophy Research Archives* by the Philosophy Documentation Center at Bowling Green, with William Alston (Rutgers) as founding editor. Early issues came out in microfiche, but a print format was added in 1982.

The journal was reorganized under the *JPR* title in 1990, when the microfiche format was eliminated. *JPR* went online in 1997, eventually converting all past issues to digital form.

Panayot Butchvarov (Iowa) succeeded Alston as editor of *JPR* in 1993, and ND's Michael DePaul succeeded Butchvarov in 2003. Whereas *JPR* is still published by the Philosophical Documentation Center (along with more than one hundred other journals), it is now cosponsored by ND and the Canadian Philosophical Association. *JPR* specializes in bibliographies, translations, and other research projects that are difficult to publish conventionally because of length. It comes out annually, and accepts material in either English or French.

Bill Alston was also founding editor of *Faith and Philosophy* (*F&P*) in 1984, continuing as editor until 1990, when ND's Phil Quinn took over. William Wainwright (Wisconsin, Milwaukee) was editor from 1995 to 2001, followed by William Hasker (Huntington College) until 2007. *F&P* then returned to ND under the editorship of Tom Flint. At that point, ND joined Asbury University and the Society of Christian Philosophers as cosponsors.

On the website of the Philosophical Documentation Center, its de facto publisher, *F&P* is billed as "The Journal of the Society of Christian Philosophers." From its beginning, *F&P* has been a major publishing venue for members of that society. Between 1984 and 2000, Alvin Plantinga, Eleonore Stump, William Hasker, and James Keller (Wofford College) each published ten articles or more in *F&P*.

One more journal edited for a brief period at ND is *Plato,* founded in 2000 by Christopher Gill (Exeter) as the online organ of the International Plato Society. ND's Gretchen Reydams-Schils was editor from 2004 through 2007, followed by Dimitri El Murr of the University of Paris. Reydams-Schils is currently chair of the PLS, and since 2003 has held a concurrent appointment in the Philosophy Department.[36] Gretchen received a BA in classics from the Catholic University of Leuven, Belgium, in 1987, an MA in classics from the University of Cincinnati in 1989, and a PhD in ancient philosophy from UC Berkeley in 1994. She then came to ND, where she achieved promotion to associate professor (in PLS) in 2000 and to professor in 2007.

From 2006 to 2009, she was associate dean for research, graduate studies, and centers in the A&L College.

Taking *NDJFL, NDPR, F&P, JPR,* and *Plato* together, we have five scholarly journals under ND editorship during the decade 2000–2009, serving broad constituencies within the community of professional philosophers. A large number of philosophers in the United States very likely have had or will have direct dealings with one or another of these publications sometime during their careers. This is good publicity for both department and university. In terms of service to the profession and the resulting publicity, diligent journal editors are worth their weight in gold.

DEVELOPING THE PRODUCT LINE

Like any other good graduate program, ND's Philosophy Department must compete to attract good graduate students and to place them in good jobs when their training is finished. The products for which it seeks a competitive edge are the PhDs it sends into the academic marketplace. Like other graduate programs, similarly, ND remains competitive by providing more concentrated training in some areas than in others. Its product line consists of the several areas of concentration in which its PhDs receive "state of the art" training.

Areas of concentration on which the department focused in developing its product line during the mid-1980s and 1990s include philosophy of religion, philosophy of science, logic, analytic metaphysics, epistemology, and continental philosophy. The first two have been discussed at length in chapter 5. Let us look more closely at the remaining four.

Logic

As already noted, the first technically trained formal logician in the department was Boleslaw Sobocinski, who edited the *NDJFL* in the 1960s and 1970s. Penny Maddy kept the journal going until she left in 1983. The next professional logician to assume leadership was Michael Detlefsen, who took over as editor in 1985 and remained in that role for more than twenty-five years.

Michael ("Mic") Detlefsen was born October 20, 1948, in Scottsbluff, Nebraska, the largest town (with a 1950 population of about eight thousand) in that part of the state.[37] He went east to Illinois for his BA (Wheaton, 1971), and further east to Maryland for his PhD (Johns Hopkins, 1976). He returned west in 1975 to start teaching at the University of Minnesota, Duluth, and moved to ND as associate professor in 1984. He was promoted to professor in 1989, and installed as McMahon-Hank Professor of Philosophy in 2008.

Mic authored *Hilbert's Program: An Essay on Mathematical Instrumentalism* in 1986, and in 1992 coedited both *Proof, Logic, and Formalism* and *Formalism and Proof and Knowledge in Mathematics*. He has published over fifty journal articles and essays in professional collections. His growing prominence as a logician has been fostered by a burgeoning series of grants and fellowships, culminating in 2007 with a Senior *chaire d'excellence* appointment funded to the tune of $2.4 million by three French universities in collaboration with the Agence nationale de la recherche. In 2011 he was appointed guest professor at the University of Paris. He continues to serve as McMahon-Hank Professor of Philosophy at ND.

During the late 1970s and early 1980s, Mic's professional activity was confined mainly to the United States. From the late 1980s onward, however, most of his invited lectures and conference presentations have taken place abroad. In the two decades between 1990 and 2010, he gave roughly sixty addresses in fifteen different foreign countries. Mic Detlefsen undoubtedly is one of the two or three best-known logicians in Europe and the United States today.

Michael Kremer was born in 1957, received his PhD from Pittsburgh in 1986, and was hired that year by ND to help Detlefsen with the *NDJFL* and to teach graduate and undergraduate courses in logic. As it turned out, he was on the editorial staff of the journal for only one year (1987–88). Although he continued to teach logic throughout his sixteen years at ND, his main interest turned out to be philosophy of language and early analytic philosophy. Although his publication list at the time was not extensive, he was promoted to associate professor with tenure in 1993. He was promoted to professor in 2001, the year before he left for the University of Chicago. By that time, he had published well over a dozen very substantial articles.

A practicing Catholic and congenial colleague, Mike lists faith and reason as one of his primary research topics. Of particular interest, I happen to know, is the mystical in Wittgenstein's *Tractatus.* His 2010 CV lists a book-length manuscript on Frege as still in process. Mike Kremer currently is the Mary R. Morton Professor of Philosophy at Chicago.

Sun-Joo Shin was considered previously. She arrived in 1991, and Timothy Bays in 1999. Both were here before Kremer left in 2002. Thus between 1999 and 2002 there were four technically trained logicians in the department including Detlefsen. After Shin left in 2003, the number went back down to two. The addition of Curtis Franks in 2006 brought it back to three, where it still remains.

Timothy Bays grew up in South Bend (his father, Phillip, was a St. Mary's chemistry professor), went to Northwestern for his BA, then proceeded to UCLA for a PhD in mathematics in 1994 and another in philosophy in 2000. Arriving at ND in 1999 as assistant professor, he was promoted to associate with tenure in 2007, on the strength of a powerful mind and seven articles. His wife, Terri, has served as director of ND's OpenCourseWare Project, and currently is studying to be an Episcopalian priest.

Curtis Franks has a BA in philosophy and mathematics from Rice University (2000) and a PhD in philosophy from UC Irvine (2006). He published *The Autonomy of Mathematical Knowledge: Hilbert's Program Revisited* in 2009,[38] three years after coming to ND. As with Mike Kremer, one of his main research interests is Wittgenstein's *Tractatus.* Within my recollection, Curtis is the only member of the department ever to wear a yarmulke to class.

Analytic Metaphysics

Philosophy of religion became a featured item in ND's product line with the arrival of Al Plantinga in 1982. Given the key roles of modal logic and possible-worlds ontology in Al's philosophy of religion, it was natural that he should become a magnet for others with similar interests in metaphysics. Mike Loux was already working in this area when Plantinga arrived. Although Loux was not particularly interested in philosophy of religion as such, his collaboration with Plantinga established analytic metaphysics as one of the department's distinctive strengths. By the end of the 1980s, the department had decided to make that somewhat arcane branch of philosophy another of its specialties and began hiring accordingly.

Dean Zimmerman joined the department in 1991, a year before receiving his PhD in metaphysics from Brown (under Roderick Chisholm). While at ND, Dean taught courses in metaphysics and philosophy of religion, developing a particular interest in the work of Peter van Inwagen. During his nine years at ND, Dean published eighteen articles and coedited *Metaphysics: The Big Questions* (Blackwell, 1998) with van Inwagen.[39] Also during that time, Dean initiated the summer workshop "Metaphysical Mayhem," which continues to meet biennially. He also organized a rock band called "Spinning Jenny," with his wife, Tami, on bass, himself on synthesizer, and two ND graduate students playing guitar. Leaving ND in 2000, Dean spent a year or two at Syracuse and then moved on to Rutgers University, where he currently is professor of philosophy and director of graduate studies.

Peter van Inwagen was born on September 21, 1942, received a BS from Rensselaer Polytechnic in 1963, and earned a PhD from Rochester in 1969. He stayed at Rochester for another year before moving to Syracuse as assistant professor in 1971. At Syracuse, he was promoted to associate professor in 1974 and to professor in 1980. In 1995, he came to ND as John Cardinal O'Hara Professor of Philosophy.

Van Inwagen is a world-class metaphysician. He has delivered over three-dozen invited presentations in fifteen different countries. He gave the F. D. Maurice Lectures at the University of London in 1999, the Wilde Lectures on Natural Religion at Oxford in 2000, and the Gifford Lectures at St. Andrews in 2004. Honors at home include election to the American Academy of Arts and Sciences in 2005, presidency of the Central Division of the APA in 2008–9, and presidency of the Society of Christian Philosophers in 2010–11. Between 1978 and 2010, he participated in over two hundred colloquia in the United States and abroad. He has authored eight books, edited or coedited five others, and published over 150 papers and critical studies.

Peter's autobiographical essay, "Quam Dilecta,"[40] recounts his spiritual odyssey from Unitarianism through agnosticism to eventual membership in the Episcopalian Church. It also discusses his challenge, all too common among philosophers, of dealing with anger at not receiving what he considered due recognition within the profession. Complicating this challenge was a difficult first marriage, which ended in divorce in 1987. Two years later he married Elisabeth (Lisette) Bolduc, one of the social mainstays of the current department. All this is relevant and worth noting because philosophers tend to be "too intellectual and introverted," as Peter says of himself, and need help bringing their intellectual and spiritual lives together. Peter's success in pulling this off is a lesson worth heeding by others trying to cope with similar issues.

Michael Rea received a BA in philosophy and economics from UCLA in 1991 and a PhD in philosophy from ND under Plantinga in 1996. He began teaching at Delaware in 1996, where he was promoted to associate professor with tenure in 2000. In 2001, he moved back to ND as associate professor with tenure. He was promoted to professor in 2008.

Mike's specialties are metaphysics and philosophy of religion. He has published two scholarly books and either edited or coedited nine others. He also has published over three dozen articles and delivered over six dozen invited lectures and conference presentations. He currently is director of ND's Center for Philosophy of Religion. Like Plantinga and Detlefsen, Mike is a member of the Christian Reformed Church.

Epistemology and Philosophy of Mind

I was the department's only trained epistemologist until Richard Foley came in 1977.[41] Five PhD theses on epistemology were written under my direction between 1965 and 1978, followed by six under Foley between 1982 and 1992. Michael DePaul came in 1982, but did not begin directing graduate theses until well after 2000. Between 2004 and 2010, however, two epistemology PhDs were completed under his direction and three under his codirection. Four additional faculty with special competence in epistemology (Leopold Stubenberg, Marian David, Ted Warfield, and Robert Audi) were hired after Foley left in 1990. Five dissertations on epistemology have been directed or codirected by this group as of 2010.

Leopold Stubenberg was born in Graz, Austria, in 1956, the son of Josef-Wilhelm M. S. J. Herr und Graf von Stubenberg and Caroline Gräfin von Nostitz-Rieneck.[42] He received his PhD from Arizona, two years after joining the ND department in 1990. He was promoted to assistant professor the year his thesis was accepted. A revised version of the thesis was published as *Consciousness and Qualia* in 1998.[43] On the basis of this anticipated publication, one coedited book, and five articles, the department promoted him to associate professor with tenure in 1997. As the title of his book suggests, Leopold was trained in the philosophy of mind as well as epistemology. Equally fluent in English and German, he is an engaging conversationalist on many topics. One of Leopold's nonacademic interests is the evolution of fuel-efficient automotive transportation. He owns an original Honda Insight and several motorcycles.

Marian David studied in Graz, Austria (his country of birth), and at the University of Colorado before receiving his PhD from Arizona in 1990. He was assistant professor at ND from 1990 to 1996, when he was promoted to associate professor with tenure. In 2003, he was made professor. Besides writing about two dozen articles in journals and collections, he coedited a German volume in honor of Roderick Chisholm with Leopold Stubenberg in 1986 and published the monograph *Correspondence and Disquotation: An Essay on the Nature of Truth* in 1994.[44] Marian is one of the most precise thinkers I have known, comparable in this respect to his fellow countryman Ludwig Wittgenstein. Like Wittgenstein as well, I suspect, he is sometimes discomfited by his own intellectual fastidiousness.

Ted ("Fritz") Warfield received his PhD from Rutgers in 1994, was a postdoc at ND's Center for the Philosophy of Religion in 1994–95, and with the strong recommendation of center director Al Plantinga was appointed assistant professor in the department the following year without external search. He was promoted to associate professor with tenure in 2001 and made professor in 2007. He has coedited three books and published about two dozen articles. He has served as codirector of five PhD theses on epistemology.

Fritz plays a key role in the department as an influential member of the Gourmet Report's editorial board. His service to the university includes three years on the A&L College Council, one year on the Faculty Senate, and one year as assistant varsity volleyball coach (Fritz is unusually agile for his size). Reminiscent of Joe Bobik forty years earlier, Fritz is a gambler with an uncanny skill at beating the odds. This may have something to do with his perennial bachelor status.

Robert Audi was Charles Mach University Professor of Philosophy at the University of Nebraska before coming to ND in 2003 as the David E. Gallo (as in wine) Professor of Business Ethics and professor of management and of philosophy. Increasing involvement with the Philosophy Department, with which he had arranged a joint appointment when he came, led to Audi's relinquishing the Gallo Chair in 2010 and settling into one of the Rev. John O'Brien Chairs of Philosophy as the department's senior epistemologist. He bills himself on his website as also specializing in religious epistemology, philosophy of mind and action, political philosophy, and ethics.

Since receiving his PhD from Michigan in 1967, Audi has published roughly 120 articles and thirteen books, three of which he either coauthored or coedited. He served as editor-in-chief of the *Cambridge Dictionary of Philosophy* from 1989 to 1995, and of the *Journal of Philosophical Research* from 1989 through 1992. He was president of the Western Division of the APA in 1987–88. Sociable by nature, he has expended considerable time and energy in his recent role of graduate placement director. One of Robert Audi's more endearing traits is that he is always looking for someone to help.

By virtue of its focus on the nature and the powers of thought, epistemology overlaps with what is now known as philosophy of mind. Robert Audi and Leopold Stubenberg work in both disciplines, as did

I during the 1970s and 1980s.[45] Another ND philosopher of mind was Bill Ramsey, who worked almost exclusively in that area.

William Ramsey came to ND in 1989 with a PhD fresh from UC San Diego. He stayed for eighteen years before departing in 2007 for the University of Utah, Las Vegas. Bill was promoted to associate professor with tenure in 1994, on the strength of one coedited book (*Philosophy and Connectionist Theory*) and seven articles. In 1998 he coedited another book with ND colleague Mike DePaul, and in 2007 authored *Representation Reconsidered.*[46] Bill's strong academic suit was teaching. According to Neil Delaney, A&L director of the Honors Program, in which Ramsey often taught, he was especially good in courses focused on issues central to the Catholic tradition.[47] Indeed, Ramsey was one of only a few ND philosophers to get high marks from the *Irish Rover,* a conservative Catholic undergraduate monthly. More orthodox recognition came with the Madden Award for first-year teaching in 1999, a Kaneb Award for A&L teaching in 2002, and the Sheedy Award for Excellence in Teaching in 2005.

For Bill Ramsey, however, the suit that trumps everything academic is rock climbing. The reason he left ND for Utah is the proximity there of superb climbing routes. Before he left, Bill had established himself as one of the premier rock climbers in the world.[48] A decade or so before leaving, he had practice walls erected both in his house and in the Rockne Memorial building. Before this, he played squash to condition his arms and legs. My contribution to rock climbing is that I taught Bill Ramsey the game of squash.

Continental

Discussion of the department's need for more strength in continental philosophy began in the early 1990s and came to a head in 1999 with the appointment of Karl Ameriks to the McMahon-Hank Professorship of Philosophy. Before 1990, Stephen Watson had been the only full-time continental person in the department, with Gary Gutting dividing his time between continental, philosophy of science, and philosophy of religion. Fred Rush joined the continental contingent in 2001, followed by Anja Jauernig in 2002.

Karl Ameriks was born in Munich in 1947, received a PhD from Yale in 1973, and proceeded directly to ND as assistant professor. Before being awarded his endowed chair, he became associate professor with tenure in 1979 and was promoted to professor in 1985. Ameriks has authored four books, coedited five, and translated two by German authors, in addition to publishing about seven dozen scholarly articles. He also is coeditor (with Desmond Clarke, a 1974 ND PhD) of *Cambridge Texts in the History of Philosophy,* which currently boasts about six dozen titles.

Karl's scholarly work has been supported by fellowships from the Alexander von Humboldt Foundation and from the Earhart Foundation. He received a Fulbright grant for study in Tübingen in 1969 and an NEH Fellowship in 1998. Between 1991 and 1994 he served as president of the North American Kant Society, and in 2004–5 he was president of the Central Division of the APA. He was elected to the American Academy of Arts and Sciences in 2009.

In addition to his professional honors, Karl has been an unusually active participant in departmental affairs. He was director of graduate studies in 1981–84 and acting chair of the department in 1988–89. During the twenty-seven years between 1983 and 2010, twenty-four students completed their PhDs under his direction. Karl has what I take to be a photographic memory. Although he speaks sparingly (in a high pitched voice), he seems to remember everything he hears or reads. His wife, Geraldine, is lecturer in the Department of Romance Languages and Literatures.

Stephen Watson received his PhD from Duquesne University in 1980. After a stint at Colgate, he came to ND in 1983 as assistant professor. He rose quickly to associate professor in 1987 and then to professor in 1992. He has authored seven books and coedited three others. He has also authored about sixty articles and chapters in edited collections. Watson has given over sixty invited papers and lectures as well, including more than a dozen in nine foreign countries. He has directed ten PhD theses and codirected two others.

Despite spending relatively little time in his office, Watson served five years (1996–2001) as chair of the Philosophy Department. It was with his help in this role that Ameriks received the McMahon-Hank

Chair in 1999. I am in Watson's debt for a different kind of favor. Also in 1999, he helped me arrange a welcome "semiretirement" to a half-time position, which I still occupy.

Fred Rush received his BA in philosophy from Washington and Lee in 1978, and for the next decade or so made his living playing guitar in rock ensembles. He left professional music in 1989 and went to Columbia to earn credentials for a career in philosophy. He received his PhD in 1996. After an additional year teaching at Columbia, Fred moved to the University of Kansas as assistant professor in 1997. He came to ND at that rank in 2001 and was promoted to associate professor with tenure in 2006. Before tenure, Fred began editing *The Cambridge Companion to Critical Theory* (2004). He also had published ten articles in professional journals. In 2009, he published the monograph *On Architecture* with Routledge Press. In addition to continental philosophy, Fred's research interests include philosophy of art.

Fred and his wife, lawyer Leslie Callahan, once owned a house near mine previously occupied by a son of old-time ND philosopher William Roemer. But then Fred inherited an elegant grand piano and needed more space to display it properly. So he moved into a grand old house in a historic neighborhood with plenty of room for his wife, two teenage sons, several professional guitars in neat array, and a grand piano with a room to itself.

Anja Jauernig joined the department as an instructor in 2002, two years before receiving her PhD from Princeton. She was appointed assistant professor in 2004, the rank she held until moving to the University of Pittsburgh as associate professor in 2011. As of 2011 she had published four articles in professional journals and three in edited collections. Her current CV lists several books on Kant and Leibniz as "in preparation." Anja is a competitive swimmer, a resolute vegetarian, and someone impeccably disciplined both personally and professionally. Having grown up near Freiburg in Germany, an ancient university town known for its high standard of living and advanced environmental practices (which she internalized), Anja found South Bend a bit too far from civilization for her liking.[49] Hence the move to Pittsburgh, which is closer to Germany.

THE DEPARTMENT ADRIFT

The decade of the 1990s was a period of malaise in ND's Philosophy Department. Attendance at department meetings was falling off, fewer people were coming to Friday colloquia, and there was increasing concern that the department was operating with conflicting agendas. In 1993, the department's endowed-chair holders convened as an ad hoc committee to consider the problem and possible remedies.[50]

One analysis of the problem, by Phil Quinn, was that the department had become fragmented because of excessive specialization. Quinn was aware that specialization was not unique to ND, but was concerned about its effects at ND in particular. "Empirical indicators of this trend," as he describes them, "include declines in attendance at such events as departmental colloquia, perspective lectures and the faculty discussion group, and the increase in numbers and importance of specialized discussion groups." Noting that "this process merely reflects what is going on in the larger arena of academic philosophy," he goes on to question whether we can "buck the trend with any prospect of success?"

A similar concern, expressed by Mike Loux, was that the department had lost its sense of a common mission. Loux had arrived during the period when the department was being transformed from the Thomism of the 1950s to the robust pluralism of the 1970s. During both of these eras the department operated with a shared sense of purpose. Although the rhetoric of pluralism was still current in the 1990s, however, by then both Thomism and robust pluralism had fallen by the wayside. And with them had gone any sense of a communal endeavor. The department of the 1990s was clearly fragmented, and just as clearly lacked a common purpose.

Another analysis was put forward by Ernan McMullin, to the effect that the department had become too large. In 1993, it had thirty-six full-time members, plus a substantial number of adjuncts and professional specialists. The main reason for this large faculty, of course, was the university requirement that all undergraduates take two courses in philosophy. With an undergraduate enrollment of approximately eight thousand students in the 1990s, about two thousand students were taking philosophy in any given term. The two-course requirement has continued to provide employment for several dozen otherwise unneeded ND philosophers up to the present.

Not coincidentally, the two-course requirement was mentioned in one way or another by several participants. One concern was how the requirement meshed with teaching on the graduate level. Although department size was dictated by this undergraduate requirement, in ways already noted, the going practice was to hire new faculty for what they could contribute to the graduate program (see the seventh section of chap. 6). One consequence was that the department was loaded with specialized researchers, many of whom were ill suited to teach required courses for undergraduates. Another previously mentioned concern was rooted in internal politics. From time to time, other departments had challenged philosophy's two-course requirement as an unwarranted privilege to an overindulged department, and these challenges became more intense as the decade proceeded. Everyone present realized that if the department were to lose its two-course requirement, it would be left with a large cadre of teachers with no courses to teach. An urgent preoccupation of the department at the time thus was to defend this requirement against would-be interlopers.

The committee of chaired professors disbanded after two or three meetings, with no effect on departmental policy that I can recall. In most practical respects, the department during subsequent years was pretty much what it had been in the early 1990s. It continued to be fragmented. It continued to hold on to its two-course requirement. And it continued to grow in size, expanding from thirty-six full-time members in 1993 to forty-two in 2009. As it turned out, the concerns expressed by the chaired professors in 1993 were not widely enough shared to prevent the department from remaining mired in the status quo for the rest of the decade.

The first department meeting in the fall of 1999 had been set aside for discussion of a memo I submitted the previous spring entitled "Conversation on matters pertaining to department identity." The memo stemmed from growing discontent with what I perceived as the department's unremitting emphasis on image over substance, reinforced by an almost reverential deference to Leiter ratings. I had converted to Catholicism in 1994, and in some vague way felt that this push for national visibility was at odds with the Catholic character of the department. The memo was written with the help of several senior colleagues who had similar misgivings.

The memo in question laid out three models among which I thought the department might choose in charting its future development. Each model was characterized in terms of its implications for undergraduate curricula, for graduate training, and for department hiring. One was the "Thomistic model," corresponding to the way the department had conceived itself during the 1950s and before. Another was the "pluralist model," epitomizing its focus during the 1960s and 1970s. Third was the "specialist model," mirroring the ethos of the department in the 1990s. Even a casual reader would have had no trouble discerning that the pluralist alternative was the one preferred by the author. The memo ended, perhaps tendentiously, with a quotation from the 1990 encyclical *Ex Corde Ecclesiae*,[51] along with an argument that the pluralist model was in harmony with papal teaching.

The meeting to discuss the memo was held on August 23, 1999, in McKenna Hall, the recently renamed Center for Continuing Education. Department chair Stephen Watson called the meeting to order at 1:00 p.m. Recognizing that the memo had been circulated almost six months earlier, I began with a short summary of its contents. An awkward silence followed the summary.

Then Al Plantinga broke the ice by reading a short statement he had penned just that morning. The burden of his remarks was that the accepted religious orientation of the department was not simply "Catholic" but "Catholic and other Christian." So much for the quotation from *Ex Corde Ecclesiae,* which had elicited no discernible reaction from my Catholic colleagues. In the fall of 1999, the department numbered thirty-eight full-time members, of whom nineteen were Catholic. No attendance was taken, and I have no sense of how many Catholics were present. I do remember, however, that roughly half the department attended the meeting.

Plantinga's correction duly noted, someone on my left raised a question about a recent challenge by the English Department to our two-course requirement. The meeting then was turned over to Fred Freddoso, the current director of undergraduate studies.

I realized at the time, of course, that there was no real hope that the department would revert to the pluralistic model of earlier decades. The intent of the memo had been to stimulate a general discussion of the department's mission, a topic that had exercised the endowed-chair holders earlier in the decade. As the fate of my memo indicated, however, a discussion of that sort was no longer deemed relevant by the department as a whole (in this case, more accurately, the half that attended meetings). Between 1990 and 1999, fifteen new full-time faculty had been added to the department, most of whom came from major graduate programs and all of whom confined their research to specialized areas of philosophy. A junior colleague told me after the meeting that the pluralist model had merit, but that people of his generation just hadn't been trained that way. The specialist model by then was firmly established in the profession, leaving ND powerless to buck the tide even if it had wanted to.

Within two or three months after the meeting, I had initiated negotiations for a new contract with the university. Beginning in the fall of 2000, I would teach half-time, at half my previous salary, and spend the time thus freed in continuing research. This turned out to be the best move of my professional career. As the next decade progressed, I published *Metaphysics and Method in Plato's* Statesman in 2006 and *Unearthed: The Economic Roots of Our Environmental Crisis* in 2010. I then began work on a comprehensive history of ND's Philosophy Department.

CHAPTER 8

Entering the New Millennium

THE 2000 EXTERNAL REVIEW

Within the five years following 1999, department size increased from 38 to 43, and Catholic membership decreased from 50 percent (19 of 38) to 40 percent (17 of 43). Remaining unchanged was its lack of a common mission and its disinclination to address the issue. A consequence was that the department moved into the new millennium with no consensus about where it should be heading. The department, in short, remained adrift.

It might seem apparent at first that this drop in Catholic membership marked a decline of Catholic influence in the department, and that its lack of a common mission resulted from this decline. But this understanding of the department's Catholic presence would be mistaken. During the early 1980s Catholics were still a clear majority, and yet their influence in department affairs was already slipping. Moreover, the department's sense of mission during this earlier period had already begun to falter, despite a preponderance of Catholics on its full-time faculty.

The source of this mistaken understanding is the assumption that strength of Catholic influence in department affairs is measured by percentage of Catholic faculty. This assumption is incorrect. And the reason it is incorrect is that Catholic membership in the department during recent decades had ceased to constitute a unified bloc. During the Thomistically dominated 1950s, Catholic members shared a common view of philosophy and acted accordingly. By the late 1970s, however, the Catholic presence in the department had become splintered into opposing factions. Within a few years after 2000, the seventeen Catholics in the forty-three-person department had become overtly divided between the conservative right, the progressive left, and the rest in between. On the conservative side was a group typified by Ralph McInerny, Fred Freddoso, and newcomer John O'Callaghan, who tended to think of Thomism as an integral part of their Catholic faith. On the opposing side were Catholics such as Phil Quinn, Paul Weithman, and Kristin Shrader-Frechette, whose practice of philosophy was bound up with advocacy of liberal causes. In between was a somewhat larger group of moderate Catholics who, though perhaps leaning in one direction or the other, took positions individually, case by case.

Similar diversity had been present among Catholic members of the department in the 1990s. Thus divided among themselves, Catholics of this era seldom voted as an integrated bloc. Once again, this is why a given proportion of Catholic members today does not translate into a corresponding degree of distinctively Catholic influence in department affairs. Catholics tend to push in opposing directions, depending on their particular religious orientations. The Catholic vote, in effect, tends to cancel itself out.

In my estimation, this is one of the main reasons ND's Philosophy Department moved into the new millennium without a shared sense of purpose. Catholics could not agree on where the department should be heading, and non-Catholics for the most part didn't really care. Having no common sense of purpose, moreover, the department also had no common ground for establishing policies and procedures that might serve in its best long-term interest. In particular, it had no commonly shared basis for evaluating the adequacy of its two-course requirement. And as it turned out, the department was about to be challenged in unequivocal terms to rethink its handling of that requirement.

In early November 2000, ND's Philosophy Department underwent its third external review. Outside members of the review committee this time were Julia Annas from Arizona, Fr. Thomas Flynn from Emory, and Jerome Schneewind from Johns Hopkins. Gerald Massey from Pittsburgh had also been appointed an external member, but was unable to attend because of illness. The internal member of the committee was Fr. Brian Daley, SJ, a distinguished scholar in ND's Theology Department.

Up to a point, Professors Annas, Flynn, Schneewind, and Daley seemed pleased with what they found. Observing that the department's faculty was "very strong on research," that "many of its members [had] international reputations," and that its curriculum was "extremely strong and varied," they remarked that in their opinion "the Department as a whole" was "excellent."[1] That said, however, they proceeded to lay out a number of rather pointed criticisms.

The first criticism concerned the two-course requirement. Having "devoted much time in . . .[their] meetings to the two required courses," the reviewers reported, they came to believe "that the Department must rethink the way it [was] carrying out its responsibility" in this regard. Elaborating on this responsibility, they cited the need for courses that enable "the transmission of Catholic traditions and the preparation of Catholics for the intellectual challenges of the future." With this in view, they recommended (1) that the department "make more of an effort to have these courses serve the purpose that underlies the requirement."

A second major criticism was (2) that the department was overly preoccupied with professional rankings. As they put it, the reviewers did "not think that aiming at 'top ten' status, and guiding recruitment by what will pay off in these rankings," was "the best way to develop the Department." Such rankings, they suggested, reflect "fashions and trends that may not be pertinent to Notre Dame's special identity." Referring back to their previous criticism, the visitors pointed out that in fact there "may be conflicts between the search for faculty who will bring higher rankings and the search for faculty who can help the University carry out its Catholic mission."

Other critical observations concerned departmental procedures and governance. Regarding the former, the external reviewers found that procedures "both for hiring and for retention are far too informal." In matters of hiring, they noted, the department votes on job candidates as a "committee of the whole." Given the many diverse interests in the department, this procedure makes it likely that "no group gets the candidate it thinks best." Concerning retention, they asked whether the department "is tough enough in assessing graduate students and younger faculty."[2] With regard to procedures, in sum, the reviewers suggested (3) that hiring procedures were too informal, (4) that the department's criteria for promotion to tenure were too lax, and (5) that graduate students were not held to sufficiently rigorous standards of achievement.

Regarding governance, the reviewers considered it "quite clear" (6) that the "Department needs to rethink the role of its chair." While "Prof. Watson has been doing an excellent job of . . . keeping the Department operating well despite strong disagreements" within it, "a different strategy seems necessary" in the current situation. What the department now needs is "a very strong leader who will be able to make decisions even when they leave one group or another unhappy."

Although forcefully articulated, criticisms (3) through (6) were not developed in further detail. More attention was given to perceived problems associated with (1) the two-course requirement and (2) obsession with department rankings. The department's response to these criticisms is treated in the following section. Before considering this response, however, let us look more deeply into problems regarding rankings and the two-course requirement. As it turned out, the reviewers' advice that the department scale back its emphasis on rankings was both relevant and timely. During the 2000s the department not only declined in PGR ranking, but began to show other symptoms of being on the wane as well. One such symptom relates to the fact that high-ranking graduate programs are generally more successful than others in placing their PhDs in desirable jobs. Among professionally oriented philosophers, jobs in universities with PhD programs are usually preferred over jobs in institutions not offering PhD degrees. From 2000 to 2009, nonetheless, ND's department experienced a sharp decline in proportion of PhDs it sent on to universities with doctoral programs.

In chapter 6, statistics were presented comparing the periods 1969–88 and 1989–2008 with respect to initial placement of new PhDs. Figures from the later period can be broken down to produce corresponding statistics for 1989–1998 in comparison with 1999–2008. Between 1969 and 1988, by way of review, 124 recipients of ND PhDs went on the job market, of whom 90 (73 percent) found academic employment. And 21 of that 90 (23 percent) went on to universities granting PhDs in philosophy. Comparable figures for 1989–1998 show a vast improvement. During that period 55 of 66 (84 percent) found academic employment and 22 of those (40 percent) were employed by universities with PhD programs in philosophy. The decade of the 1990s, of course, was the first to show the influence of the Gourmet Report. ND's success in playing the rankings game during that decade is reflected in the jump from 23 percent to 40 percent of fresh PhDs landing jobs in universities offering advanced philosophic training.

The corresponding figures for 1999–2008 are sobering, to say the least. While the percentage of fresh PhDs finding academic employment is essentially the same as before (62 of 73, or 85 percent), the proportion of those employed by universities with PhD programs falls off dramatically. In contrast with 40 percent for the period 1989–1998, only 18 percent (11 of 62) find jobs in institutions offering PhDs in philosophy. This is even less than the 23 percent for the combined 1970s and 1980s. Despite the fact that the department ranked fourteenth nationwide moving into the new millennium,[3] its performance on this score was worse than before the rankings game began. It was still highly successful in placing its PhDs in colleges and MA-level philosophy programs, but the department was not providing whatever extra boost it took to give its PhDs an auspicious shot at jobs in research universities.

Another arena in which the department's relatively high ranking was not producing benefits that might be expected is that of faculty recruitment. Given that jobs at high-ranking departments usually are considered especially desirable, these departments typically have a fairly easy time recruiting new faculty. Despite its favorable rankings, however, ND was having trouble filling the faculty slots it happened to have available. Vicissitudes in the hiring of new faculty are amply documented in the minutes of department meetings held during the decade 2000–2009.

Between fall of 2000 and spring of 2009, 16 people were added to the department, more than compensating for the 11 who left during the same period. In order to recruit these 16 people, however, the department made no less than 37 offers. Put the other way around, 57 percent of the department's offers during the decade of the 2000s were declined.

Further breakdown of the 16 accepted offers is both pertinent and informative. For one thing, 6 of the accepted offers included tenure. Three of these 6 were at the level of associate professor (Dumont, O'Callaghan, Rea), 1 at the level of professor (Joy), and 2 at the level of professor with endowed chair (Audi, Cross). Of these 3 higher-level offers, moreover, 2 were extended to people who had previously indicated a desire to join the department. This leaves only 1 professorial-level appointee with tenure that involved an active recruitment effort.

Of the 21 offers that were rejected, on the other hand, 8 had been at the level of professor and 8 at professor with endowed chair. Thus a total of 10 offers of endowed chairs were made between 2000 and 2009, of which just 2 (to Audi and Cross) were accepted. This does not fit the standard recruitment profile of a department benefiting from high Gourmet rankings. Also relevant is that, of the 37 offers made during 2000–2009, only 8 were to Catholic candidates. And of these 8 offers, only 3 (Dumont, O'Callaghan, Speaks) were accepted. Of the 5 offers to Catholics that were rejected, 2 were at the level of endowed chair.[4]

Of particular interest is the department's failure to recruit new women into senior positions. Lynn Joy came back as professor in 2000, and Janet Kourany was promoted from adjunct to associate in 2001, but both had been in the department previously. The only new women recruited from 2000 through 2010 were Anja Jauernig in 2002 and Katherine Brading in 2004, both fresh out of graduate school. A sustained effort to recruit senior women was made in 2007, when the department personally invited 34 senior women to apply for the open position advertised that year. But as recorded in the department minutes for September 7, 2007, only 3 of the 34 submitted applications. And none of these 3 received a job offer.

Whether by coincidence or not, these signs of a research department in decline were accompanied by an actual drop in Gourmet rankings during the decade in question. The department's highest ranking came in 2004, when it was tied for twelfth with Cornell, Arizona, and UC Berkeley.[5] In 2006, it was ranked thirteenth with two other departments. By 2009, it had fallen into a two-way tie for fifteenth place, and had slipped even farther to eighteenth by 2011. Declining from its peak in 2004, the department had dropped six ranks within the next seven years. To repeat, there was something prophetic in the review committee's advice that the department not tie its future to high Gourmet rankings.

The other criticism developed at length by the external reviewers concerned the two-course requirement. This requirement, we may recall, is a relic of the four-course sequence of the early 1950s and the six-course requirement of the preceding era. In these earlier manifestations, the rationale of the requirement was to prepare students for intelligent participation in the life of faith. With the initiation of the two-course version in 1970, however, the ostensive purpose shifted to one of ensuring that students were cognizant of major moments in the Catholic philosophic tradition. The two-course philosophy sequence eventually became part of the university's academic tradition, on a par with the Freshman Year of Studies and A&L's College Seminar.

This time-honored status, however, did not protect it from periodic attacks, directed from both inside and outside the A&L College. Inside attacks came from departments such as the PLS, which had philosophically trained people on its faculty who wanted part of the action. Outside attacks came by and large from the Business School, which had developed ethics courses of its own that it wanted to substitute for the philosophy requirements. The typical departmental response to such attacks was a skillfully honed defense of the status quo by Neil Delaney, Philosophy's elder statesman.

On one memorable occasion, however, representatives of the Business School argued before the assembled university faculty (with

President Jenkins presiding) that the second philosophy requirement should be replaced by a course of their own in business ethics. Defending philosophy's monopoly on this occasion was Alasdair MacIntyre, widely recognized then as the world's foremost moral philosopher. His response boiled down to the claims (1) that ethics courses can be morally damaging to students, (2) that a rigorous course in mathematics can be morally more edifying than most ethics courses, and (3) that ethics courses taught by philosophers are less likely to be morally damaging than courses taught by nonphilosophers. MacIntyre's oration was followed by a stunned silence. The two-course requirement had been successfully defended once again.

The external reviewers brought the controversy up to date by observing that "outside the Department the requirement is viewed by some individual faculty members with envy and even with anger." They also asserted that the initial course "should not be just the sort of introductory course that one can find in any good secular school," and that both courses "should use texts and address problems that are pertinent to Catholic beliefs and traditions." The department's response is examined in the following section.

THE DEPARTMENT'S RESPONSE

The primary author of the response was Paul Weithman, who joined the department in 1991 and served as chair from 2001 to 2007. An accomplished scholar, compassionate colleague, and meticulous administrator, Paul kept the department on even keel through what would prove to be one of its more taxing periods. His first major challenge was to soothe the department's displeasure with the external report and to prepare a diplomatic rebuttal for consumption by the upper administration. Let us consider how Weithman's response deals with the six criticisms itemized in the previous section.

Criticisms (4) (criteria for tenure) and (5) (graduate student assessment), it so happens, are not addressed at all,[6] whereas (2) (concerning rankings) receives a scant one-sentence reply. This latter is a forthright assertion that the department must be filled "with philosophers whose contributions to scholarship will help . . . maintain its place in the profession."[7] Critical points concerning (1) (the two-course requirement), (3) (loose hiring procedures), and (6) (stronger leadership), on the other hand, are discussed extensively. Following the order of Paul's treatment, we begin with the latter two issues.

As presented by the external reviewers, the emphatic advice that the department needed stronger leadership was coupled with the observation that informality in matters of hiring seemed "to have gone to extremes." Of particular concern was the department's acting as a "committee of the whole" in voting on job candidates. Quite understandably, Weithman took these charges as an affront to the department's pervasively democratic mode of operation. The departmental response proceeds accordingly.

After a cursory introduction, the response begins with the statement, "Our department is proud of its democratic heritage." The procedures of the department, it continues, "should function . . . to further [its] commitments to self-governance." Quoting Churchill's famous remark that democracy is the worst form of government except for the alternatives, Weithman goes on to observe that democracy "in the department, like democracy elsewhere, can lead to decision-making which is often messy and, on rare occasions, unfortunate." Nonetheless, he affirms, "the department would be very reluctant to put authority for decision-making in the hands of a few," for this "would fly in the face of our conception of philosophy."

Although himself a proven leader, Paul Weithman is proclaiming for all to hear that he is not about to step into the role of the "very strong leader" envisaged by the external reviewers. What the department needs by way of leadership, his response intimates, is what it has already—a skillful moderator of democratic procedures. The department will continue to vote on job candidates as a "committee of the whole," despite whatever "extreme informality" that might entail.

To put this stand against autocratic leadership in context, we need to know a few things about Paul Weithman's own intellectual formation. After earning a 1981 BA at ND, he received his PhD from Harvard in 1988. His thesis on the political thought of Saint Thomas Aquinas was codirected by John Rawls in philosophy and Judith Shklar in government. Paul describes himself as a Catholic liberal,[8] by which he means a Catholic with "an overriding concern for the rule of law and for the political liberties of conscience, speech, assembly, and of the press."[9] Paul's version of Catholic liberalism is influenced by the political liberalism of Rawls himself, which calls for the disinterested participation (under a "veil of ignorance") of rational agents in establishing principles that will structure the political order in which they live. Such rational deliberation is possible only when democracy prevails.

Paul's response to the reviewers' doubts about the department's handling of the two-course requirement was governed by the key liberal principle of egalitarian decision-making. To appreciate the significance of the departmental response to the external evaluators, accordingly, we need to read it as a principled response of a liberal Catholic rather than as an opportunistic defense of the status quo. As Rawls's student, Paul considered it important that people have a hand in formulating the procedures by which their professional activity is guided. Given the likelihood that all department members would be affected by changes in the two-course requirement, Paul wanted the entire department to decide whether changes should be made.

Paul's strategy for getting the entire department involved comprised three stages. The first was carried out during the summer of 2001, shortly after the external reviewers' report had been received, when Paul met with a small committee to study existing courses that satisfied the two-course requirement. As stated in the departmental response, this committee found that the department's introductory courses "[covered] . . . central problems of the philosophical tradition," "read predominantly classic texts," and "[seemed] solidly in line with what the Dean and the external reviewers [recommended]." Upon receiving the report of this committee, the department voted to hold a meeting devoted to the two-course requirement.

In preparation for this meeting, Paul circulated a position statement on which discussion would be based.[10] The statement was formulated with advice from (past chair) Neil Delaney, (past dean) Mike Loux, and (eminent moral philosopher) Alasdair MacIntyre. It is hard to imagine any group of Catholic philosophers better qualified as advisers. Formulation of this statement was second of the three stages.

"Because Notre Dame is a Catholic university," the statement begins, its purposes "include the preservation, extension, and transmission of Catholic thought." Accordingly, its "students should learn to think in depth about the intellectual and existential problems posed by a life of faith," should have "the opportunity to learn how the great thinkers of the Catholic tradition approached those problems in the past," and should also learn "what Catholicism has to say about these problems as they arise in the contemporary world." The two required courses in question, it goes on to say, are directed expressly towards these ends.

Additional goals mentioned for the first course are to impart a "basic cultural literacy" regarding "seminal philosophical texts," to make students aware that many "concepts they pre-reflectively employ . . . generate significant philosophical questions," and to foster the acquisition of "argumentative and analytical skills." The second required course might be on various topics including ethics, philosophy of science, philosophy and religion, and philosophy of mind. Whatever its topic, the second course should presuppose "that the goals of the introductory course have been achieved," and should aim at further development of "the argumentative and analytical skills" acquired at the introductory level. Moreover, students in this second course "should be held to the highest standards of philosophical argument and inquiry," standards comparable to those "accorded recognition at the best philosophy departments." In both beginning and second courses, the statement continues, students should demonstrate that they have met the applicable standards both "orally and in writing." Several department members interpreted this subsequently as requiring oral examinations in beginning courses.

The third stage of the department's deliberation was a formal discussion of Paul's position statement. This discussion took place during two department meetings, held on December 11, 2003, and February 11, 2004. Most of the December meeting was given over to a conversation with Dean Roche regarding philosophy's role in the strategic plan he was developing for the A&L College. When attention finally turned to the two-course requirement, several faculty members raised objections to the apparent stipulation that oral examinations would be required in introductory courses. Since by then the hour was late, further discussion of the topic was postponed to the second meeting. On this subsequent occasion, two months later, the department agreed to eliminate reference to oral evaluations and to set slightly lower standards for the second required course. And that was it. With a vote of eighteen to zero, the department then signed off on the two-course requirement and turned its attention to other matters. Nothing else in the position statement was ever discussed by the department as a whole.

Paul had penned his official response to the external report in November 2001. His position statement on the two-course requirement had been discussed and approved roughly two years later. At no stage in the process did the department have anything substantial to say about the two-course requirement other than that it should not involve oral examinations in beginning courses. The position statement was approved unanimously by eighteen members of a forty-five-member department. This means that three-fifths (twenty-seven of forty-five) of the department became bound by a vote on the two-course requirement in which they did not participate. Such was the character of democratic decision-making among ND philosophers in the middle of the decade following 2000.

Paul Weithman relinquished the helm in 2007, having kept the department afloat through six often-turbulent years. His successor was Stephen Dumont, a moderate Catholic who joined the department in 2001. Stephen received his PhD from Toronto in 1983, spent three years at the Catholic University of America, and then returned to Toronto for sixteen years before coming to ND as associate professor. He was promoted to professor in 2006.

As noted in minutes dated January 31, 2007, Stephen was the department's unanimous choice as chair. The eighteen members voting for him were won over by his frank protestation that (1) he lacked the "administrative and social skills" necessary to run such a large department, (2) he had not been at ND long enough to know the other administrators he would be working with, and (3) he would much rather spend his time on genuine academic projects. Despite his three years as chair, by the end of the decade Stephen had published twenty-two articles on medieval philosophy, several quite substantial.

THE CENTER FOR ETHICS AND CULTURE

Paul Weithman's response to the external review epitomized the liberal Catholic vision of the Philosophy Department's mission. Neither the reviewers' report nor Weithman's response mentioned the Center for Ethics and Culture (CEC), newly founded by David Solomon in 1999. The CEC was soon to become the institutional rallying point of the conservative Catholic vision. David Solomon's center underwent its own external review in 2008. Here is an account of circumstances leading up to that event.

Nathan Hatch became provost of the university in 1996, the year after Alasdair MacIntyre left for Duke. Although himself a member of Al Plantinga's Christian Reformed Church, Hatch was fully committed to promoting ND's Catholic character. He considered MacIntyre's departure a major loss to the university, and began looking for ways to compensate for it. To this end, it was natural for him to consult David Solomon, ranking moral philosopher on campus after Alasdair left. David and Alasdair had been close friends for decades, dating from the two years (1975–77) David spent at Boston University under Alasdair's tutelage. Although Southern Baptist by background, David attended services at St. Andrew Greek Orthodox Church with his wife, Mary Lou, during most of his time at ND.

After more than a year of informal conversation on the matter, Nathan and David began serious discussion of an ND ethics center in 1998. Eschewing the concept of an "ivory tower" research group, David thought that ND needed something with a predominantly practical orientation, focusing on the interaction between theory and practice in the manner of MacIntyre's signature work *After Virtue.* In David's words, the primary goals of the center would be "(1) to bring Alasdair MacIntyre's conception of practical rationality and Pope John

Paul II's substantive ethical vision into contact with the best contemporary scholarship in moral philosophy, moral theology, and the social sciences; and (2) to sponsor campus events that would make these ideals available to Notre Dame students."[11] Hatch agreed with these goals, but seemed hesitant about funding an actual center.

Meanwhile, David had been in touch with friends from Baylor, his undergraduate alma mater, who wanted him to form a "Baptist version" of the proposed center at their institution. Despite the offer of a chaired appointment, David replied that he was not interested in leaving ND. Baylor then proposed a three-year visiting appointment to get the center started, after which David could return to ND if he wanted. When David asked the provost for a three-year leave of absence, however, Hatch refused, saying he was not going to let David "take his intellectual capital away." As he told me later, David interpreted this to mean that Hatch still wanted to entice MacIntyre back to ND and considered David's friendship with Alasdair the "capital asset" most likely to make that happen. Fearing that his refusal of a leave of absence would encourage David to go to Baylor permanently, Hatch moved quickly to establish the CEC at ND with David as founding director.

Provided office space on the tenth floor of Flanner Hall, with an annual budget of $25,000 to cover staff and operating expenses, ND's CEC got underway in the fall of 1999. By that stage in the life of the Philosophy Department, David had lost confidence in its ability to represent the traditional Catholic viewpoint on moral issues confronting contemporary culture. His new center was free from departmental influence and reported directly to the Provost's Office. With the provost's backing, David now was in charge of a group "resolutely and unapologetically committed to articulating and defending traditional Catholic positions" on matters pertaining to social justice and the sanctity of human life.

In this manner, a non-Catholic provost and a non-Catholic moral philosopher collaborated in establishing a center dedicated to the defense of traditional Catholic moral and social values. Things went well as long as Nathan Hatch remained in the Provost's Office. When non-Catholic Hatch was replaced by Catholic Thomas Burish in 2005,[12] however, dark clouds began to gather on the horizon. We return soon to the resulting thunderstorm.

Before getting down to the business of "defending traditional Catholic positions," the CEC's first big event was a conference celebrating Ralph McInerny and his recent accomplishments. A collection of essays in honor of Ralph had just been published by Thomas Hibbs and John O'Callaghan, two of Ralph's PhD students, and Ralph himself was midway through his Gifford Lectures in Glasgow.[13] To top off the event, David Solomon arranged a Mass (celebrated by Bishop D'Arcy), a reception, and a lavish banquet. The banquet was attended by hundreds of guests, including most members of the Philosophy Department accompanied by spouses and special friends. Fr. Marvin O'Connell of the History Department gave the after-dinner speech, sharing some charming reminiscences about times he and Ralph spent together as seminarians.

The CEC got down to its appointed business with a conference in the fall of 2000 on the theme "A Culture of Death," inspired by John Paul II's *Evangelium Vitae*. Among the sixteen invited speakers this first year, predictably including Alasdair MacIntyre and Ralph McInerny, were Sidney Callahan of Mercy College and Judge John Noonan on the Ninth U.S. Circuit Court of Appeals. Judge Noonan would return in 2009 to share the commencement stage with President Barack Obama.

This first conference was followed by two others on related topics, "A Culture of Life" in 2001 and "From Death to Life" in 2002. Twenty-six speakers were invited to the former, including Francis Cardinal George of Chicago and Stanley Hauerwas of Duke University. High-profile speakers at the latter included Bishop John D'Arcy (the local ordinary), and ND president Edward A. Malloy, contributing to a total of twenty-eight invited speakers in all. These first three conferences were funded by a $250,000 gift from the Mass Family Foundation, based in Washington, DC.

Encouraged by these early successes, the CEC continued its series of fall conferences through the remainder of the decade. By mid-decade, individual conferences regularly included about twenty invited addresses and over one hundred submitted papers (almost all those submitted were accepted). Hundreds of people would also attend who were not reading papers. From 2000 onward, these annual assemblies were held in McKenna Hall, the largest venue on campus designed specifically for conference use. By the end of the decade, CEC conferences were filling this facility to near capacity.

Another ongoing series of meetings sponsored by the CEC during this period was the Notre Dame Medical Ethics Conference. Solomon had directed this series for about fifteen years previously before bringing it under the wing of the CEC in 2000.[14] In his own words, the purpose of this series is to explore "a variety of complex ethical issues in health care through the prism of the Catholic ethical and cultural tradition." These conferences attracted scholars from various disciplines, including law and theology, and featured open discussion of case studies contributed by participants. Over five hundred case studies from past conferences have been posted on the CEC website.

Most other activities of the CEC catered to undergraduate students. Notable among these was an undergraduate-organized series of lectures on Catholic authors, ranging from Sigrid Undset and G. K. Chesterton to Flannery O'Connor and Walker Percy. A second undergraduate-led activity is called "Breaking Bread" and consists of sizable numbers of students and faculty sharing dinner and conversation in the press box of the ND football stadium. The CEC also has sponsored several undergraduate publications, notably *The Catholic Idler* and *Vita, Dulcedo, et Spes* (both short-lived), and has been credited with playing a role in establishing the markedly conservative *Irish Rover*.[15] The byline of the last-named periodical is: "It behooves a watchdog to bark. Good Rover."

An explicit understanding between Provost Hatch and David Solomon in setting up the center was that it "provide a central clearing house for information, decisions, and programs developed by the many ethics organizations spread across the colleges" (italics deleted). To fulfill its role of disseminating information, the CEC began compiling a *Notre Dame Ethics Bulletin* that was sent weekly to all faculty on campus. This bulletin listed not only lectures on ethics but also films and artistic events of ethical significance. The task of coordinating events with ethical bearing "across the colleges," however, was not easy to accomplish. Success in such a venture requires willing participation of the groups involved, which in this case was not always forthcoming.

This problem was pointed out in the "External Review Report" submitted to the CEC in April 2008. Outside members of the review committee were Christine Hinze, Fordham professor of theology, and Fr. John Langan of Georgetown's Department of Philosophy. Associate Professor Jennifer Herdt of ND's Department of Theology was the internal member. The review had been requested by Provost Thomas Burish, Nathan Hatch's replacement, to whom the CEC reported directly. Although the report was generally favorable, it mentioned a few respects in which change was needed. In particular, the report observed that the "vision of a coordinating . . . clearing house for decision making . . . in ethics . . . has not been realized."

One explanation of this failure considered by the reviewers was that ethics-related centers and programs at ND simply do not want to be coordinated. Another reason suggested was that the center's "John Paul II culture-of-life/MacIntyrean ethics-and-culture" focus brings with it "an ideological narrowness" at odds with its mandate to act as an umbrella organization that would integrate ethics-related initiatives across the various colleges. This role requires "an impartial broker," a description which the CEC's particular "Catholic ethics and culture" self-conception renders it unable to meet.

A second substantial criticism by the external reviewers had to do with the annual conference series. As phrased in their report, there was "a certain repetitive, 'ingrown' character to the list of scholars, speakers, participants and advisors featured at [the CEC's] fall conferences," and sometimes in other programs as well. This claim is supported by lists of invited speakers for the eight conferences held from 2000 to 2007. One person (Tristram Engelhardt of Rice and Baylor) spoke at all eight, two (Ralph McInerny and Alasdair MacIntyre) at seven, one (Margaret M. Hogan of Portland) at six, one (Thomas Hibbs of Boston College) at five, and six (Russell Hittinger of Tulsa, Laura and Jorge Garcia from Boston College, Wilson Miscamble of ND's History Department, Michael Beaty of Baylor, and Gilbert Meilaender of Valparaiso) at four. In the summary view of the external reviewers, the center needed "to increase its collaboration and conversation with scholars and practitioners representing relevant but differing ways of addressing its focal issues and concerns."

Although critical of its hallmark conferences, the reviewers had nothing but praise for the center's undergraduate activities. The CEC had been "especially good," they said, "at responding to and support-ing programming interests among undergraduate students who [were] part of its constituency." Singled out for explicit commendation were the "Breaking Bread" dinners, the CEC's various student publications, and its newly instituted Ralph McInerny Essay Contest.

A more recent undergraduate service provided by the CEC is the "Fund to Protect Human Life," established a few months after the ex-ternal review had been completed. Expenditures from this fund are su-pervised by a five-person committee appointed by the director and have been used to defray expenses of students participating in Right-to-Life marches in Washington, DC, as well as to underwrite various campus events pursuant to the fund's general purpose.[16] One such event was the alternative commencement of 2009, to which we turn presently.

FR. JENKINS AND *THE VAGINA MONOLOGUES*

Phil Quinn was ultraliberal, Ralph McInerny ultraconservative. If I read the signs correctly, John Jenkins is neither liberal nor conserva-tive, but rather occupies a middle ground where he can communicate effectively with both extremes. This enabled him to guide the univer-sity safely through two of the most intense Catholic-culture skirmishes in its history. First was the flap over *The Vagina Monologues*; second, the commencement of 2009. Before looking into these events, how-ever, we should know more about John Jenkins himself, the man, the philosopher, and the CSC priest.

John Ignatius Jenkins was born on December 17, 1953, in Omaha, Nebraska, third of a dozen siblings. He went to high school at Omaha's Creighton Prep, where he was senior captain of the swim team.[17] After a year at Creighton University, John transferred to ND, where he earned a BA in philosophy in 1976 and an MA in 1978. He spent most of the next five years in Moreau Seminary and was ordained a CSC priest in 1983. By 1989 he had earned a BPhil and a DPhil from Oxford. In the meanwhile, he had completed an MDiv and a Licentiate in Sacred Theology from the Jesuit School of Theology in Berkeley, both in 1988. His DPhil thesis, entitled "Knowledge, Faith and Philosophy in Thomas Aquinas," was directed by Master of Balliol College and ex-priest Sir Anthony Kenny.

Fr. Jenkins's professional CV is only four pages long and reflects his joint commitment to both an academic and an administrative calling. Among academic appointments, it lists his membership in the Philosophy Department, which began in 1990 and continues to the present. On the administrative side, he served as director of the CSC seminarian program from 1991 to 1993 and was religious superior of the Holy Cross priests and brothers at ND from 1997 to 2000. In 2000 he was appointed associate provost and vice-president of the university, a position he held until becoming ND's seventeenth president on July 1, 2005.

Despite this load of administrative duties, Fr. Jenkins has published a book, *Knowledge and Faith in Thomas Aquinas,*[18] and at least six substantial articles. He has received honorary degrees from Benedictine College (2006), the University of San Francisco (2010), and Aquinas College (2011). In 2010 he was elected to the American Academy of Arts and Sciences. One of his fondest honors, I would guess, was being named Senior Class Fellow of 2009. This award was presented three days before the 2009 commencement, when ND conferred an honorary degree on President Barack Obama in the midst of raucous protests around the university's perimeter.

John Jenkins's distinction as a philosopher, however, lies not in honors and scholarly accomplishments but in the set of character traits he brings to the task. In book 6 of Plato's *Republic,* Socrates identifies a number of attributes that mark a person as ideally suited for the pursuit of philosophy. Prominent among them are proficiency in learning, impartial behavior, and a gentle disposition. Sometimes in tension with these, but also essential, are the attributes of steadfastness and courage. To become an accomplished philosopher, Socrates states, one must possess both sets of distinguishing features. In our time, as presumably in Plato's, it is hard to find individual philosophers who exhibit both sets of characteristics. Yet during his time as ND's president, Fr. Jenkins has come to exhibit both in a way Plato might have considered exemplary.

Proficiency in learning is a standard trait among trained academicians, amply illustrated by Fr. John's having earned four advanced degrees within five years after ordination. His impartiality, in turn, was evident at a meal I shared with him in the late 1960s while he was working on his DPhil in Oxford. At the time I was staying with my wife, Patti, at Merton College, where dinner at High Table is attended by self-effacing waiters and a professional steward to keep things running smoothly. One evening John invited Patti and me to dinner at Campion Hall, the Jesuit academic residence where he was then staying. Although Campion, unlike Merton, had no high table, it had the usual complement of dinner attendants. When dinner was over, John got up and helped clear the tables. Although other help was available, it somehow seemed natural for this inherently modest priest to step into the role of a menial servant.

Fr. John's gentle disposition was common knowledge around the university even before he became president. As described in the previously cited *Notre Dame Magazine* article published a year before he took office, John Jenkins is not only dutiful but also "humble, sincere, warm, friendly, selfless, thoughtful, [and] genuine."[19] The same article includes a remark by John Affleck-Graves, his soon-to-be executive vice-president: "When you first meet John, you see him as a very soft, kind, and gentle person, and he is. But when you work with John you realize that there's an inner toughness that isn't always readily apparent." Affleck-Graves's remark about inner toughness takes us back to Plato's second set of characteristics. Gentle and fair-minded as he certainly is, would John Jenkins be able to muster the steadfastness and courage essential to being a good university president?

The answer was not immediately apparent. A recurring topic of faculty conversation after his election by the Board of Trustees was whether Fr. John would play the role of pawn in power-struggles within the university or whether he would stay aloof from the fray and be his own man. Doubts began to mount a few months before he took office. Tyrone Willingham, ND's first African American football coach, was fired in 2004, three years into his six-year contract. The decision to let him go was made by the Board of Trustees in consultation with the incoming president.[20] A few weeks later, Fr. Jenkins and Athletic Director Kevin White made a late-night flight to Salt Lake City in an attempt to persuade one-time ND assistant coach Urban Meyer to sign on as Willingham's successor. Meyer went to the University of Florida instead, and ND settled for the ill-fated Charlie Weis (who also was fired before his contract expired). Faculty were not alone in viewing the whole episode as a matter of the new president being commandeered by the Athletic Department.

Nonetheless, Fr. Jenkins's reputation as a minion of the-powers-that-be began to dissipate within a year after his inauguration. For the courageous and evenhanded way he handled the controversy surrounding *The Vagina Monologues* was clearly a matter of his own initiative. *The Vagina Monologues* (*TVM*) was first performed at ND in 2002 and returned regularly to campus in subsequent years. In 2004, local Bishop John D'Arcy declared *TVM* "antithetical to Catholic teaching" and reprimanded President Malloy for allowing its performance on campus.[21] Fr. Jenkins gave his first public statement on the matter in a speech before the assembled ND faculty on January 23, 2006, when he declared the play to be empty of and contrary to "central elements of Catholic sexual morality." After viewing the play himself in February and attending a subsequent panel discussion, however, Fr. Jenkins said that, while its portrayal of sexuality opposed Catholic teaching, the discussion had led him to see the play in a new light. An extended series of meetings with faculty and students followed which eventually persuaded him that performance of *TVM* merited protection in the name of free speech.

On April 5, 2006, Fr. Jenkins announced that *TVM* would be permitted to continue, with the caveat that it was to be presented not as entertainment but within an explicitly academic setting. In explaining his decision, he stated that although he was determined never to "suppress or neglect the Gospel that inspired this university," he also was "very determined that we not suppress [free] speech on this campus."[22]

As might be expected, Fr. Jenkins's decision elicited mixed reactions. Supporters of *TVM* were pleasantly surprised, applauding what they saw as a marked improvement in Fr. Jenkins's perspective. The conservative sector, on the other hand, was predictably outraged. Bishop D'Arcy led off with an official pronouncement that he was "deeply saddened" by Fr. Jenkins's decision.[23] Ralph McInerny followed by decrying Fr. Jenkins's "incredible waffling" in allowing "campus presentations of the infamous and pornographic play *The Vagina Monologues*."[24] The objection with the greatest local impact, however, came from Fr. Jenkins's erstwhile friend and ally, the director of ND's CEC. In an April 14, 2006, piece in the *Wall Street Journal* ("A President's Retreat"), David Solomon declared that "the debate initiated by Father Jenkins exposed a great deal of hostility among faculty members toward traditional Catholic teachings," and remarked that Fr. Jenkins's *TVM* decision was "one more step in a long process of secularization" at ND.[25] Perhaps not coincidentally, the CEC was called upon to give an account of its expenditures two days after the *Wall Street Journal* article appeared. A few months later it was told to begin preparations for the external review that took place in 2008.[26]

The Catholic hierarchy chimed in once again in February 2008, when the U.S. Bishops Committee on Doctrine moved its February 11 meeting off campus in protest of a *TVM* performance scheduled for March 24–26 (Easter that year was on March 23).[27] As it turned out, the 2008 performance was the last at ND. The sponsors of the projected 2009 performance canceled on their own initiative, ostensibly because of the unfavorable local publicity the expected event had encountered.

By this time it was clear to all concerned that Fr. Jenkins was not taking orders from anyone else about how to run the university. Although he had alienated many conservative Catholics, both lay and clerical, no doubts remained about his steadfastness and courage once he had reached a principled stand on the issue. The *TVM* controversy had been his trial by fire, and in the eyes of most of the university he had passed with flying colors. But a much larger controversy began to brew in the months ahead. For President Obama was about to accept ND's invitation to be its 2009 commencement speaker.

THE ALTERNATIVE COMMENCEMENT

At the end of the 2010–11 academic year, I had an hour-long conversation with John Jenkins on topics ranging from his views about philosophy at ND to circumstances surrounding the 2009 commencement. One surprise that emerged in this conversation was that President Obama was not the first person asked to be the 2009 commencement speaker. After the first person declined in the preceding November or December, feelers were sent out to Obama representatives in Chicago to determine whether the president might be interested. It turned out that he was, and the university announced his official acceptance on March 20, 2009.

Strong reactions ensued almost immediately, both positive and negative. Most graduating seniors were thrilled to hear that the newly elected president would address their commencement. A vast majority of faculty were pleased as well. Whereas faculty attendance at commencement exercises usually is relatively sparse, this year the university set up a lottery that admitted only about half of the faculty who were eager to attend. Alumni reaction was mixed. But given that about 54 percent of voting Catholics chose Obama in 2008, it seems likely that ND alumnus and former *Newsweek* religion editor Kenneth Woodward spoke for the majority in his *Washington Post* article welcoming the invitation.[28] As he put it, Woodward was "adamantly pro-life, independent as a voter—and greatly pleased that Obama has agreed to speak at my alma mater."

Negative responses were motivated for the most part by Obama's political stance on reproductive issues. As a carryover from Republican campaign tactics in 2004, the term "pro-abortion" was taken to be synonymous with "Democratic" in right-wing rhetoric. This, combined with the fact that he had recently lifted the ban on federal funding of embryonic stem cell research imposed by his Republican predecessor, meant that Barack Obama came to ND burdened with a partisan reputation of being the "most pro-abortion" president in U.S. history.

Different negative reactions came from different quarters. Most prominent from a church perspective was the reaction of local ordinary John D'Arcy, who within days after Obama's acceptance was announced released a statement saying that he would not attend the commencement.[29] Not surprisingly, the bishop saw the honorary degree for which the president was slated as a violation of the U.S. Catholic Bishops' mandate in 2004 that Catholic institutions should not honor those who act in defiance of the church's moral principles. A fact too seldom noted in this regard is that, although Bishop D'Arcy did not appear at the official commencement (he spoke at the alternative commencement instead), he gave a homily at the official Baccalaureate Mass the day before. On this occasion he said a number of favorable things about ND, among them that ND is "a great Catholic university" and that it remained "a privilege for him to be associated with it."[30]

Support for D'Arcy's stand began to grow among his fellow bishops, including several with prominent Catholic colleges and universities in their dioceses. By the time of the actual commencement, more than eighty bishops had publicly endorsed D'Arcy's position. The remaining roughly two hundred U.S. prelates remained mostly silent, for reasons about which one can only speculate.[31]

Although unmistakably negative, the public reaction of the dissenting bishops was measured and dignified. Comparably temperate was Professor Mary Ann Glendon's rejection of the 2009 Laetare Medal. Glendon had received an ND honorary degree in 1996, had taught Barack Obama at Harvard Law School, and was a former U.S. ambassador to the Vatican. She had been selected as Laetare Medalist well before Obama had been invited to speak, and was looking forward to receiving the actual medal on stage at commencement. In the meanwhile, unfortunately, ND had issued a list of "talking points" for its trustees to use in responding to criticism, two of which mentioned Glendon and made her feel that she was being exploited as a counterpoise to Obama's appearance.[32] She sent a letter to Fr. Jenkins declining the medal on April 27, just three weeks before the commencement.

Another group of actors in the commencement drama were the itinerant antiabortion agitators who set up camp on the university's perimeter. In sharp contrast with the responses of Professor Glendon and the bishops, that of the protestors on the periphery was raucous in the extreme. Trucks roamed the streets displaying pictures of aborted fetuses, protestors pushed baby carriages containing artificially bloodied dolls, bands of pedestrians carried anti-Obama posters, and a roaring airplane circled the university day after day towing banners with disgusting images. The general cacophony may have been intensified by the fact that the main organizers of the protest were vying for positions of prominence within the pro-life movement. The Center for Bio-Ethical Reform (CBR) was responsible for the horrendous images, and Randall Terry was egging on the pedestrian demonstrators. Despite hostile words they had exchanged previously, neither Terry nor CBR could pass up the opportunity to gain publicity by exposure in the national media. Other notable pro-life demonstrators on this occasion were Alan Keyes,[33] a black politician who claimed Obama was born in Kenya, and born-again-Christian Norma McCorvey, the "Jane Roe" of the 1973 *Roe vs. Wade* decision.

There were strident voices within the university as well. Charles Rice of the Law School, in a March 30, 2009, *Observer* article entitled "No Confrontation Necessary," suggested that Fr. Jenkins should "resign or be removed." In his more urbane manner, Ralph McInerny accused the administration of "sleeping with the enemy" and (alluding to priestly duplicity during the Indian wars) described Jenkins as a "white father" speaking with a "forked tongue." Ralph went on to praise students who boycotted the main commencement for refusing "to sup with the devil."[34]

No less insistent but more respectful was the reaction of several hundred students who objected to an Obama honorary degree. Dubbing themselves "NDResponse," this group requested support from CEC Director David Solomon in arranging an alternative to the official ND commencement. David complied by offering to pay all expenses out of his "Fund to Protect Human Life." With this financial backing, the students themselves took charge of organizing and managing the alternative events. They were assisted, however, by Elizabeth Kirk, then associate director of the CEC. Elizabeth is the wife of William Kirk, then associate vice-president for residence life. Bill Kirk was the only high-level ND administrator on the platform of the alternative commencement.[35]

From the perspective of NDResponse, everything on the appointed weekend went according to plan. On Saturday evening there was a Rosary in the Grotto said by Bishop D'Arcy, followed by Eucharistic Adoration in Alumni Hall chapel which continued through the night.

The following morning was auspicious for an outdoor ceremony. A makeshift platform had been assembled on the west end of the South Quad, perhaps a hundred feet in front of Rockne Memorial.[36] Lavishly bedecked with flowers, the platform was equipped with a podium, two recording microphones, and chairs for the platform party. No chairs were provided for the audience, although some brought their own. Somewhere between two and three thousand people attended.

The day's events began with an onstage Mass, celebrated by Fr. Kevin Russeau, CSC, and assisted by nine other priests. After Mass, several speakers, both lay and clerical, addressed the assembled crowd. Whether by plan or not, the "keynote" speaker turned out to be Fr. John Raphael, a ND alumnus and then principal of New Orleans' mostly black St. Augustine High School. Fr. Raphael's talk was loud and clear, delivered in a manner reminiscent of Martin Luther King Jr. Bishop D'Arcy, who had decided to attend at the last minute, gave a short and apparently extemporaneous talk with his arms leaning on the podium. This was the last of his twenty-five commencement speeches at ND. Perhaps because the wind was blowing in his face, Bishop D'Arcy's words were hard to understand. Even harder to understand was 1993 ND Law graduate Christopher Godfrey, the former New York Giants Super Bowl champion who founded Life Athletes (a group of sports stars dedicated to "virtue, abstinence, and respect for life"). To judge from his gestures, Godfrey's talk was mainly about Knute Rockne and football.

Featured speakers from the ND faculty were CSC priest Wilson Miscamble and David Solomon. Fr. Miscamble, a historian, spoke mainly about ND's storied past and the need for present-day ND to live up to its former promise. The final talk was given by David Solomon, one of the most engaging public speakers I have ever heard. Dressed in full academic garb, mortarboard and all, David began by inviting all attending ND faculty members up to the stage. According to his own recollection, about twenty professors responded, including fellow philosophers Fred Freddoso and John O'Callaghan. David spoke primarily in praise of NDResponse, students who endeavored to "speak truth to power" and, by that witness, to serve as a beacon to the rest of the university.

Circumstances surrounding the speeches of the alternative commencement were no less remarkable than the speeches themselves. For the first half-hour or so, the ceremony on the South Quad was attended by several security personnel, equipped with tear gas and handcuffs. The online video of Fr. Raphael's speech reminds viewers why such precautions were needed. Interspersed with images of the scattered audience and of Fr. Raphael himself are extensive shots of protests simultaneously underway just outside the university. We see people with bull horns, signs vilifying Obama, and pictures of aborted fetuses, all providing an unseemly visual background for the uninterrupted soundtrack of Fr. Raphael's speech. As the ceremony continues, however, the police officers move discreetly away from the quad, inasmuch as nothing about the congregation at the Mass itself proved remotely threatening.

The makeup of the audience was interesting in its own right. A large portion consisted of family groups, many seeming to have no direct connection with the university. Apart from an occasional faculty member in formal attire, few people with academic paraphernalia were evident. Although a fair number of graduating seniors attended, most came without cap and gown. Despite its billing as an alternative commencement, nothing about the occasion seemed to call for academic garb. Another notable fact about the audience is that it offered little sustained applause. In sharp contrast with what happened in the Joyce Center a few hours later, there was no suggestion of a standing ovation. Most people were standing throughout the ceremony, but that was because they had no chairs.

After the speeches on the South Quad, several hundred people gathered at the Grotto to hold a "Vigil for Life" in honor of the class of 2009. The grotto service consisted of a Rosary with reflections after each decade by Fr. Frank Pavone, the world renowned pro-life evangelist whom "Jane Roe" Norma McCorvey credited with guiding her into the Catholic Church. Following Fr. Pavone's reflections were hymns, pro-life prayers, and "official tassel-flipping" by the roughly twenty-five seniors in attendance who wore mortarboards. With this, the alternative commencement came to an end. About the same time, President Obama was beginning his speech in the Joyce Center.

THE OBAMA COMMENCEMENT: THREE SPEECHES

President Obama's speech was being revised up to the morning before delivery. Like other U.S. presidents of recent times, Obama relies heavily on speechwriters. The main speechwriter on this occasion was Jon Favreau, a graduate of the College of the Holy Cross in Worcester, Massachusetts. Favreau had been a student of David J. O'Brien, a history professor at Holy Cross specializing in Catholic political thought who later moved to Dayton University. O'Brien is a friend of ND historian Scott Appleby, currently Director of ND's Kroc Institute for International Peace Studies. At Fr. Jenkins's request, Appleby contacted O'Brien, who then contacted Favreau. As it turned out, ND exercised considerable influence on the content of Obama's commencement speech, with Appleby and Favreau in email contact from an early stage in its inception.[37]

One suggestion by Appleby which Favreau readily accepted was that President Obama acknowledge Fr. Hesburgh's work with the Civil Rights Commission and his contribution to the historical events that led to Obama's election as the nation's first black president. The result was an extended tribute, toward the end of Obama's speech, to Fr. Hesburgh and his work with the original Civil Rights Commission.

Less easy to work into the speech was Appleby's request that Obama say something to clarify his stance on health care and the Provider Refusal Rule, better known as the "conscience clause." Decreed by President Bush just days before he left office, this provision allows health care providers to refuse participation in procedures they find religiously or morally objectionable. Primarily at stake was whether Catholic hospitals would have to provide abortions and sterilizations to patients with federally funded insurance. Recently inaugurated President Obama had not yet taken a public stand on the matter, and ND officials were hopeful that he would use his commencement address as an occasion to voice support of the conscience-clause provision.

Although Appleby had requested earlier that Obama's speech say something about the conscience clause, the draft copy he received from Favreau the day before commencement still contained nothing specific about it. Appleby consulted Fr. Jenkins and his advisers immediately, and by 4:00 Saturday afternoon had replied to Favreau saying that the university was under fire for appearing to endorse Obama's pro-choice views and really needed a strong statement on the conscience clause. The final version of Obama's speech was emailed to Appleby Sunday morning at 10:00. Approximately four hours later, President Obama spoke the following words for the world to hear: "Let's honor the conscience of those who disagree with abortion, and draft a sensible conscience clause, and make sure that all of our health care policies are grounded in sound science and clear ethics, as well as respect for the equality of women." While still not as strong as ND wanted, this statement was enough to enable the university to say that it had given Obama a platform to reinforce the conscience provision. As Appleby told me later, even Cardinal George of Chicago, a vocal critic of Obama's visit up to that point, acknowledged that ND had "moved the ball forward" with Obama's speech.

Apart from occasional football games, no event I can recall from my more than fifty years at ND was more eagerly awaited than the 2009 commencement. In order to ensure a seat, I had volunteered to serve as Marshall for the A&L College. After leading A&L graduates and professors (those lucky enough to get tickets from the lottery) to their places, I took a seat right next to the platform, maybe twenty feet from front-center and less than ten from the chair reserved for my old friend, John Noonan. The packed auditorium was pulsating with anticipation.

President Obama entered the auditorium to thunderous applause that lasted until the entire platform party was seated. Following a rousing rendition of "America the Beautiful" and an invocation by graduating senior Adrienne Murphy, Provost Thomas Burish took over as master of ceremonies. The valedictorian's address, given by Ms. E. Brennan Bollman, lasted about fifteen minutes and was followed by a standing ovation. Provost Burish then passed out the honorary degrees. Obama's came first. In the official citation, he was lauded for being willing to enter into conversation with those who disagree with him. Again the audience arose in ovation.

Other honorary degree recipients that day were Randall T. Shepard of the Indiana Supreme Court; Don Michael Randel, president of the Andrew W. Mellon Foundation; Cindy Parseghian (daughter of former ND coach Ara) of ND's College of Science Advisory Council; Patrick Finneran, vice-president of Boeing Integrated Defense Systems; ND trustee Fritz L. Duda; and Purdue University president emeritus Steven Beering. An honorary Doctor of Laws was also conferred in absentia on Myles Brand, former president of Indiana University, Bloomington, and currently president of the National Collegiate Athletic Association, with which ND is so closely involved.[38]

University President John Jenkins's address came next. Unlike Obama, Fr. Jenkins wrote his own speech. But because controversy was already rampant, Jenkins had asked President Clinton's former press secretary, Mike McCurry, for tips on how to handle it. McCurry's advice was to avoid using the speech as an occasion to respond to specific attacks. In effect, the advice was to say what you want to say without yielding time to your opponents. And so, instead of fretting over the escalating attacks from outside, Jenkins had spent long hours sorting out what exactly he wanted to say.

Fr. Jenkins's commencement address was divided into three parts. First was his charge to the graduating seniors. The basic message was that they should help heal a world torn by division, avoiding pride in self and contempt for others. Easing "the hateful divisions between human beings is the supreme challenge of this age," he said, adding that if we can solve this problem, "we have a chance to come together and solve all the others."

Next was a call for reasoned dialogue as a means of resolving differences. As part of this call, President Jenkins quoted Pope Benedict XVI urging American Catholics to find inspiration in their religion "to pursue reasoned, responsible and respectful dialogue" in an effort to build a more humane society. Pope John Paul II was also quoted as saying that a Catholic university is meant to be "a primary and privileged place for a fruitful dialogue between the Gospel and culture." Fr. Jenkins added that the sort of dialogue that might accomplish this does not arise spontaneously. It rather is a process that requires "listening carefully and speaking honestly," abetted by "many acts of courtesy and gestures of respect."

In the final part of his address Fr. Jenkins turned directly to President Obama. "As we all know," he said, "a great deal of attention has surrounded President Obama's visit to Notre Dame." But less "attention has been focused on the president's decision to accept." This remark was followed by extended applause. He accepted, Jenkins continued, even though he knew that Notre Dame is "fully supportive of the Church's teaching on the sanctity of human life" and that "we oppose his policies on abortion and embryonic stem cell research" (applause). Whereas others might have been dissuaded for that reason, "President Obama is not someone who stops talking with those who differ with him" (applause, as Obama nods in agreement). "Mr. President: This is a principle we share" (applause).

Disagreements thus acknowledged, Fr. Jenkins begins a list of things about the president worthy of admiration and honor. He is a leader with "great respect for the role of faith and religious institutions in public life." As "the first African American to be elected president" (extended applause, marked by cheers and a few boos), "he has been a healer" in a country "deeply wounded by racial hatred." He has set an agenda for extending health care coverage to millions lacking it, for improving education of those who most need it, and for "promoting renewable energy for the sake of our economy, our security, and our climate" (applause). "He has declared the goal of a world without nuclear weapons" (applause), and "has pledged to accelerate America's fight against poverty . . . and to advance America's merciful work in fighting disease in the poorest places on earth" (applause).

"As commander-in-chief and as chief executive," Fr. Jenkins concludes, "he embraces with confidence both the burdens of leadership and the hopes of his country." "Ladies and Gentlemen: The President of the United States" (sustained applause, as Jenkins and Obama embrace).

President Obama advanced to the podium in front of a standing audience. "Thank you—thank you—thank you—please—thank you." The president began speaking before the applause had ended. (As the audience sat down, the camera focused on the stern face of a Secret Service agent in full academic garb standing directly behind him.) "Thank you, Fr. Jenkins, for that generous introduction. You are doing an outstanding job as president of this fine institution" (applause). "You have already said much of what I want to say" (laughter). "Good afternoon to Fr. Hesburgh, to Notre Dame trustees, to faculty, and to families. I am honored to be here today (applause, while the camera focuses on Fr. Ted seated in the audience) and grateful to all of you for allowing me to be part of your graduation.

"I also want to congratulate the class of 2009 for all of your accomplishments. And since this is Notre Dame . . ." At the mention of Notre Dame, three or four hecklers stood up and started shouting from seats high to the left of the speakers' platform. Before the camera could catch them, a handful of students, acting individually, stood up in protest, facing the intruders. Within seconds, the entire body of graduating seniors was standing up and shouting in unison "We are ND" (with an emphasis both on "We" and "ND"). Although an appreciable number of seniors had symbols on their mortarboards indicating support of the antiabortion movement, they too were pumping their fists in the air proclaiming their ND identity. A moment or two later, security forces ushered the intruders out of the building.

Completely unflapped, President Obama made an offhand remark about not being put off by uncomfortable situations (cheers from the audience), completed his interrupted sentence with some remarks about ND athletics, and got down to serious business. Given the great diversity in culture and belief in our ever-shrinking world, he told the graduates, we must find a way of reconciling these differences "to live together as one human family." The question we must face is how as individuals we can "remain firm in our principles and fight for what we consider right," all the while following Fr. Jenkins's advice not to demonize "those with just as strongly held convictions on the other side." And nowhere, he observed, does this question "come up more powerfully than on the issue of abortion."

Frankly acknowledging that the opposing sides on this issue "at some level . . . are irreconcilable," he urged that each side should make its case to the public "without reducing those with differing views to caricature." The debate will continue. But each side should speak with "open hearts," "open minds," and "fair-minded words." Being fair-minded, the president said, is "a way of life that has always been the Notre Dame tradition" (applause). In the words of Fr. Hesburgh, ND is both a "lighthouse" shining with traditional Catholic wisdom and a "crossroads . . . where . . . differences of culture and religion and conviction can coexist with friendship, civility, hospitality, and especially love." "And I want to join him and Fr. John in saying how inspired I am by the maturity and responsibility with which this class has approached the debate surrounding today's ceremony." Looking over the thousands of graduates seated before him, the president added: "You are an example of what Notre Dame is about." At this point, the entire audience rose to its feet and applauded for almost a minute.

The president then moved on to an account of his work in impoverished Chicago neighborhoods, inspired by Cardinal Archbishop Joseph Bernardin. Cardinal Bernardin, he said, was "congenial and gentle in his persuasion, always trying to bring people together, always trying to find common ground." Like Fr. Hesburgh's ND, Cardinal Bernardin "stood as both a lighthouse and a crossroads—unafraid to speak his mind on moral issues ranging from poverty . . . and abortion to the death penalty to nuclear war."

President Obama's speech drew to a close with the story of Fr. Hesburgh's work on the Civil Rights Commission that made it possible for a black man to be elected president. As he noted, it was the "twelve resolutions recommended by this commission that would ultimately become law in the Civil Rights Act of 1964." Frequently interrupted by cheers and sustained applause, Obama spoke of the commission's difficulties in finding places to meet in the South (because of black member J. Ernest Wilkins, then U.S. undersecretary of labor), of Hesburgh's flying them all to ND's retreat at Land O'Lakes, Wisconsin, and of their coming to agreement on key issues while fishing on the lake. When cheers following this story subsided, Obama summed it up saying: "They fished, and they talked, and they changed the course of history."

The lessons of Cardinal Bernardin and Fr. Hesburgh, he said in conclusion, should help us to work together and "shoulder each other's burdens," thus enabling America to "continue on its precious journey towards that more perfect union." "Congratulations, class of 2009. May God bless you, and may God bless the United States of America."

The crowd arose at this point for an extended ovation, with Fr. Jenkins clapping enthusiastically until the general applause ended. After the president's address, Provost Burish presented him with a copy of the picture, now hanging in Washington's National Gallery, of Martin Luther King Jr. and Fr. Hesburgh joining hands and singing "We Shall Overcome."

Next in order was the Laetare presentation. As already noted, Mary Ann Glendon had declined the medal a scant three weeks before commencement. Rather than drop this part from the ceremony, however, the administration invited the 1984 Laetare Medalist, the Honorable John Noonan, to give a Laetare-related address. Despite the short notice, Judge Noonan accepted.

Then eighty-two years old, Judge Noonan had a voice that was still resonant and a message that was timely. "As the president has so well put before you," he said, we face matters of moral urgency in "the turbulent modern world." There are some things on which most of us have reached moral agreement. "Genocide is wrong; torture is wrong (applause); slavery is wrong (applause)." These are "great moral causes where the truth ultimately prevailed."

However, there is another great moral debate in this country, he continued, which has yet to be resolved. It concerns "the inviolability of human life in a mother's womb, the rights of a woman with respect to her own body . . . and the role of government in a decision that is patently personal and significantly social." The matter of this debate, he said pointedly, is "too serious to be settled by pollsters and pundits . . . or by banners and slogans, pickets and placards." At the center of the debate "are the claims of conflicting consciences," those indispensable guides that govern our moral lives.

But "all consciences are not the same," and that is why we have different moral visions. "I am here to confirm," said Judge Noonan, "that we live in a country . . . where our president is a man of conscience" (applause). Moreover, we can rejoice "that we live in a country where dialogue, however difficult, is doable" (applause). We can rejoice with you, class of 2009, "as your voices join the dialogue and declare your own consciences on the urgent moral matters that will be settled only when they are settled right."

Never once in Judge Noonan's fifteen minute speech did he use the word "abortion" or the divisive terms "pro-life" and "pro-choice." Neither did he mention Mary Ann Glendon by name, referring to her only as a friend who "is not here today, whose absence I regret." Equally balanced between liberal and conservative, this speech called on all interested parties to engage in dialogue and work together. Echoing Obama's campaign mantra, he concluded "Yes! We can work together, serenely secure in that trust that the truth will out!" (applause, as the platform party stands followed by an uncertain audience).

Ceremonies ended with the official conferring of degrees by deans of the several colleges. Provost Burish thanked both President Jenkins and President Obama for their unstinting participation, and declared the commencement officially over. The platform party descended to sustained applause and vanished into the bowels of the Joyce Center. President Obama, attended by his Secret Service agents, soon was on his way back to the South Bend Regional Airport.

Neil Delaney encountered Fr. Hesburgh on their way out of the building. As Neil recalls, Fr. Ted said he considered what had just happened to be "one of the greatest events in the history of the university."

TIME PRESENT AND TIME FUTURE

The President's Faculty Dinner has been held on the Tuesday evening after commencement for as long as I remember. This is the occasion on which promotions are announced, awards conferred, and the faculty sips wine while listening to the president reminisce. I had attended only sporadically during recent years. But I made a point of being present on May 19, 2009.

Hundreds of faculty and their guests had been ushered into the North Dining Hall and were chatting at their seats awaiting President Jenkins's arrival. When he appeared around 7:30, everyone in the room arose and began cheering and clapping. His face was aglow with appreciation. I had never seen a Roman collar juxtaposed to such a radiant face. Moving confidently across the room, he proceeded directly to the table where I was sitting with a dozen or so other philosophers. He shook hands with all of us and thanked us for our support. The applause continued for another several minutes while he greeted people at nearby tables and took his assigned place at the front of the room. The dinner itself occupied a good two hours. The part I remember best, however, was the exuberant support shown a fellow philosopher whose interchange with the nation's president had made a lasting mark in ND's history. ND no longer was just a place with an outstanding football program. It had become a place where major problems of contemporary society could be seriously addressed on a public stage.

Although Fr. Jenkins might reject the comparison, I regard his current presidential role as similar to that of the statesman in Plato's dialogue by that name. In this dialogue, Plato argues that a state governed by its hawkish sector would constantly be fighting, whereas one governed by docile citizens would be in constant danger of annihilation. Neither condition is compatible with a robust and healthy social order. A statesman's primary task, accordingly, is to weave "hawks" and "doves" together into the fabric of a well-ordered and durable state.

Similarly, a university dominated by conservative Catholicism would subordinate acquiring new knowledge to defending old doctrines, while one dominated by Catholic liberals would risk losing its Catholic identity. John Jenkins's most critical task as ND's president is to steer the university on a course that avoids both unacceptable outcomes. The opposing persuasions must work together for the university to flourish, and Fr. Jenkins's role as president is to do the best he can to foster this cooperation.

Toward the end of our aforementioned conversation in the spring of 2011, I asked Fr. John whether he has any thoughts of returning to the Philosophy Department when his term as president is over. His quick response, with a laugh, was that he would love to return. He misses the life of a full-time philosopher. Although he enjoys his current job, he said he enjoys teaching every bit as much.

I then asked him for reflections he might want to share about great moments in the department's history. After a brief mention of its Thomistic origins, he proceeded directly to the time he first arrived in the early 1970s. Fr. Ernan McMullin, of course, had been chair from 1965 to 1972, followed by Neil Delaney and Richard Foley. He remembered both Delaney and Foley with appreciative comments. But among ND philosophers, Fr. John recalled, it was Ernan McMullin who had put the department on the map of American philosophy. It was Fr. Ernan's "vision of a philosophy department appropriate to a Catholic university," moreover, that had set the department on the path that leads to the present.

Thus prompted, I asked Fr. John what he thought of ND's Philosophy Department today. "An interesting question," he remarked, and paused reflectively before answering. "Philosophy is an important department at ND," he said. "It always has been and will continue to be." When he first came, he recalled, the department was characterized by "a healthy pluralism." Now it's mainly analytic. During its pluralist days it was more historical, which he tended to favor. "Personally," he said, "I find analytic philosophy a bit stale the way it's done today." There are some great philosophers at ND now, he hastened to add, and they're doing what good philosophers do in other universities. But the way "philosophy is done here today is not clearly better for ND than the way it was done in the 1970s."

This led to a discussion of the role of rankings in departmental affairs. "The rankings game," he said, "is something you can't ignore." But neither can you "let it determine who you are and what you do." Rankings provide only "a one-dimensional measure." The department needs another standard to shape its self-conception and to serve as a gauge of what it accomplishes. It is particularly important, Fr. John added, that we have an overview of philosophy's role in undergraduate education and that we understand the department's responsibility in that regard.

I then remarked that the department's external evaluators had said essentially the same thing a decade earlier. Instead of focusing on national rankings, they said, the department should focus on its mission as part of a Catholic institution. In particular, it should become more reflective about the role of its two-course requirement. Thus reminded, Fr. John nodded his head and expressed emphatic agreement.

Fr. John's agreement with the advice of the external reviewers struck me as curiously prescient. In the year 2000, the department had been advised to downplay the competition for national rankings and to pay more attention to how it handles its undergraduate requirements. In early 2011, the university president, himself a philosopher, expressed his preference for the same priorities. Sooner or later, I cannot help thinking, the department will see the wisdom of these revised priorities and act accordingly.

Disengaging from the ranking game does not imply reverting to the posture of the 1950s, when the department paid little attention to what was happening at major secular universities. Nor should it occasion a lack of interest in how ND's graduate program compares in quality with programs at peer institutions. The point is that faculty scholarship and graduate training should be judged on intrinsic merit, rather than on external impressions of professional prominence like those that drive the Leiter reports.

Paying more attention to the rationale of its two-course requirement, in turn, does not mean reverting to a curriculum based on the Thomism of earlier years. Courses in Thomism obviously should be offered as options, but a wide range of other courses should be involved as well. Rather than inculcating a particular worldview, their purpose would be to help students think philosophically for themselves about matters of faith.

Recalibrating the department's required course offerings, moreover, does not require that only Catholics teach the courses in question. For one thing, since dozens of such courses would be taught each term, there probably would not be enough Catholic teachers in the department to go around.[39] For another, there are non-Catholics in the department who can teach such courses no less effectively than their Catholic colleagues. For a department member to teach these courses, it should be required only that he or she be well versed in the history of philosophy and be in sympathy with the university's Catholic mission.

It is not unduly speculative to predict that the future of ND's Philosophy Department hinges on how it responds to this call for a change in priorities. There is room in the profession today for a strong-minded and well-balanced department that is guided by its own internal purposes rather than by the perceptions of outsiders with other interests. We at ND are in a position to become such a department. And if we take the lead, philosophy departments at other institutions may follow.

To cope with these issues, however, the department will have to forge a new sense of identity. It will have to realign itself with a mission in view that is distinctive enough to bring its various factions together. In effect, it will have to take a lesson from Fr. Jenkins's leadership of the university and find a way to restore harmony between its liberal and conservative sectors.

HEARTWOOD AND SAPWOOD, BOTH PARTS OF A LIVING TREE

There have been conservatives and liberals in the Philosophy Department since at least the 1940s. Conservative Thomists during that time included Herman Reith and Vincent Smith, with Leo Ward and John FitzGerald in the liberal wing. These men worked well together and enjoyed each other's company, probably unaware of the distinction they instantiated. This rapport continued through the era of pluralism, with ready cooperation between conservatives like John Oesterle and Joseph Bobik and liberals like Ernan McMullin and David Burrell. Even Ralph McInerny, for a time, was part of this congenial mix. It was during the early 1960s, after all, that Ralph and Ernan were working together in preparation of the "Philosophy in the Age of Christian Renewal" conference, inspired by what Ralph then referred to as "the wisdom of Pope John XXIII."[40]

But tensions between these two wings of the department began to arise in the aftermath of Vatican II. First came the "Land O'Lakes statement" in 1967, previously described (quoting ND historian Philip Gleason) as "a declaration of independence from the [Catholic] hierarchy."[41] Ralph was horrified by this statement, beginning a period of alienation from his liberal colleagues which seemed to intensify as the years went by. Then in 1979 Ralph became director of the Jacques Maritain Center, which led to his own "declaration of independence" from the Philosophy Department itself. Liberal and conservative Catholics thenceforth tended to work at cross-purposes, to the distinct misfortune of the department as a whole.

Recourse to an analogy can help make the nature of this misfortune clear. Oak saplings are highly vulnerable in early days of growth. They can be stepped on, uprooted, or eaten by herbivores. As they mature, however, they escape these hazards by developing a hard core that gains strength as the tree grows larger. Because of its interior location, this stable core is known as the tree's heartwood. Heartwood is a source of structural stability, helping protect the tree from destruction by outside forces. It is through its sapwood, on the other hand, that the tree performs most of its vital functions. Located between the heartwood and the bark, a tree's sapwood conveys water from the roots to the leaves and stores nutrients needed for further growth. The sapwood of a living tree is constantly replenished, sustaining its vital functions as long as the tree remains alive.

Heartwood and sapwood work together for the good of the tree. If either fails in its proper function, the tree will soon die.[42] And neither can survive the death of the tree. The healthy function of one part thus requires that the other part function in a healthy manner as well. Heartwood and sapwood, quite literally, are interdependent.

Conservative Catholicism corresponds to the heartwood of this analogy. The more solid its conservative base, the more resistant the church at large to disruptive influences from outside. Maintaining a solid base is the joint function of the magisterium (popes and bishops) and of lay people dedicated to strict observance of the magisterium's teachings. In terms of the analogy, the church's heartwood is composed of conservatives like Ralph who routinely translate church doctrine into practices of daily life. People like Ralph help preserve the church's identity as it adapts to changing times and social conditions.

Like all other living things in the world, however, the church itself changes with its changing environment. While its doctrines remain mostly stable, thanks to heartwood persistence, its interactions with the rest of the world are in constant flux. Keeping the church abreast with changing circumstances is the role of the sapwood. Without sapwood, the church would lose sensitivity to the world around it. And without this sensitivity the church would ossify and eventually die.[43]

The analogy of heartwood and sapwood applies not only to the church at large but also to Catholic universities. George Bernard Shaw famously remarked that a Catholic university is a contradiction in terms. What Shaw presumably had in mind was a university completely dominated by heartwood Catholicism. Heartwood Catholicism is preoccupied with doctrine and orthodoxy, to which it tends to subordinate other matters relevant to a vital faith. To the extent that the heartwood factor is dominant, it impedes the full academic freedom essential to a mature university. Given this understanding of a Catholic university, Shaw's well-known remark seems basically on target. An institution dominated by heartwood orthodoxy probably would not qualify as a full-fledged university.

Comparably famous in Catholic circles, however, is Fr. Hesburgh's observation that a Catholic university is where the church does its thinking. In Fr. Hesburgh's ideal university, although heartwood is a necessary part of the mix, inquiry proceeds without restriction by doctrinal boundaries. The university in which the church does its thinking is one in which heartwood and sapwood play complementary roles. Sapwood engages the freedom typical of a good secular university, while heartwood holds the university true to its Catholic identity. Heartwood's distinctive contribution to the academic part of the enterprise is to put forward topics of inquiry with specifically Catholic significance (e.g., the interaction between faith and reason). But the university imposes no antecedent requirements on the direction responsible inquiry into those topics might take.

Let us return to the interaction between heartwood and sapwood in the Philosophy Department itself. Up through the mid-1960s, by way of brief review, heartwood and sapwood sectors of the department worked together harmoniously. With Ralph's amassing of heartwood resources in the Maritain Center later in that decade, however, a split developed that persisted into the new millennium. When Ralph left the Maritain Center in 2006, heartwood leadership passed to David Solomon in the Center for Ethics and Culture. The split continued through 2009, showing itself in the unrest surrounding President Obama's visit.

Given the major challenges ahead, it is high time for heartwood and sapwood partisans to set aside their grievances. One urgent challenge is to break the hold of Leiter rankings on department deliberations. Another is to bring the department's required courses in line with the university's Catholic mission. Success in both tasks will depend on all sectors of the department working together with a unified purpose. In particular, it will require that both heartwood and sapwood Catholics heed the advice of the 2009 commencement speakers to start working together with open hearts and open minds. If the two sectors continue to work at cross-purposes, this will only exacerbate the conditions that led to this unhappy predicament in the first place.

Along with others in the department, of course, Ralph was an instigator of this predicament. He regrettably is no longer here to help set matters right. Yet Ralph offered a few canny hints, in the months before his death, about how the predicament might be resolved. As a public figure, he was still outspoken in his heartwood opposition to President Obama's being given an honorary degree. In the privacy of his personal life, nonetheless, there were signs that he was beginning to reach out across partisan barriers.

One sign was an incident involving South Bend's Catholic Worker community. People familiar with church politics will recognize the Catholic Worker movement, founded by pacifist Dorothy Day, as typifying a left-wing branch of Catholic social activism. Yet Ralph provided significant financial support to that community in the year or two before he died. Michael Baxter, an ND theologian and prominent community member, remembers telling Ralph that his group was in dire need of $15,000 to pay down a construction debt. Without further ado, Ralph stepped to his desk and wrote out a check for the entire amount.[44] Nor was this Ralph's only support of the Catholic Worker cause. Baxter recalls an earlier contribution accompanied by a note, "written in the handwriting of an aging man well aware of what lay ahead," on which were penned the words: "Pray for an old sinner." This benevolence on Ralph's part was an act of Christian charity, bespeaking friendship transcending ideological boundaries.

Another little-known gesture on Ralph's part might be thought of as an act of prudence, sometimes typified as the "mother of all virtues." To no one's surprise, Ralph did not attend the official commencement where President Obama received his honorary degree. But he did not attend the alternative commencement either, thereby disallowing that event any symbolic value it might have gained by his presence.[45] Since Ralph already was struggling with esophageal cancer, the natural supposition was that he was too ill to attend. What is not commonly known, however, is that he sat though the entire Graduate School commencement ceremony the previous day (followed by an outside reception) at which his doctoral advisee Patrick Gardner received his PhD.[46] My surmise is that Ralph had realized that he was not strong enough for two extended ceremonies in a row. The implication seems to be that he judged loyalty to his student a better cause than symbolic support of an overtly partisan event.

These episodes culled from Ralph's declining months are merely anecdotal, and subject to various interpretations. The interpretation I prefer ties in with the words on the last page of his novel *Gate of Heaven*. The words are recalled as having been spoken by Father Cullen, the recently deceased founder of the ill-fated Society of St. Brendan. This wise old man is portrayed as urging those left behind to give up on failed intentions that have no chance of success. The words Ralph puts in Father Cullen's mouth are: "Let go. Who can guarantee the results and consequences of our efforts? The living write a story unreadable by them, entering and exiting without knowledge of the ultimate script. It does not matter. Let go, let go." Ralph's dominant intention throughout his adult life had been to win the day for heartwood orthodoxy, and this intention willy-nilly had fallen short. As his life drew to a close, it was time to let go. Redemption, one might think, for a proud warrior like Ralph, could amount to letting go of vain intentions.

As a warrior for orthodoxy, Ralph's hopes may have been colored by a nostalgia for earlier, perhaps simpler, times. David Solomon tells a story about visiting Ralph during his last days in the hospital. Ralph asked David to go to his house and bring back his copy of St. Louis de Montfort's *The Secrets of the Rosary*. The book had Ralph's name inscribed on the title page, but in unfamiliar handwriting. When David asked Ralph about this, Ralph replied that he had signed the book after buying it with money received on his eleventh birthday. Eighty-year-old Ralph had returned to devotional reading that once fed the simple faith of an eleven-year-old boy.

Nostalgia looks backward, and holds one to the past. Letting go can free one to look ahead. On the day before he died (the feast of Saint Thomas) Ralph wrote his final words on a piece of paper in the presence of his family.[47] These words were "I commend my soul to God." With these words, one may believe, Ralph broke the hold of the past and turned his vision to what comes next.

Ralph died on January 29, 2010. Ernan McMullin, the standard-bearer of Ralph's sapwood opposition, died a year and a few days later. The one task remaining before I relinquish the story to other narrators is to recount the events surrounding Ernan's memorial Mass.

Epilogue
Ernan's Memorial Mass

Synne is behovely
but alle shalle be wele

[All thynge] and alle maner
of thynge shalle be wele.
—Julian of Norwich, *A Book of Shewings*

Ernan officially retired from the university in 1994 at the age of sixty-nine, but retained his previous office in Decio Faculty Hall. His home then was at the end of Oak Park Drive in South Bend, where he had lived for over twenty years. In 2001 he moved with the department to another office in newly constructed Malloy Hall, occupying a space on the first floor to avoid walking up stairs.

As part of the ceremony marking the opening of Malloy Hall, the university had granted Ernan an honorary degree. Other dignitaries receiving honorary degrees on this occasion were his friend Bas van Fraassen of Princeton, well-known Cardinal Avery Dulles of Fordham, and liberation theologian Fr. Gustavo Gutiérrez, also of ND. At the time, Fr. Gutiérrez and Ernan were the only faculty granted ND honorary degrees while still in residence.

Although retired, Ernan remained active in departmental affairs as long as he occupied the office in Malloy. He attended faculty meetings, spent time in the Reilly Center, and entertained graduate students in his home and elsewhere. Then within months after Fr. Malloy resigned as president in 2005, Ernan's ties with the university were mysteriously severed. Colleagues in Malloy were puzzled to find his office vacated overnight. He put his house up for sale within weeks thereafter, moving it quickly in mid-2006 before the market collapsed. Furniture had to be disposed of, books had to be packed, and letters of fond memory had to be shredded. The more laborious of these tasks were completed with the help of former colleagues from various departments in the university.

Ernan then set off for an apartment in St. Paul, Minnesota, which had been rented with the help of longtime friends Dick and Annette Conklin. Dick had been ND's associate vice-president of university relations until he retired in 2001. Annette is the sister of Anita Pampusch, who had received a PhD under Ernan's direction in 1972 and who served as president of nearby St. Catherine's College from 1984 to 1997. Dick Conklin is one of my two primary sources of information about Ernan's time in the Twin Cities.

Ernan's apartment was a ten-minute drive from the Minneapolis-St. Paul International Airport. Proximity to the airport was important, inasmuch as he continued to give talks around the country and still enjoyed going to professional meetings. Before long, Ernan had established a travel routine to which he adhered for the rest of his life. Home base during fall and spring was his St. Paul apartment. Most of his academic travel took place during these two seasons. Between trips there was time for frequent social interchanges with the Conklins and other close friends in the Twin Cities area. On Sunday Ernan would go to Mass in the largely African American parish of St. Peter Claver, where Fr. Kevin McDonough was pastor.

The two priests first met when Fr. McDonough was vicar general of the Archdiocese of St. Paul and Minneapolis. Ernan had approached Fr. McDonough to "give notice of his residence" in the diocese, but did not request "ecclesiastical authorization for ministerial work" such as saying Mass in public.[1] The two subsequently became firm friends and met periodically for dinner and conversation. Fr. McDonough is my other main source of information about Ernan's life in the Twin Cities.

Ernan spent winters and summers during this time in the more temperate climate of Northern Ireland. Ernan's sister Maire and her husband (a veterinarian) had built a house on a hill overlooking Donegal Bay, and later added an apartment for Ernan's use. Maire once had been women's golf champion of Ireland, but recently had begun showing signs of dementia and did not leave the house frequently. It so happened that her husband died about the time Ernan sold his house in South Bend. So during the time Ernan was in Donegal, brother and sister set up housekeeping together. Ernan would go shopping and do routine maintenance, while Maire did the cooking and provided loving companionship. According to David Burrell, my informant on this phase of Ernan's life, daily practice of the household included a Mass said by Ernan before dinner and a glass of wine together at 10:00 in the evening. These home Masses, David said, were a great comfort to Ernan, who missed saying Mass for larger congregations after leaving South Bend.

The sad fact of the matter is that by this time Ernan's faculties had diminished significantly. During the last year or two of his life, his hearing loss progressed so rapidly that he cut back on conferences and spent more and more time with his family in Donegal. His memory for details also began to falter, and his back problems (which dated from the 1960s) progressed to the point of requiring treatment at the Mayo Clinic. But his power of intellect remained as clear as his vision. The audiotapes he dictated for me in 2010 are no less sharp and to the point than his comments at colloquia some forty years earlier. And as far as I know, he never had trouble reading without glasses.

In his prime, Ernan McMullin was one of the most captivating human beings I have known. To borrow a phrase he sometimes used to describe Fr. Hesburgh, this Irish priest from Donegal could "charm a bird out of a tree." To quote again from his Maynooth College obituary, the "humorous twinkle in his eyes" was often visible from "the remotest rows of a lecture hall."[2] The lilt and brogue of his speech were such, I remember thinking, that he could mesmerize an audience just by reading from a phone book. There was something enthralling about his personal presence, whether in speaking before a group or in private interchange.

I recall personal conversations with Ernan in which he would advance within a foot of where I was standing. This struck me instinctively as a violation of personal space, prompting me to retreat as quickly as I could without appearing impolite. Although some women reacted as I did, there were also some who had the opposite reaction. This might help explain why Ernan formed so many close relationships with women. He had a deep love for opera, and was frequently seen escorting one or another female friend to musical performances.

Ernan's charisma was also evident in his relationships with children, particularly those with developmental problems. He was involved for almost three decades with the L'Arche community in South Bend, beginning sometime in the 1970s. The local branch met first in Moreau Seminary, and later in the Logan Center for people with disabilities. Sometimes Ernan would officiate at Mass, and sometimes he would come just to offer companionship. According to a friend of mine who was also involved, Ernan was "wonderful with handicapped people—so gentle, so loving, so pastoral." Another friend tells of walking with Ernan around St. Joseph's Lake when a group of children with Down syndrome came up shouting "Father, Father" as they rushed into his arms. As part of his funeral announcement in early February 2011, Ernan's family encouraged people who wished to send memorial donations to Down Syndrome Ireland.

Although he never had a parish of his own, Ernan functioned in pastoral roles for numerous ND faculty and students.[3] He baptized many faculty children, including a son from my first marriage. In a eulogy appearing in the 2011 issue of *Notre Dame Magazine,* Star Trek actor Sean Griffin ('65) recalls how Ernan officiated at baptisms, weddings, and funerals for three generations of the Griffin family. "The amazing thing about him," Griffin relates, "was that as brilliant as he was, he was also a . . . compassionate man and incredible listener." Ernan loved life, he loved children, and (said Griffin) "he loved my folks and family—with all our flaws and imperfections, he never judged any of us." Fr. McDonough gives similar testimony in telling me that he "never heard Ernan speak in criticism of anyone but himself."

I have had numerous conversations with Fr. David Burrell about the final years of Ernan's life, including the circumstances of his move to the Twin Cities. As may be recalled, David was one of Ernan's main allies in shaping the pluralistic department of the 1960s. David thinks that Ernan's leaving the university was "the best thing that ever happened to him."[4] His reason for thinking this is that "Notre Dame asks so much of people that leaving its centripetal intensity can often free one to become oneself." I have similar thoughts, but mine go back to an interview with Ernan recorded for the television series *Closer to Truth*.[5]

One of Ernan's themes in this interview is that we go before a judging God with a "tapestry" amounting to what we have made of our lives. The tapestry of every life is woven under certain limitations, such as poverty, cultural conditions, and various addictions. But we are judged, Ernan said, not by a checklist of vices and virtues, but by what we have made of the gifts we are given. If what we have done with our lives is found pleasing, then we are judged worthy of God's timeless presence. Heaven, Ernan suggests, is a state of beatific vision, which is the ultimate state of everyone whose tapestry God looks on favorably. I like to think that the events surrounding Ernan's death helped make his tapestry worthy of a favorable final judgment. Speculation aside, Fr. McDonough summed it up well by remarking that Ernan "was grateful for many opportunities and mercies shown him, and died in peace."

Ernan McMullin died on February 8, 2011, as a result of a thoracic aneurysm suffered two days earlier at his sister's house in Mountcharles, Donegal. He had spent Thanksgiving with family in Washington state and Christmas with friends in Minnesota. On his way back to Donegal in late December, he began experiencing severe pain in his lower back and remained housebound until being taken to hospital on Sunday, February 6. Soon after he arrived at Letterkenny Hospital, the pain moved to his upper back and he went into respiratory arrest. Early Monday morning he returned to consciousness and his heartbeat strengthened. He spent a brief time sharing memories with immediate family. Then vital signs progressively weakened. His family gave permission to remove life-support on early Thursday morning.

Ernan passed in the presence of ten family members, who held his hand, stroked his forehead, and cried for the happy times they had shared together. His remains lay at rest in his room at Mountcharles until being moved for the funeral Mass at St. Agatha Church near Donegal town. He was buried next to his parents on Saturday, February 12, 2011.

Among the events surrounding Ernan's death was a memorial Mass held at ND on March 3, 2011. The Mass was organized by former chair Paul Weithman, acting both on his own behalf and on behalf of the Philosophy Department. Recognizing the importance of scheduling it on a weekday after working hours, Paul also realized that use of Sacred Heart Basilica was ruled out by the 5:15 Mass held there each weekday of the term. As he told me afterwards, however, he received full cooperation from the Basilica's rector, who made available the chapel of newly completed Ryan Hall. The Mass was scheduled for 5:45 of the designated day. Fr. David Burrell agreed to officiate.

After the Mass, there was a reception in the nearby Eck Visitors' Center, followed by a party (by invitation) at David and Mary Lou Solomon's house that went on past midnight. David Solomon was the department's most outspoken advocate of heartwood orthodoxy after the death of Ralph McInerny, and Fr. David's sapwood views were equally well known. Despite previous disagreements, however, the two Davids were able to collaborate on an event that all parties concerned found edifying and congenial. Ernan surely would have been pleased, since cooperation of this sort between heartwood and sapwood is something he advocated all along.

Ryan chapel seats about 240 people, and was filled almost to capacity before I arrived at 5:40. Upon entering the chapel, I spotted a seat in the front row to the left of the altar (from the celebrant's perspective) and went to it immediately. While sitting down, I noticed Fr. John Jenkins seated directly to my left and David and Mary Lou Solomon to my right in the row behind. As David remarked to me afterward, in order to see Fr. Burrell at the alter he had to look between my head and that of the university's president. Fr. Burrell had flown in from England that morning, and would fly back to Uganda the following day. Seated beside the altar was ninety-three-year-old Fr.

Hesburgh, whom Fr. Burrell had helped onto the dais before the service began.

Readers at the Mass were Ernan's sister, Ailis, and Ani Aprahamian of ND's Physics Department, with whom Ernan often stayed during recent visits to South Bend. The Prayer of the Faithful was written and delivered by Sr. Kathleen Cannon, associate provost under Tim O'Meara and current associate dean of the College of Science. Music was provided by the ND Folk Choir, which sang in both English and Gaelic.

Fr. Burrell's brief homily touched on Ernan's Christian faith, his "penetrating philosophical wit," his love of opera, and the joy he found in being with family. Coming in for special note was the "modest yet comfortable home" of his sister Maire that overlooks Donegal Bay. This is the place to which Ernan gravitated, the homily continued, "when time at Notre Dame and South Bend had summarily run out."

Fr. Hesburgh's eulogy came next. Fr. Ted was one of Ernan's real-life heroes. And Fr. Ted admired Ernan in turn as the person who, perhaps more than anyone else, had helped realize Fr. Ted's goal of making ND a great research university. On Ernan's last visit to South Bend before his death, he had asked for and received Fr. Ted's blessing. According to one of Ernan's confidants who confided in me later, Ernan was almost beside himself with joy during the hours after that happened. Reflecting on this event afterward, it strikes me unmistakably as redemption in the making.

Fr. Ted's voice was firm, but both his eyesight and his memory were unreliable. Speaking without notes, he gave his own version of how he and Ernan first met. As he tells it, their first meeting was in Ireland when Ernan was working with Erwin Schrödinger in the newly founded Dublin Institute for Advanced Studies. Ernan had grease on his face, was dressed in dirty coveralls, and was working on the construction of a nuclear reactor. I had heard this version of their meeting during a previous conversation with Fr. Ted and had checked it with Ernan afterwards. According to Ernan, they first met in Louvain during one of Fr. Ted's recruiting trips. Although Ernan did have contact with Schrödinger in Dublin, the only apparatus he worked on there was a cosmic ray detector. And he never went to work in dirty clothing.

Despite a few discrepancies of this sort, however, Fr. Ted's memories of Ernan were fond and appreciative. Ernan was a fine philosopher, a devoted colleague, and a good priest. Fr. Ted found occasion several times to emphasize that last assessment. As I gathered from conversations afterward, a number of people in the congregation took special note of that repeated emphasis.

After wine and wafers were brought to the altar and consecrated, Fr. Burrell realized that he needed help distributing them. The reader will recall that Fr. Jenkins and I were seated in the front row directly next to the altar. Quite spontaneously, Fr. Burrell asked Fr. Jenkins to help with the hosts and deputized me to join Ernan's niece Petria as cup minister. Fr. Jenkins and Petria took stations to the left of the altar, while I stood with Fr. Burrell to the right. My cup was almost drained while there were members of the Folk Choir still waiting to receive it, but perhaps some consecrated moisture reached their lips nonetheless.

Following communion, the choir sang a traditional Irish prayer. The memorial Mass ended with a pro forma rendition of "Notre Dame, Our Mother," celebrating the tenderness of the Lady atop the Golden Dome and the glory of the university it symbolizes. More than fifty years in its presence had left me no more in awe of the Golden Dome than when I arrived in 1958. But I joined the singing anyway, and managed to avoid cracking on the final high note.

Philosophy Faculty, 1950–2010

(with institutions granting PhDs, or comparable degrees, where applicable)*

Present in 1950

Anderson, James F. (Toronto)	1948–55
Boyle, Fr. Jerome M., CSC	1945–52, 1966–75
Brennan, Fr. Thos. James, CSC (Gregorian)	1931–73
Brennan, Fr. Thos. Joseph, CSC (Notre Dame)	1946–63
Broughal, Fr. Lawrence V., CSC	1920–51
Caponigri, A. Robert (Chicago)	1946–81
Chroust, Anton-Hermann (Munich)	1946–72
Denissoff, Fr. Elias (Louvain)	1948–58
FitzGerald, John James (Louvain)	1937–77
Glanville, John (Notre Dame)	1949–54
Johnston, Herbert L. (Toronto)	1948–77
Kreilkamp, Karl (Catholic Univ.)	1946–58
Leahy, Fr. James, CSC	1939–55
McAvoy, Fr. Bernard L., CSC	1950–52, 1964–66
Miltner, Fr. Charles C., CSC (Gregorian)	1922–52
Moore, Fr. Philip S., CSC (Catholic Univ.)	1933–52
Morrison, John J. (Notre Dame)	1947–56
Mullahy, Fr. Bernard I., CSC (Laval)	1939–55
Mullally, Joseph P.	1943–51
O'Grady, Daniel C. (Ottawa)	1926–56
O'Reilly, Fr. Peter	1948–60
Phelan, Fr. Gerald B. (Louvain)	1946–52

Reith, Fr. Herman R., CSC (Laval)	1945–81	
Riter, Fr. Regis H., CSC	1949–60	
Roemer, William F. (Notre Dame)	1922–59	
Scanlon, Fr. William S., CSC	1949–51	
Smith, Vincent E. (Catholic Univ.)	1950–60	
Thompson, Richard J. (Toronto)	1948–51	
Ward, Fr. Leo R., CSC (Catholic Univ.)	1928–63	
Woodward, Fr. Robert, CSC	1949–51	

New Arrivals	Arrivals' Years in Department	Departures
	1951	
Evans, Joseph (Notre Dame)	1951–79	Broughal, Fr. Lawrence V., CSC
		Mullally, Joseph P.
		Scanlon, Fr. William S., CSC
		Thompson, Richard J.
		Woodward, Fr. Robert, CSC
	1952	
Golebiewski, Fr. Casimir (Kraków)	1952–54	Boyle, Fr. Jerome M., CSC
Havey, Fr. William, CSC (Gregorian)	1952–60	McAvoy, Fr. Bernard L., CSC (Gregorian)
		Miltner, Fr. Charles C., CSC
		Moore, Fr. Philip S., CSC
		Phelan, Fr. Gerald B.
	1953	
Boarman, Fr. Glenn, CSC	1953–61	
Pouillon, Fr. Henri, OSB (Louvain)	1953–56	
	1954	
McMullin, Fr. Ernan (Louvain)	1954–57, 1961–94	Glanville, John
Oesterle, John (Laval)	1954–77	Golebiewski, Fr. Casimir
	1955	
Bochenski, Fr. Joseph I. M., OP (Anglicum)	1955–56	Anderson, James F.

Marrero, Alvin	1955–58	Leahy, Fr. James, CSC
		Mullahy, Fr. Bernard I., CSC

1956

Bobik, Joseph (Notre Dame)	1956–2009	Bochenski, Fr. Joseph I. M., OP
McInerny, Ralph (Laval)	1956–2009	Morrison, John J.
		O'Grady, Daniel C.
		Pouillon, Fr. Henri, OSB

1957

Downs, Fr. Richard J., CSC	1957–61	McMullin, Fr. Ernan
Fisk, Milton (Yale)	1957–63	
FitzGerald, John Joseph (Tulane)	1957–66	
Nielsen, Harry (Nebraska)	1957–68	
O'Halloran, Fr. James A., CSC	1957–62	
Sobocinski, Boleslaw (Warsaw)	1957–77	

1958

Buckley, Fr. James, CSC	1958–68	Denissoff, Fr. Elias
Sayre, Kenneth (Harvard)	1958–	Kreilkamp, Karl
Thomas, Fr. Ivo, OP	1958–59	Marrero, Alvin

1959

Manier, Edward (St. Louis)	1959–2007	Roemer, William F.
Weiher, Fr. Charles, CSC (Notre Dame)	1959–2005	Thomas, Fr. Ivo, OP

1960

De Koninck, Thomas (Louvain)	1960–64	Havey, Fr. William, CSC
Lobkowicz, Nikolaus (Fribourg)	1960–72	O'Reilly, Fr. Peter
		Riter, Fr. Regis H., CSC
		Smith, Vincent E.

1961

Francis, Richard	1961–66	Boarman, Fr. Glenn, CSC
Gavin, Fr. Michael J., CSC	1961–69	Downs, Fr. Richard J., CSC
McMullin, Fr. Ernan (Louvain)	1954–57, 1961–94	

1962

Küng, Guido (Fribourg)   1962–73   O'Halloran, Fr. James A.
Turley, Robert S. (Notre Dame)   1962–66

1963

Doig, Fr. James, CSC (Gregorian)   1963–68   Brennan, Fr. Thomas
                                                 Joseph, CSC
                                              Fisk, Milton
                                              Ward, Fr. Leo R., CSC

1964

Deku, Henry (Berlin)   1964–67   De Koninck, Thomas
McAvoy, Fr. Bernard L., CSC   1950–52,
                              1964–66

1965

Burrell, Fr. David, CSC (Yale)   1965–2006
Hund, Fr. William, CSC   1965–71
 (Fribourg)
Versfeld, Martin   1965–67

1966

Boyle, Fr. Jerome M., CSC   1945–52,   FitzGerald, John Joseph
                            1966–75
Kamitz, Reinhard   1966–72   Francis, Richard
McKim, Vaughn R. (Yale)   1966–2009   McAvoy, Fr. Bernard L., CSC
                                      Turley, Robert S.

1967

Ballestrem, Karl (Fribourg)   1967–71   Deku, Henry
Canty, John T. (Notre Dame)   1967–70   Versfeld, Martin
Delaney, Cornelius (St. Louis)   1967–
Gerber, Rudolf (Louvain)   1967–71

1968

Loux, Michael (Chicago)   1968–2010   Buckley, Fr. James, CSC
Solomon, William (Texas)   1968–   Doig, Fr. James, CSC
                                   Nielsen, Harry

1969

Donnelly, John (Brown)	1969–71	Gavin, Fr. Michael J., CSC
Glick, Daryl (Notre Dame)	1969–71	
Gutting, Gary (St. Louis)	1969–	
Pahi, Biswambhar (Yale)	1969–75	

1970

Binkley, Timothy (Texas)	1970–73	Canty, John T.

1971

Brennan, Sheilah (Laval)	1971–91	Ballestrem, Karl
Goodpaster, Kenneth E. (Michigan)	1971–80	Donnelly, John
Ludman, Earl (Chicago)	1971–72	Gerber, Rudolph
		Glick, Daryl
		Hund, Fr. William, CSC

1972

		Chroust, Anton-Hermann
		Kamitz, Reinhard
		Lobkowicz, Nikolaus
		Ludman, Earl

1973

Ameriks, Karl (Yale)	1973–	Binkley, Timothy
Davis, Charles C. (Notre Dame)	1973–81	Brennan, Fr. Thomas James, CSC
Larson, Bruce	1973–77	Küng, Guido
Mellema, Paul (MIT)	1973–80	
Sterba, James P. (Pittsburgh)	1973–	

1974
(no changes)

1975

Garson, James (Pittsburgh)	1975–80	Boyle, Fr. Jerome M., CSC
Post, John (UC Berkeley)	1975–77	Pahi, Biswambhar
Thomas, Laurence (Pittsburgh)	1975–79	

1976
(no changes)

	1977	
Bayless, David (Cambridge)	1977–79	FitzGerald, John James
Crosson, Frederick (Notre Dame)	1977–84	Johnston, Herbert L.
Duffy, Michael (Temple)	1977–79	Larson, Bruce
Foley, Richard (Brown)	1977–90	Oesterle, John
Moore, Harold (Fordham)	1977–80	Post, John
Pojman, Louis (Union Theological)	1977–79	Sobocinski, Boleslaw
Simon, Lawrence (Boston University)	1977–87	
Stephens, Lynn (Massachusetts)	1977–79	

	1978	
Maddy, Penelope (Princeton)	1978–83	

	1979	
Domingo, Willis (Oxford)	1979–83	Bayless, David
Freddoso, Alfred (Notre Dame)	1979–	Duffy, Michael
Lepore, Ernest (Minnesota)	1979–81	Evans, Joseph
Wachsberg, Milton (Princeton)	1979–84	Pojman, Louis
		Stephens, Lynn
		Thomas, Laurence

	1980	
Bricker, Phillip (Princeton)	1980–81	Garson, James
Flint, Thomas (Notre Dame)	1980–	Goodpaster, Kenneth E.
Garcia, Jorge L. (Yale)	1980–89	Mellema, Paul
O'Neill, Eileen (Princeton)	1980–83	Moore, Harold
Sartorelli, Joseph (Oxford)	1980–81	

	1981	
Edidin, Aron (Princeton)	1981–92	Bricker, Phillip
Lee, Richard (Stanford)	1981–82	Caponigri, A. Robert
McClelland, Richard (Cambridge)	1981–85	Davis, Charles C.
Morris, Thomas V. (Yale)	1981–96	Lepore, Ernest
Robinson, John (Notre Dame)	1981–88	Reith, Fr. Herman R., CSC
Stern, Cindy (Syracuse)	1981–84	Sartorelli, Joseph

	1982	
DePaul, Michael (Ohio)	1982–	Lee, Richard
Plantinga, Alvin (Yale)	1982–2010	

1983

Mellon, Joseph (MIT)	1983–85	Domingo, Willis
Watson, Stephen (Duquesne)	1983–	Maddy, Penelope
Wettstein, Howard K. (NYU)	1983–89	O'Neill, Eileen

1984

Blackburn, Thomas S. (Pittsburgh)	1984–88	Crosson, Frederick
Detlefsen, Michael (Johns Hopkins)	1984–	Stern, Cindy
		Wachsberg, Milton

1985

Kent, Bonnie D. (Columbia)	1985–86	McClelland, Richard
O'Connor, David K. (Stanford)	1985–	Mellon, Joseph
Quinn, Philip L. (Pittsburgh)	1985–2004	

1986

Bicchieri, Cristina (Cambridge)	1986–89	Kent, Bonnie D.
Heffernan, George (Cologne)	1986–90	
Kremer, Michael (Pittsburgh)	1986–2002	

1987

| Mercer, Christia (Princeton) | 1987–89 | Simon, Lawrence |

1988

| Joy, Lynn S. (Harvard) | 1988–95, 2000– | Blackburn, Thomas S. |
| MacIntyre, Alasdair | 1988–95 | Robinson, John |

1989

Ramsey, William M. (UC San Diego)	1989–2007	Bicchieri, Cristina
		Garcia, Jorge L.
		Mercer, Christia
		Wettstein, Howard K.

1990

David, Marian (Arizona)	1990–	Foley, Richard
Jenkins, Fr. John, CSC (Oxford)	1990–	Heffernan, George
Kennedy, John B. (Stanford)	1990–98	
Stubenberg, Leopold (Arizona)	1990–	

1991

Shin, Sun-Joo (Stanford)	1991–2003	Brennan, Sheilah
Stump, Eleonore (Cornell)	1991–93	
Weithman, Paul (Harvard)	1991–	
Zimmerman, Dean (Brown)	1991–2000	

1992

Edidin, Aron

1993

Blanchette, Patricia (Stanford)	1993–	Stump, Eleonore

1994

McMullin, Fr. Ernan

1995

Klima, Gyula (Eötrös Loránd)	1995–99	Joy, Lynn S.
van Inwagen, Peter (Rochester)	1995–	MacIntyre, Alasdair
Warfield, Ted (Rutgers)	1995–	

1996

Morris, Thomas V.

1997

Abramson, Kate (Chicago)	1997–99	
Howard, Don (Boston)	1997–	

1998

Shrader-Frechette, Kristin (Notre Dame)	1998–	Kennedy, John B.

1999

Bays, Timothy (UCLA)	1999–	Abramson, Kate
Moss, Lenny (Northwestern)	1999–2006	Klima, Gyula

2000

Joy, Lynn S.	1988–95, 2000–	Zimmerman, Dean

2001

Dumont, Stephen (Toronto)	2001–	
Franks, Paul (Harvard)	2001–5	

Kourany, Janet A. (Columbia)	2001–	
Rea, Michael (Notre Dame)	2001–	
Rush, Fred (Columbia)	2001–	
	2002	
Jauernig, Anja (Princeton)	2002–11	Kremer, Michael J.
	2003	
Kelly, Thomas (Harvard)	2003–4	Shin, Sun-Joo
O'Callaghan, John (Notre Dame)	2003–	
	2004	
Audi, Robert (Michigan)	2004–	Kelly, Thomas
Brading, Katherine (Oxford)	2004–	Quinn, Philip L.
	2005	
		Franks, Paul
		Weiher, Fr. Charles, CSC
	2006	
Franks, Curtis (UC Irvine)	2006–	Burrell, Fr. David, CSC
Newlands, Samuel (Yale)	2006–	Moss, Lenny
Speaks, Jeffrey (Princeton)	2006–	
	2007	
Cross, Richard (Oxford)	2007–	Manier, Edward
Ramsey, Grant (Duke)	2007–	Ramsey, William M.
	2008 (no changes)	
	2009	
Karbowski, Joseph (UC Berkeley)	2009–	Bobik, Joseph
Kelsey, Sean (Princeton)	2009–	McInerny, Ralph
		McKim, Vaughn R.
	2010	
		Loux, Michael
		Plantinga, Alvin

* Not included are professional specialists, adjunct faculty, concurrent faculty from other departments, and most faculty who stayed less than three years.

CAP Membership, 1967–2010

(Department chair is listed first, with elected members in alphabetical order.)

(1967–68) McMullin, Bobik, Caponigri, FitzGerald, Johnston, McInerny, Oesterle

(1968–69) FitzGerald, Bobik, Caponigri, FitzGerald, Johnston, McInerny, Oesterle

(1969–70) McMullin, Bobik, Caponigri, Johnston, McInerny, Sayre

(1970–71) (unavailable)

(1971–72) McMullin, Burrell, FitzGerald, Johnston, Küng, McInerny, Oesterle

(1972–73) Delaney, Bobik, Burrell, FitzGerald, McInerny, Oesterle, Sayre

(1973–74) Delaney, Bobik, Burrell, FitzGerald, McInerny, Oesterle, Sayre

(1974–78) (unavailable)

(1978–79) Delaney, Crosson, Gutting, Loux, McInerny, Sayre, Solomon

(1979–80) Loux, Ameriks, Crosson, McInerny, Sayre, Solomon, Sterba

(1980–81) Delaney, Ameriks, Gutting, McInerny, McMullin, Solomon, Sterba

(1981–82) Delaney, Ameriks, Foley, Gutting, Loux, McKim, McMullin

(1982–83) Loux, Ameriks, Delaney, Foley (spring), Gutting, McKim, McMullin (fall), Solomon

(1983–84) Foley, Burrell, Delaney, Freddoso, McMullin (spring), Plantinga, Sayre (fall), Solomon

(1984–85) Delaney, Burrell, Freddoso, McMullin, Plantinga, Sayre, Solomon

(1985–86) Foley, Burrell, Delaney, Freddoso, Plantinga, Quinn, Sayre

(1986–87) Foley, Burrell, Delaney, Freddoso, McMullin, Quinn, Solomon

(1987–88) Foley, Ameriks, McKim, McMullin, Plantinga, Quinn, Solomon

(1988–89) Ameriks, Burrell, Delaney, Detlefsen, Gutting, Plantinga, Sayre

(1989–90) Foley, Ameriks (fall), Burrell, Detlefsen, Gutting, McMullin, Plantinga, Solomon (spring)

(1990–91) Gutting, Delaney, DePaul, Detlefsen, Freddoso, Joy, McMullin

(1991–92) Gutting, Ameriks, Delaney, DePaul, O'Connor, Plantinga, Solomon

(1992–93) Gutting, Ameriks, Delaney, DePaul, Detlefsen, Joy, Plantinga

(1993–94) Gutting, Detlefsen, O'Connor, Plantinga, Quinn, Solomon, Watson

(1994–95) Gutting, Burrell, Delaney, DePaul, Joy, O'Connor, Watson

(1995–96) Gutting, Burrell, Delaney, Freddoso, O'Connor, Solomon, Watson

(1996–97) Watson, Ameriks, Burrell, Delaney, Freddoso, Plantinga, van Inwagen

(1997–98) Watson, Freddoso, O'Connor, Plantinga, Solomon, van Inwagen, Weithman

(1998–99) Watson, O'Connor, Plantinga, Quinn, Solomon, van Inwagen, Weithman

(1999–2000) Watson, Delaney, DePaul, Detlefsen, O'Connor, Quinn, Solomon

(2000–2001) Weithman, Ameriks, Delaney, DePaul, Detlefsen, Howard, Quinn

(2001–2) Weithman, Ameriks, Blanchette, Delaney, Detlefsen, Gutting, Howard

(2002–3) Weithman, Ameriks, Gutting, Howard, Joy, Quinn, Warfield

(2003–4) Weithman, Blanchette, Franks, Gutting, Joy, Quinn, Warfield

(2004–5)* Weithman, David, Delaney, DePaul, O'Callaghan, Ramsey, Warfield, Watson

(2005–6) Weithman, Blanchette, David, Delaney, DePaul, Detlefsen, Dumont, Stubenberg

(2006–7) Weithman, Blanchette, David, Delaney, DePaul, Dumont, Ramsey, Warfield

(2007–8) Dumont, Bays, Joy, O'Callaghan, Rea, Stubenberg, van Inwagen, Warfield

(2008–9) Dumont, Bays, Cross, Delaney, Joy, Stubenberg, van Inwagen, Weithman

(2009–10) Dumont, Blanchette, Cross, David, Delaney, Rush, Stubenberg, Weithman

*In 2004–5 the number of elected members of the CAP increased to seven. This change was made to avoid ties in voting among those members. With the chair ex officio, committee membership now numbered eight.

Administrators

PHILOSOPHY DEPARTMENT CHAIRS, 1920–2010

Years	Chairs
1920–37	Miltner, Fr. Charles C., CSC
1937–42	Brennan, Fr. Thomas J., CSC
1942–49	Moore, Fr. Philip S., CSC
1949–52	Phelan, Fr. Gerald B.
1952–55	Mullahy, Fr. Bernard I., CSC
1955–64	Reith, Fr. Herman R., CSC
1964–65	Nielsen, Harry A.
1965–72	McMullin, Fr. Ernan
(1968–69)	FitzGerald, John (Acting Chair)
1972–82	Delaney, Cornelius
(1979–80)	Loux, Michael (Acting Chair)
1982–83	Loux, Michael
1983–90	Foley, Richard F.
(1984–85)	Delaney, Cornelius (Acting Chair)
(1988–89)	Ameriks, Karl (Acting Chair)
1990–96	Gutting, Gary
1996–2001	Watson, Stephen
2001–7	Weithman, Paul J.
2007–10	Dumont, Stephen
2010–	Cross, Richard

ARTS AND LETTERS DEANS, 1919–2010

Years	Deans
1919–23	Carrico, Fr. Joseph Leonard, CSC
1923–35	Miltner, Fr. Charles C., CSC
1935–36	Campbell, T. Bowyer
1936–40	Miltner, Fr. Charles C., CSC
1940–43	Boland, Fr. Francis J., CSC
1943–51	Cavanaugh, Fr. Francis P., CSC
1951–69	Sheedy, Fr. Charles E., CSC
1969–75	Crosson, Frederick J.
1975–81	Charles, Sr. Isabel, OP
(1981–83)	Burns, Robert E. (Acting Dean)
1983–91	Loux, Michael J.
(1988–89)	Hatch, Nathan (Acting Dean)
1991–97	Attridge, Harold
1997–2008	Roche, Mark W.
(1999–2000)	Fox, Christopher (Acting Dean)
2008–	McGreevy, John T.

UNIVERSITY PROVOSTS, 1970–2010

Years	Provosts
1970–78	Burthchaell, Fr. James, CSC
1978–96	O'Meara, Timothy
1996–2005	Hatch, Nathan
2005–	Burish, Thomas G.

UNIVERSITY PRESIDENTS, 1946–2010

Years	Presidents
1946–52	Cavanaugh, Fr. John J., CSC
1952–87	Hesburgh, Fr. Theodore M., CSC
1987–2005	Malloy, Fr. Edward A., CSC
2005–	Jenkins, Fr. John I., CSC

NOTES

CHAPTER ONE

1. The passage quoted (in translation) and other content of this paragraph come from sec. 15 of *Aeterni Patris*. In following paragraphs, sections of papal encyclicals from which quotes are taken will be indicated parenthetically.

2. Joseph Bobik, *Jokes, Life after Death, and God* (South Bend, IN: St. Augustine's Press, 2011).

3. Although not a Thomist, Caponigri was a Catholic who attended Mass daily, often acting as server for priests high up in the administration. Anthony Simon (son of Yves Simon), a generous source of much material in this chapter, has told me that his father was once asked to vet Caponigri's philosophic views for orthodoxy, and that they were judged favorably.

4. The succession was not entirely broken even with Hesburgh, whose father was German and mother Irish. It was renewed with President Edward Malloy (1987–2005) and current president John Jenkins.

5. Leo XIII's promulgation of Thomism as the "normative" Catholic philosophy was repeated in one way or another by his successors Pius X (1903–1914), Benedict XV (1914–1922), Pius XI (1922–1939), and Pius XII (1939–1958). John XXIII (1958–1963) was the first pontiff in the twentieth century to remain silent on the place of Thomism in Catholic thought. (See Jose Pereira's "Thomism and the Magisterium: from *Aeterni Patris* to *Vertatis Splendor*," *Logos* 5, no. 3 [2002]: 147–83). When Joe Bobik said he was a Thomist "because the Pope said so," he may have had the series of popes from Leo XIII to Pius XII in mind.

6. In 1908 the name of this tribunal was changed to "Supreme Sacred Congregation of the Holy Office," and in 1965 to "Congregation for the Doctrine of the Faith."

7. Anton-Hermann Chroust, *Socrates, Man and Myth* (Notre Dame: University of Notre Dame Press, 1957).

8. Jacques Maritain, *The Person and the Common Good,* trans. John J. FitzGerald (New York: Charles Scribner's Sons, 1947).

9. This is from the Yves René Marie Simon Papers in the University of Notre Dame Archives, as reported in https://sites.google.com/a/nd.edu/the-notre-dame-center-for-ethics-and-culture. Sources for these paragraphs on Yves Simon are that website; Leo R. Ward, *My Fifty Years at Notre Dame* (Notre Dame: Indiana Province of the Priests of Holy Cross, 2000), chap. 8 (http://archives.nd.edu/ward); and personal communication with his son, Anthony.

10. Ward, *My Fifty Years,* chap. 8.

11. Ibid.

12. Best known among these probably are *Prévoir et savoir: Études de la nécessité dans la pensée scientifique et en philosophie* (Montréal: Éditions de l'Arbre, 1944) and *Philosophy of Democratic Government* (Chicago: University of Chicago Press, 1951).

13. *Notre Dame Scholastic,* October 16, 1931. His return visit the following year is noted in the *Scholastic* of December 2, 1932.

14. Florian Michel, *La pensée catholique en Amérique du Nord* (Paris: Éditions de Brouwer, 2010), 396.

15. Details of this story come from Laurence Shook, *Étienne Gilson* (Toronto: Pontifical Institute of Mediaeval Studies, 1984), and from personal communication with Anthony Simon.

16. Maritain's house at 26 Linden Lane was bequeathed to the University of Notre Dame when Jacques and Raïssa moved back to France in 1960. For two decades or so it was used as a residence for ND professors spending time in Princeton on university business. I occupied it for a week in the late fall of 1978. A few years later ND sold the property, having decided that taxes and upkeep exceeded its value as a temporary residence for traveling faculty.

17. *Notre Dame Scholastic,* October 26, 1934. Anthony Simon informed me that Maritain made a brief earlier visit to ND in 1933.

18. Leo R. Ward, "Meeting Jacques Maritain," *Review of Politics* 44, no. 4 (October 1982): 483–88.

19. Anthony Simon said that Maritain preferred staying in the infirmary because it allowed him privacy, rest, and seclusion from social events. He recalls having spent several hours with Maritain in 1955 at the Morris Inn, during which time Maritain expressed regret that there was no room for him in the infirmary.

20. This quote and other details in this section on Gödel come from John W. Dawson Jr., "Kurt Gödel at Notre Dame," http://math.nd.edu.

21. Menger and Simon coauthored "Aristotelian Demonstration and Postulational Method," *Modern Schoolman* 25, no. 3 (1948): 183–92.

22. Carl W. Grindel, "Vincent Edward Smith, 1915–1972," *Proceedings and Addresses of the American Philosophical Association* 45 (1971–72): 225–26.

23. Ralph McInerny recalls that she was pushed by an intruder; see his *I Alone Have Escaped to Tell You* (Notre Dame, IN: University of Notre Dame Press, 2006), 99.

24. See "Albuquerque Journal Obituaries: Denissoff," *Albuquerque Journal,* March 18, 1998, http://obits.abqjournal.com/obits/show/136943.

25. See "Archimandrite," *Wikipedia,* last modified March 13, 2013, http://en.wikepedia.org/wiki/Archimandrite, and Martha Liles, "Archimandrite," Melkite Greek Catholic Church Information Center, http://www.mliles.com/melkite/archimandrites.shtml.

26. In 1950 specifically, according to the *University Bulletin,* there were thirty philosophy faculty teaching eighteen hours of required courses to 2,689 A&L and business students.

27. Jacques Maritain, *An Introduction to Philosophy,* trans. E. I. Watkins (Sheed & Ward, 1937), 107. The subsequent quotation is from p. 108.

28. From Fr. Hesburgh's preface to Ward, *My Fifty Years.*

29. Fr. Virgil Michel, OSB, was a monk at St. John's University and Abbey in Minnesota. He founded the magazine *Orate Fratris* (now *Worship*) in 1926, and cooperated with Dorothy Day in the Catholic Worker Movement.

CHAPTER TWO

1. Fr. O'Hara was appointed bishop of Buffalo, NY, in 1945, and archbishop of Philadelphia in 1951. He was elevated to Cardinal in 1958 by Pope John XXIII.

2. Philip Gleason, *Contending with Modernity: Catholic Higher Education in the Twentieth Century* (New York: Oxford University Press, 1995), 272.

3. Arthur J. Hope, *Notre Dame, One Hundred Years* (UNDP, 1943), chap. 31.

4. In his autobiography, *God, Country, Notre Dame* (UNDP, 1990), Fr. Theodore Hesburgh mentions O'Hara's removal of "certain sociology books" (61). Gleason, *Contending,* 272, refers only to books O'Hara "found improper." Without mentioning names, Fr. Leo Ward reports knowing "a high official" who made off with books from the library (*My Fifty Years,* chap. 9).

5. Hesburgh, *God, Country,* 62.

6. Information on President John J. Cavanaugh comes from chapter 33 of Hope, *Notre Dame,* added after the 1943 edition; from Hesburgh, *God, Country*; and from an interview with Fr. Cavanaugh reported in Dorothy V. Corson's *A Cave of Candles: The Story behind Notre Dame's Grotto* (Nappanee, IN: Evangel Publishing House, 2008). According to Corson, Fr. Cavanaugh's story was an inspiration behind Rudy Ruettiger's 1993 film *Rudy,* in which Fr. Cavanaugh himself figures.

7. Hesburgh, *God, Country,* 64.

8. Before Challenge I, ND's fund-raising drives had seldom garnered more than $1.5 million annually (see Michael O'Brien's *Hesburgh: A Biography* [Washington, DC: Catholic University of America Press, 1998], 91). Challenge II (1963–66), responding to another conditional offer of $6 million by the Ford

Foundation, raised about $22 million. Subsequent drives were increasingly successful. SUMMA (1967–72) totaled $62.5 million, Campaign for Notre Dame (1975–81) $180.5 million, Notre Dame: A Strategic Moment (1987–90) $463 million, Generations (1991–2000) $1.1 billion, and Spirit of Notre Dame (2004–11) more than $2 billion. (Campaign totals are from the July 12, 2011, press release "Notre Dame Campaign Raises $2.014 Billion.")

9. ND had a number of truly outstanding teachers at the time—Willis Nutting of the General Program of Liberal Education, Thomas Stritch of American Studies, Frank O'Malley of English, Joe Evans of Philosophy—but none was a particularly strong scholar. I remember an A&L Advisory Council meeting at which English professor Rufus Rauch, another acclaimed teacher, argued emphatically in defense of the practice of counting class preparation as scholarly research.

10. O'Brien, *Hesburgh*, 284.

11. This and the following quotation are from O'Brien, *Hesburgh*, 92.

12. Unless noted otherwise, material in this section comes from Hesburgh, *God, Country.* Quotations in the text come from pages indicated in parentheses after the quotations themselves.

13. Gleason, *Contending*, 295.

14. In his *Hesburgh*, Michael O'Brien describes Fr. Ted's "exceptional capacity to motivate. Optimistic, energetic, his attitude inspired the faculty and staff. . . . He made subordinates feel that their work was significant." O'Brien then quotes Provost Timothy O'Meara, who recalls that "it is not [just] the words he uses. . . . It is the whole way in which . . . his presence communicates. He gives people the feeling of being important" (22).

15. This despite the book's having received a *nihil obstat* from Fr. Leo R. Ward and an *imprimatur* from Bishop F. Noll of Fort Wayne. Details in this paragraph come directly from Hesburgh's *God, Country* (224–26). Gleason gives a comprehensive background of this incident in *Contending* (274–82).

16. John Courtney Murray was given an honorary degree at ND's commencement the following spring. Further vindication came with the ratification of a statement on religious freedom written by Fr. Murray as an official document of Vatican II.

17. So goes the account in his autobiography. In retelling the story to me later, Fr. Ted claimed only to have flown faster than all but a small number of Air Force pilots. Other details of the story fluctuate with other retellings. As noted by Michael O'Brien (*Hesburgh*, 192), Fr. Ted tends to turn his stories into parables. Historical truth may be elusive, but the truth of the parable remains.

18. When Sheedy died in 1990 of chronic lung disease (he was a heavy smoker), Hesburgh commissioned a bust of him to be installed in O'Shaughnessy's Great Hall. There it remains to the present.

19. Not mentioned in Hesburgh's account is that Nieuwland's research on synthetic rubber also resulted in the discovery of the deadly "Lewisite" gas.

Lewisite's properties were similar to those of mustard gas, except that it causes blistering immediately after contacting the skin. In Fr. Nieuwland's view (see Joel A. Vilensky, "Father Nieuwland and the 'Dew of Death,'" *Notre Dame Magazine,* Winter 2002–3), Lewisite was a humane weapon, in that it could be used to incapacitate instead of kill, and that with prompt treatment the victim has a chance of recovery. Large quantities were produced in the United States for use against the Germans, but were eventually dumped into the Atlantic Ocean after the Germans surrendered in 1918. The gas was subsequently used by Japan against the Chinese in World War II, and Iraq is suspected of using Lewisite in its 1980 war against Iran.

20. Bochenski went by several given names during his lifetime. He was born Józef Franciszek Emanuel Lansdorff de Rawicz Bochenski. When he joined the Dominicans, he took the name "Innocent Maria" and began signing his publications "I. M. Bochenski." Subsequently he added his original Christian name to become Joseph I. M. Bochenski. But when asked what the "M" stood for, he would insist it was short for "Moses." The most common form of his name today is probably "Joseph M. Bochenski." He also went by various pseudonyms, including "Emil Majerski," "Bogusław Prawdota," "P. Banks," and "K. Fred." I owe this information to Jarosław Kozak, "Joseph (Innocent Maria) Bochenski OP (1902–1995)," *Studies in East European Thought* 49, no. 4 (1997): 287–303, and to personal correspondence with Guido Küng.

21. Professor Küng is my main source of information on Bochenski's military career.

22. Material concerning Fr. Bochenski's academic career comes from Guido Küng, "In Memoriam: Joseph (Innocent) M. Bochenski, O. P. 1902–1995," *Review of Metaphysics* 49, no. 1 (1995): 217–18; from personal email correspondence with Professor Küng; from Kozak, "Bochenski"; from Jan Parys's *Entre la logique et la foi,* trans. from Polish by Eric Morin-Aguilar (Warsaw: Les Éditions Noir sur Blanc, 1990), esp. 9, 27, 93, 137, 161–62; and from several conversations with Fr. Ernan McMullin.

23. According to Kozak, "Bochenski," 293, Bochenski's philosophic career extended through four periods: Neo-Thomism (1934–45), history of logic (1945–55), Sovietology (1955–70), and analytic philosophy (1970–95).

24. Bochenski drew a basic distinction between ontology and metaphysics. Metaphysics studies transcendent objects, typified, for example, by Kant's transcendental ideas (ego, world, God). Other metaphysicians he mentions are Spinoza and Whitehead, along with Maritain and the Thomists he studied in seminary. Ontologists, on the other hand, study the structures of reality and do so with the help of formal logic. Bochenski viewed himself as an ontologist, in the company of Leśniewski, Quine, and the early Wittgenstein. Done properly, he believed, ontology is the purest form of analytic philosophy; ontology boils down to formal logic.

25. Parys, *Entre.*

26. Parys, *Entre,* 25. This estimation may have been a bit biased. In 1986, W. V. O. Quine and Burton Dreben were still at Harvard, and Charles Parsons was about to return in 1989.

27. Ralph McInerny, in his nostalgic unpublished lecture "Notre Dame and Dame Philosophy" (1992), refers to Parys's *Entre* as a "fascinating, outrageous, marvelous book" containing memories of "an octogenarian" who found objectivity "elusive." Being a sexagenarian himself, Ralph remarks facetiously, he can remember only what actually happened. Ralph purported to find Bochenski's ND unrecognizable from the few things said about it in this book.

28. Sources for this section on Fr. McMullin include obituary notices, conversations with several colleagues who knew him well (particularly Vaughn McKim, Don Howard, and Paul Weithman), and my own interactions with him dating back over fifty years. In the last year of his life he granted me five or six prearranged interviews and corrected an early draft of the present chapter.

29. Otto Bird, Head of GPLE, had conducted a survey of student reaction to courses taught in his program. Upon hearing of results unfavorable to the Philosophy Department, Fr. Hesburgh had asked Ernan to summarize them in perspicuous form. When Ernan submitted his summary to Hesburgh, the latter sent a copy to A&L Dean Sheedy, who in turn (injudiciously) sent a copy to the philosophy teachers affected. The young upstart from Ireland was blamed for the department's discomfiture.

30. See "Rev. Ernan McMullin, Distinguished Alumnus of Maynooth College," St. Patrick's College, Maynooth, 2011, http://maynoothcollege.ie/news /InMemoriamRevErnanMcMullan.shtml.

31. Ernan McMullin, ed., *Galileo: Man of Science* (New York: Basic Books, 1968).

32. This view of the primacy of theology in Catholic higher education was articulated in Fr. Leo R. Ward's *Blueprint for a Catholic University* (St. Louis: B. Herder, 1949), 97–104. For further background, see Gleason, *Contending,* 163–66, 252, 257–64.

33. *The Curriculum of a Catholic Liberal College,* internal report of the College of Arts and Letters, University of Notre Dame Archives, 1953. Page numbers of passages quoted are noted in the text.

34. Gleason, *Contending,* 298.

35. From Ernan McMullin's presidential address "Who Are We?," *Proceedings of the American Catholic Philosophical Association* 41 (1967): 11.

36. Gleason, *Contending,* 298.

37. McMullin, "Who Are We?," 374.

38. "Curriculum: Departure at DePaul," *Time,* October 23, 1964, http:// time.com/time/magazine.

39. McMullin, "Who Are We?," 10.

40. W. Norris Clarke, SJ, "The Future of Thomism," in *New Themes in Christian Philosophy*, ed. Ralph McInerny (UNDP, 1968),187–207; quotation from 203–4.

41. See Fr. Weisheipl's "The Revival of Thomism as a Christian Philosophy," in McInerny, *New Themes*, 164–85; quotations from 185.

42. McMullin, "Who Are We?," 192.

43. See Gerald A. McCool, preface to *The Future of Thomism*, ed. Deal W. Hudson and Dennis W. Moran (Mishawaka, IN: American Maritain Association, 1992), 1.

44. McMullin, "Who Are We?," 11.

45. Gleason, *Contending*, 297.

CHAPTER THREE

1. This unpublished lecture presented a brief history of philosophy at ND, as Ralph then saw it, from the university's founding in 1842 to its sesquicentennial in 1992. As he remarked toward the end of the lecture, its title was intended to evoke *The Consolation of Philosophy*, by Boethius, "in which Dame Philosophy addresses the complaint of Boethius that the innocent suffer while the ways of the wicked prosper."

2. Ralph's recollection in this regard is corroborated by the statement in the 1957 *University Bulletin* that the aim of the Philosophy Department's basic courses was "to perpetuate the Thomistic tradition not only for itself but with a view to relating it to contemporary problems and discoveries."

3. McInerny, *I Alone Have Escaped*, chap. 3. The present account of Ralph's life relies heavily on this book and on my personal memories. Other sources are indicated when relevant.

4. Matthew Rogerson, the hero of the story, is a mediocre teacher at a mediocre college who attempts to avoid involuntary failure by actually trying to fail. This effort itself fails, as Rogerson's antics turn him into a resoundingly popular teacher. For reasons I can't quite put my finger on, the novel strikes me as autobiographical, perhaps because in later years Ralph devoted less and less time to his academic duties while gaining in academic distinction. More recent novels featuring the same character are *Rogerson at Bay* (1976) and *The Search Committee* (1991).

5. McInerny, *I Alone Have Escaped*, 33.

6. As it turned out, both ND and St. Louis were in the process of incorporating under boards of trustees with predominantly lay memberships. Other institutions represented at the meeting were soon to follow.

7. Gleason, *Contending*, 317. Gleason goes on to characterize it as "a symbolic turning point" in the church's "cold war on modernity."

8. In chap. 9 of *I Alone Have Escaped,* dealing mainly with Vatican II, Ralph admits that, given the definition of a conservative Catholic "as one who accepted the magisterium of the Church," he became "willy-nilly a conservative Catholic."

9. Ralph McInerny, *What Went Wrong with Vatican II: The Catholic Crisis Explained* (Manchester, NH: Sophia Institute Press, 1998).

10. See "Thomistic Institute: Summer 1998," Jacques Maritain Center, http://maritain.nd.edu/jmc/ti98.htm. Ralph directed the Thomistic Institute from 1993 to 2006, with a year off following Connie's death in 2002.

11. See "International Catholic University," http://home.comcast.net/~icu web/icu1.htm.

12. See "McInerny Center for Thomistic Studies," http://www.thomasinter national.org/ralphmc/philostudies/philostudies.htm.

13. According to rumors circulated by subsequent students at ND (my source here is Charles Quinn), Sobocinski brought valuable papers with him in a brief-case acquired from an SS officer he had killed during clandestine operations. Imagine how logic by day might have mixed with homicide at night.

14. Papers by ND faculty were just assumed to be both true and interesting. Perhaps this is the reason Harry Nielsen's "Language as Existent" was published in 1961, and my "Propositional Logic in Plato's *Protagoras*" in 1963, although neither has much to do with formal logic.

15. Otto Bird, "In Memoriam: Ivo Thomas (1912–1976)." *Notre Dame Journal of Formal Logic* 18, no. 2 (1977): 193–94.

16. According to Charles Quinn, Lobkowicz had to give up his title of "Prince" when he left Czechoslovakia. But he continued to refer to his wife as countess.

17. Promotion to associate professor at that time generally required publication of at least one book. Guido's book was *Ontologie und logistische Analyse der Sprache: Eine Untersuchung zur zeitgenössischen Universaliendiskussion* (Vienna: Springer, 1963), which was translated into English by E. C. M. Mays (Dordrecht: D. Reidel, 1967). This is Guido's only book-length publication. However, he has translated one book from Russian (*Philosophical Problems of Many-Valued Logic,* by A. A. Zinov'ev, with D. D. Comey [Dordrecht: D. Reidel, 1963]) and one from French (*Formale Logik,* by J. Dopp [Einsiedeln: Benziger Verlag, 1969]) and published over five dozen articles in topflight journals, including *Nous, Dialectica, Monist, Synthese, Review of Metaphysics, American Philosophical Quarterly, Studies in Soviet Thought,* and *NDJFL.*

18. Thomas, a son of Ralph's revered teacher Charles De Koninck, taught at ND from 1960 to 1964, after which he joined his father on the philosophy faculty at Laval. Charles died early in 1965. There is a durable rumor that young Thomas served as the model for the juvenile hero of Antoine de Saint-Exupéry's *Le Petit Prince.* See Mario Asselin, "Thomas De Koninck," http://blogue.marioasselin .com/2002/12/thomas_de_konin/.

19. Dates and places here come from Gleason's *Contending,* 306. The text of Hans Küng's speech, "The Church and Freedom," appears in *Commonweal,* June 21, 1963, 339–53.

20. The quote is from Parys's *Entre,* 27. For Bochenski's classifications cited in this paragraph, see pp. 27 and 93.

21. Kenneth M. Sayre, *Recognition: A Study in the Philosophy of Artificial Intelligence* (UNDP, 1965).

22. Harry A. Nielsen, *Methods of Natural Science: An Introduction* (Englewood Cliffs, NJ: Prentice-Hall, 1967).

23. Milton Fisk, *Nature and Necessity: An Essay in Physical Ontology* (Bloomington: Indiana University Press, 1974).

24. Milton Fisk, *A Modern Formal Logic* (Englewood Cliffs, NJ: Prentice-Hall, 1964).

25. See "'Analytic' and 'Continental' Philosophy," *Philosophical Gourmet Report* 2011, http://www.philosophicalgourmet.com/analytic.asp.

26. Ralph returned to Harry's administrative ineptitude and his idiosyncratic view of the department's mission in a beautiful eulogy delivered in the Malloy Hall chapel a week after Harry's death. He was "uniquely unqualified for administrative work," Ralph observed, and "had many other virtues" as well. "When he was chairman," Ralph went on, "he suggested that the main purpose of the department was to arm students against being bamboozled out of their faith." To this I may add something I once heard Harry say, to the effect that religious belief is a matter of what one refuses to deny.

27. See "Milton Fisk: Biography," http://www.miltonfisk.org/biography.

28. Kenneth M. Sayre, *Plato's Analytic Method* (Chicago: University of Chicago Press, 1969).

29. Kenneth M. Sayre, *Plato's Late Ontology: A Riddle Resolved* (Princeton: Princeton University Press, 1983); *Plato's Literary Garden: How to Read a Platonic Dialogue* (UNDP, 1995); *Parmenides' Lesson: Translation and Explication of Plato's* Parmenides (UNDP, 1996); and *Metaphysics and Method in Plato's* Statesman (Cambridge: Cambridge University Press, 2006).

30. Maritain, *Introduction to Philosophy,* 181.

31. Frederick Copleston, *Aquinas* (New York: Penguin Books, 1955), 243.

32. Jude Dougherty, "One Hundred Years of Philosophy by the Catholic University of America," *Fellowship of Catholic Scholars Newsletter,* December 1996. Dougherty then was dean of Catholic University's School of Philosophy.

33. John D'Arcy, then Bishop of Fort Wayne and South Bend, said Mass on the occasion of a lavish dinner for Ralph celebrating his 1999–2000 Gifford Lectures. I was there. The bishop appeared fully decked out with crosier and mitre. When asked by a clerical friend why he engaged in such heraldry for a simple Mass, D'Arcy answered, "Because Ralph is Ralph."

34. See the mimeographed "Progress Report Prepared for the Dean and Faculty by the Special Committee, October, 1961," in the University of Notre Dame Archives.

CHAPTER FOUR

1. Gleason, *Contending,* 297–98.
2. McMullin, "Who Are We?" Relevant facts and figures in this address came from a comprehensive survey McMullin had conducted the year before of philosophy departments in American Catholic colleges and universities, reported under the title "Philosophy in United States Catholic Colleges" in McInerny, *New Themes.* Enjoying a 63 percent response rate, this survey gathered information about faculty size and background, courses taught, use of textbooks, and similar matters.
3. This quotation and the figures behind it are from McMullin's "Philosophy in United States Catholic Colleges," 404. While some contemporary feminists may take exception with the phrasing of this observation, others might welcome it as an acknowledgment by a quintessentially male philosopher that women bring a distinctive set of sensibilities to the profession.
4. McMullin, "Who Are We?," 15.
5. This estimate takes both tenured and nontenured faculty into account. Tenured faculty by themselves were about 60 percent Thomist during this period. However, the department brought in numerous temporary instructors to help teach the four courses required of all A&L undergraduates. These courses at that time were almost exclusively Thomistic in orientation and required teachers trained in that tradition.
6. Three other CSCs were assigned to teach philosophy at ND by their religious superiors and subsequently reassigned without departmental oversight. Fr. Michael J. Gavin was in the department from 1961 to 1969 and Fr. Jerome M. Boyle from 1966 to 1975, both after time spent at the CSC's Portland University in Oregon. In a similar situation was Fr. Bernard L. McAvoy, who administered ND's undergraduate seminary from 1948 to 1954, taught theology at Catholic University from 1954 to 1960, and then went to Portland after a brief stint teaching philosophy at ND from 1964 to 1966. Although I overlapped each of these older priests for several years, I don't recall having met any of them.
7. I was a member of Charlie Weiher's thesis defense board, my first duty in this capacity. The oral examination, chaired by Fr. Reith, ended with a vote by show of hands. Fr. Reith had made it known in advance that Fr. Weiher was destined to teach philosophy at ND. I hesitated for a moment when the vote was called, but soon was persuaded by the chairman's glare to raise my hand and make the vote unanimous.

8. Tantur (Arabic for "hilltop"), known officially as the Ecumenical Institute for Theological Research, was built by ND in the late-1960s at the request of Pope Paul VI. The site in Israel was purchased by the Vatican from the Order of Knights Hospitallers in response to the call for ecumenism of Vatican II. Construction of Tantur led to the abandonment of previous plans to erect an Institute of Advanced Religious Studies on the banks of ND's St. Mary's Lake.

9. Best known among Fr. Burrell's earlier works are *Analogy and Philosophical Language* (New Haven: Yale University Press, 1973) and *Aquinas: God and Action* (UNDP, 1979). His publications after 1980 included three books on Islamic theology and three on cross-cultural religious studies. A similar pattern is evident in his shorter writings. By time of retirement, he had written more than one hundred articles.

10. This and following quotes are from the manuscript of an autobiography tentatively titled "A Philosophical-Theologian's Journey." It is especially fitting that David's autobiography contain the word "journey" in its title.

11. With the exception of Fr. Hesburgh himself, David Burrell is the most widely traveled person I have known. A hackneyed joke about the former declares that the main difference between Fr. Hesburgh and God is that God is everywhere whereas Hesburgh is everywhere except ND. A similarly exaggerated witticism about David is that he feels most grounded when in the air. David has hundreds of friends around the globe whom he visits when in their vicinity. He has a habit of formulating his travel plans in terms of people he will visit on a given day. I once asked him how he could stand all that time in the air. His answer was that flying provides the only time he has for thinking, the rest of his waking hours being spent in conversation.

12. Anticipated membership included David, John Gerber, CSC, and Elena Malits, CSC, among religious, and Kenneth Goodpaster and his wife, Harriet, among lay people. Goodpaster and I bought land for the project early in 1978, and I started building a solar house on my portion a few months later. The whole thing fell apart in 1980, with Lucille's death in an auto accident, Goodpaster's failure to get tenure, and David's being transferred to Tantur. I gradually completed the solar house and have been living in it ever since.

13. Ludwig Wittgenstein, *Philosophical Investigations,* trans. G. E. M. Anscombe (New York: Macmillan, 1953).

14. A characteristic theme of the *PI* is that the philosopher's aim is "to shew the fly the way out the fly-bottle" (309)—that is, to escape the confusions of language that lead to philosophic problems. Harry told us that when one of Bouwsma's students would leave the field, Bouwsma would interpret this as an escape from the "fly-bottle" and throw a party in celebration.

15. John Austin gave the William James Lectures at Harvard in 1955, later published as *How to Do Things with Words* under the editorship of J. O. Urmson. I had attended these lectures faithfully and admired Austin's ability to improvise

from a set of notes recently scribbled on legal-sized yellow paper. In the course of the lecture series, his audience dwindled from roughly two hundred to maybe two dozen people. As an admirer of the "ordinary language" approach to philosophy which he represented, I probably held Austin in higher esteem than did most of my ND colleagues.

16. According to department minutes, faculty began meeting to hear each other read papers in the late spring of 1955. No commentators were involved at that point, and the meetings were not officially sponsored by the department. Paper readers that year included John Oesterle, Otto Bird, and newly arrived Ralph McInerny. Ernan McMullin, who also arrived in 1955, soon took it upon himself to organize these occasions. It is recorded in minutes for the spring of 1957 that McMullin turned this role over to John Oesterle when he left for Yale.

17. See Michael Detlefsen's "Logic at Notre Dame: Skolem at Notre Dame," http://math.nd.edu/; also Kenneth M. Sayre, "Gasking on Arithmetical Incorrigibility," *Mind* 71 (1962): 272–76.

18. Skolem visited ND several times between 1957 and 1962, teaching courses on set theory and combinatorial logic. Fred Crosson and I took one of his courses (for credit) in 1960, which led to his commenting on my paper.

19. This section is based on department newsletters, my own memories, and those of Fr. McMullin himself.

20. Four other ND people were invited to take part in the discussion but did not make formal presentations: John Oesterle and Ralph McInerny from philosophy, Catesby Taliaferro from mathematics, and Fr. Edward O'Connor from theology.

21. Rorty and I struck up a friendship of sorts after his hard-hitting comments on my conference paper. I watched the legendary 1979 Cotton Bowl game in Rorty's living room in Princeton. At the end of the game, ND made one of the greatest comebacks in its entire football history. It was trailing 34–12 midway through the final quarter, which prompted me to stop watching the TV, to thank Dick for his hospitality, and to return to my Princeton quarters. (I was staying in Maritain's house, then owned by ND, preparing lectures for our upcoming Perspective Series.) I did not learn of ND's final 35–34 win over Houston until I read about it in the paper two days later.

22. See McMullin's "Philosophy in the United States Catholic College," in McInerny, *New Themes,* 370–409.

23. The Perspective Series resembled the earlier conference on the concept of matter in both respects. The title of the series, McMullin often reminded me, was suggested by unwavering Thomist John Oesterle, in view of its intended effect of broadening the perspectives of ND's resident philosophers.

24. Vaughn's seventy-page "Social and Environmental Values in Power Plant Licensing: A Study in the Regulation of Nuclear Power," in *Values in the Electric*

Power Industry (UNDP, 1977), which I edited, and which also contains an essay by Alasdair McIntyre, is probably the most powerful essay in that volume.

25. Michael Loux, *Primary Ousia: An Essay on Aristotle's Metaphysics Z and H* (Ithaca, NY: Cornell University Press, 1991); *Metaphysics* (New York: Routledge, 1997), and *Nature, Norm and Psyche: Explorations in Aristotle's Philosophical Psychology* (Pisa: Scuola Normale Superiore, 2004).

26. Gary Gutting, *Michel Foucault's Archeology of Scientific Reason* (Cambridge: Cambridge University Press, 1989).

27. While expressing admiration for Saint Thomas, neither John XXIII nor Paul VI insisted on Thomism as a basis for Catholic theology or philosophy. The Thomist mandate imposed by Popes Leo XIII through Pius XII was subsequently rescinded by Pope John Paul II in his encyclicals *Veritatis Splendor* and *Fides et Ratio*. In *Veritatis Splendor* (1993) he proclaimed that "certainly the Church's Magisterium does not intend to impose upon the faithful any particular theological system, still less a philosophical one" (sec. 29). Then in *Fides et Ratio* (1998) he announces that "the Church has no philosophy of her own nor does she canonize any one particular philosopher in preference to others" (sec. 49), and that the term "Christian philosophy" should not be understood "to suggest that there is an official philosophy of the Church, since the faith as such is not a philosophy" (sec. 76).

28. Given that philosophical analysis was to be part of McMullin's pluralistic synthesis, one can almost hear him insist that ND should favor an "analytic philosopher" with a broad vision like that of Aristotle or Saint Thomas. In 1960, to be sure, he had persuaded the ACPA to hold a session on analytic philosophy and recommended Sellars for the job. My guess is that Ernan classified Sellars as an analytic philosopher on the basis of his editing (with Herbert Feigl) the 1949 volume *Readings in Philosophical Analysis*. Recently arrived from Harvard, I found that classification bizarre.

29. Documents involved are "Report of the Visitors to the Notre Dame University, Department of Philosophy, April 14–15, 1975," "Response to the External Evaluation of the Graduate Program," and "Report of the Review Committee for the Graduate Program in Philosophy," all on file in the Philosophy Department office. All quotations in this section are from these documents.

CHAPTER FIVE

1. Data in this paragraph come from the University of Notre Dame Archives and from Marina Smyth, "The Medieval Institute Library: A Brief History," in *What Is Written Remains: Historical Essays on the Libraries of Notre Dame,* ed. Maureen Gleason and Katherina J. Blackstead (UNDP, 1994), 211–29.

2. Fr. Phelan's ND residence was a room in the Main Building, the predecessor of which had been destroyed by fire in 1879. In the spring of 1952, smoke was detected coming from Phelan's quarters. It turned out that the priest was in an advanced state of inebriation and had let some tobacco fall on flammable material. To make matters worse, this was the second time he had set fire to his living quarters. Phelan spent a few days in the infirmary as a cover-up for this intolerable misadventure, and soon was shipped back to Toronto. For these and other details on Fr. Phelan, see Michel, *Penseé catholique,* 416–17.

3. Biographical material on Canon Gabriel is from a death notice by Marina Smyth ("Rt. Rev. Astrik L. Gabriel, O.Praem," Rare Books and Special Collections, Hesburgh Libraries, University of Notre Dame, http://www.library.nd .edu/rarebooks), and from an online obituary ("Abbot Canon Dr. Astrik L. Gabriel O.Praem.," Tributes.com, http://www.tributes.com/show/Abbot-O.Praem .-87771264).

4. The Ambrosiana Collection is a result of a conversation Fr. Hesburgh had with Giovanni Battista Cardinal Montini (later Pope Paul VI) on the occasion of ND's 1960 commencement, when Cardinal Montini, President Dwight D. Eisenhower, and iconic humanitarian Dr. Thomas Dooley all received honorary degrees. Montini and Hesburgh were walking past the hole being excavated for ND's new Memorial Library on their way to the exercises when Montini remarked (as paraphrased by Hesburgh in a recent interview): "Padre, you're going to need some books to put in it. Send somebody to Milan." Fr. Hesburgh's choice of emissary was Canon Gabriel. (I was present at this commencement ceremony and remember vividly the deferential treatment Dr. Dooley received from other members of the platform party, who seemed unaware of his countercultural reputation as an active homosexual.)

5. This description is from the online obituary http://www.tributes.com /show/Abbot-O.Praem.-87771264.

6. Canon Gabriel was reputed as prone to paying unwelcome attention to young women. Successive generations of female graduate students passed on the caution that when you come across this portly cleric in the library stacks you had better move quickly in the other direction.

7. Information on the search committee's activities was provided by Michael Loux, Neil Delaney, and Timothy O'Meara.

8. This account of Ralph's interest in the Medieval Institute position is based on conversations with then provost Timothy O'Meara and then department chair Neil Delaney.

9. Ralph McInerny, *I Alone Have Escaped,* 146.

10. Another account of the firing, due to David Solomon, has Dean Loux visiting Ralph's home to inform him of the provost's impending action, to the great consternation of Connie (Ralph's wife) and Fr. Marvin O'Connell, who were also present. Mike Loux disavows this version of the story. Whatever the details, hard

feelings against Loux persisted among Ralph's close friends and family for years to come. This was an additional factor contributing to Ralph's alienation from the Philosophy Department, of which Mike remained a prominent member.

11. Information on the founding of the JMC comes from letters written during 1958 by Joe Evans and Fr. Herman Reith to Academic Vice-President Philip Moore, CSC, conveying Maritain's detailed wishes for the proposed center, and from a letter from Fr. Moore to Joe Evans appointing Joe director. I have copies of these letters. Other sources are conversations with Alice Osberger, administrative assistant of the center since its inception, and the current JMC website, http://www2.nd.edu/.

12. This and the following paragraph rely on information provided by Maritain scholar Bernard Doering, ND professor emeritus of Romance languages.

13. Several decades after the fact, Alice Osberger remarked half-humorously that Joe's sister in Montreal, whom he had visited just before his death, was afraid that the sugar-rich pie she had baked for him might have been a contributing factor.

14. One of Ralph's first official acts as joint director of the JMC and the MI was to have a door cut in the wall between their two offices. This was tangible evidence of his expanding sense of empire. The door was removed when Ralph left the MI.

15. Up to his time at Stanford, Novak had been an advocate for liberal causes. By the time of his collaboration with Ralph in the JMC, however, he had published his well-known *The Spirit of Democratic Capitalism* (New York: Simon and Schuster, 1982), which promotes the virtues of capitalism as a basis for a democracy incorporating Christian virtues. On a recent AEI website (SourceWatch, http://www.sourcewatch.org/index.php?title=American_Enterprise_Institute, last modified July 11, 2012 [see under "Personnel"]), he is described (in terms obviously intended to be complimentary) as a "neoconservative Catholic who strongly favors capitalism and criticizes . . . liberal Catholic initiatives."

16. Ralph's ambition for the journal, stated in his *I Alone Have Escaped* (138), had been "to engage *America* and *Commonweal* frontally." *Commonweal* responded, somewhat belatedly, in an editorial entitled "'Crisis' Averted," dated September 14, 2007, by pointing out that among the journal's "driving ambitions" from the beginning were not only to condemn Catholic "dissenters" but to rebuke the bishops who failed to silence them. In the first issue Ralph had criticized the National Council of Catholic Bishops for opposing the Reagan administration's support (through the CIA) of the Nicaraguan contras who were attempting to overthrow the left-leaning Sandinista government.

17. I have copies of documents cited in this and the following two paragraphs.

18. Deal Hudson is a thrice-married former Baptist minister who converted to Catholicism in 1984 and taught at Fordham University from 1989 to 1995. He

was fired from Fordham as a result of sexual impropriety with a female undergraduate (in 1994), which eluded public notice until graphically disclosed by the *National Catholic Reporter* on August 19, 2004 (Joe Feuerherd, "The Real Deal," http://www.nationalcatholicreporter.org/update/bnHOLD081904.htm). Hudson subsequently became an adviser on the Catholic vote to Karl Rove during President George W. Bush's 2004 reelection campaign. Rove's strategy in that regard was to target churchgoing Catholics with alarmist sound bites pertaining to same-sex marriage and right-to-life issues, a strategy that probably contributed substantially to Bush's reelection. In this regard, see "'Crisis' Averted."

19. It is not clear from available records how much of this money was processed through regular channels of the university's Office of Research.

20. The decade of the 1980s had been a dry period for Ralph as a thesis director, with only one PhD completed (in 1983). There were also complaints about the quality of his teaching during this period, as well as about his frequent absences from the university. It is probably not coincidental that his greatest involvement with Novak and their contentious journal occurred during this time.

21. In 1989, for example, the JMC received $44,580 from the Bradley Foundation for student support (beneficiaries were Terry Hall, Brian Kelly, and Stephen Werner). This is one of the few grants to the center documented in department records. Fellowship money came in from private donors as well, reputedly including Michael Novak.

22. John's appointment to the department in 2003 was controversial. At stake was the disposition of the newly available John and Jean Oesterle Professorship of Thomistic Studies. Many tenured faculty argued that John, with his 1996 ND PhD, had insufficient seniority for the position. The issue was resolved by conferring the titled professorship on Fred Freddoso and using the endowment to fund John's appointment as associate professor with tenure.

23. Michael Scriven's "The Mechanical Concept of Mind" was published in 1953, Hao Wang's "Toward Mechanical Mathematics" in 1960, and John Lucas's "Minds, Machines, and Gödel" in 1961. My friend Bert Dreyfus had begun to pester AI researchers in the halls of MIT as early as 1960.

24. Kenneth M. Sayre, "Human and Mechanical Recognition," *Methodos* 14, no. 54 (1962): 27–40; Kenneth M. Sayre and Joseph Bobik, "Pattern Recognition Mechanisms and St. Thomas' Theory of Abstraction," *Revue Philosophique de Louvain* 61 (1963): 24–43; Kenneth M. Sayre and Frederick Crosson, eds., *The Modeling of Mind: Computers and Intelligence* (UNDP, 1963).

25. Dozens of current websites can be found citing Sayre's paradox by name, although not always stating it in its original form.

26. High-level ND administrators at this point were beginning to push interdisciplinary research. Our group included participants from four universities, five ND colleges, and ten disciplines overall. A regrettable outcome in our case is

that Neil Schilmoeller subsequently was denied tenure, for the apparent reason that his particular department at the time did not approve of interdisciplinary work.

27. For several years after the beginning of our power-industry studies, the group had continued to use the title "Philosophic Institute for Artificial Intelligence" in correspondence. By the end of the 1970s, reference to AI had been dropped from the title.

28. This estimate is due to Michael Loux, A&L dean from 1983 to 1991.

29. Not mentioned in the narrative above is an NSF grant of $4,841 in 1973 to Harold Moore (then of GPLE) and me for an exploratory study in medical ethics. Moore enrolled in ND Law School in 1974, but continued teaching. He moved to Philosophy in 1977, where he taught until receiving his JD in 1980 (graduating at the top of his class). He then moved to New York as a corporate finance lawyer. Also not mentioned are several excellent secretaries who served the institute during that period.

30. Center for Philosophy of Religion, 2012, http://philreligion.nd.edu.

31. Although Catholic University had a PBK chapter dating from 1941, Fred was not elected as an undergraduate. He became an honorary faculty member shortly after ND received a chapter in 1968. Fred was the only PBK member I have known to wear his key as part of his daily attire.

32. This sketch of CRC origins comes from "Christian Reformed Church" at http://www.crcna.org/pages/history_of_crc.cfm.

33. Alvin Plantinga, "Spiritual Autobiography," 20.

34. Although I never heard him use the term *aggiornamento,* Al clearly agreed with Ralph that the "updating" of the church following Vatican II was moving in the wrong direction. Al was particularly concerned that the biological sciences were threatening Christian orthodoxy in their reliance on the evolutionary model. Al's common cause with Ralph in this general regard continued well into the first decade of this century, when they had a falling out on matters of departmental hiring.

35. Some of Al's arguments and accompanying concepts became so well known that they gained name-recognition on their own. Consider The Great Pumpkin Objection (to Reformed Epistemology) and The Free Will Defense (based on the notion of Transworld Depravity).

36. Al himself admits being confuted once by David Lewis. See Alvin Plantinga, "Self Profile," in *Alvin Plantinga,* ed. James E. Tomberlin and Peter van Inwagen (Dordrecht: D. Reidel, 1985), 49–50.

37. Plantinga, "Spiritual Autobiography," 6–7.

38. Ibid., 7–8.

39. Ibid., 17.

40. An eagerly anticipated bout took place between Plantinga and Daniel Dennett (Tufts) during the 2009 meeting of the APA in Chicago. Both contestants had a gallery of supporters, each of which claimed victory when the dust settled.

A blow-by-blow account of this match is given in Andrew Moon's "An Opinionated Play-by-Play of the Plantinga-Dennett Exchange," *The Prosblogion: A Philosophy of Religion Blog,* February 23, 2009, http://prosblogion.ektopos.com.

41. I still have a photo from that occasion of Anscombe and myself sitting together, both dressed in then-acceptable masculine attire. Despite her mannish ways (she also smoked cigars), Elizabeth was happily married to Peter Geach and mother of seven children. Among many droll stories about Anscombe, my favorite has to do with attire. Once when attending an upscale Boston restaurant, she was told by the headwaiter that women in pants were not allowed to be seated. Elizabeth promptly took off her pants and proceeded to a table in her (quite modest) underclothing.

42. Proceedings of the 1988 conference were published as *Christian Philosophy* (UNDP, 1990), under the editorship of Tom Flint. Proceedings of the 1986 conference, "Philosophy and the Christian Faith," had been published by the same press two years earlier, under T. V. Morris's editorship.

43. Distrust between CPR philosophers and ND theologians was rampant, the former thinking the latter too liberal and the latter thinking the former too conservative. Collins and his cohorts actually put pressure on the university to cancel the conference before it was convened. Tom Flint appealed successfully to President Monk Malloy, and the conference went on as scheduled.

44. Unlike the MI, the JMC, and the PIAI, the CPR at the time had little external funding. These postdocs in 1984 were funded by a grant from the Pew Charitable Trusts, with additional support from the Philosophy Department itself. Continuity in funding was provided for several years by the Dean's Office (while Mike Loux was dean), but the CPR came under increasing pressure to find outside funding for itself. Al extended little effort of his own in this regard, maintaining that his job was to direct the center but not to finance it.

45. The first substantial grant from the outside ($1.4 million) came in 2009 from the Templeton Foundation, when Mike Rea was director of the CPR. This grant was worked out with the help of Templeton contact Michael J. Murray, who received a philosophy PhD from ND in 1991 and was CPR Plantinga Fellow in 2003–4.

46. Jack Reilly had gained prominence at ND previously as a supporter of the Snite Museum of Art. In the early 1980s he donated the Wisdom-Reilly Collection of master drawings, purchased intact for the museum from art scholar John Minor Wisdom. This initial collection of sixty-five pieces served as a nucleus for the highly acclaimed and still-growing John D. Reilly Collection, consisting mostly of nineteenth-century drawings by Degas, Millet, and Ingres, among others, and now numbering over five hundred items. Still an active benefactor of the university, Jack donated a room dedicated to his brother (James J. Reilly) in Stinson-Remick Hall, the engineering building opened in 2010.

47. McKim has different recollections from those of Mike Loux about the extent of his and McMullin's involvement in setting up the Reilly Center. Be this as it may, McKim was not invited to the center's inauguration and believes that McMullin also was not invited.

48. Ernan McMullin, ed., *Construction and Constraint: The Shaping of Scientific Rationality*, with an introduction by Vaughn McKim (UNDP, 1988); Ernan McMullin and James Cushing, eds., *Philosophical Consequences of Quantum Theory: Reflections on Bell's Theorem* (UNDP, 1989).

49. Between 1995 and 2010, a total of 27 PhD degrees were granted by the program, 14 in history and 13 in philosophy. As of 2010, all 13 degree-holders in philosophy were holding academic positions, compared with 10 in history. Ernan often spoke with pride of Alisa Bokulich, who received her HPS PhD in 2001 and was appointed director of Boston University's Center for Philosophy & History of Science in 2010.

50. Already mentioned are proceedings from conferences held before the PhD program got underway, appearing under McMullin's editorship in 1988 and 1989. These are listed in the public record as volumes 1 and 2 of the Reilly Center's Studies in Science and the Humanities. The next three volumes of this series, all published by UNDP, are as follows: (3) *The Social Dimensions of Science* (1992), edited by Ernan McMullin; (4) *Causality in Crisis? Statistical Methods and the Search for Causal Knowledge in the Social Sciences* (1997), edited by Vaughn McKim and Stephen P. Turner (a sociologist from the University of South Florida); and (5) *Controlling Our Destinies: Historical, Philosophical, Ethical, and Theological Perspectives on the Human Genome Project* (2000), edited by Phillip Sloan.

51. McMullin's interest in Galileo traces back to his early years in the department. As noted previously, he had organized a conference at ND in 1964 marking the four-hundredth anniversary of Galileo's birth. The proceedings of that conference, *Galileo: Man of Science,* had become a standard reference work in many areas of Galileo studies. As the title might suggest, however, this earlier work left the Vatican's treatment of Galileo largely unexamined.

52. Geoffrey Cantor, "Galileo and the Church: Then and Now," *Metascience* 15 (2006): 345–48.

53. A somewhat disgruntled discussion of how this performance fit into the agenda of the conference may be found in Wendy Arons's "Interdisciplinarity, Performance, Power: 'Galileo' in the Academy," *Theatre Topics* 14, no. 1 (March 2004): 275–91. Arons, at the time, was an ND professor of film, television, and theater.

54. Ernan McMullin served as the original director of the Reilly Center from 1986 to 1994. Subsequent directors were Vaughn McKim (1995–97), Phillip Sloan (PLS, 1997–98), again McKim (1999–2003), and then Gerald McKenny (theology, 2004–10). Don Howard took over in 2011. These same people took turns

heading up the center's constituent HPS program. McMullin was the first director of HPS after it became a PhD program (1990). McKim then became acting director in 1991–92 and director from 1993 to 1994. Sloan served as director from 1995 to 1997. Don Howard became director in 1998, the year after he joined the Philosophy Department, serving until 2010. As for the undergraduate STV program, its first director was McKim (1986–94), followed by Chris Hamlin (History, 1995–97), Kristin Shrader-Frechette (1998), and then Phil Sloan (1999–2001). Between 2001 and 2011, STV lacked a regular director and was managed by acting directors instead. Edward Jurkowitz, an administrator without departmental affiliation, took over as education director in 2011.

CHAPTER SIX

1. Statistics in this section for the most part pertain to incoming faculty who received PhDs before the end of their first year at ND and who stayed at least three years. Excluded are most visiting faculty who stayed only one year, and several CSC priests who were assigned to the department by their nonacademic superiors. No distinction is made here between tenure-track faculty who left because not reappointed and those who left for other reasons. Professional specialists, adjunct professors, and concurrent professors from other departments also are not included.

2. From Joe Evans in 1950 to John O'Callaghan in 2003, the ND department has hired fourteen of its own PhDs into tenure-track positions. Of these, at least one (Michael Rea) was not Catholic at time of hiring.

3. Information about jobs after leaving ND from 1960 on comes from the Internet, augmented by my own memory. With occasional exceptions, I am confident that this information is reliable. Nonetheless, the percentages in the text should be read as close approximations.

4. See Anja Jauernig, "About Me," http://www.pitt.edu/~jauernig/About Me.html.

5. Christian B. Miller, editor of *Essays in the Philosophy of Religion / Philip L. Quinn* (Oxford: Clarendon, 2006), lists fifty-five. Data in this and the next few paragraphs are from this source and from Phil's CV.

6. Other members of the department elected to the AAAS before Phil were Alvin Plantinga, Alasdair MacIntyre, and Ernan McMullin, as well as former member Penelope Maddy. ND philosophers elected after Phil are Peter van Inwagen, Karl Ameriks, and Fr. John Jenkins.

7. Philip L. Quinn and Charles Taliaferro, eds., *A Companion to Philosophy of Religion* (Malden, MA: Blackwell, 1997); Philip L. Quinn and Kevin Meeker, eds., *The Philosophical Challenge of Religious Diversity* (Oxford: Oxford University Press, 2000).

8. When not traveling to conventions, Phil spent most of his leisure time in his crowded apartment. A speed-reader with a voracious literary appetite, he had thousands of books stacked on shelves both at home and in his office. On a typical evening at home he would leaf rapidly through professional literature, read an entire mystery novel, and then take a glass of scotch to help put him to sleep.

9. As far as I know, there was no public indication of Phil's own sexual orientation. Like Ernan McMullin, he had a conspicuous number of good friends among women but relatively few among men. In point of fact, however, his presence conveyed an impression of disinterest in amorous involvement of any sort.

10. Quotations and other relevant material in this paragraph are taken from an April 2, 2009, letter by David Hoekema (Calvin College), 1984–92 executive director of the APA, to Kwame Anthony Appiah, 2008–9 chair of Board of Officers of the APA (http://www.calvin.edu/academic/philosophy), and from "A Letter to the American Philosophical Association Board of Directors" drafted by Mark C. Murphy, May 18, 2009 (http://www9.georgetown.edu/faculty/murphym/APAStatement-Murphy.htm).

11. Hesburgh, *God, Country*, 182.

12. Ibid., 183.

13. Sheilah and Ralph McInerny were graduate students together at Laval and completed their PhDs the same year. Unlike Ralph, Sheilah had little enthusiasm for the brand of Thomism represented by Charles De Koninck. I first encountered Sheilah O'Flynn (her maiden name) at Harvard when she was interviewing for the Woodrow Wilson Fellowship that took her to Oxford in 1955.

14. Also present at this time was Adjunct Professor Janet Kourany, wife of James Sterba. Janet was a visiting instructor at ND during the academic year 1975–76. After receiving her PhD from Columbia in 1977, she taught at the University of Utah for the next four years, reaching the rank of associate professor. She returned to ND in 1981, serving as adjunct associate professor until 2001, when she became an associate professor on the regular faculty.

15. For reasons it chooses not to discuss publicly, ND is not legally on record as opposed to what was termed "level-two discrimination" in the fourth section of this chapter. As a legally nonbinding substitute, the administration issued a document entitled "The Spirit of Inclusion at Notre Dame" in 1997. The upshot of "The Spirit," as stated in the student handbook, is that ND welcomes "all people, regardless of color, gender, religion, ethnicity, sexual orientation, social or economic class, and nationality." Moreover, the statement says, ND values "gay and lesbian members of this community as we value all members of this community," and goes on to condemn "harassment of any kind." Whether ND eventually will follow the lead of other Catholic universities (including Fordham, Georgetown, and Loyola) in adding a sexual orientation clause to its official nondiscrimination policy remains to be seen.

16. A sign of unsettled times in religious orders after Vatican II is the fact that four of the last six nuns to receive PhDs in the department returned to secular life and eventually married. Along with Shrader-Frechette and Pampusch, a notable example is Dolores Dooley. Dr. Dooley's husband, Dr. Desmond Clarke, is a former priest who received an ND PhD in philosophy the same year as she (1974). Both subsequently found teaching positions in the University of Cork, Ireland. David Solomon told me of his astonishment when the two, still in religious garb, came up after class one day to announce their engagement.

17. It is hard to imagine Stuart Hampshire, Thomas Kuhn, Paul Benacerraf, and Richard Rorty (a partial roster of Princeton philosophers at the time) spending a day together working on a colleague's house.

18. I also recall that during my time at Harvard (1952–58), roughly half of the incoming graduate students failed the prelims each year and were dropped from the program. The failure rate for ND's comps, by contrast, averaged somewhere around 15 percent, even during their more rigorous years in the 1970s.

19. Montey Holloway received an ND PhD in philosophy in 1981, and from 1982 to the present has served as professional specialist in the role of assistant to the chair. Montey has been the stabilizing element through the years that has protected the department from being swamped by computerized bureaucracy.

20. This was the case even at wealthier universities, Harvard included. Apart from a few Junior Fellows (Burton Dreben, Marshall Cohen, Stanley Cavell, Charles Parsons), I was not aware of any philosophy graduate students during my time who received financial aid from the university. After paying room, board, and tuition out of savings my first year, I was enabled to complete my PhD by a half-time appointment as assistant dean of Harvard's Graduate School of Arts and Sciences (1953–56) and a nine-to-five job with MIT's Lincoln Laboratory (1956–58).

21. As soon became evident, faculty were not inclined to teach survey courses on the graduate level, preferring courses in their own specialized areas. After a few years of vacillation, the upshot of the new system was that PhD candidates took written exams in the history of philosophy and in their own areas of projected specialization, along with specialized courses in the three systematic areas. Providing the broad competence in these areas that prepared candidates for undergraduate teaching had disappeared from the department's agenda.

22. The graduate-student proposal was drafted by Tim Hurley, who taught for six years as assistant professor at Furman University and now is a lawyer in South Carolina.

23. These data come from a list, issued by the ND Graduate School, of PhDs earned in the department between 1934 and 2009, and from a careful name-by-name Internet search. Because of possible errors in both sources, figures given in the text should be treated as best-available approximations.

24. Minor changes were made in the 1980s and 1990s to modify the open-list approach with a few prerequisites. Moving into the 2000s, requirements

(beyond the two-course base) have included a fixed set of three courses (history of ancient and medieval, history of modern, formal logic), three electives from the intermediate or advanced level, and two advanced seminars. These latter five are chosen from what happens to be available, with no guidelines regarding sequence or degree of difficulty.

25. Comparisons on this score are complicated by lack of uniformity in classifying faculty entering the count. The only thing certain about such a count is that the largest philosophy department in the country will be at a Catholic university.

26. Through the 1970s and 1980s, the Philosophy Department was treated by the Dean's Office as the "plum" of the A&L College.

27. A case in point is the majors course I taught in the fall of 1992 on Plato's *Parmenides*. I had taught a previous graduate course on this dialogue during the 1970s. But the dialogue is so difficult, and my interpretation was so slow in developing, that I was still working on it two decades later. Although only five signed up for the majors course in 1992 (there were also several auditors), they were very good students, and some of my remaining problems with the dialogue were resolved during that semester. *Parmenides' Lesson: Translation and Explication of Plato's* Parmenides was finally published in 1996.

28. This quotation comes from a message of ND's executive vice-president, John A. Affleck-Graves, introducing ND's 2011 *Annual Report Online*. Wording of the blurb changes from year to year. For a subsequent version, see "Advancing Our Vision" at http://advancingourvision.nd.edu.

CHAPTER SEVEN

1. The National Research Council had been publishing rank orderings of graduate programs since the early 1980s. These rankings came out infrequently and were soon overshadowed by those of PGR.

2. Leiter had earned a JD from Michigan Law School before beginning work on his philosophy PhD. After receiving the PhD, he held a tenure-track position in the Texas Law School from 1995 to 1997 and then occupied four different endowed chairs sequentially in law and philosophy between 1997 and 2008. In 2008 he moved to the Law School of the University of Chicago, where currently he is John P. Wilson Professor of Law and director of the Center for Law, Philosophy, and Human Values.

3. Kim was McMahon-Hank Visiting Professor at ND during the fall terms of 1999 and of 2001–5, all the while occupying his regular position of William Herbert Perry Faunce Professor of Philosophy at Brown. This time at ND is not mentioned on his Brown CV.

4. By 2004, ND had far outstripped other Catholic programs in the country. Georgetown, the only other Catholic department to appear in the rankings

that year, was in a six-way tie for forty-fourth (see Philosophical Gourmet Report 2011, http://www.philosophicalgourmet.com/overall.asp). In the 2008 PGR rankings of the top fifty philosophy programs in the English-speaking world, only Oxford and St. Andrews (Scotland) among foreign universities ranked higher than ND.

5. The open letter in question was drafted by Richard Heck, then of Harvard University, and signed by almost two hundred other philosophers across the country. This letter was reported and discussed in Katherine S. Mangan, "175 Philosophy Professors Blast Rankings of Graduate Programs," *Chronicle of Higher Education,* January 18, 2002. One complaint was that PGR had become too influential to be controlled by one individual. Leiter subsequently established an advisory board of five dozen or so professional philosophers to help him construct and administer the surveys on which the rankings are based. Despite this diversification of influence, a recent news release in the *Boston Globe* described Leiter (then of Chicago's Law School) as still "the most powerful man in academic philosophy" (see Mark Oppenheimer, "The Philosopher Kingmaker," *Boston Globe,* April 20, 2008).

6. Leiter himself had stressed from the first that his rankings amount to an "attempt to capture . . . professional reputations" based on publication counts, "professional honors, job offers, and conversations." The quotation is from "Description of the Report" in the 1991–92 hard-copy PGR (DOC#49718 on file in ND's Philosophy Department).

7. Born in 1947 in Fern Creek, Kentucky, Kristin Shrader graduated from a high school run by the Sisters of Mercy and at age seventeen joined the order herself. Her superiors asked her to major in mathematics at Edgecliff College, and then sent her to ND for a PhD in philosophy. After two years of course work, she completed her thesis in a record two additional years. Shortly after completing her PhD, Kristin was released from her vows. She subsequently married Maurice Frechette, a laicized Christian Brother with a PhD in mathematics from ND.

8. Release time as research professor at South Florida enabled Shrader-Frechette to increase her publication rate almost threefold. This was in addition to her outspoken advocacy for female-faculty rights, which led to increasing involvement in unsavory campus politics. Her personal (and sometimes chilling) account of the latter is included as chap. 9 in *Singing in the Fire: Stories of Women in Philosophy,* ed. Linda Martin Alcoff (Lanham, MD: Rowman & Littlefield, 2003).

9. See the website of the Center for Environmental Justice and Children's Health, http://www3.nd.edu/~kshrader/cejch.html.

10. Sterba's CV would be even longer if it included details such as page numbers of journal articles and volumes in which they appear.

11. Sterba joined the Christian Brothers (a Catholic teaching order) as a teenager, but left before taking final vows. As mentioned in personal conversation,

his belief in a Christian God had been subverted by his failure to find a rationally convincing solution to the problem of evil.

12. Thomas V. Morris, *Understanding Identity Statements* (Aberdeen: Aberdeen University Press, 1986).

13. See "Wisdom Retreats," Morris Institute for Human Values, http://www.morrisinstitute.com.

14. In his eulogy on March 3, 2011 (see the epilogue), Fr. Hesburgh acknowledged Ernan as the single faculty member who did most to advance his goal of excellence in research.

15. My PIAI (chap. 5) is a case in point. Between 1962 and 1972, we brought roughly $113,000 in grant money into the university. By 1980, we had brought in another $233,000. This adds up to more than a million 2010 dollars.

16. ND's organizational chart circa 2010 is on the Internet at http://www.nd.edu/about/leadership/pdf/orgchart.pdf, under the title "ND Online Directory."

17. See "Doing Business South Bend," at http://www.southbendin.gov/business/ideal_bsns_envmt/avlble_prop/innov_pk.asp.

18. This opaque statement comes from the "OTT Mission and Vision" page of the OTT website, http://ott.nd.edu.

19. In its current instantiation, Innovation Park is an imposing three-story brick building across from ND's new hockey complex. It remains mostly vacant two years after completion. A second building, dedicated to research in nanotechnology, was originally scheduled to be completed in 2012, but was not yet under construction by the beginning of that year.

20. See National Science Foundation, "In Service to Society: NSF Strategic Areas," http://www.nsf.gov.

21. ND sports arenas, classroom buildings, and residence halls are usually named after donors. Other buildings are sometimes funded by more self-effacing benefactors and named for prominent CSC priests, such as Hesburgh Library, Joyce (Athletic and Convocation) Center, and Malloy Hall. In point of fact, most public facilities at ND (so far excluding water fountains and water closets) are named after people. A campaign was recently underway to find donors willing to contribute $1,500 in return for having their names attached to individual seats in the new Phillip J. Purcell (basketball) Pavilion. These would be endowed chairs, economy class.

22. McInerny and Loux are anomalous in this regard and perhaps should be classified separately. Although veteran philosophers, both initially received chairs outside the department. McInerny's chair came through the Medieval Institute, and Loux was installed as O'Shaughnessy Dean of A&L before returning to the department. Three years after returning, he became the George Shuster Chair of Philosophy.

23. Alasdair MacIntyre, *Marxism: An Interpretation* (London: SCM, 1953; reissued as *Marxism and Christianity,* 1968); Alasdair MacIntyre and Anthony Flew, eds., *New Essays in Philosophical Theology* (London: SCM, 1955); Alasdair MacIntyre, *The Unconscious: A Conceptual Analysis* (New York: Humanities Press, 1958); *Difficulties in Christian Belief* (London: SCM, 1959); *A Short History of Ethics* (New York: Macmillan, 1966); *Secularization and Moral Change* (London: Oxford University Press, 1967); *The Religious Significance of Atheism* (New York: Columbia University Press, 1969); *Herbert Marcuse: An Exposition and a Polemic* (New York: Viking, 1970).

24. See Kelvin Knight, *Aristotelian Philosophy: Ethics and Politics from Aristotle to MacIntyre* (Cambridge: Polity Press, 2007), 2.

25. Mark C. Murphy, on page 1 of his biography *Alasdair MacIntyre* (Cambridge: Cambridge University Press, 2003), quotes from an interview in which Alasdair distinguishes three phases in his life as an academic philosopher. The early phase, from 1949 to 1971, is one "of heterogeneous, badly organized, sometimes fragmented and often frustrating and messy enquiries from which nonetheless in the end [he] learned a lot." The second phase is from 1971 to 1977, which was "an interim period of sometimes painfully self-critical reflection." The third phase, from 1977 onwards, finds him engaged in a single project "to which *After Virtue, Whose Justice? Which Rationality?*, and *Three Rival Versions of Moral Enquiry* are central."

26. Alasdair MacIntyre, *Against the Self-Images of the Age: Essays on Ideology and Philosophy* (London: Duckworth, 1971).

27. Alasdair and Lynn were married in 1977. He had two daughters by his first wife, to whom he was married from 1953 to 1963, and a son and daughter by his second, whom he married in 1963 and divorced in 1977. As previously noted, Alasdair described the years 1971 to 1977 as the part of his life when he was engaged in "sometimes painfully self-critical reflection."

28. The department prepared a request that Alasdair be made an offer in the fall of 1986, but Fr. Hesburgh refused to approve it for two specific reasons (with which Alasdair was rumored to have agreed). One was that Alasdair was known to have a severe drinking problem. In 1975, I believe it was, he had delivered one of his Perspective lectures while visibly intoxicated (although, remarkably, the lecture was quite coherent). The other is that Hesburgh considered it inappropriate to have a twice-divorced person in a chaired position teaching ethics at ND. The request was resubmitted, and quickly approved, when Fr. Malloy took over as university president in 1987. As Fr. Malloy explained later, MacIntyre had converted to Catholicism and had stopped drinking a few years previously. (Alasdair was said to have agreed with this reasoning as well and accepted the offer.)

29. Lynn Sumida Joy, *Gassendi the Atomist, Advocate of History in an Age of Science* (Cambridge: Cambridge University Press, 1987).

30. Ethical theory was not a strong suit among top Catholic philosophers of this period. Among Alasdair's putative peers in this group, only Canadian Charles Taylor had overlapping interests; and Taylor has a history of rebuffing overtures from departments in the United States.

31. From Hauerwas's biographical essay, "The Virtues of Alasdair MacIntyre," *First Things,* October 2007, http://www.firstthings.com.

32. Out of love and respect for the Oesterles, Ralph found ways of keeping Jean occupied after her health began to fail. Her title of associate editor provided justification for her retaining office space in the Maritain Center.

33. Editors listed between 1981 and 1988 include philosophers and logicians from both inside and outside the university. Penelope Maddy and Michael Detlefsen were trained logicians from ND's Philosophy Department. ND philosophers listed on the masthead with specialties other than logic were Phillip Bricker, Ernest LePore, and Howard Wettstein. LePore came to ND in 1979 with a PhD from Minnesota. He left for Rutgers in 1981, where he currently is professor of philosophy and acting director of the school's Center for Cognitive Science. Wettstein was at ND from 1985 to 1989. His PhD is from the City University of New York. He subsequently was coeditor of *Midwest Studies in Philosophy,* with Peter French of Arizona State. He is now professor of philosophy at UC Riverside.

34. See "How Can Notre Dame Philosophical Reviews Publish Nonsense Like This?," in *Leiter Reports: A Philosophy Blog,* May 2007, http://leiterreports .typepad.com.

35. See Catherine Grant, "Back from Vac with Notre Dame Philosophical Reviews," *Film Studies for Free* (blog), August 5, 2009, http://filmstudiesforfree .blogspot.com.

36. Concurrent faculty are not full-time members of the Philosophy Department and hence not treated in this account. Reydams-Schils enters the account because of her role as editor of a philosophy journal. Other concurrent faculty in 2010 were John Finnis (Law), Stephen Gersh (Medieval Institute), Vittorio Hösle (German and Russian Languages and Literatures [GRLL]), G. Felicitas Munzel (PLS), Robert Norton (GRLL), and Mark Roche (GRLL).

37. Mic and I were born in the same Scottsbluff hospital, roughly twenty years apart.

38. Curtis Franks, *The Autonomy of Mathematical Knowledge: Hilbert's Program Revisited* (Cambridge: Cambridge University Press, 2009).

39. Dean Zimmerman and Peter van Inwagen, eds., *Metaphysics: The Big Questions* (Malden, MA: Blackwell, 1998).

40. See Peter van Inwagen, Quam Dilecta, http://informationphilosopher .com/solutions/philosophers/vaninwagen/quam_dilecta.html.

41. My PhD thesis, written under Roderick Firth, was titled "Phenomenalism and the Selective Theory." In the late 1960s I left epistemology as a research topic and started dividing my time between Plato and cybernetics. I returned to

epistemology in the late 1990s with the publication of *Belief and Knowledge: Mapping the Cognitive Landscape* (Lanham, MD: Rowman & Littlefield, 1997).

42. As recorded in The Peerage, "Leopold Ernst Herr und Graf von Stubenberg," http://thepeerage.com/p11614.htm.

43. Leopold Stubenberg, *Consciousness and Qualia* (Amsterdam: J. Benjamin, 1998).

44. Marian David, *Correspondence and Disquotation: An Essay on the Nature of Truth* (Oxford: Oxford University Press, 1994).

45. The only ND PhD thesis expressly on philosophy of mind in the department to date was completed in 1990 by Steven Horst under my direction.

46. William M. Ramsey, *Representation Reconsidered* (Cambridge: Cambridge University Press, 2007).

47. At the end of the term, Ramsey would announce an extra session in which he gave his own atheistic views on these issues. More students would show up for these "off the record" sessions than regularly attended his scheduled lectures.

48. For a scarcely believable video of his rock-climbing prowess, see "Bill Ramsey—Reverse Polarity (5.14b)," DPM Climbing video, http://www.dpmclimbing.com/climbing-videos.

49. See Anja Jauernig, "About Me."

50. No minutes were taken at these meetings. My information comes from position statements submitted by Professors Plantinga, Burrell, Quinn, Loux, and McMullin, copies of which were given me by McMullin. There was no written input from either McInerny or MacIntyre.

51. Included among the research activities of a Catholic university, the encyclical emphasized, "will be a study of *serious contemporary problems* in areas such as the dignity of human life, the promotion of justice for all, the quality of personal and family life, the protection of nature, the search for peace and political stability, a more just sharing in the world's resources, and a new economic and political order that will better serve the human community" (English translation, sec. 32, emphasis original).

CHAPTER EIGHT

1. These and other quotations in this section are from "Report of the Committee to Visit the Philosophy Department, University of Notre Dame, Nov. 5–8, 2000," on file in the Philosophy Department office.

2. The external reviewers omitted details on both counts. With respect to faculty retention, however, it is relevant to note that only four of the seventeen junior faculty given tenure during the 1980s and 1990s had book-length publications before being promoted, a majority having fewer than ten published articles. Regarding graduate-student assessment, it is also noteworthy that graduate

students were seldom dropped from the program because of poor performance after the written comprehensives were abolished in 1989.

3. This figure is from then department chair Paul Weithman's "Department Response to the Reports of the Reviewers [of the] Department of Philosophy," subsequently cited by description rather than title.

4. The two chair-level offers to Catholics that were rejected went to Eleonore Stump, who by then had converted to Catholicism, and to Jean-Luc Marion of the Sorbonne, described in the department minutes of October 31, 2007, as "the most prominent Catholic philosopher in Europe." The source of this glowing description was not documented.

5. Rankings for 2004, 2006, 2009, and 2011 come from Leiter, "Overall Rankings," Philosophical Gourmet Report 2011, http://www.philosophical gourmet.com/overall.asp.

6. On May 5, 2004, Provost Hatch convened a group of interested parties, including Paul Weithman, Fr. Brian Daley, and Jeffrey Kantor, vice-president for graduate studies and research, to discuss Weithman's response to the external reviewers' recommendations. The Graduate School's official summary of this meeting ("Summary of the Three-Year Follow-Up Meeting for the Department of Philosophy Review") states perfunctorily that the department "has improved the quality of the tenure and promotion packets it presents to the College" and "has improved the procedure for evaluating graduate students." No specifics are given.

7. In the mid-1990s, both Dean Harold Attridge and Provost Nathan Hatch strongly supported the department's efforts to improve its rankings. Unanimity on this matter ended when Mark Roche replaced Attridge as dean in 1997. Roche (a concurrent member of the department) had studied philosophy for two years in Tübingen before going to Princeton for a PhD in German literature, and was unhappy with the American style of philosophy that puts a premium on prestige. Weithman's near silence on the topic may have been due to an understandable reluctance to get involved in a disagreement between dean and provost.

8. See his review of *Catholicism and Liberalism,* ed. R. Bruce Douglass and David Hollenbach, in *Faith and Philosophy* 13, no. 1 (1996): 144.

9. Paul Weithman, "Toward an Augustinian Liberalism," *Faith and Philosophy* 8, no. 4 (October 1991): 461–62.

10. Entitled "The Two-Course Requirement in Philosophy," this statement is included in the department minutes of December 11, 2003.

11. Unless otherwise noted, quotes in this section are from the CEC's (unpublished) 2008 "Self-Study Document, Notre Dame Center for Ethics and Culture," prepared in advance for its external review.

12. Hatch left ND to become president of Wake Forest, a formerly Baptist and still conservative university in Winston-Salem, North Carolina.

13. As quoted in the Philosophy Newsletter of fall 2000, David also intended the event to acknowledge Ralph's approaching fiftieth year in the department.

David jumped the gun a bit on this one. Ralph's actual fiftieth anniversary was celebrated with another lavish banquet thrown by the CEC in 2006. Joe Bobik, who had arrived at ND the same year as Ralph, was honored on this same occasion. While the event was still underway, Joe confided in me that he found the whole thing a bit overdone.

14. John Robinson, David's friend and longtime associate, has been extensively involved in this conference from its beginning. John received a 1975 PhD in philosophy from ND and a 1979 JD from UC Berkeley, Law School, and then joined ND's Philosophy Department in 1981. He served as assistant professor of law and philosophy from 1984 through 1988, when he moved to ND's Law School full-time. He currently is associate professor of law and associate dean of the Law School. John has a natural wit rivaling that of his deceased friend, Ralph McInerny, save that John's is more restrained than extroverted and more dry than effervescent.

15. This credit comes from Nicholas Capaldi of New Orleans' Loyola University, in a testimonial letter to David Solomon dated December 22, 2007, included in the CEC's "Self-Study Document."

16. According to its 2012 website, headed "Notre Dame Fund to Protect Human Life" (http://sites.google.com/a/nd.edu/the-notre-dame-fund-to-protect-human-life), the purpose of the fund is "to educate Notre Dame students in the rich intellectual tradition supporting the dignity of human life, especially in its beginning stages, and to prepare those students, through personal witness, public service, and prayer, to transform the culture into one in which every human life is respected." This rather visionary description happens to be part of an Internet solicitation for contributions. When I last spoke to David about this in mid-2011, the fund had received direct gifts totaling about $500,000 and two legacy gifts (in wills) each in excess of $1,000,000.

17. John still swims in winter, but prefers running in summer. In the fall of 2003, he completed his first marathon in Chicago, running with John Affleck-Graves (soon to be his executive vice-president), who had completed ninety-two marathons previously. Biographical information in this and the next two paragraphs is from Ed Cohen's "Genuine John Jenkins," *Notre Dame Magazine,* Summer 2004, 5–9.

18. John Jenkins, *Knowledge and Faith in Thomas Aquinas* (Cambridge: Cambridge University Press, 1997).

19. Cohen, "Genuine John Jenkins."

20. Outgoing president Monk Malloy strongly opposed Willingham's ouster, describing it as the only time he had "been embarrassed to be president of Notre Dame." See Pete Thamel, "Outgoing President Opposed Firing Willingham," *New York Times,* December 9, 2004, http://www.nytimes.com.

21. See Bishop John D'Arcy's statement "Vagina Monologues Presentation at Notre Dame," Catholic Diocese of Fort Wayne-South Bend, February 12, 2004, http://diocesefwsb.org.

22. See Neela Banerjee, "Notre Dame's President Allows 'Monologues' and Gay Films," *New York Times,* April 6, 2006, http://www.nytimes.com.

23. See Jeff Mirus, "The *Monologues* Revisited: Bishop D'Arcy and Notre Dame," Catholic Culture.org, April 25, 2006, http://www.catholicculture.org.

24. See the retrospective April 4, 2011, account "The Teacher, the University and Sycamore," Sycamore Trust, April 4, 2011, http://www.projectsycamore.com /bulletins/110327.php.

25. See David Solomon, "A President's Retreat," *Wall Street Journal,* April 14, 2006, http://online.wsj.com/article/SB114496644011725536.html.

26. This is from a personal conversation with former A&L dean Michael Loux.

27. Dates and other details are from LifeSiteNews, "Catholic University of Notre Dame President Approves Vulgar Pro-Lesbian Play Vagina Monologues," LifeSiteNews *Daily News,* March 11, 2008, http://www.lifesitenews.com.

28. Kenneth Woodward, "Why Notre Dame Should Welcome Obama," *Washington Post,* March 30, 2009, http://articles.washingtonpost.com/2009 -03-30.

29. See David Gibson's *Commonweal* posting "Bishop D'Arcy to boycott Obama at Notre Dame," March 24, 2009, http://www.commonwealmagazine .org/blog/?p=2961.

30. See John M. D'Arcy, "Baccalaureate Mass Homily," *ND Report,* May 16, 2009, http://ndreport.nd.edu/archives/2008-2009 (the bishop's address follows that of President Jenkins).

31. In his "Bishop Decries 'Combative Tactics' of a Minority of U.S. Bishops," *National Catholic Reporter,* August 26, 2009, Tom Roberts reports Archbishop Michael Sheehan of Santa Fe as saying that he disagreed with the "combative tactics" of "a minority of U.S. bishops" who publicly opposed Obama's visit to ND, adding that the majority of Catholic bishops in the United States shared his disagreement. Citing the influence of the late Cardinal Joseph Bernardin of Chicago, with whom he had worked, Archbishop Sheehan expressed his belief that "building bridges" with politicians who oppose church teachings is more productive than "burning them."

32. These talking points are listed in Kathleen Gilbert, "Revealed: Obama Commencement Talking Points for University of Notre Dame Trustees," LifeSite-News *Daily News,* April 7, 2009, http://www.lifesitenews.com.

33. Keyes and Terry were among eighty-eight protestors arrested for trespassing on campus before the commencement. Their cases were initially assigned to Judge Jenny Pitts Manier, wife of retired philosophy professor Ed Manier, who later recused herself. Charges against the "Notre Dame 88" were dismissed in May 2011 before their cases came to trial, denying them another moment of national publicity. See "Charges Dropped for ND Protesters," *South Bend Tribune,* May 5, 2011, http://articles.southbendtribune.com.

34. See Charles Rice, "No Confrontation Necessary," *Observer,* March 30, 2009, http://www.ndsmcobserver.com/2.2756/search-7.35315?q=rice&from=20 09&to=MM%FDD%2FTY. For the McInerny quotes, see Ralph McInerny, "A House Divided," *The Catholic Thing,* May 19, 2009, http://www.thecatholic thing.org.

35. It is hard to escape the conclusion that Kirk's participation in this extraordinary event had something to do with his being fired a year later. A further factor relevant to his firing, perhaps, is that Kirk had developed a reputation for taking unusually stern disciplinary actions against errant football players. Yet another source of administrative ire may have been his crackdown on the use of alcohol at tailgate parties, which had unwittingly netted a few ND trustees. (I owe this last tidbit to Neil Delaney.)

36. My description of the alternative commencement events is based (1) on interviews with David Solomon and Fred Freddoso, who were there, (2) on email correspondence with Andrew Chronister, who helped organize the event, (3) on "ND Rally Celebrates Graduates, Praises 'Sanctity of Life,'" Catholic News Agency, May 18, 2009, http://www.catholicnewsagency.com/news/nd_rally _celebrates_graduates_praises_sanctity_of_life, and (4) on a series of videos on YouTube, notably (i) "Fr. John Raphael speaks at Notre Dame at the 2009 Commencement," June 9, 2009, http://www.youtube.com/watch?v=koLCg1A0qHs& feature=relate, (ii) "Bp. John D'Arcy Speaks at Notre Dame at the 2009 Commencement," June 9, 2009, http://www.youtube.com, and (iii) "Chris Godfrey Speaks at Notre Dame at the 2009 Commencement," June 9, 2009, http://www .youtube.com.

37. These and subsequent details regarding the composition of Obama's speech come from an interview with Professor Scott Appleby.

38. Before entering administration, Brand had taught philosophy at Pittsburgh, the University of Illinois, Chicago, and the University of Arizona. He died of cancer in September 2009.

39. In his departmental response of 2002, Paul Weithman gave persuasive arguments why a topflight philosophy department with a majority of Catholic members is not a practical goal. The main reasons are that relatively few Catholic undergraduates go on to major graduate programs, and that of those who do the more successful tend to take jobs at secular institutions.

40. McInerny, *New Themes,* ix. As convener of Vatican II, with its emphasis on *aggiornamento* ("bringing up to date"), John XXIII was a distinctly liberal pope, in contrast with, say, conservative Pius IX of Vatican I.

41. Gleason, *Contending,* 317.

42. It is true that a tree's sapwood can sometimes sustain itself for a few years after the heartwood decays and the tree becomes hollow. But without a solid core the tree eventually falls. It is also true that interrupting the upward flow of nutrients through the sapwood, perhaps by girdling the tree's circumference, will kill

the whole organism within a single season. Although sapwood comes closest to being self-sustaining in the short term, both are necessary for long-term viability.

43. In *Liberal Faith: Essays in Honor of Philip Quinn,* which he edited, Paul Weithman said that liberal faith "is more a sensibility than a set of creedal commitments" (2). This is as it should be. Sensibility is a form of sensitivity, and all living things must be sensitive to changes in their environments in order to make adjustments necessary for staying alive.

44. For this and the quotation following, see Michael Baxter, "An Old Sinner," in *O Rare Ralph McInerny,* edited by Christopher Kaczor (South Bend, IN: St. Augustine's Press, 2011), 100–103.

45. This symbolic value might have been considerable. Within a few years after 2000, Ralph had become a darling of Washington's powerful right-wing political establishment. In 2006, friends and former students founded the McInerny Center for Thomistic Studies in his honor. The first McInerny Banquet (at the Capital Hilton), marking the end of the center's first year, was organized by a committee including Robert Bork, Fr. Richard J. Neuhaus, Robert Royal, and Mary Ann Glendon. See McInerny Center for Thomistic Studies, announcement of the first McInerny Banquet, Thomas International Project, http://www.thomasinternational.org/ralphmc/annualbanq/2006/annualbanq2006.htm.

46. See Patrick Gardner, "His Last Class, His Last Graduation," in Kaczor, *O Rare Ralph,* 59–61.

47. See D. Q. McInerny, "The Last Written Words of Ralph McInerny as Recounted by His Brother D. Q. McInerny" in Kaczor, *O Rare Ralph,* 148.

EPILOGUE

1. This information is from an email from Fr. McDonough dated April 14, 2012. All quotations attributed to Fr. McDonough in this epilogue are from this email and with his permission.

2. "Rev. Ernan McMullin."

3. From ordination to death, Ernan's diocese was that of Raphoe, Donegal. Once he took up permanent residence in the United States, he was too far afield for regular oversight by his diocesan superior. Indeed, he became so adept at staying beneath diocesan radar that other secular priests at ND would consult him for tips on how to "manage" their bishops.

4. From an email dated March 16, 2012, quoted with permission.

5. One of twelve recorded by Ernan for this series, the interview in question is entitled "What Is God's Judgment?" and can be viewed at http://www.closertotruth.com/video-profile/What-is-God-s-judgment-Ernan-McMullin-/1127.

BIBLIOGRAPHY

"Abbott Canon Dr. Astrik L. Gabriel O.Praem." Obituary, d. May 16, 2005. Tributes.com. http://www.tributes.com/show/Abbott-O.Praem.-87771264.

"Advancing Our Vision." University of Notre Dame, 2011. http://advancing ourvision.nd.edu.

"Albuquerque Journal Obituaries: Denissoff." *Albuquerque Journal,* March 18, 1998. http://obits.abqjournal.com/obits/show/136943.

Alcoff, Linda Martin, ed. *Singing in the Fire: Stories of Women in Philosophy.* Lanham, MD: Rowman & Littlefield, 2003.

"American Enterprise Institute." *SourceWatch,* 2012. Last modified July 11, 2012. http://www.sourcewatch.org/index.php?title=American_Enterprise _Institute.

"Archimandrite." *Wikipedia.* Last modified March 13, 2013. http://en.wikipedia .org/wiki/Archimandrite.

Arons, Wendy. "Interdisciplinarity, Performance, Power: 'Galileo' in the Academy." *Theatre Topics* 14, no. 1 (March 2004): 275–91.

Austin, John L. *How to Do Things with Words.* Cambridge, MA: Harvard University Press, 1962.

Banerjee, Neela. "Notre Dame's President Allows 'Monologues' and Gay Films." *New York Times,* April 6, 2006. http://www.nytimes.com.

"Bill Ramsey—Reverse Polarity (5.14b)." DPM Climbing video. http://www .dpmclimbing.com/climbing-videos.

Bird, Otto. "In Memoriam: Ivo Thomas (1912–1976)." *Notre Dame Journal of Formal Logic* 18, no. 2 (1977): 193–94.

"Bp. John D'Arcy Speaks at Notre Dame at the 2009 Commencement." June 9, 2009. YouTube video. http://www.youtube.com.

Burrell, David B. *Analogy and Philosophical Language.* New Haven: Yale University Press, 1973.

———. *Aquinas: God and Action.* Notre Dame: University of Notre Dame Press, 1979.

Cantor, Geoffrey. "Galileo and the Church: Then and Now." *Metascience* 15, no. 2 (2006): 345–48.

Center for Environmental Justice and Children's Health. http://www3.nd.edu
/~kshrader/cejch.html.

Center for Philosophy of Religion. http://philreligion.nd.edu/about.

"Charges Dropped for ND Protesters." *South Bend Tribune,* May 6, 2011. http://
articles.southbendtribune.com.

"Chris Godfrey Speaks at Notre Dame at the 2009 Commencement." June 9,
2009. YouTube video. http://www.youtube.com.

Clark, Kelly, and Michael Rea. *Reason, Metaphysics, and Mind: New Essays on the
Philosophy of Alvin Plantinga.* Oxford: Oxford University Press, 2012.

Clarke, W. Norris. "The Future of Thomism." In *New Themes in Christian Philosophy,* edited by Ralph McInerny, 187–207. Notre Dame: University of
Notre Dame Press, 1968.

Cohen, Edward. "Genuine John Jenkins." *Notre Dame Magazine,* Summer 2004,
5–9.

Copleston, Frederick. *Aquinas.* New York: Penguin Books, 1955.

Corson, Dorothy V. *A Cave of Candles: The Story behind Notre Dame's Grotto.* Nappanee, IN: Evangel Publishing House, 2008.

"'Crisis' Averted." *Commonweal,* September 14, 2007, 3.

"Curriculum: Departure at De Paul." *Time,* October 23, 1964. http://www.time
.com/time/magazine/.

"The Curriculum of a Catholic Liberal College." Internal report of the College of
Arts and Letters, University of Notre Dame, 1953. University of Notre Dame
Archives.

D'Arcy, John M. "Baccalaureate Mass Homily." *ND Report,* May 16, 2009.
(Bishop D'Arcy's homily follows that of President Jenkins.) http://ndreport
.nd.edu/archives/2008-2009.

————. "Vagina Monologues Presentation at Notre Dame." Catholic Diocese of
Fort Wayne-South Bend, February 12, 2004. http://www.diocesefwsb.org.

Dawson, John W., Jr. "Logic at Notre Dame: Kurt Gödel at Notre Dame." http://
math.nd.edu.

"Description of the [Leiter] Report." Hard copy on file as DOC#49718 in the
Philosophy Department of the University of Notre Dame.

Detlefsen, Michael. "Logic at Notre Dame: Skolem at Notre Dame." http://math
.nd.edu.

"Doing Business South Bend." City of South Bend publicity web article. http://
www.southbendin.gov/business/ideal_bsns_envmt/avlble_prop/innov_pk
.asp.

Dougherty, Jude. "One Hundred Years of Philosophy by the Catholic University
of America." *Fellowship of Catholic Scholars Newsletter,* December 1996.

Feigl, Herbert, and Wilfred Sellars, eds. *Readings in Philosophical Analysis.* New
York: Appleton-Century-Crofts, 1949.

Feuerherd, Joe. "The Real Deal." *National Catholic Reporter,* August 19, 2004. http://www.nationalcatholicreporter.org/update/bnHOLD081904.htm.

Fisk, Milton. "Milton Fisk: Biography." http://www.miltonfisk.org/biography.

"Fr. John Raphael Speaks at Notre Dame at the 2009 Commencement." June 9, 2009. YouTube video http://www.youtube.com/.

Gibson, David. "Bishop D'Arcy to boycott Obama at Notre Dame." *Commonweal,* March 24, 2009. http://www.commonwealmagazine.org.

Gilbert, Kathleen. "Revealed: Obama Commencement Talking Points for University of Notre Dame Trustees." LifeSiteNews Daily News, April 7, 2009. http://www.lifesitenews.com.

Gleason, Maureen, and Katharina J. Blackstead, eds. *What Is Written Remains: Historical Essays on the Libraries of Notre Dame.* Notre Dame: University of Notre Dame Press, 1994.

Gleason, Philip. *Contending with Modernity: Catholic Higher Education in the Twentieth Century.* New York: Oxford University Press, 1995.

Grant, Catherine. "Back from Vac with Notre Dame Philosophical Reviews." *Film Studies for Free* (blog), August 5, 2009. http://filmstudiesforfree.blogspot.com.

Grindel, Carl W. "Vincent Edward Smith, 1915–1972." *Proceedings and Addresses of the American Philosophical Association* 45 (1971–72): 225–26.

Hauerwas, Stanley. "The Virtues of Alasdair MacIntyre." *First Things,* October 2007. http://www.firstthings.com.

Hesburgh, Theodore. *God, Country, Notre Dame.* With Jerry Reedy. Notre Dame: University of Notre Dame Press, 1990.

"History: Christian Reformed Church." http://www.crcna.org/welcome/history.

Hoekema, David K., to Kwame Anthony Appiah. April 2, 2009. http://www.calvin.edu/academic/philosophy.

Hope, Arthur J. *Notre Dame, One Hundred Years.* Notre Dame: University of Notre Dame Press, 1943.

Hudson, Deal W., and Dennis W. Moran, eds. *The Future of Thomism.* Mishawaka, IN: American Maritain Association, 1992.

International Catholic University. http://home.comcast.net/~icuweb/icu.htm.

Jacques Maritain Center, University of Notre Dame. "Introduction." http://www2.nd.edu.

Jauernig, Anja. "About Me." http://www.pitt.edu.

Jenkins, John. "Baccalaureate Mass Homily." *ND Report,* May 16, 2009. http://ndreport.nd.edu.

John Paul II, Pope. *Ex Corde Ecclesiae.* Encyclical letter. 1990.

———. *Fides et Ratio.* Encyclical letter. 1998.

———. *Veritatis Spendor.* Encyclical letter. 1993.

Kaczor, Christopher, ed. *O Rare Ralph McInerny.* South Bend, IN: St. Augustine's Press, 2011.

Knight, Kelvin. *Aristotelian Philosophy: Ethics and Politics from Aristotle to Mac-Intyre.* Cambridge, UK: Polity Press, 2007.

Kozak, Jarosław. "Joseph (Innocent Maria) Bochenski OP (1902–1995)." In *Studies in East European Thought* 49, no. 4 (1997): 287–303.

Küng, Guido. "In Memoriam: Joseph (Innocent) M. Bochenski, O. P. 1902–1995." *Review of Metaphysics* 49, no. 1 (1995): 217–18.

Küng, Hans. "The Church and Freedom." *Commonweal,* June 21, 1963, 343–53.

Leiter, Brian. "'Analytic' and 'Continental' Philosophy." *Philosophical Gourmet Report* 2011. http://www.philosophicalgourmet.com/analytic.asp.

———. "How Can Notre Dame Philosophical Reviews Publish Nonsense like This?" *Leiter Reports: A Philosophy Blog,* May 7, 2007. http://leiterreports .typepad.com/blog.

———. "Overall Rankings." *Philosophical Gourmet Report* 2011. http://www .philosophicalgourmet.com/overall.asp.

Leo XIII, Pope. *Aeterni Patris.* Encyclical letter. 1879.

———. *Rerum Novarum.* Encyclical letter. 1891.

LifeSiteNews. "Catholic University of Notre Dame President Approves Vulgar Pro-Lesbian Play Vagina Monologues." LifeSiteNews Daily News, March 11, 2008. http://www.lifesitenews.com.

Liles, Martha. "Archimandrite." Melkite Greek Catholic Church Information Center. Last updated August 22, 2010. http://www.mliles.com/melkite /archimandrites.shtml.

Lindberg, David C. Review of *Galileo: Man of Science,* by Ernan McMullin. *Physics Today* 21, no. 12 (1968): 75–77.

Mangan, Katherine S. "175 Philosophy Professors Blast Rankings of Graduate Programs." *Chronicle of Higher Education,* January 18, 2002.

Maritain, Jacques. *An Introduction to Philosophy.* Translated by E. I. Watkins. New York: Sheed & Ward, Inc., 1947.

McCool, Gerald A. Preface to *The Future of Thomism,* edited by Deal W. Hudson and Dennis W. Moran, 1–5. Mishawaka, IN: American Maritain Association, 1992.

McInerny Center for Thomistic Studies. Announcement of the first McInerny Banquet. Thomas International Project. http://www.thomasinternational .org/ralphmc/annualbanq/2006/annualbanq2006.htm.

McInerny Center for Thomistic Studies. Mission page. http://www.thomasinter national.org/ralphmc/mission.htm.

McInerny, Ralph. "A House Divided." *The Catholic Thing,* May 17, 2009. http:// www.thecatholicthing.org.

———. *I Alone Have Escaped to Tell You.* Notre Dame: University of Notre Dame Press, 2006.

———, ed. *New Themes in Christian Philosophy.* Notre Dame: University of Notre Dame Press, 1968.

McKim, Vaughn. "Social and Environmental Values in Power Plant Licensing: A Study in the Regulation of Nuclear Power." In *Values in the Electric Power Industry,* edited by Kenneth Sayre, 30–99. Notre Dame: University of Notre Dame Press, 1977.

McMullin, Ernan, ed. *Construction and Constraint: The Shaping of Scientific Rationality.* Notre Dame: University of Notre Dame Press, 1988.

———. "Philosophy in the United States Catholic College." In *New Themes in Christian Philosophy,* edited by Ralph McInerny, 370–409. Notre Dame: University of Notre Dame Press, 1968.

———."What Is God's Judgment?" Interview of Ernan McMullin by Robert Lawrence Kuhn. http://www.closertotruth.com/video-profile/What-is-God-s-judgment-Ernan-McMullin-/1127.

———. "Who Are We?" *Proceedings of the American Catholic Philosophical Association* 41 (1967): 1–16.

McMullin, Ernan, and James Cushing, eds. *Philosophical Consequences of Quantum Theory: Reflections on Bell's Theorem.* Notre Dame: University of Notre Dame Press, 1989.

Melkite Greek Catholic Church Information Center. http://www.mliles.com/melkite.

Menger, Karl, and Yves Simon. "Aristotelian Demonstration and Postulational Method." *Modern Schoolman* 25, no. 3 (1948): 183–92.

Michel, Florian. *La pensée catholique en Amérique du Nord.* Paris: Éditions de Brouwer, 2010.

Mirus, Jeff. "The *Monologues* Revisited: Bishop D'Arcy and Notre Dame." Catholic Culture.org, April 25, 2006. http://www.catholicculture.org.

Moon, Andrew. "An Opinionated Play-by-Play of the Plantinga-Dennett Exchange." *The Prosblogion: A Philosophy of Religion Blog,* February 23, 2009. http://prosblogion.ektopos.com.

Murphy, Mark C. *Alasdair MacIntyre.* Cambridge: Cambridge University Press, 2003.

———. "A Letter to the American Philosophical Association Board of Directors." May 18, 2009. http://www9.georgetown.edu/faculty/murphym/APA Statement-Murphy.htm.

National Science Foundation. "In Service to Society: NSF Strategic Areas." In *NSF in a Changing World: The National Science Foundation's Strategic Plan.* Arlington, VA: National Science Foundation, 1995. http://www.nsf.gov.

"ND Rally Celebrates Graduates, Praises 'Sanctity of Life.'" Catholic News Agency, May 18, 2009. http://www.catholicnewsagency.com.

Notre Dame Fund to Protect Human Life. Last updated 2012. http://sites.google.com/a/nd.edu/the-notre-dame-fund-to-protect-human-life.

O'Brien, Michael. *Hesburgh: A Biography.* Washington, DC: Catholic University of America Press, 1998.

Oppenheimer, Mark. "The Philosopher Kingmaker." *Boston Globe,* April 20, 2008.

Parys, Jan. *Entre la logique et la foi.* Warsaw: Les Éditions Noir sur Blanc, 1990.

The Peerage. "Leopold Ernst Herr und Graf von Stubenberg." http://thepeerage .com/p11614.htm.

Pereira, José. "Thomism and the Magisterium: From *Aeterni Patris* to *Veritatis Splendor.*" *Logos* 5, no. 3 (2002): 147–83.

Pius XII, Pope. *Humani Generis.* Encyclical letter. 1950.

Plantinga, Alvin. "Self Profile." In *Alvin Plantinga,* edited by James E. Tomberlin and Peter van Inwagen, 3–97. Dordrecht: D. Reidel, 1985.

———. "Spiritual Autobiography." In *Reason, Metaphysics, and Mind: New Essays on the Philosophy of Alvin Plantinga,* edited by Kelly Clark and Michael Rea, 1–39.

"Progress Report Prepared for the Dean and Faculty by the Special Committee, October, 1961." Archives of the University of Notre Dame.

Quinn, Philip L. *Essays in the Philosophy of Religion.* Edited by Christian Miller. Oxford: Clarendon, 2006.

"Rev. Ernan McMullin, Distinguished Alumnus of Maynooth College." St. Patrick's College, Maynooth, 2011. http://www.maynoothcollege.ie/news /InMemoriamRevErnanMcMullan.shtml.

Rice, Charles. "No Confrontation Necessary." *Observer,* March 30, 2009.

Roberts, Tom. "Bishop Decries 'Combative Tactics' of a Minority of U.S. Bishops." *National Catholic Reporter,* August 26, 2009.

Sayre, Kenneth, ed. *Values in the Electric Power Industry.* Notre Dame: University of Notre Dame Press, 1977.

Shook, Laurence. *Etienne Gilson.* Toronto: Pontifical Institute of Mediaeval Studies, 1984.

Smyth, Marina. "The Medieval Institute Library: A Brief History." In *What Is Written Remains: Historical Essays on the Libraries of Notre Dame,* edited by Maureen Gleason and Katherina J. Blackstead, 211–29. Notre Dame: University of Notre Dame Press, 1994.

———. "Rt. Rev. Astrik L. Gabriel, O.Praem." Obituary, d. May 16, 2005. Rare Books and Special Collections, Hesburgh Libraries, University of Notre Dame. http://www.library.nd.edu/rarebooks.

Soloman, David. "A President's Retreat." *Wall Street Journal,* April 14, 2006. http://online.wsj.com/article/SB114496644011725536.html.

"The Teacher, the University, and Sycamore." Sycamore Trust, April 4, 2011. http://www.projectsycamore.com/bulletins/110327.php.

Thamel, Pete. "Outgoing President Opposed Firing Willingham." *New York Times,* December 9, 2004. http://www.nytimes.com.

"Thomistic Institute: Summer 1998." Jacques Maritain Center. http://maritain .nd.edu/jmc/ti98.htm.

Tomberlin, James E., and Peter van Inwagen, eds. *Alvin Plantinga*. Dordrecht: D. Reidel, 1985.

Van Inwagen, Peter. "Quam Dilecta." http://informationphilosopher.com/solutions/philosophers/vaninwagen/quam_dilecta.html.

University of Notre Dame. "ND Online Directory." http://www.nd.edu/about/leadership/pdf/orgchart.pdf.

University of Notre Dame Office of Technology Transfer. "FAQs and Answers." http://ott.nd.edu/.

Ward, Leo R. "Meeting Jacques Maritain." *Review of Politics* 44, no. 4 (October 1982): 483–88.

———. *My Fifty Years at Notre Dame*. Notre Dame: Indiana Province of the Priests of Holy Cross, 2000. http://archives.nd.edu/ward.

Weisheipl, James A. "The Revival of Thomism as a Christian Philosophy." In *New Themes in Christian Philosophy*, edited by Ralph McInerny, 164–85. Notre Dame: University of Notre Dame Press, 1968.

Weithman, Paul J. *Liberal Faith: Essays in Honor of Philip Quinn*. Notre Dame: University of Notre Dame Press, 2008.

———. Review of *Catholicism and Liberalism,* edited by R. Bruce Douglass and David Hollenbach. *Faith and Philosophy* 13, no. 1 (1996): 140–46.

———. "Toward an Augustinian Liberalism." *Faith and Philosophy* 8, no. 4 (October 1991): 461–80.

"Wisdom Retreats." Morris Institute for Human Values. http://www.morris institute.com.

Wittgenstein, Ludwig. *Philosophical Investigations*. Translated by G. E. M. Anscombe. New York: Macmillan, 1953.

Woodward, Kenneth. "Why Notre Dame Should Welcome Obama." *Washington Post,* March 30, 2009. http://articles.washingtonpost.com/2009-03-30.

"Yves R. Simon (1903–1961)." Notre Dame Center for Ethics and Culture. https://sites.google.com/a/nd.edu/the-notre-dame-center-for-ethics-and-culture.

INDEX

and Thomism, 5, 71, 78, 104, 107, 108, 109, 144, 350n13

and Vatican II, 82, 155, 160, 163, 346n34

McIntire, Michael, 168

McIntosh, Robert, 168

McKenny, Gerald, 348n54

McKeon, Richard, 68, 126, 127

McKim, Carole, 137

McKim, Vaughn, 113, 123, 129, 130–31, 136, 193, 214

administrator, 138, 146, 155, 348n54

and the Philosophic Institute for Artificial Intelligence, 168, 169, 341n24

and the Reilly Center, 185–86, 188–89, 348n47

and the Sellarsians, 120, 137–38, 142–43, 210

McMullin, Fr. Ernan, 2, 5, 6, 39, 62, 63, 64, 65–69, 70, 71, 83, 89, 94, 118, 119, 120, 123, 182, 197, 216, 242, 261, 303, 335n28, 341n16, 342n28, 349n6, 354n14, 357n50

and the Carnegie Summer Institute, 128–30

and the Concept of Matter Conference, 68, 125–27

department chair, 69, 84, 88, 99, 105, 110, 116, 135, 143, 144–45, 172, 205, 210, 214, 236, 301

early alienation from the department, 66, 73–74, 77

estrangement from the university, 6, 69, 310, 312–13, 315 (*see also* McDonough, Fr. Kevin)

family, 65, 311, 314, 316

—parents, 65

—sisters, 311, 315

and the Graduate Program in History and Philosophy of Science, 138

love of opera, 312

Memorial Mass, 308, 309–16

and the Philosophical Perspective series, 69, 130, 132, 134

publications and addresses, 46, 76, 110–11

and the Reilly Center for Science, Technology, and Values, 138, 185–89, 348n47

and the Sellarsians, 137, 142, 143

social life, 210, 310, 362n3

—charismatic persona, 5, 68, 311

—women friends, 310, 312, 315, 350n9

Thomism, attitude toward, 74, 75, 84, 112

without priestly faculties, 310, 311

Meeker, Kevin, 198

Meilaender, Gilbert, 281

Mellon, Joseph, 213

Menger, Karl, 34, 35, 48, 57, 60

Menzel, Christopher, 183

Mercer, Christia, 196, 206–7, 213

Merleau-Ponty, Maurice, 111, 119, 173

Meyer, Susan Suavé, 194–95

Meyer, Urban, 285

Mezei, Balazs, 184

Michel, Fr. Virgil, 45, 332n29

Miller, Christian, 198

Miltner, Fr. Charles, 41

Miscamble, Fr. Wilson, 281, 290

Mitchell, Msgr. Gerard, 67

Montini, Cardinal Giovanni Battista, 343n4. *See also* Paul VI, Pope

Moore, G. E., 115

Moore, Harold, 119, 211, 346n29

Moore, Fr. Philip S., 48, 79, 151–52

Morris, Thomas, 183, 233–34

Mullahy, Fr. Bernard, 58, 79, 152

Mullally, Joseph, 41

Munzel, Felicitas, 356n36

Murdock, Charles, 169

Murphy, Adrienne, 294

KENNETH M. SAYRE is professor of philosophy and director of the Philosophic Institute at the University of Notre Dame. He is the author of numerous books, including *Unearthed: The Economic Roots of Our Environmental Crisis* (University of Notre Dame Press, 2010).